Customer Knowledge Management:
People, Processes, and Technology

Minwir Al-Shammari
University of Bahrain, Bahrain

INFORMATION SCIENCE REFERENCE

Hershey · New York

Director of Editorial Content: Kristin Klinger
Director of Production: Jennifer Neidig
Managing Editor: Jamie Snavely
Assistant Managing Editor: Carole Coulson
Typesetter: Kim Barger
Cover Design: Lisa Tosheff
Printed at: Yurchak Printing Inc.

Published in the United States of America by
            Information Science Reference (an imprint of IGI Global)
            701 E. Chocolate Avenue, Suite 200
            Hershey PA 17033
            Tel: 717-533-8845
            Fax: 717-533-8661
            E-mail: cust@igi-global.com
            Web site: http://www.igi-global.com/reference

and in the United Kingdom by
            Information Science Reference (an imprint of IGI Global)
            3 Henrietta Street
            Covent Garden
            London WC2E 8LU
            Tel: 44 20 7240 0856
            Fax: 44 20 7379 0609
            Web site: http://www.eurospanbookstore.com

Library of Congress Cataloging-in-Publication Data

Al-Shammari, Minwir, 1962-

  Customer knowledge management : people, processes, and technology / by Minwir Al-Shammari.

      p. cm.

  Includes bibliographical references and index.

  Summary: "This book introduces an integrated approach to analyzing and building customer knowledge

management (CKM) synergy from distinctive core advantages found in key organizational elements"--Provided

by publisher.

  ISBN 978-1-60566-258-9 (hardcover) -- ISBN 978-1-60566-259-6 (ebook)

  1. Customer relations. 2. Relationship marketing. I. Title.

  HF5415.5.A424 2009

  658.4'038--dc22

                              2008037389

British Cataloguing in Publication Data
A Cataloguing in Publication record for this book is available from the British Library.

All work contributed to this manuscript is new, previously-unpublished material. The views expressed in this
manuscript are those of the authors, but not necessarily of the publisher.

*If a library purchased a print copy of this publication, please go to http://www.igi-global.com/agreement for
information on activating the library's complimentary electronic access to this publication.*

*In memory of my parents who have unknowingly practiced
'honesty is the best policy' for enduring relationships*

Table of Contents

Section II:
Reinventing (3 Rs)

Section III:
Capitalizing (3 Cs)

Section IV:
Mastering (3 Ms)

Foreword

In order to survive in an increasingly dynamic and complex world, many organizations are attempting to redefine themselves in order to gain sustainable competitive advantage and better respond to new marketing demands. As competition grows, delivering high-quality products and services that meet customers' needs and expectations becomes an important way to success. Since the added value and quality of a product or service is perceived by the customer, it is paramount that companies have a thorough understanding of customer needs and expectations. To achieve such a level of understanding, companies are arranging processes and deploying systems for storing customer data, managing customer interactions, building and managing customer knowledge.

In the current economy, customer knowledge has become a valuable asset for organizations. Customer knowledge provides organizations with a reference for improving customer experience, as it allows companies not only to effectively identify customer needs and preferences, but also compares performance against customer expectations. Managing customer knowledge is no longer something that only leading-edge companies use to gain sustainable competitive advantage. It is now a managerial necessity for all types of organizations.

Increasing "customer share" is a better strategy than increasing "market share." The more companies know about their customers, the better they can serve them. To convince customers to give more of their attention and business, let them know about your business very well. To work with quality, it is necessary to continually observe the expectations and perceptions customers have about the products and services you deliver. Due to the availability of current information and communication technologies such as the Internet, mobile, and wireless resources, customers are now able to get more information than they usually were able to a few years ago, and they usually know very well the companies they regularly deal with. Online access to databases, chat resources, and bulletin boards put customers in contact with staff and with other customers so that they can mutually help each other.

The adoption of customer-focused strategies and practices may significantly increase an organization's capacity to generate knowledge. In this context, customer knowledge management (CKM) can be seen as an enabler for the development of organizational capabilities that allow the adoption of business approaches that support knowledge creation and sharing mechanisms. Although the adoption of technical solutions makes it feasible for organizations to systematically manage knowledge, strategic and cultural aspects should be carefully observed prior to any technical investment. The adoption of customer-focused strategies is of crucial importance to the processes of knowledge acquisition, conversion, and application. In this context, CKM practices provide powerful resources to improve an organization's ability to recognize not only customer demands, but also to identify patterns and trends that can guide future strategies.

CKM regards customers as the focal point of the organization. A fundamental notion of CKM is that it is not something that can be bought and installed in an off-the-shelf manner. It should be seen as a broad-business strategy that implies the redevelopment of organizational structures, systems, and processes in a way that services and product offerings are arranged around a refreshed understanding of customer needs and expectations. The real concept of CKM implies deep strategic and operational concerns. More professional approaches to CKM are necessary and the contribution that this book makes is very welcomed. The book provides a comprehensive and holistic view of CKM by addressing managerial and technological aspects of the matter, including issues concerning strategies, human resources, processes redesign, ICT systems, customer relationship management, and change management. This multidisciplinary feature of the book makes it a valuable source for academics and managers at all levels who wish to become active players in today's dynamic and complex business world.

Dr. Luciano Batista
The Open University Business School, UK

Dr. Luciano Batista is a lecturer in operations management at the Open University Business School, The Open University, UK. His academic degrees comprise a BSc in computer science, an MSc in management and a PhD in information systems management. After graduating in computer science, he worked in the industry for 11 years. During this period, he worked 3 years as computer programmer, 4 years as systems analyst and 4 years as CIO. After obtaining a master's degree in 1998, he moved his career from industry to academia. Dr. Batist a obtained his PhD from the Manchester Business School, The University of Manchester, UK. His PhD research focused upon the applicability of CRM systems in the government context. During his PhD, he has actively contributed to the development of the CRM National Project in the UK, a government project commissioned by the Department for Communities and Local Government (DCLG), former Office of the Deputy Prime Minister (ODPM). After his PhD, he worked as associate research fellow at the School of Business and Economics, University of Exeter, UK, where he developed research on service processes and integrated CRM / BPM approaches, as well as taught operations management. Throughout his academic career, Dr. Batista has co-authored important government reports and published in journals and international conferences in Europe, USA and Latin America. At the Open University, he has been teaching and researching operations management-related issues concerning CRM, process innovation, applicability of digital technologies, and logistics and supply chain management.

Preface

OVERVIEW

In facing the 21st Century's competitive, dynamic, and complex business environments, organizations seek to create a "difficult-to-imitate" sustainable competitive advantage (SCA) through effective leveraging of organizational distinctive core competencies (DCCs). In dynamic business environments, enterprises face the challenge of rapidly adapting to, that is, increasing demands of customers concerning quality and innovativeness of products and services. In combination with global competition, customers change the rules of the market and force companies to adapt swiftly (Österle, 2001). This challenge and rising internal pressures, for example to improve efficiency of operations, also require enterprises to redesign their competitiveness model to focus on value-adding customer processes. Focusing on customer processes requires knowledge of considerable extent. Customer-centric companies need to provide knowledge that customers require, process the knowledge that customers pass to the company and possess knowledge about customers. As a consequence, knowledge is considered a DCC in the competition of the 21st Century (Drucker, 1999; Davenport and Prusak, 1998).

Due to the dramatic shifts in the knowledge economy and global competition, the most valuable resource that creates SCA for a business organization is becoming what it *knows* not what it *owns*. Customers are the lifeblood of any business organization. The importance of customers to business firms in the digital economy has created tough "rivalries" over acquiring new customers and/or retaining/expanding relationship with current ones. Customer-driven companies need to harness their capabilities to manage the knowledge of those who buy their products (Baker, 2000; Davenport and Klahr, 1998). In the accelerating shift towards customer-centric organizations, strategies are redesigned, organizations restructured, and a process view of a business replaces functional perspective as a means of organizing work around customer processes, that cut across functional areas, with the aim of developing Customer Knowledge (CK) from information flow via advanced Information and Communication Technologies (ICTs). CK, in turn, is becoming a major weapon for providing value-adding products and/or services that seek to serve each customer in his/her preferred way and to enhance customer satisfaction and loyalty.

In facing dynamic and complex business environments, proponents of the resource-based view to strategy have proclaimed that a company can be best conceptualized as a bundle of unique resources, or competencies, rather than as a bundle of product market positions (Barney, 1991). Nonetheless, many contributors to the resource-based view of the firm question this one-sided thinking about the locus of competence (Prahalad and Ramaswamy, 2000; Inkpen, 1996). It has recently been claimed that such competence actually moved beyond corporate boundaries, and that it is worthwhile to also look for competence in the heads of customers, rather than only in the heads of employees. Although Customer Relationship Management (CRM) has been traditionally popular as a means to tie customers to the company, but left perhaps the greatest source of value under-leveraged, viz. the knowledge residing in customers (Gibbert et al., 2002).

In the context of CK, customer is broadly defined as an organization's stakeholders such as consumers, suppliers, partners, joint ventures and alliances, and competitors. In some cases, a customer may not have a current relationship with the organization, but one is likely to develop in the future (Paquette, 2005a). CK can be explicit or tacit, and individual or group knowledge based on the model presented by Cook and Brown (1999). Explicit knowledge is easily codified, transferred, and understood by multiple individuals, where tacit knowledge requires experience and practice in order to flow from one individual to another. Both of these forms of knowledge can reside at the individual level, or be created and transferred between different groups. Knowledge derived from customers through an interactive and mutually beneficial process is referred to as CK. CK can be composed of a combination of CK, supply chain knowledge, joint venture specific knowledge, and so forth. This knowledge is created within a two-way flow of knowledge which creates value for both parties (Paquette, 2005a). CK gave birth to a relevant field of research as it supports customer processes and cultivates concepts and technologies of Knowledge Management (KM) and CRM (Romano and Fjermestad, 2002).

CK can also be divided into four types (Davenport et al., 2001; Garcia-Murillo and Annabi, 2002; Gibbert et al., 2002; Desouza and Awazu, 2005; and Smith and McKeen, 2005): knowledge for, from, about, and co-creation with customers. Knowledge *for* customers is a continuous flow of knowledge directed from the company to its customers in order to support customers in their buying cycle. Knowledge *from* customers refer to customers' needs or consumption patterns of products and/or services that have to be incorporated by the company for product and/or service innovation and development. Knowledge *about* customers encompasses the customer's past transactions, present needs and requirements, and future desires. Knowledge *co-creation (with customers)* refers to a two-way business-customer relationship for the development of new knowledge or a new product, for example Microsoft shares its "beta-ware" version with customers in order to learn with them and debug the software.

CRM is a relationship-based strategy that has flourished in recent years. CRM integrates order and sales, marketing, and service processes, in order to establish a profitable and longer relationship with customers or suppliers. CRM itself should not be only seen as a technological solution, although ICT is required to enable the integration of customer-facing processes. CRM *content* technology enables a company to integrate a large volume of customer information and to efficiently transform this information into useful knowledge. CRM *contact* technology also enables a company to interact with its customers in ways that provide value to the customer as well as to make it easier for the customer to do business with the company.

As companies grow and interact with more and more customers through increasingly diverse media and channels, having a systematic approach to manage CK becomes critical. Customer Knowledge Management (CKM) is needed not to capture simple transactional information, that is by CRM systems, but to extend the formation of strategic partnerships and to develop new products. CKM refers to the methodologies and systems employed in the acquisition and distribution of valuable customer derived information and knowledge concerning the provisioning of customer services or products throughout an enterprise. CKM is described as the creation of new knowledge gained by companies and their customers sharing platforms and processes (Paquette, 2005b).

CKM is also different from traditional KM in the objective pursued. Whereas traditional KM is about efficiency gains that avoids "re-inventing the wheel", CKM is about innovation, and creation of growth opportunities for the corporation through partnering with existing customers (e.g., cross-selling and up-selling), or through acquiring new customers and getting engaged in an active and value-creating relationship with them. CKM contrasts the desire of traditional CRM to maintain and nurture existing customers and the belief that "retention is cheaper than acquisition". However, retention often becomes increasingly difficult in an age where competitors' offerings are close imitations and only three mouse-clicks away (Gibbert et al., 2002).

THE CHALLENGES

Building the customer-centric knowledge-intensive enterprise is not a simple task and it poses real challenges to organizations. Although transformation to a CKM-based organization is sound theoretically, its implementation suffers in practice from some pitfalls. Implementing a CKM strategy represents a real challenge as it does not happen over a short period of time like implementation of any ICT-based project. CRM systems frequently have been accused for over-promising but under-delivering. The transformation towards a knowledge-enabled, customer-centric organization may face a number of challenges in such areas as absence of an overall KM strategy, knowledge hoarding corporate culture, inaccurate identification of business requirements, stovepipe or functional structure, lack of business process integration, weak customers' expectations and satisfaction, shortage in meeting knowledge needs of power users, poor quality of data, inertia/resistance to change, fear of job loss, excessive vendors' involvement, and ineffective formal organizational roles (Al-Shammari, 2005).

The most significant challenges in implementing CKM effectively are organizational, not technical. Smith and McKenn, (2005) found that the four major hurdles that must be overcome: structural challenges, cultural challenges, competency challenges, and privacy concerns. Transforming a product-centric organization into a customer-centric organization is easier said than done as companies may end up becoming customer-focused only by terms that are defined by the companies themselves not by their customers. Some companies may be concerned about the profitability of focusing on customers rather than on selling products, or may have poor alignment of their rewards and goals with a customer perspective. Some companies may shy away from customer-centricity because of corporate narcissism, that is, a sense that "we know better than our customers" (Gibbert et al., 2002). Furthermore, not all companies want to hear what their customers really think of their products, services, image, and credibility. Skills and competencies for CKM must be used in the collection, creation, dissemination, and usage of CK. However, companies do not often take full advantage of the knowledge sources they have, for example, communities of practice, alumni, retirees, and front line workers. Since much of CKM is based on developing a trusting relationship with each customer, organizations should take privacy dimension into consideration. Companies must understand not only the legal guidelines around how customer data is protected but also how customers feel about how a firm uses their information. For example, too much customization may make some customers feel uncomfortable with what a company knows about them (Smith and McKenn, 2005).

Paquette (2005a) identified several cultural challenges in CKM implementation. He argued that CKM faces cultural challenges of sharing CK at the individual, group, or organizational level. Firms may experience a challenge of perceiving customers as a source of knowledge, not just revenue as reflected in the "not invented here" concept, which demonstrates an unwillingness to accept externally generated ideas (Paquette, 2005a). Other companies fear showing internal processes to customers such as suppliers or alliance partners, so they control what the customer sees to be afraid of giving away strategic secrets to the marketplace (Gibbert et al., 2002).

Besides cultural influences, a firm may face the obstacle of not having the competency required to absorb and utilize the external knowledge. Cohen and Levinthal (1990) argue that a firm's absorptive capacity, or its ability to absorb new knowledge, is a function of the firm's prior knowledge that allows it to recognize and synthesize new knowledge. Also, ICTs may not be able to handle the transfer of knowledge from external sources, as most knowledge sharing support systems are only designed for internal use. Control of content may be lost, as external knowledge transfer can push the locus of control beyond a firm's boundaries (Gibbert et al., 2002). Thus, organizations can be quite reluctant to open up these systems, as technical challenges occur without a universal integration and security mechanism that interfaces with both parties' systems (Paquette, 2005a).

Desouza and Awazu (2005) identified four major challenges to CKM: segmentation, integration, distribution, and application. The challenge in information-rich cultures is to find the right categories on which to segment data prior to analysis. The attributes used to segment customer data are transient; an attribute that is important today and may not be so tomorrow. The problem with dialogue is that customers cannot articulate what they want – they don't realize they need something until the innovative product offers it to them. Novice computer shoppers differ from superior ones in terms of CK needs. So providing the same level of knowledge to both customer groups will lead to frustrated user experiences. In the context of knowledge from customers, the business firm must be able to segment its users based on how they consume the product and/or service; into beginners, intermediate, expert and lead users. Segmenting users in this manner allows the business firm to get a better sense of how to manage the incoming knowledge from each group. The challenge for knowledge from customers is to integrate the various contact/delivery channels. It is more common to find discrepancies in the information than to find that customer information coming from multiple sources synchronized. The challenge is to integrate the various channels, media, and methods for delivery of CK. The Internet and mobile phones allow customers to no longer be restricted in the media they can use to find information about products and/or services. To ensure a company can communicate with its customers through disparate mediums and in multiple languages, its CRM systems must be compatible with multiple environments, platforms, and systems. The challenge in distribution of knowledge about customers is to communicate it in usable formats according to different requirements and uses. A significant problem with knowledge about customers is privacy. How does a company ensure it uses the information it gathers in a responsible way? Customers share information willingly when they believe it will be used to provide them with better support, products, and/or services. They are reluctant to share it when they think it will be used in unauthorized or hidden ways.

SEARCHING FOR A SOLUTION

Change occurs frequently in most large and small companies. The problem arises when it is not always well planned or deliberately executed. This is especially true when change is reactive to events rather than proactive in anticipating or even creating them. The situation aggravates when organizations do not invest much in planning, pursue change haphazardly, and adopt ICT-based generic or ready-made change initiatives. Companies usually benefit more from change they are prepared for versus change that is imposed on them. In order to prepare for change, companies should also learn how to identify the need for change and how to manage it successfully. This learning capability will allow companies to address future problems and take advantage of opportunities more quickly and effectively than their competitors.

In the search for a suitable solution, the role of researchers is to redefine and refine frontiers of knowledge and research by pushing a line of argument to develop an alternative approach to things rather than to prove a particular approach as a more absolute truth. Several approaches and directions have been taken by researchers in managing CK as a source of developing durable and profitable relationships with customers. This book discusses and analyzes these approaches and proposes CKM as a "multiple-paradigms one-solution" holistic business framework. A business model or framework is conceived as a high-level approach to conduct business, wherein a company can leverage its DCCs to create an SCA. The model clearly outlines how a company adds value by creating new, or revising existing, products, services, and/or processes. The CKM framework is thought to be helpful in organizing thoughts related to building blocks of several interdisciplinary subjects and identifying the interacting relationships between these building blocks. The strategic point of the CKM framework is that businesses are looked at as a vertical value chain, moving from resources through to the customer, and broken down into tiny segments with the SCA achievement as an ultimate aim.

CKM has been recently utilized as the main proactive approach to face drastic and too fast globalization, competitive environments, and changing customer's preferences. The basic theme behind CKM is to utilize DCCs of organizations, that is, knowledge, to add value to customers as well as to companies by delivering the *right* product and/or service, at the *right* price, to the *right* customer, at the *right* time and location, and through the *right* distribution channel. CKM results from the integration of intervention techniques and methodologies rooted in people, process, and technology, viz. Business process Reengineering (BPR), ICTs, KM, and CRM, and aims at maximizing value for customers and creating profitable and enduring relationship with them. Successful CKM change requires transformation of organizations from "product-centric" to "customer-centric" strategy, from "vertical" to "network" structure, from "individualistic" to "collective" work, from "hoarding" to "sharing" culture, from "ceremonial" to "results-oriented" practices, from "functional" to "process" work orientation, and from "centralized" to "distributed" computing.

While CRM systems are typically used to target daily customer transactions, CKM is presented to leverage knowledge-enabled customer-business transactions from a strategic level, viz. generating, sharing, and applying CK. CKM is not a tool (like CRM), but a strategic process that is designed to capture, create, and integrate knowledge about and for customers dynamically. CKM is introduced as a principal approach that amalgamates BPR ICTs, KM, and CRM and in order to leverage DCCs in the quest for achieving SCA in today's competitive business world. CKM is a strategic process that seeks to gather and analyze customer data from customer-facing business processes, and then to generate knowledge needed to create value to customers through providing customized products, services, and/or processes.

CKM is not just about customer data nor is it just about customer relationships, viz. social (people-based) or transactional (technology-based); rather, CKM is a knowledge-based business strategy enabled by a holistic organizational reinvention manifested by changes in people, structure, processes, and technology. Research specifically on the concept of CKM has shown growing appearance in the literature. Major CKM contributions include Garcia-Murillo and Annabi, (2002), Gibbert, et al. (2002), Rowley (2002 a,b), Kolbe, et al. (2003), Roscoe (2003), Bueren, et al. (2005), Desouza and Awazu (2005), Paquette (2005), Smith and McKen (2005), Chen and Su (2006), Su and Chen (2006), and Lopez-Nicolas and Molina-Castillo (2008).

The proposed CKM framework (Figure P0.1) presents a unified frame of reference that integrates dynamic interactions among basic organizational pillars of people, processes, and technology in pursuit of the enrichment of the CK wealth of organizations. Double-arrow flows are used to show intra- and inter-connections and integration between different parts, or elements, of the framework, and also serve as unifying glue for various elements of the framework. Double-arrow flows are needed to reflect the fact that building the value of customers increases the value of the demand chain knowledge and the stream of business activities that flow in the opposite direction to the supply chain knowledge, that is from the customer up through the retailer all the way to the manufacturer. However, it should be noted here that boundaries or dichotomies between or within different parts of the framework are blurred. Therefore, an imaginary blurred rather than definite line needs to continue to be kept in mind when analyzing CKM.

Figure P0.1. A schematic diagram for the CKM framework

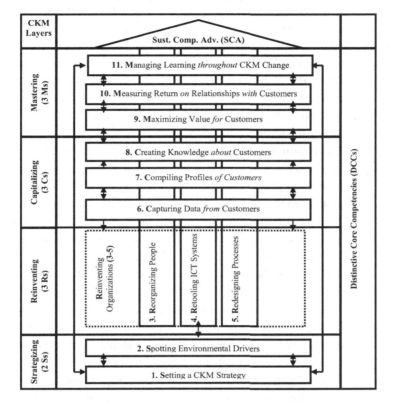

BOOK STRUCTURE

This particular four-stage perspective of the CKM framework is adopted as a base for organizing the book into various chapters. The CKM layers are organized in four coherent parts abbreviated as SRCM (Strategizing, Reinventing, Capitalizing, and Mastering), with each part divided into two or three chapters as follows:

Section I – Strategizing –This section explores concepts, issues, and trends surrounding the strategy and its environmental drivers of the CKM change (2 Ss): The chapters belonging to this section are chapter I and II.

Chapter I addresses background concepts, critical issues, and future trends related to the blueprinting of a CKM strategy. CKM is a knowledge-based strategy for anticipating and meeting customers' needs profitably. It deals with issues such as major organizational components (people, structure, process, and technology), intellectual (staff) capital and relationship (customers) capital of organizations.

Chapter II examines the importance of business environmental conditions in driving organizational change, such as CKM. The basic premise of the chapter is that business organizations need to strive to adapt to opportunities as well as challenges brought by constant, complex, rapid, and discontinuous environmental changes.

Section I of Chapter II discusses basic concepts related to organizational environments and the relationship between organizations and their environments. It identifies and explains major types of environments (the general and the task environments), typologies of environmental changes, organizational change programs, and the relationship between environments and organizational effectiveness. Section II of Chapter II addresses the major issues that surround environmental conditions and organizational responses to their environments.

Section II – Reinventing – It looks into changes in the role of three major organizational pillars or enablers of CKM (3 Rs): reorganizing people, retooling ICT systems, and redesigning processes. It is composed by chapter III, IV, and V.

Chapter III looks into the reorganization of people in teams as a major pillar of CKM. Chapter IV examines the role of ICTs in retooling legacy systems in order to enable CKM change strategy. The main focus of this chapter is on the hardware, software, and network components of ICTs. Chapter V explores the last section in infrastructural changes, viz. the role of business processes in CKM change. Section I provides a theoretical background to the redesign of business processes. It examines the need for business process orientation, the anatomy of a process, the concept of BPR, pillars of BPR, principles of BPR, results of BPR, followed by a BPR example from the banking industry. This chapter discusses the strategic importance of process change and innovation in adapting to complex, dynamic and competitive business environments by leveraging process-based DCCs of organizations.

Section III – Capitalizing – This analyzes the first three stages of CKM value chain (3 Cs): capturing data from customers, compiling profiles of customers, and creating knowledge about customers. It is composed of chapters VI, VII, and VIII.

Chapter VI examines the concepts, issues, and trends related to capturing customer data and routing it to, or sharing it with, people in other units within the organization. Chapter VII discusses the strategic, or analytical side of CKM. This chapter focuses on the information discovery tools. Chapter VIII seeks to discuss various concepts, issues, and trends concerning composition of knowledge about customers.

Section IV – Mastering – This section includes the last three stages of CKM value chain (3 Ms): maximizing value for customers, managing relationships with customers, and managing learning throughout CKM change. It is composed by chapters IX, X and XI.

Chapter IX discusses the efforts to improve the experience of customers and to boost customer satisfaction and loyalty if businesses fail to connect with customers and anticipate their needs. Chapter X addresses customer value reciprocity for business represented by durable and profitable customer relationship. Chapter XI is concerned with learning and adapting throughout the life of CKM change. It focuses on the accumulated knowledge and experience in CKM implementation, wherein end product learning is back channeled into the early planning stages of CKM.

POTENTIAL AUDIENCE

The book is of immediate interest to academics and practitioners alike. It targets both advanced students and business managers'. This holistic view of the book could be useful for CRM professionals drill-down for CKM.

CONTRIBUTION OF THE BOOK

The review of the conceptual foundations of BPR, ICTs, KM, and CRM shows that there is no shortage in the number of contributions devoted to the exploration of each concept. However, this book seeks to add value to existing literature by offering a one integrated enterprise-wide CKM paradigm that cuts-across traditional business silos to generate CK. The book provides a holistic approach for an inherently interdisciplinary subject matter. Different perspectives, frameworks, methods, techniques, models, and systems have been integrated into a unified CKM framework that tells a coherent story. Concepts, issues, and recommended solutions are described, explained, and illustrated using first-hand diagram and metaphors. In particular, two recommended solutions have identified new dimensions of CKM for mass customization and for customer life cycle that are unique to the existing models and theories of CKM.

This book presents a new conceptual framework that provides a holistic view of CKM. The book discusses and analyzes the approaches concerning CK and proposes CKM as a "multiple-paradigms one-solution" holistic business framework. The book introduces a strategic full-fledged multi-faceted, customer-oriented, and knowledge-intensive integrated framework to enterprise-wide business change. This framework is the basis of the organization of the book as it helps in organizing thoughts related to building blocks of several interdisciplinary subjects and identifying the interacting relationships between these building blocks. The CKM framework can also be used as a blue-print for CKM implementation.

The framework weaves together the various stages of CKM strategic change in a simple and practical framework. The unified framework helps readers to understand key CKM fundamental concepts (related to the "*What, Who,* and *Where*" questions), and interpret and analyze the reasoning behind initiating a CKM change strategy (related to the "*Why*" question), as well as CKM implementation (related to the "*How*" question).

The book introduces a comprehensive, yet simple and integrated approach to analyze and build CKM synergy from DCCs in key organizational elements: strategy, people, structure, processes, technology, and information in a way that advances the cause of system thinking in search of SCA. It also emphasizes the importance of strategic alignment *with* external environment, *among* organizational components, and *within* organizational components.

In each chapter, before the discussion of issues, a presentation of the most relevant concepts regarding the topic under discussion is conducted. The adopted framework provides continuity for the concept of CKM throughout the whole book. Each chapter starts with a scheme, that was presented in the preface, and that accompanies the reader throughout the book, telling him/her where he/she is and to where he/she is going and what still misses to be discussed. This scheme helps the reader navigate through the manuscript. The chapters are well integrated with each other; every chapter provides a foundation for understanding subsequent chapters, and subsequent chapters are interwoven with preceding chapters.

REFERENCES

Al-Shammari, M. (2005). Implementing a knowledge-enabled CRM strategy in a large company: A Case study from a developing country. In M. E. Jennex (Ed.), *Case studies in knowledge management* (pp. 249-278). Hershey, PA: Idea Group Publishing.

Baker, M. (2000) Creating an alliance between employees and customers. *Knowledge Management Review, 3*(5), 10-11.

Barney, J. B. (1991). Firm resources and sustained competitive advantage. *Journal of Management, 17*(1), 99-120.

Bueren, A., Schierholz, R., Kolbe, L. M., & Brenner, W. (2005). Improving performance of customer-processes with knowledge management. *Business Process Management Journal, 11*(5), 573-588.

Chen, Y-H., & Su., C-T. (2006). A Kano-CKM model for customer knowledge discovery. *Total Quality Management, 17*(5), 589-608.

Cook, S. D. N., & Brown, J. S. (1999). Bridging epistemologies: The generative dance between organizational knowledge and organizational knowing. *Organization Science, 10*(4), 381-400.

Davenport, T. H., & Klahr, P. (1998) Managing customer knowledge. *California Management Review, 40*(3), 195-208.

Davenport, T. H., & Prusak, L. (1998). *Working Knowledge: How Organizations Manage What They Know*. Harvard Business School Press, Boston, MA.

Davenport, T. H., Harris, J. G., & Kohli, A. K. (2001). How do they know their customers so well? *Sloan Management Review, 42*(2), 63-73.

Desouza, K. C., & Awazu, Y. (2005). What do they Know? *Business Strategy Review, 16*(1), 41-.45.

Drucker, P. F. (1999). Knowledge worker productivity – the biggest challenge. *California Management Review, 41*(2), 79-94.

Garcia-Murilo, M., & Annabi, H. (2002). Customer knowledge management. *Journal of the Operational Research Society, 53*, 875-884.

Gibbert, M., Leibold, M., & Probst, G. (2002). Five styles of customer knowledge management and how smart companies use them to create value. *European Management Journal, 20*(5), 459-469.

Inkpen, A. C. (1996). Creating knowledge through collaboration. *California Management Review, 39*(1), 123-139.

Kolbe, L., et al. (Eds). (2003). *Customer knowledge management*. Berlin: Springer.

Lopez-Nicolas, C., & Molina-Castillo F. J. (2008). Customer Knowledge Management and E-commerce: The role of customer perceived risk. *International Journal of Information Management, 28*(2), 102-113.

Österle, H. (2001), Enterprise in the information age, in H. Österle, E. Fleisch, & R. Alt (Eds), *Business Networking: Shaping Collaboration between Enterprises* (pp.17-54), Springer, Berlin.

Paquette, S. (2005). Customer knowledge management. In D. Schwartz (Ed.), *The Encyclopedia of knowledge management* (pp. 90-96), Hershey, PA: Idea Group.

Paquette, S. (2005a). Customer knowledge management. In D. Schwartz (Ed.), *The Encyclopedia of knowledge management* (pp. 90-96), Hershey, PA: Idea Group.

Paquette, S. (2005b). The impact of customer-centric knowledge management systems on strategic decision-making. *AMCIS 2005 Proceedings*. Paper 366.

Prahalad, C., & Ramaswamy, V. (2000). Co-opting customer competence. *Harvard Business Review, 78*(1), 79-87.

Romano, N. C., & Fjermestad, J. (2002). Electronic commerce customer relationship management: an assessment of research. *International Journal of Electronic Commerce, 6*(2), 61-113.

Rowley, J. (2002a). Eight questions for customer knowledge management in E-Business. *Journal of Knowledge Management, 6*(5), 500-511.

Rowley, J. (2002b). Reflections on customer knowledge management in E-Business, *Qualitative Market Research, 5*(4), 268-280.

Smith, H. A., & McKeen, J. D. (2005). Developments in Practice XVIII - Customer Knowledge Management: Adding Value for Our Customers. *Communications of the Association for Information Systems, 16,* 744-755.

Su, C-T., Chen, Y-H., & Sha, D. Y. (2006) Linking innovative product development with customer knowledge: a data-mining approach. *Technovation, 26*(7), 784-795.

Acknowledgment

The inherently interdisciplinary nature of CKM has made the development process of this book extraordinarily hectic and bumpy, although extremely exciting and enriching. The writing-up journey passed through several iterations and revisions over the past four years, and left behind more gray hairs, but hopefully more professional exploits. In writing this book, the pain lies in presenting a viable frame of reference for the book, while then joy comes in being able to make different parts of the framework fit well and be neatly integrated within the overall picture.

I am indebted to many individuals who were kind enough to provide assistance in taking up this arduous endeavor. I especially appreciate the efforts of colleagues who have provided insights which were extremely useful in the preparation of the manuscript of this book: Dr. Mohamad Ali Abdulla from Bahrain's Economic Development Board (EDB) for his constructive critiques and meticulous insights on earlier versions of the CKM framework and throughout the book's development process, and Dr. JoAnn Long from the University of Bahrain for her valuable and diligent comments on an earlier draft of this book. Many friends and colleagues have been a constant source of support and encouragement through this academic endeavor and were eager to seeing it published.

I wish also to acknowledge the help of three anonymous reviewers of the book for their rigorous and challenging but value-adding comments that have made it possible to produce a better final product. Last but not least, thanks are also due the wonderful people at IGI Global who provided editorial help and advice: Rebecca Beistline, our assistant editor for her continuous support and guidance throughout the writing-up journey, Christine Bufton, administrative editorial assistant, and Jamie Snavely, production managing editor.

My small family has lived with me through the ups and downs of this endeavor. I am grateful to my wife and children for their patience and understanding, and for giving-up many week-end plans, providing moral support and occasionally typing support, and creating a conducive atmosphere needed to preserve the writing-up momentum.

The spirit of my grandparents has not been very far from this journey. The remaining memories of their 'boundary-transcending' migration journey, at the beginning of last century, from Al-Owshidziyah of Hayil cutting across the Nofoud desert, have significantly inspired in me the cross-functional process orientation essential for undertaking such an interdisciplinary CKM endeavor.

Minwir Mallouh Al-Shammari
(Ibn-Owaishidz)
August 2008

Section I
Strategizing (2Ss)

Chapter I
Setting a CKM Strategy

INTRODUCTION

In today's dynamic business environment, change is omnipresent. Organizations have to develop sound change management strategies in order to counter the same. Transition to knowledge-based economies made establishment of effective knowledge management (KM) mechanisms within companies crucial to achieve business competitiveness. This chapter addresses background concepts, critical issues, and future trends related to the blueprinting of CKM as a knowledge-based strategy for anticipating and meeting customers' needs profitably. Crafting CKM requires a set of activities, i.e. plan, design, build, and implement, which seek to create or leverage the firm's distinctive core competencies (DCCs) in order to attain a sustainable competitive advantage (SCA).

This chapter advocates the premise that successful businesses are those that have both vision and commitment to make that vision a reality. The vision might be customer-oriented, e.g. the strategy is CKM, the processes include CKM value chain primary activities (capture data from customers, create profiles of customers, compose knowledge about customers, maximize value for customers, measure return on relationships with customers, and master the learning throughout CKM change), and CKM value chain support activities: reorganizing people, reconfiguring processes, and retooling Information and Communication Technologies (ICTs).

CONCEPTUAL FOUNDATIONS

This section covers background concepts related to competitiveness strategies, viz. strategic thinking, strategic planning, and tools for strategic planning.

Strategic Thinking

Attaining SCA requires the development of an effective business strategy. The prerequisite to the development of an effective business strategy is logical, critical, dynamic, and creative thinking. The basic problem in the search for SCA is how to determine from which resources, competencies, or core competencies SCA may originate. The answer to how firms would propose, analyze, and select strategic actions is through strategic thinking (Swift, 2001).

Strategic thinking, as illustrated in Figures 1.1, 1.2, and 1.3, is a creative and dynamic synthesis that involves three dimensions (Boar, 1994; Swift, 2001):

1.   Time: People think across different timelines (past, present, and future).
2.   Substance: People think between the concrete and the abstract.
3.   Concurrence: People may think about one or more issues simultaneously.

Most of the time, people engage in point thinking to solve daily problems, wherein all problem solving efforts converge on one point. In point thinking, an average person, or a mundane thinker, thinks uni-dimensionally (one issue in concrete terms in the present) (Figure 1.1). In contrast, strategists think dynamically within the thought bubble of the three strategic dimensions (Figure 1.2). Since the combinations of strategic ideas are boundless, strategic thinking is a very powerful way to develop deep and far-reaching insights, rather than tactical and short-term views, about problems and to solve them in novel, unanticipated, and creative ways. SCA is born and nourished from this kind of thinking (Swift, 2001).

When faced with hyper-competitive business environments, more advanced strategic thinking needs to be added. A strategist thinker may adopt four-dimensional dynamic thinking about multiple issues in multiple dimensions, at higher

Figure 1.1. Mundane/ordinary thinking model

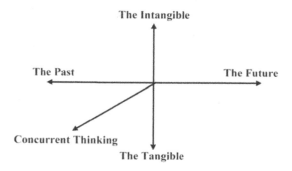

Figure 1.2. Three-dimensional dynamic strategic thinking model

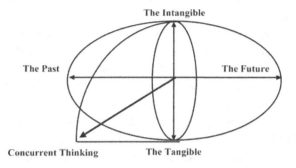

Figure 1.3. Four-dimensional advanced strategic thinking model

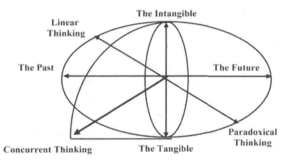

Source (Figures 1.1, 1.2, and 1.3): Adapted from Swift (2001). Accelerating Customer Relationships: Using CRM and Relationship Technologies, NJ: Prentice-Hall.

levels of abstraction and detail over time (Figure 1.3). The thought bubble may be extended to a fourth dimension of linear logic versus paradoxical thinking (Board, 1994):

- Logical thinking: relates to the logic of solving daily problems using common sense, deductive/inductive reasoning, and concern for economies of time, cost, and effort to problem solving. Daily life applauds the logical, the economical, and the utilization of common sense. For example, customer teams may engage in extensive and exhaustive linear logic justification (i.e., cost/benefit exercises) to convince decision makers to approve Customer Relationship Management (CRM) technologies, i.e. Data Warehouse (DW). While cost-conscious capital budgeting methods are appropriate for things that are readily cost-justifiable (things that are concrete, obvious, and known to all), strategic vision has been the required ingredient to create it. In the CRM example, the cost and benefits are often dispersed across wide gaps of time and space (Swift, 2001).

- Lateral thinking: hyper-competition and intelligent counter-measures cause strategic paradoxical actions to take place by taking creative and paradoxical actions that are contrary to routine business sense. When a linear logic action evolves into a reverse of itself or of opposites, such as an advantage becomes a disadvantage, and doing the reverse of what linear logic would dictate. As business competition migrates from industrial economies of scale to ICTs, CRM achieve optimal results when used as weapons of competitive advantage to discover new things that were never known or thought about before. When the weaponry shifts to ICT fighting, CRM becomes subject to strategic paradox and must be excessively utilized and leveraged in order to create new opportunities and achieve maximum benefits (Swift, 2001).

Strategic Planning

Business organizations must always be prepared to respond creatively to marketplace dynamics through strategic planning that leads to business actions. Strategic planning is is equal to direction plus focus (concentration of effort) plus perseverance (constancy of purpose) plus adaptability (flexibility). Business actions are of no strategic interest if they do not lead to the development of an advantage (Swift, 2001). The process of strategic planning involves systematic examination of opportunities and threats in the business environment to identify or create opportunities that need to be exploited and the threats that need to be avoided by matching resources and capabilities to the changing environment (Johnson et al., 2005).

Development of a strategic plan is based on the firm's mission, and requires policies, programs activities, processes, and resources to carry out strategies. The core of the strategic planning process is to identify what your organization can do best and about making choices between competing priorities. This means creating or utilizing existing DCC in order to create a SCA. The process of strategic planning commonly ends with the development of a set of performance targets and measures of success, i.e. key performance indicators (KPIs) and critical success factors (CSFs), tracking and learning from progress in performance, and striving for high improvement in outcomes.

Mintzberg et al. (2005) offered the 'Ten Schools of Thought' model that can be used to categorize strategy development. They discuss prescriptive (the first three) and descriptive (the last seven) schools which follow:

- The Design School *(*Strategy as a Process of Conception) is the most influential view of the strategy-formation process. In this process, the internal situation of the organization (strengths and weaknesses) is matched to the external situation of the environment (threats and opportunities). Major limitations of the school are: a) simplification may distort reality, b) strategy has multiple and complex variables, and c) weak in dynamic environments.

- The Planning School *(*Strategy as a Formal Process) is discussed in the third chapter. A rigorous set of formal steps are taken, such as formal procedure, formal training, and formal analysis. Major limitations of the school are: a) strategy can become too static, b) the risk of 'groupthink', and c) development of strategy from the ivory tower of top management.

- The Positioning School *(*Strategy as an Analytical Process) is similar to the planning school which made strategic development into a science. It places the business within its industry and economic marketplace and looks at how the organization can improve its strategic positioning within that industry. The school's major limitations are: a) strategy becomes too systematic and rigid, and b) focus is on hard (economic) facts, neglecting culture, power, politics, and social elements of the organization.

- The Entrepreneurial School *(*Strategy as a Visionary Process) introduces the first descriptive school of strategy development. The school stresses the most innate of mental states and processes - intuition, judgment, wisdom, experience, and insight. The visionary process takes place within the mind of the charismatic chief executive or founder of an organization especially in its early or difficult years. Major limitations of the school are: a) may blind leaders to potential unexpected dangers, b) may be difficult to find the right leader with the right qualities, and c) leadership becomes an extremely demanding function in this school of thought.

- The Cognitive School *(*Strategy as a Mental Process) sees strategy as a cognitive process. It concentrates on what is happening in the mind of the strategists and how they process patterns and process information. Strategies emerge as concepts, maps, schemas, and frames of reality. Stresses the creative side of the strategy process. Major limitations of the school are: a) low viability beyond the conceptualization stage, b) not very practical to conceive high-level thoughts, and c) not very useful in guiding collective strategy development.

- The Learning School *(*Strategy as an Emergent Process) suggests that people learn over time about a situation as well as about their organization's capability to deal with it. Management pays close attention to what works, and what doesn't work. Strategies emerge in small steps, as organizations adapt, learn, and incorporate these 'lessons learned' into their overall action plans. This school questions severely the basic assumptions and premises of the design, planning, and position schools of strategy development. It is applicable in strong complex and dynamic environmental conditions, as well as in professional organizations. The school's major imitations are: a) could lead to having no strategy or just doing some tactical maneuvering, b) not as useful during crises as in stable conditions, and c) taking many incremental steps may not necessarily add up to a sensible ground strategy.

- The Power School (Strategy as a Process of Negotiation) is an overt process of negotiation between power holders within the company and/or between the company and its external stakeholders. This perspective is particularly useful in understanding strategic alliances and joint-venture decisions. Major limitations of this school are: a) politics can sometimes be divisive, b) uses a lot of energy, c) causes wastage and distortion and is costly, d) can lead to having no strategy or just doing some tactical maneuvering (muddling through), and e) overstates the role of power in strategy development.

- The Cultural School (Strategy as a Collective Process) is the reverse image of the power school. Strategy formation is viewed as a fundamentally collective and cooperative process that is developed as a reflection of the organization's corporate culture. Emphasizes the crucial role that social processes, beliefs and values play in decision-making, strategy formation, and resistance to strategic change. Major limitations of the school are: a) can feed resistance to change and can be misused to justify the status-quo and b) gives few clues on how things should evolve.

- The Environmental School (Strategy as a Reactive Process) unlike the other schools that see the environment as a factor, the environmental school sees it as an actor. Seeing the strategy as a response to the challenges imposed by the external environment, this school merits a detour on the strategy safari. It positions environment alongside leadership and organization as one of the three central forces in the process. The school's major limitations are: a) the frequently vague environmental dimensions make it less useful for strategy formation and b) denial of real strategic choice of organizations in strategy formation is unrealistic.

- The Configuration School (Strategy as a Process of Transformation) is an "all of the above" strategy formation school that offers the possibility of reconciling and integrating the messages of the other schools. It is a process of transforming the organization from one type of decision-making structure into another. It is important to note that there are two complementary sides to this school, structure versus strategy. One describes states as configurations (more descriptive), whilst the other describes the strategy-making process as transformation (more prescriptive). The key to successful change management is to sustain stability and success, or at least adaptable strategic change. However, the stability period is occasionally interrupted by a need for transformation. In order to be able to manage that disruptive process without destroying the organization, a sort of stable, balanced transformation (dynamic equilibrium) in organizational change is needed.

An organization can be described in terms of some stable configuration of its coherent clusters of characteristics and behaviors in a particular type of context, and so serves as one way to integrate the perspectives of other schools. Examples of configuration are planning in machine-type organizations under conditions of relative stability, and entrepreneurship organizations under dynamic configurations of start-up and turnaround. But if organizations can be described by such states, then change must be described as rather dramatic transformation from one state to another. Nonetheless, these two very different practices and perspectives complement one another and so belong to the same school. The limitations of this school are: a) the existence of several, not just a limited number of, valid configurations, and; b) if the reality is being described by using configuration, then reality is being destroyed in order to explain it.

Strategic Planning Tools

One of the most important strategic planning tools that may be used by the 'Design School', as well as in other schools that emphasize the role of external/internal environment in their formation, is the SWOT (Strengths, Weaknesses, Opportunities, and Threats) analysis (Andrews, 1971). Analysis of strengths and weaknesses is used to analyze internal environment strengths and weaknesses (i.e., structure, culture, as well as resources and competencies in such areas as marketing, finance, research and development, operations and logistics, human resources, and ICTs). The external audit of opportunities and threats analyzes macro environment opportunities and threats (i.e., socio-economical, technological, and market environment) (Figures 1.4, 1.5, and 1.6).

A SWOT analysis is a powerful strategy planning tool employed to identify strategic options available to organizations to meet objectives and to maintain sustainable growth. This analysis helps to match organizational resources, capabilities, and distinctive competencies to the competitive environment in which a firm operates. Organizations seek to cultivate their strengths and avoid exposure from their weaknesses. External opportunities need to be exploited with internal strengths. Further extension of the SWOT analysis can be conducted (Figure 1.7) by incorporating two additional factors: performance against competitors and importance of competitive factors for customers (Martilla and James, 1977; and Slack, et al., 2006).

The key to a successful SWOT analysis is to be realistic. In looking at organizational strengths or weaknesses, one should evaluate their strengths relative to those of other competitors, and also face any unpleasant truths regarding their weaknesses. For example, if all competitors offer on-line customer-care services, then a competitive advantage may be downgraded to a competitive necessity. Carrying out a SWOT analysis is often enlightening in terms of putting internal weaknesses or shortages into perspective, pointing out what needs to be done to attract and retain potential customers. However, a SWOT analysis should be used with some caution, as it is a normative model that can help in diagnosing current customers' situations as is rather than a prescriptive model that suggests what ought to be done.

Despite the fact that strategic planning is considered crucial to a successful utilization of corporate DCCs and the achievement of a SCA, it has come under severe attack. Mintzberg (1994) argues that strategy has set out to provide uniformity and formality when none can be created, and that strategy is not the consequence of strategic planning but the opposite - its starting point. Strategy, to him, is sensitive

Figure 1.4. SWOT analysis matrix

	Opportunities (O)	Threats (T)
Strengths (S)	S-O Strategies Pursue opportunities that are a good fit to the firm's strengths.	S-T Strategies Use strengths to counter threats.
Weaknesses (W)	W-O Strategies Overcome weaknesses to pursue opportunities.	W-T Strategies Overcome weaknesses to counter threats.

Source: Adapted from Weihrich (1982). The TOWS Matrix - A Tool for Situational Analysis, Long-Range Planning, 15 (2), 52-64.

Figure 1.5. Strengths-weaknesses intersections with importance-performance ratings

Importance				Performance		
Strengths		Weaknesses		High	Medium	Low
Major	Minor	Major	Minor			

Figure 1.6. Opportunities-threats intersections with probabilities of external conditions

External Conditions				Probability		
Opportunities		Threats		High	Medium	Low
Major	Minor	Major	Minor			

Figure 1.7. Importance-performance priority quadrants

		Performance	
		High	Low
Importance	High	Quadrant I: Appropriate	Quadrant II: Urgent Action
	Low	Quadrant III: Overdoing	Quadrant IV: Not Important

Source: Adapted from Martilla, J. & James. J. (1977). Importance-Performance analysis, Journal of Marketing, 41 (1), 77-79.

to the management process which is intuitive and humane, based on immediate responses. He argues that we must re-conceive the process by which strategies are developed by emphasizing informal learning and personal vision and the roles that can be played by planners. He emphasizes the creative and spontaneous, the right-side of the brain rather than the left side with its predilection for analysis and rationality. Instead of seeing strategy as the elevation of rationalism, Mintzberg (1994) sees strategy as being deliberately, delicately, and dangerously implanted as a potter making a pot. He advocates the notion that strategy cannot be planned because planning is about analysis and strategy is about synthesis. He believes that strategy is more likely to emerge, through a kind of organizational osmosis, than be produced by a group of strategists sitting around a table believing they can predict the future. That is why, he asserts, the process has failed so often and so dramatically. He diagnoses the failure of strategic planning as the failure of formalization, and adds that we are fascinated by our ability to program things, identifying formalization as the fatal mistake of modern management.

Although strategic planning is useful, it is not essential to every organization in every context. It is beyond imagination that business organizations operating in fast changing and complex environmental conditions would categorically give up strategic planning. Instead, a dynamic, creative, and less-formalized strategic planning process is likely to replace conventional strategic planning in the future. More discussion on this point is provided in the 'Future Trends' section of this chapter.

CRITICAL ISSUES

This section discusses the critical competitive strategy development issues; namely, strategic positioning, leveraging competitiveness strategies, reconciling competitiveness strategies, balancing bases of competitiveness, and sustaining competitive advantage.

Creating Difficult-to-Imitate Competitive Strategies

As today's business organizations exist and operate in environments that are rife with turbulence and uncertainty, it is becoming imperative for them to adapt to changing environments by developing long-term scenario plans and innovations that enable them to strategically position themselves in the marketplace. In the real business world, strategic issues are numerous, complex, and may involve trade-offs among pros and cons of different strategic choices. Strategic positioning is about matching a company's strategy to a company's situation in order to exploit core competencies that differentiate a company from its competitors and create a competitive advantage. The delicate balance of vision and action in the face of resource constraints is a strategy that will allow individuals and teams to excel (Kanter, 1989).

Strategic positioning relates to the task of matching strategy to the situation and industrial environment. It involves consideration of the following factors related to the industry's environment (Thompson et al., 2007):

- The maturity stage of the industry (emerging, rapid growth, mature, or declining).
- The industry's structure (fragmented or concentrated).
- The relative strength of competitive forces; forces that could endanger a company's competitive position, i.e. intra-industry rivalry, bargaining power of buyers, bargaining power of suppliers, threat of new entrants, and threat of substitute products or services (Porter, 1985).
- The scope of competitive rivalry (regional or international).

Besides, matching strategy to a company's situation takes into consideration the following company-specific categories of positions (Thompson et al., 2007): a) firms in industry leadership positions that normally range from stronger-than-average to powerful competitive positions), b) firms in runner-up positions such as firms with smaller market shares than the industry's leader(s), and c) firms that are competitively weak or crisis-driven.

A business strategy depends not only on its external environment but on its organizational context as well. In order to set direction for future actions of organizations, a capstone business strategy needs to integrate many interrelated organizational components, viz. strategy, people, structure, processes, and technology that need to be in alignment or dynamic 'equilibrium' with each other (Scott-Morton and Allen, 1994). A successful business strategy offers a unified approach with balanced emphasis on technology and business perspectives. Any change in one of the components would entail a need for a change in another. This alignment is considered as one of the critical factors for a successful implementation of a business strategy.

The way people are organized in a structure should reflect and be compatible with the business strategy, i.e., when firms are transforming into a customer-oriented business, their legacy pyramid and rigid functional structures need to be given up and in turn adopt a process-centered structure. As a result, processes and technology will have to be reconfigured in order to reflect the customer-centric strategy. As structure, processes, and technology dynamically interact with business strategy, and strategy interacts externally with environment, there is a huge potential as well as challenge of business organizations for having a far more internal and external congruency through innovative and ongoing organizational learning and adjustment activities.

Leveraging Competitive Strategies

Competitive strategy is an enterprise's plan for achieving SCA over, or reducing the edge of, its adversaries. Models of business competitiveness have shifted their focus from external factors related to the market to internal factors based on tangible and intangible assets of organizations. Drucker (1993) pointed out that the most valuable assets of the 21st century enterprise are its knowledge and knowledge workers. Tiwana (2001) argued that knowledge is the only source for innovation and SCA. Therefore, effective development, maintenance, and expansion of customer knowledge (CK) and relationships are becoming a strategic imperative for companies in virtually every industry (Park and Kim, 2003). The salient feature of CK assets is that their competitive advantage is difficult-to-imitate.

Market-Based View

Competition has been traditionally based on external environmental factors. Porter (1980) developed his traditional market-based view (MBV) of competitive strategy to understand and analyze a firm's competitive advantage based on its external business environment and the threats of competition. He argues that competition in an industry is based on five forces: intra-industry rivalry, bargaining power of buyers, bargaining power of suppliers, threat of new entrants, and threat of substitute products or services. The strategic business manager seeking to develop an edge over rival firms can use this model to better understand the industry context in which the firm operates.

Although market requirements are important, they are usually short-lived and of different levels of importance for customers and performance against competitors in terms of providing what the customer requires. Hill (1993) differentiated between two types of competitive factors, 'order qualifiers' and 'order winners'. Order winners are the competitive factors that directly and significantly contribute to performance of the organization (i.e., quality, speed, dependability, and flexibility). Order qualifiers are those aspects of competitiveness where the operations performance has to be above a particular level just to be considered by a customer (i.e., price). Being great at qualifiers is unlikely to attract new customers, but being bad at them can lead to customer dissatisfaction (Salck, et al., 2006).

Resource-Based View

The roots of the resource-based view (RBV) of organizations go back to Wernerfelt (1984), Porter (1985), and Barney (1991). The RBV of the firm recognizes the importance of internal organizational resources (such as people, capital, facilities, and technology) capabilities as a principal source of creating and sustaining competitive market position. According to this approach, resources are the main source of an organization's capabilities, whereas capabilities are the key source of its competitive advantage (Grant, 1991). Javidan (1998) differentiates between resources, capabilities, competencies, and core competencies based on two factors of difficulty and value. Figure 1.8 shows organizational capabilities continuum alongside usage level (operational, tactical, and strategic) and expected value.

At the bottom end of the continuum are resources, and at the top end, distinctive core competencies. Resources represent the 'building blocks' of competencies and are made up of tangible and intangible assets. Tangible resources of a firm include financial assets as well as physical assets such as technology, machines, equipments, buildings, and facilities; whereas intangible resources include knowledge about customers or suppliers, knowledge and experience in handling process technologies, skills and expertise in research and development, and financial know-how in acquiring and raising capital. Capabilities are the second block in the continuum and represent an organization's ability to exploit its resources in handling business processes that cut across functional areas such as marketing, production, and finance. Capabilities are reflected in a firm's shared values, assumptions, and beliefs, which are manifested not only through its strategic focus, structures, and systems, but also through the management styles, skills, and behaviors of its people (Graetz, et al., 2006). Competencies come next to capabilities in the continuum and are followed by core competencies and distinctive core competencies. Competencies represent strategic skills necessary to create cross-functional coordination and integration of business processes. Core competencies follow next to competencies in the continuum and represent a collection of skills that are widespread across an organization and confer a competitive advantage (Javidan, 1998).

Core competencies commonly represent the organization's value chain and relate directly to the value-added to external customers, and subsequently to business organizations. Core competencies evolve slowly through collective learning and information sharing and are required to carry out a mission-critical business of the organization (Shoemaker, 1992; Dalkir, 2005). At the top end of the continuum come distinctive core competencies (DCCs) that represent unique and important core competencies that enable organizations to understand their customers and deliver

Figure 1.8. Organizational capabilities continuum

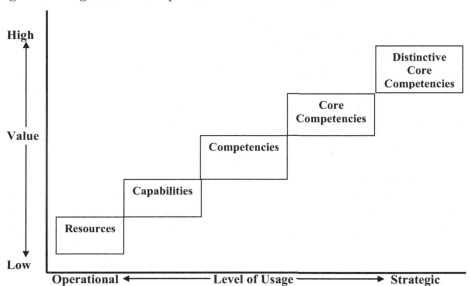

value-adding products or services. DCCs enable organizations to create SCA that make them better than their rivals and help them win in the marketplace.

In the past, economic winning was associated with inventing new products. But in the 21st century, SCA will come more out of new processes and much less out of new products. New products can be easily reproduced, but new processes cannot. What used to be primary (inventing new products) becomes secondary, and what used to be secondary (inventing and perfecting new processes) becomes primary (Peppard and Rowland, 1995).

The RBV of the firm differs from the more traditional view of strategy that sees firms as seeking to create or protect their competitive position through external factors such as their control of the market by creating barriers or constraints to the threat of new competitors, bargaining power of suppliers, bargaining power of customers, threat of substitute products or services, and the rivalry among existing competitors (Porter, 1985). By contrast, the RBV sees companies as being able to protect their long-term competitive advantage through the development of new capabilities that represent barriers to imitation, substitution, or transfer. Barriers to automation are created through the use of scarce, imperfectly mobile, imperfectly imitable, or imperfectly substitutable resources (Slack et al., 2006).

Knowledge-Based View

During the early 1990s, a number of streams of research converged to produce a new theory of the firm, viz. the knowledge-based view (KBV) of the firm. These streams include the RBV of the firm, epistemology, and organizational learning (Grant, 2002). Today's world economy has shifted its focus from tangible to intellectual resources. Although some intellectual resources are more visible than others, i.e., patents, intellectual property, etc., the majority consist of know-how, know-why, experience, and expertise that tend to reside in the head of one or a few employees (Klein, 1998; Stewart, 1997). The only SCA that a firm achieves usually comes from what it knows, how quickly it acquires new knowledge, how efficiently it uses what it knows, and how quickly it applies new knowledge (Davenport and Prusak, 2000). In the KBV of a firm, competitive advantage or positioning is created through knowledge-intensive competencies that maximize value-adding offerings to customers.

The increasing dominance of knowledge as a basis for improving efficiency and effectiveness of organizations triggered many companies to find new ways of utilizing knowledge they had gained in devising or improving their business practices (Awad and Ghaziri, 2004). However, sometimes the two terms 'effectiveness' and 'efficiency' are used to refer to two different things. Although related, the two terms can be differentiated as follows:

- Effectiveness: focuses on the success of the interactions with the external environment (doing right things), e.g., encouraging customer-centric business strategies and goals that that lead to increased creation of value-adding offerings to customers and, in turn, increased customer satisfaction and loyalty.
- Efficiency: reflects the success of the internal operations (doing things right), e.g., reducing wastage, reducing usage of resources, and improving integration and sharing of resources.

Firms need to select the competitive focus of their KM initiatives, i.e. product/service and leadership, operational excellence, and/or customer relationships, the nature of their product or services, e.g. standardized/customized or mature/innovative, and the type of knowledge used, i.e. explicit or tacit knowledge to solve problems. For instance, in facing shrinking business cycles, organizations seek to create and exploit people, process and technology-based knowledge faster and better and maximize their profitability by having product leadership through shorter time to market and, if possible, a longer product life cycle. Therefore, the product development cycle must shrink through delivering changeable knowledge-based capabilities and features.

The world's economy is shifting from a traditional one towards a knowledge-based economy. A traditional economy is known for resource scarcity, tangibility, imitability, increasing marginal cost, and decreasing marginal utility. In contrast, a knowledge-based economy enjoys resource abundance, intangibility, inimitability, and diminishing marginal cost. Increasing marginal knowledge, unlike other resources, does not diminish with continuous usage. Rather, it grows once split, shared, or used (Figure 1.9).

Reconciling Competitiveness Strategies

The aforementioned views of competitiveness may not be looked at as substitutes for each other, but they represent two sides of a strategic equation that need to be reconciled. The MBV is an externally focused (outside-in) approach to competitiveness, whereas the RBV is an internally focused (inside-out) approach (Salck et al., 2006, Greasley, 2006). Competitive strategies must be able to meet external dynamic market requirements, and at the same time, need to continue to develop internal knowledge-based capabilities that make firms able to create difficult-to-imitate value for customers through its value chain activities.

However, as the nature of competition nowadays has remarkably changed from what it has been before, production efficiency and the quality of products will not be the differentiator; organizations must turn to the only remaining source of dif-

Figure 1.9. Knowledge-based resources vs. marginal utility

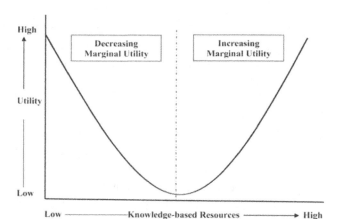

ferentiation: knowledge based innovation in the design, manufacture, and marketing of products or services that customers will value.

Kim and Mauborgne (1999) consider the market-based competition as a second-best, zero-sum strategy because it does not create sustainable long-term wealth. On the other hand, a knowledge based value-innovation strategy is a 'first-best' strategy that stimulates demand by expanding existing markets and creating new ones. Value-innovation strategy is based on knowledge-rich infinite intangible resources, i.e. know-how, know-why, learning, and skills, rather than finite resources such as physical and financial assets. Key to innovation will be a new style of leadership, cross-functional teams and empowerment of employees, both leading to customized products (Boyett and Boyett, 1995).

The ability to reconcile dichotomy among different views of competitiveness helps in leveraging all possible means to achieve a SCA to organizations. In dynamic and turbulent environments, companies try to create SCA through creating knowledge-based, value-adding relationships with customers. Many companies are migrating towards knowledge-intensive, customer-focused competitive organizations. A knowledge-based SWOT analysis of external environmental conditions and assessment of internal strengths and opportunities (Zack, 2002) should be a precondition for building a knowledge-based strategy. Instead of basing competition on traditional factors, such as price or location, firms may start with general domains of knowledge into competitive positioning.

Firms may start with identifying competitive knowledge positioning in line with the three 'Value Discipline Triad' strategic frameworks proposed by Treacy and

Wiersema (1995). Product differentiation or innovation is now being based on product/technology knowledge (an internal RBV of competition), operational excellence (internal RBV of competition) is now being based on operations knowledge, and level of trust and intimacy in customer relationships (external MBV of competitiveness) is now being based on customer/market knowledge (Zack, 2002). However, in order to rap up the three scenarios of reconciliation among different competitive views of competitiveness, a set of three-dimensional business competitiveness scenarios that integrate market, resource, and knowledge-based views of competitiveness is developed (Figure 1.10). Possible scenarios for reconciling different views of competitiveness include resource versus knowledge, market versus resource, and resource versus knowledge-based competitiveness scenarios.

Balancing Competitiveness Strategies

In their pursuit of DCCs, some companies may become unbalanced in their bases of competitiveness. Miller (1990) identified four major categories of companies according to their orientation towards competitive advantage; "craftsmen," "builders," "pioneers," and "salesmen". The "craftsmen," may be represented by Texas Instruments and Digital Equipment Corporation, two companies achieving early success through engineering excellence. But once they became so obsessed with engineering details, they lost sight of market realities. Among the "builders" are Gulf & Western and ITT, which built successful, moderately diversified companies. However, they then developed such a fetish for diversification that they continued to diversify far beyond the point at which it was profitable to do so. The third category is the "pioneers" like Wang Labs that was obsessed with its own originally brilliant innovations, but ended up producing novel but completely useless products. The final group comprises the "salesmen," exemplified by Procter & Gamble and Chrysler. They became so concerned with high sales levels but paid scant attention to product development and manufacturing excellence, and as result, generated a proliferation of inferior quality products (Miller, 1990).

The delineation of a competitive priority is not always a sort of 'either-or' decision. Business organizations operating in dynamic, complex, and fast-changing environments need to take a balanced focus on their bases of competitiveness in order to avoid failure in their pursuit of SCA. Based on strategic analysis and positioning decision, companies may develop a particular base for competitiveness (core base), but coupled with other supporting bases. For example, it is possible for one company to emphasize cost, time, and volume flexibility or emphasize quality and design flexibility.

Figure 1.10. 3D business competitiveness scenarios: Integrating market, resource, and knowledge perspectives

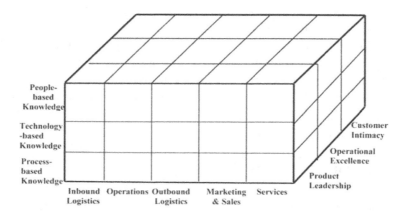

RECOMMENDED SOLUTION: A PROPOSED CKM FRAMEWORK

This section introduces the proposed CKM framework as well as its building-blocks and conceptual roots.

A Proposed CKM Framework

In order to face turbulent and competitive business environments, the development of a CKM change framework is recommended (Figure 1.1). A framework is a brief set of ideas and assumptions for organizing our thoughts about a particular situation or event, and enables us to make sense of the world's complexity (Alter, 2002). It may also be looked at as a simplified and systematic approach for representing and understanding components and interrelationships among components of a certain situation or event. A review of the literature clearly shows that there is a lack of a clear and simple conceptual framework for understanding CKM. This creates a wide variety of possibilities for understanding and implementing CKM as a concept or an approach.

CKM is conceived as a holistic business model that results from the integration of several interrelated concepts, techniques, and methodologies rooted in people, process, and technology, and is aimed at creating profitable and loyal customers. The book creates a CKM paradigm that integrates several models, theories, and methods of strategic thinking, business process reengineering (BPR), ICTs, KM, and CRM (Figure 1.11). The strategy framework may also be decomposed into a four-step high-level road map (Figure 1.12) abbreviated as Strategic Relationship Customer Management (SRCM): Strategizing, Reinventing, Capitalizing, and Mastering.

The CKM framework is introduced as a strategic change, systematic approach that seeks to answer eleven sets of questions, and examines the relevant conceptual foundations, critical issues, future trends, and a recommended solution of each:

1.   How to develop a CKM strategic change in response to business environmental pressures? ?
2.   How to environmental conditions in the context of CKM?
3.   How to change people as a major organizational enabler of CKM?
4.   How to change ICT systems to enable CKM?
5.   How to develop a customer-focused business process orientation to enable CKM?
6.   How to capture data from customers on their current and future needs?
7.   How to develop profiles of customers?
8.   How to utilize business capabilities to develop knowledge about customers?
9.   How to deliver the highest value to customers, and to ensure their loyalty and retention?
10.   How to measure return on relationships with customers?
11.   How to manage learning throughout the implementation of CKM change?

Figure 1.11. Roots of CKM

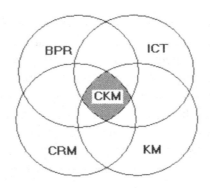

Figure 1.12. Higher level CKM process development model

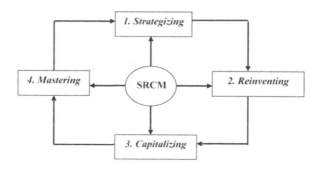

Building Blocks of the CKM Framework

The framework is divided in 4 parts as follows:

- Section I - *Strategizing*: This is the first stage in the CKM process. It deals with *diagnosing* drivers for CKM in the external as well as internal environment and planning of a strategic change. This part consists of two chapters (2 Ss):

    - Setting a CKM Strategy (Chapter I)
    - Spotting Environmental Drivers (Chapter II)

- Section II - *Reinventing*: This phase addresses the *enabling* role of reinvention of organizational infrastructure in successful implementation of CKM. This level deals with reinvention of the major organizational pillars: people, processes, and technology. The three organizational pillars represent the CKM value chain *enabling* activities that transcend CKM primary activities to reflect the fact that they enable these activities, and they continue to cut across these activities in Parts (III) and (IV). The successful integration of these pillars into a holistic CKM framework is the driving force behind successful CKM. The three CKM enabling tools are as follow (3 Rs):

    - Reorganizing People (Chapter III): refers to the *'who'* element of CKM and represents a change in the human resources and organizational structure.
    - Retooling ICT Systems (Chapter IV): refers to the *'what'* element of CKM and represents changes in the ICT infrastructure.

- ○ Redesigning Processes (Chapter V): refers to the *'how'* element of CKM and represents changes in business processes as well as CKM value-chain activities.

- Section III - *Capitalizing*: This part is concerned with the *analysis and blueprinting* of CKM value chain. CKM value chain focuses six activities (3 Cs and 3 Ms) This level includes the following value chain activities (3 Cs):

  - ○ Capturing Data *from* Customers (Chapter VI): represents the customer interaction component of CKM.
  - ○ Compiling Profiles *of* Customers (Chapter VII)
  - ○ Creating Knowledge *about* Customers (Chapter VIII)

- Section IV - *Mastering*: This part represents end results of the *implementation* of CKM. The aim is to create a customer-centric business strategy that seeks to create value for a particular customer or a particular segment of customers, with the aim of achieving a return on this value provided, i.e. winning, keeping, and expanding relationship with profitable customers. The arrowhead at the end of the CKM value chain represents the profit margin. This level includes the following value chain activities (3 Ms):

  - ○ Maximizing Value *for* Customers (Chapter IX)
  - ○ Measuring Return *on* Relationships *with* Customers (Chapter X)
  - ○ Managing Learning *throughout* CKM Change (Chapter XI)

Conceptual Roots of the CKM Framework

The following contributions have participated directly or indirectly, and at various levels, to the development of the CKM framework (Figure 1.1):

- The Socio-technical Systems Model (Emery, 1959) which views an organization as a system of coordinated human and technical components (tasks, activities, and tools) that interact with each other as well as with its external environment to accomplish the organization's purpose.
- The Environmental and Organizational Impacts of IS Model (Scott-Morton and Allen, 1994; Turban et al., 2002) whose framework is based on five organizational pillars, viz. strategy, people, process, technology, and structure, and their surrounding external environment conditions.

- The Work System Framework (Alter; 2002, 2006), the elements of the which are based on business results for customers, products and services, business processes, people, information, technology, context, and infrastructure.
- The Process-oriented KM Strategies (Davenport et al., 1996; Maier and Remus, 2003) which intend to bridge the gap between human- and technology-driven KM approaches by emphasizing process-oriented knowledge content.
- Corporate Knowledge Resources Model (Edvisson and Malone, 1997) which includes human (people), structural (process and technology), and customer relationship (data) knowledge.
- The 'IDIC' CRM Implementation and Management Framework (Peppers and Rogers; 1999; Peppers et al., 2004) which is based on identifying customers, differentiating them, interacting with them, and customizing offerings. The framework is supported with process, organization, technology, and culture.
- BPR Implementation Methodology (Hammer, 1990; Hammer and Champy, 2003; and Turban et al., 1999) in which key activities of reinventing are organized into three phases referred to as the 3 R's, which include redesign, retool, and re-orchestrate.
- Customer Acquisition and Management Model (Formant, 2000) which creates a customer-oriented enterprise, by suggesting that firms move across three distinct stages of evolution and propel their growth with information-driven, strategic marketing and processes, structure and systems that are aligned with customer and prospect customer value. The three stages of customer acquisition and management are: identification of broad customer segments, clarification of customer needs and behaviors, and achieving intimacy with customers.
- A revised 'DIKAR' Model (Murray, 2000) - the original DIKAR model prevents a 'technology-push' KM strategy, by starting at the 'results end', identifying the business results and locating KM within a demand side, not supply side, knowledge context. The model is used in a customer context and starts with data then proceeds through information, knowledge, action, and ends with results.
- CRM Implementation Model (Chen and Popovich, 2003) looks at CRM as an integrative approach that combines people, process and technology, and seeks to manage relationships by focusing on customer retention and relationship development.
- A Strategic Framework for CRM (Knox et al., 2003) includes five major processes: strategy development process, value creation process, channel and media integration process, information management process, and performance assessment process.

- The CRM Value Chain Model (Buttle, 2004) identifies five primary stages: customer portfolio analysis, customer intimacy, network development, value proposition development, and manage the customer lifecycle.

FUTURE TRENDS

In this section, we discuss three expected future trends in CKM: a shift from internally focused to externally focused strategies, a shift from conventional to creative strategic planning, and a shift from technological-based to transformational-based strategies.

A Shift from Internally Focused to Externally Focused Competitive Strategies

Today's business competition is witnessing a shift from internal and supply-push strategies (product-based) to demand-pull externally focused strategies (customer-based), from traditional development of tangible and imitable products to the generation of difficult-to-imitate knowledge-based customization of products and services that fit customers' needs and preferences.

Although some business organizations are still competing based on traditional factors such as product, price, physical location, and physical distribution channel, it is foreseeable that, in the future, the vast majority of business organizations would find it inevitable to shift towards customers as a crucial factor behind the achievement of SCA.

A Shift from Conventional to Creative Strategic Planning

Strategic planning is one of the most difficult, challenging, and dynamic tasks in organizations. The ability to plan for selection and establishment of a successful business strategy, i.e. CKM, is a process driven by creative thinking and results in innovative actions. In the years ahead, more technology-intensive industries, e.g. the telecommunications industry, will be witnessing hyper-competition and constant turbulent changes. A future result will be that companies will realize that, in order to be able to add value for customers, they will require systemic, dynamic, creative, innovative, and strategic thinking rather than conventional, structured, systematic, and prescriptive programming that is confined to a fixed set of processes and a fixed time interval, i.e. annually, bi-annually, or quarterly. The adoption of non-conventional business solutions is becoming a strategic imperative in non-conventional business settings.

Creative and dynamic strategic planning requires a continuous, responsive, and intuitive learning process that articulates vision and devises solutions to enable companies to adapt to changing business requirements resulting from highly turbulent, uncertain, and competitive future environments. Creativity in strategic planning requires not only the ability to offer new products and/or services, but also to continue to learn how, when, and for whom to create new customer value-adding offerings. Such learning comes through integration of soft insights and experiences of people as well as hard data from the environment, and then synthesizes that learning experience into a creative vision of the firm. Furthermore, flexibility, responsiveness, and dynamism in major organizational pillars of people, processes, structure, and technology are needed in order to be able to meet discontinuous environmental changes.

A Shift from Technology-Based to Transformation-Based Strategies

There is no evidence of a shortage of tools and infrastructural technologies for CKM. However, the challenge is to recognize the fact that CKM is a business strategy that will not be achieved only by putting in place a technological solution. As it is very risky for a firm to plunge into a new CKM system without careful business strategizing, business should be conceived as the driver for adoption of CKM, whereas ICT would be its enabler.

Although requiring high-quality customer databases or DWs in addition to other advanced ICT solutions, CKM is converging business and technology rather than being a 'technology-driven' solution alone. The holistic organizational transformation focus of CKM should continue to be preserved in the future. Although business managers and their staff are the knowledge users of CKM systems and are responsible for generating knowledge about different aspects of the business and its customers, active involvement, support, and participation from senior-management levels and ICT managers are also essential for a successful implementation of KM strategy.

CONCLUSION

Contemporary organizations are experiencing significant changes caused by dynamic growth in the marketplace that cannot be met by traditional competitive strategies. Price or products have traditionally been a base of competition for businesses, but today's bases of competition have shifted towards speed, quality, flexibility, and customer intimacy. Many organizations are realizing that a competitive position cannot be taken for granted as local and global market conditions change constantly.

The traditional market-based view of competitive strategy is based on the firm's external business environment and the threats of competition. Resource-based models of the firm would argue that a firm can only achieve competitive advantage when its resources are rare and difficult-to-imitate. In the knowledge-based view of a firm, competitive advantage or positioning is created through knowledge-intensive competencies that maximize value-adding offerings to customers.

The long purpose of crafting a business strategy is the nurturing of long-lasting competitive advantage. The ability of organizations to compete successfully in dynamic business environments and to maximize profitability is becoming highly related to organizational ability to leverage distinctive core competencies that cannot be easily emulated by others, e.g. the ability to continue to use CK to maximize the experience of customers through new or revised products or services. Current competitive challenges induced by turbulent and complex business environments have forced companies to identify and create knowledge-based distinctive core competencies to secure a long-term competitive advantage, i.e. enduring relationship with customers to maximize profitability.

CKM has been introduced within the context of a customer-centric, knowledge-based holistic business change model that is designed to leverage the firm's DCCs in order to deliver highest value for both customers and companies. The proposed CKM framework provides a detailed, clear, accessible, and comprehensive coverage of CKM. Unlike traditional stimulus-response relationships (i.e., product, price, place, and physical distribution), CKM considers network relationships with customers and suppliers. Devising a strategy that is built upon enduring and profitable relationships with customers requires the creation of knowledge about customers and making intelligent decisions on the creation of value-adding products or services to those same customers.

Adoption of CKM strategic change demands changes in processes, as well as the social, structural, and technical elements of an organization. In their effort to add value for customers, organizations may face several issues such as dealing with CKM as a business program, not just an ICT project, aligning CKM with major organizational components (people, structure, process, and technology), and emphasizing intellectual (staff) capital as much as relationship (customers) capital of organizations.

So, organizations, be they private or public sector, that want to create and sustain success in the 21st century must act in a way that continues to provide value for clients and profit to themselves through resources, i.e. knowledge, that are difficult-to-imitate, non-transferable, and immobile. Organizations may need to shift their orientation from internal focus (products) to external focus (customers), from conventional to creative strategic planning, from a technology to 'tech-knowledgy' emphasis and from single to dual control of company-customer relationships.

REFERENCES

Alter, S. (2002). *Information systems: Foundation of e-business.* 4th edition, Upper Saddle River, NJ: Prentice Hall.

Alter, S. (2006). *The work system method: Connecting people, processes and IT for business results.* Larkspur, CA: Work System Press.

Andrews, K. R. (1971). *The concept of corporate strategy.* Homewood, IL: Irwin

Awad, E., & Ghaziri, H. (2004). *Knowledge management.* Upper Saddle River, NJ: Prentice-Hall.

Barney, J. B. (1991). Firm resources and sustained competitive advantage. *Journal of Management, 17*(1), 99-120.

Boar, B. (1994). The *art of strategic planning for information technology.* NY: John Wiley.

Bolton, M. (2004). Customer centric business processing. *International Journal of Productivity and Performance Management, 53*(1), 44-51.

Boyett, J. H., & Boyett, J. T. (1995). *Beyond workplace 2000: Essential strategies for the new American corporation.* New York: Dutton.

Bueren, A., Schierholz, R., Kolbe, L. M., & Brenner, W. (2005). Improving performance of customer-processes with knowledge management. *Business Process Management Journal, 11*(5), 573-588.

Buttle, F. (2004). *Customer relationship management: Concepts and Tools.* Oxford, England: Elsevier Publishing.

Chen, I., & Popovich, K. (2003). Understanding customer relationship management (CRM): People, process and technology. *Business Process Management Journal, 9*(5), 672-688.

Dalkir, K. (2005). *Knowledge management in theory and practice.* Amsterdam: Elsevier Butterworth-Heinemann.

Davenport, T. H., Javenpaa, S. L., & Beers, M. C. (1996). Improving knowledge processes. *Sloan Management Review, 37*(4), 53-65.

Davenport, T., & Prusak, L. (2000). *Working knowledge.* 2nd edition, Boston, MA: Harvard Business School Press.

Drucker, P. (1993). *Post-capital society.* New York: Harper & Collins.

Earl, M. (1994). The new and the old of business process redesign. *Journal of Information Systems, 3*(1), 5-22.

Edvinsson, L., & Malone, M. S. (1997). *Intellectual Capital: Realizing Your Company's True Value by Finding Its Hidden Roots.* New York, NY: Harper Business.

Emery, F. (1959). *Characteristics of sociotechnical systems.* London: Tavistock Institute.

Formant, C. (2000). Customer Acquisition and CRM: A Financial Services Perspective. In S. A. Brown (Ed.), *Customer relationship management: A strategic imperative in the world of e-business* (pp.87-105). Toronto, Canada: John Wiley & Sons.

Gebert, H., Geib, M., Kolbe, L., & Brenner, W. (2003). Knowledge-enabled customer relationship management and knowledge management concepts. *Journal of Knowledge Management, 7*(5), 107-123.

Grant, R. M. (1991). The Resource-based theory of competitive advantage: Implications for strategy formulation. *California Management Review, 33*, 113-135.

Grant, R. M. (2002). The knowledge-based view of the firm. In N. Bontis & C. W.Choo (Eds.), *The strategic management of intellectual capital and organizational knowledge.* Oxford, U.K.: Oxford University Press.

Graetz, F., Rimmer, M., Lawrence, A., & Smith, A. (2006). *Managing organizational change.* 2nd Edition, Milton, Australia: John Wiley.

Hammer, M. (1990). Reengineering work: don't automate, obliterate. *Harvard Business Review,* July-August, 104-112.

Hammer, M., & Champy, D. (2003). *Reengineering the corporation: A manifesto for business revolution.* New York: HarperCollins Publishers.

Heizer, J., & Render, B. (2006). *Operations management.* 8th edition, New Jersey: Prentice-Hall.

Hill, T. (1993). *Manufacturing strategy.* 2nd edition, New York: Macmillan.

Hill, C. W., & Jones, G. R. (2007). *Strategic management: An integrated approach.* Boston, MA: Houghton Mifflin.

Javidan, M. (1998). Core competence: What does it mean in practice? *Long Range Planning, 31*(1), 60-71.

Johnson, G., Scholes, K., & Whittington, R. (2005). *Exploring corporate strategy: Text and Cases.* 7th edition, Essex, England: FT Prentice Hall.

Kanter, R. M. (1989). *When giants learn to dance.* New York: Simon & Schuster.

Kim, W. C., & Mauborgne, R. (1999). Strategy, value Innovation, and the knowledge economy, *Sloan Management Review, 40*(3), 41-54.

Klein, D. (1998). *The strategic management of intellectual capital.* Oxford, UK: Butterworth-Heinemann.

Knox, S., Maklan, S., Payne, A., Peppard, J., & Ryals, L. (2003). *Customer relationship management: Perspectives from the marketplace.* Oxford, UK: Butterworth-Heinemann.

March, J. G. (1991). Exploration and exploitation in organizational learning. *Organization Science, 2*(1), 71-87.

Maier, R., & Remus, U. (2003). Implementing process-oriented knowledge management strategies. *Journal of Knowledge Management, 7*(4), 62-74.

Martilla, J., & James, J. (1977). Importance-Performance analysis. *Journal of Marketing, 41*(1), 77-79.

Miller, D. (1990). *The Icarus paradox: How exceptional companies bring about their own downfall.* New York: Harper Collins Publishers.

Mintzberg, H. (1994). *The rise and fall of strategic planning.* Hemel Hempstead, Hertfordshire, England: Prentice-Hall.

Mintzberg, H., Lampel, J., & Ahlstrand, B. (2005). *Strategy safari: A guided tour through the wilds of strategic management.* New York: The Free Press.

Murray, P. (2000). How smart companies get results from KM. In D. Marchland & T. Davenport (Eds.). *Mastering information management: Your single-source guide to becoming a master of information management (pp. 187-192).* London, U.K.: FT Prentice-Hall.

Park, C., & Kim, Y. (2003). A framework of dynamic CRM: Linking marketing with information strategy. *Business Process Management Journal, 9*(5), 652-671.

Peppard, J., & Ronald, P. (1995). *The essence of business process re-Engineering.* Upper Saddle River, NJ: Prentice-Hall.

Peppers, D., & Rogers, M. (2004). *Managing customer relationships: A strategic framework*. Hoboken, NJ: John Wiley.

Peppers, D., Rogers, M., & Dorf, B. (1999). *The one-to-one field book*. New York: Doubleday.

Porter, M. E. (1980). *Competitive strategy: Techniques for analyzing industries and competitors*. New York: The Free Press.

Porter, M. E. (1985). *Competitive advantage: Creating and sustaining superior performance*. New York: The Free Press.

Porter, M. (1998). *Competitive strategies*. New York: The Free Press.

Rainer, K., Turban, E., & Potter, R. (2007). *Introduction to information systems*. Hoboken, NJ: John Wiley.

Scott-Morton, M., & Allen, T. J. (1994). *Information technology and the corporation of the 1990s*. New York: Oxford University Press.

Shoemaker, P. J. (1992). How to link strategic vision to core capabilities. *Sloan Management Review, 34*(1), 67-81.

Slack, N., Chambers, S., Johnston, R., & Betts, A. (2006). *Operations and process management: Principles and practice for strategic impact*. Essex, England: Pearson Education.

Stewart, T. (1997). *Intellectual capital*. New York: Doubleday.

Swift, R. (2001). *Accelerating customer relationships: Using CRM and Relationship Technologies*. Upper Saddle River, NJ: Prentice-Hall.

Thompson, A., Strickland, A., & Gamble, J. (2007). *Crafting and executing strategy: Text and cases*. Boston, MA: McGraw-Hill.

Tiwana, A. (2001). *The essential guide to knowledge management: E-business and CRM applications*. Upper Saddle River, NJ: Prentice-Hall.

Treacy, M., & Wiersema, F. (1995). *The Discipline of market leaders: Choose your customers, narrow your focus, and dominate your market*. Boston, MA: Addison-Wesley.

Turban, E., McLean, E., & Wetherbe, J. (1999). *Information technology for management: Making connections for strategic advantage*. 2nd edition, New York: John Wiley.

Turban, E., McLean, E., & Wetherbe, J. (2002). *Information technology for management: Transforming business in the digital economy.* 3rd edition, New York: John Wiley.

Weihrich, H. (1982). The TOWS matrix - a tool for situational analysis. *Long-Range Planning*, 15(2), 52-64.

Wernerfelt, B. (1984). A resource-based view of the firm, *Strategic Management Journal*, 5, 171-180.

Zack, M. H. (2002). A strategic pretext for knowledge management. *Proceeding of the Third European Conference on Organizational knowledge, learning and capabilities,* Athens, Greece, April 5.

Chapter II
Spotting Environmental Drivers

INTRODUCTION

The only constant in life is change, and business organizations are not different. Environmental uncertainties made transition to knowledge-based economies made establishment of effective CKM mechanisms within companies crucial to business competitiveness. This chapter examines the importance of business environmental conditions in driving an organizational change, viz. CKM. The basic premise of the chapter is that business organizations need to strive to adapt to opportunities as well as challenges brought by constant, complex, rapid, and discontinuous environmental uncertainties. In their quest for SCA, organizations need to leverage their DCCs in scanning environmental drivers for CKM as well as in the crafting a holistic CKM strategy.

CONCEPTUAL FOUNDATIONS

This part of the chapter discusses basic concepts related to organizational environments and the relationship between organizations and their environments. It identifies and explains major types of environments (the general and the task environments), typologies of environmental changes, organizational change programs, and the relationship between environments and organizational effectiveness.

Organizational Environment: The General Environment

Organizations' environments include external drivers that affect business delivery of products or services, and in turn customer satisfaction. Business external environments are becoming increasingly dynamic, competitive, and complex, carrying with them both challenges and opportunities. Adaptability to environmental conditions is becoming a key prerequisite to survival and success in today's turbulent environments.

Corporations in the 21st century face unprecedented complex and dynamic business environments, and have developed newly emerging organizational characteristics (Table 2.1). New ways of doing business, coupled with fast paced markets and continuous information generation, require knowledge-based skills to be consistently utilized and improved in order to achieve SCA (Bontis, 2004).

Conducting an analysis of political, economic, social, technological, international, and legal (PESTIL) conditions may identify general environmental conditions that impact a business. Major environmental conditions in today's marketplace include increased power of customers, growing competition, globalization of business, technological advancements, and government interventions.

The Political-Legal Environment

Government's role in the economy is beginning to shrink as more markets are being liberalized and many new players are entering into those new markets. Several areas may be controlled by government regulations such as telecommunications, health, safety, employment, wage rates, housing, market entry, and environmental control. Government regulations are usually viewed as constraints on all firms affected as they cost money and make it more difficult for some countries to compete with other countries that lack such regulations. On the other hand, government deregulations, or liberalization of markets, can be a blessing to one firm but a curse to another that loses regulation protection.

The role of governments in the new world economy is very limited, invisible, and often regulatory in nature. Even in developing countries, shrinking role of governments is becoming very noticeable. For instance, for so many years the telecommunications industry has been liberalized in many countries, with the hope for better customer welfare and higher levels of economic performance. As telecommunications networks form a country's 'nervous system', no country can develop and progress in the absence of such a system. The role of telecommunications in economic development is growing in industrial countries, in particular, but in all countries around the world. The developing countries have realized that 'wealth does not create telephone density, but that telephone density creates wealth' (Wilson, 2000).

Table 2.1. Traditional and emerging characteristics of organizations

20ᵗʰ Century Corporation	21ˢᵗ Century Corporation
Product-focused	Customer-focused
Mass production	Mass customization
Goal-oriented	Vision-oriented
Price-focused	Value-focused
Quality control	Total quality management
Stockholder-focused	Stakeholder-focused
Finance-directed	Speed-directed
Physical Assets	Knowledge Assets
Vertical Integration	Virtual Integration
Hierarchical	Flat
Functional	Cross-functional
Rigid	Flexible
Formal	Informal
Incremental Improvements	Revolutionary Improvements
Domestic	Global
Efficient	Innovative

Sources: Adapted from Wind and Main (1999), Byrne (2000), and Turban et al. (2002).

The primary rationale introduced by governments to regulate telecommunications was that because of the high infrastructure costs, network harmonization requirements and the obligation to provide universal service, telecommunication is a 'natural monopoly.' It was thought that competition or market forces could not effectively safeguard the consumers' interest. Therefore, prompted by the desire to safeguard consumers' interests, governments introduced regulation as a 'substitute for competition' (Wilson, 2000). On the other side, regulatory bodies can impose, on a frequent basis, restrictions that adversely affect business operations and success. Intensified competition in deregulated markets can lead to the loss of competitiveness without appropriate partnering.

The Economic Environment

Companies nowadays are facing the increasing challenge of shifting the power from the producer to the consumer, as well as changes in consumer trends. Consumer trends manifest themselves in increasingly changeable and diverse consumer preferences, more demanding consumers, an increasing interest for things such as status, reputation, brand names, logos, greater product design flexibility, higher responsiveness, user-friendliness, and an increasing interest in after-sales service provided for products and the shortening of the life span of products and services (Jacobs, 1996; Burlton, 2001).

The intensity of competition in today's marketplace is spiraling in both volume and velocity. Some of the major economic conditions that may be spotted are increased power of customers, shrinking business cycles, the commoditization of products and services, differentiation of products or services by knowledge, and globalization of business. Growing competition has been intensified due to the following (Burlton, 2001): shrinking business cycles, commoditization of products and services, and differentiation of products and services by knowledge.

- *Shrinking Business Cycles:* Since the mid-1980s, it has become clear that products and services do not remain unchanged for very long. Since then, the time to market and product life cycle have continued to shrink. Products or services nowadays last for months, not for years, before they have to be dropped or renewed. When this occurs, it decreases the opportunity to recover investment costs. Business organizations could improve their profitability through faster time to introduce a new capability that the marketplace would love (Burlton, 2001).

- *Commoditization of Products and Services:* Unlike products of a few years ago, many of today's products or services look much alike as many organizations learn from one another. Many newly added features seem to be limited in adding value to customers, and many products are becoming mature. Products with similar functionality were assessed by their quality. If a product's functionality and quality are comparable, customers usually look to convenience and customization (Burlton, 2001). Therefore, in the future, tailor-made (make-to-order) customization is thought to pose a real challenge to ready-made (make-to-stock) commoditization, as will be discussed in the future trends section of this chapter.

- *Differentiation of Products and Services by Knowledge:* Many organizations are now realizing that providing great products or services is important, but by itself cannot guarantee success. Knowledge can be provided as a product, such as in training organizations and consulting firms, or incorporated as a major component of products or services. Knowledge incorporated in products or services is needed in order to make it easy for customers to use the product with confidence, and in order to help differentiate products or services from those of other competitors. An example is the availability of knowledgeable staff to answer customers' queries, or operating manuals and reference materials in physical or electronic form (Burlton, 2001). One famous example of knowledge incorporated in products is the Progressive Insurance model of service to automobile insurance policyholders. Progressive Insurance adjusters can go to the accident scene with their technology-equipped vehicles, survey the damage, arrange for personal transportation and towing of the vehicle, and give a check to close the insurance claim case on the spot (Hammer and Champy, 1993).

The Socio-Cultural Environment

The term 'culture', in its wider context, displays a notion of shared attributes (such as language, religion, beliefs, traditions, heritage), and values that distinguish one group or society from another (Schein, 1990). Hofstede (2003) describes culture as the collective programming of the mind (the way people think and interpret information) which distinguishes one group of people from another. Because of its pervasive nature, culture can undoubtedly be perceived among a group of people just as personality can be perceived in an individual (Usoro and Kuofie, 2006). Differences in individuals' values, perceptions, attitudes, motivations, and behaviors from one country to another may be partially explained by differences in national cultures. Hofstede (1980, 1994) studied 116,000 people working in different countries and identified five dimensions across cultures, each of which varies on a continuum, with two extreme points: social orientation, power orientation, uncertainty orientation, goal orientation, and time orientation.

A brief description of dimensions of international societal cultures is given below:

- *Social Orientation*: a person's belief about the relative importance of the individual compared to groups to which the person belongs, i.e. individualism versus collectivism. Individualism is the cultural belief that the individual comes first; whereas collectivism is the belief that the group comes first. Hofstede found that the relatively individualistic societies such as the United States, the United Kingdom, Australia, Canada, New Zealand, and the Netherlands tend to be relatively individualistic. On the other hand, he found that societies that are relatively collectivistic in their values are Mexico, Greece, Hong Kong, Taiwan, Peru, Singapore, Colombia, and Pakistan.
- *Power Orientation*: the beliefs of people about the acceptance of differences in authority and power of people in the hierarchy, i.e. high power distance versus low power distance. Hofstede's work found that people in France, Spain, Mexico, Japan, Brazil, Indonesia, and Singapore are relatively power accepting. In contrast, Hofstede found that individuals that are more willing

to question a decision or mandate from someone at a higher level, or may even refuse to accept it, are found in countries such as the United States, Denmark, Norway, Germany, and New Zealand.

- *Uncertainty Orientation*: refers to the extent to which people accept or avoid uncertain and ambiguous situations, i.e. uncertainty avoidance versus uncertainty acceptance. People in cultures with uncertainty acceptance are stimulated by change and thrive on new opportunities, whereas people in cultures of uncertainty avoidance dislike and avoid uncertainty whenever possible. Hofstede's work found that people that tend to accept uncertainty come from countries such as the United States, Denmark, Sweden, Canada, Australia, and Hong Kong; whereas people that tend to avoid uncertainty whenever possible are found in Austria, Japan, France, Germany, Peru, and Columbia.

- *Goal Orientation*: is the extent to which people are motivated toward different kinds of goals, i.e. career success versus quality of life. In fact, Hofstede initially labeled this dimension 'masculinity versus femininity'. At one extreme, people may exhibit aggressive goal behavior by placing high value on materialistic possessions, money, and assertiveness. In contrast, other people may show passive goal orientation by placing high value on social relationships, quality of life, and welfare of others. Hofstede found that relatively aggressive goal behaviors are exhibited by Japanese, moderately aggressive goal behaviors by people in countries such as the United States, Germany, Mexico, and Italy, whereas relatively passive goal behaviors tend be exhibited by people from the Netherlands and the Scandinavian countries of Norway, Sweden, and Finland.

- *Time Orientation*: is a newly identified dimension (Hofstede, 1994) in which people adopt a short-term versus long-term outlook on work, life, and other elements of society. 'Western' countries such as the United States and Germany tend to focus on immediate problem solving, whereas 'eastern' countries such as Japan, South Korea, and Hong Kong tend to exhibit a longer-term time orientation aim for the survival in the long run, and do not mind too many mistakes, provided subsequent attempts bring improvements.

The Technological Environment

In addition to today's rapidly changing markets, ICTs are rapidly evolving and is changing the way organizations do business. The proliferation of technology, data communications, networking and wireless transmission has revolutionized the way employees store, communicate, and exchange knowledge at high speed (Awad and Ghaziri, 2004). ICTs have the power to change the way business functions and interacts with customers, and to change the meaning of space to process information from around the world in real time through the convergence of different types of media, e.g. voice, data and video - known as 'multimedia'. This introduces the concept of an 'information superhighway' into various business applications such as carrying telephone calls, interactive shopping, electronic banking, and electronic entertainment.

Technological advancements create new business opportunities. Business conducted over electronic networks, or e-business, involves dramatic changes in physical distance and time that allowed for provision of products or services anywhere at anytime. E-business is faster, cheaper, more convenient to customers, and more scalable to accommodate business growth than physical "brick and mortar" business. E-business transactions require organizational structure to be designed around business that cut across business functions (Burlton, 2001).

The International Environment

It has been estimated that two-thirds of today's businesses operate globally (Edmonson, 2000). Marketplaces liberalized by free trade policies and agreements alongside advanced ICTs and the Web technology have opened up the world market for companies in different parts of the world. The global marketplace has dramatically increased international trade and global supply chain transactions. Global business transactions include selling, producing, purchasing, or partnering that take place in global marketplaces in order to take advantage of favorable costs of labor and materials and access to international markets.

Increased globalization of business has driven many companies to concentrate on their core strengths, or competencies, and outsource non-core ones. An example of core competencies is the special skills of workers, such as expertise in providing customized services or knowledge of a particular information system. More and more jobs in the United States and Europe are shifting to other parts of the world. Customer-service call centers of many American companies have been outsourced to Indian companies based in Bangalore, while processing of insurance claims takes place in the Philippines. Caltex Petroleum moved its headquarters from Dallas to Singapore, accounting to Manila, and its Web development to South Africa. Cognizant Technologies does sales and marketing in New Jersey and virtually everything else in Madras and Calcutta. Bell Labs, Microsoft, and Motorola operate large R&D labs in India (Clifford and Kripalani, 2000).

Organizational Environment: The Task Environment

Our discussion to this point identified and described the components of the high-level general environment. In this section, a low-level new classification of environment is provided, viz. the task environment. This classification is not very different from the first one in terms of the type or nature of its components, but in terms of its level of detail. Because the impact of the general environment sometimes is vague, imprecise, and long term, most organizations tend to focus their attention on their detailed and observable task environment.

The task environment includes five components: competitors, customers, suppliers, strategic partners, and regulators. The task environment more readily provides useful information to the organization because managers can identify environmental factors of specific interest to the organization, rather than having to deal with the high-level and more abstract dimensions of the general environment (Griffin, 2005).

Environmental Change Typologies

Organizations operate in environments with a wide range of changes that create a wide range of complexities and uncertainties. Thompson (1967) proposed a typology of environment that is based on two dimensions: its degree of change and its degree of homogeneity. The degree of change is the extent to which the environment is relatively stable or relatively dynamic, whereas the degree of homogeneity is the extent to which the environment is relatively simple (few elements, little heterogeneity), or relatively complex (many elements, much segmentation).

The interactions between different degrees of homogeneity and different degrees of change make up the following levels of uncertainty faced by the organization: least uncertainty, moderate uncertainty, and most uncertainty (Figure 2.1).

- Least uncertainty caused by a simple and stable environment (e.g., clothes manufacturers such as Levi, Wrangler, and Lee).
- Moderate uncertainty caused by a dynamic and simple environment, or by a stable and complex environment (e.g., car makers such as Ford, DaimlerChrysler, and GM).
- Most uncertainty caused by a dynamic and complex environment (e.g., electronics manufactures such as Intel, Compaq, and IBM).

CRITICAL ISSUES

This section addresses the major issues that surround environmental conditions and organizational responses to their environments. Issues discussed are the internal versus external environmental drivers, objective versus subjective scanning of environments, haphazardly versus planned change, institutionalized versus de-

Figure 2.1. Classification of organizational environments

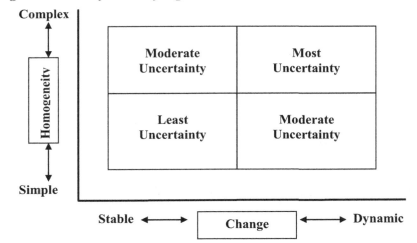

Source: Adapted from Thompson (1967). Organizations in Actions. New York: McGraw-Hill.

institutionalized organizational change, incremental versus radical organizational change, and partial versus total organizational change.

Internal vs. External Environmental Drivers

In order to understand the impacts of the business environments on organizations we will use a classical management framework, as shown in Figure 2.2, that was developed by Leavitt (1965) and modified by Scott-Morton and Allen (1994) and Turban et al. (2002). Organizations are composed of five major interrelated components, viz. organizational structure/culture, management process, ICT, organizational strategy, and individuals and roles, and surrounded by an environment.

Organizations may be also looked at as socio-technical systems, composed of human (people) and technical elements (processes, structure, strategy, and technology). The socio-technical components of the system, although different, are interdependent and are in a stable condition (equilibrium) unless there are external forces or internal forces for change (i.e., a shift to a customer-centric strategy necessitates a shift to a customer-centric structure).

Besides focusing on uncontrollable environmental contingencies (e.g., task, environment, technology, and people), organizations may focus on controllable drivers of change (e.g., learning, efficiency, or innovation motives). The Balanced Score Card (BSC), developed by Kaplan and Norton (1996), helps to manage and

Figure 2.2. Five forces influence the organization

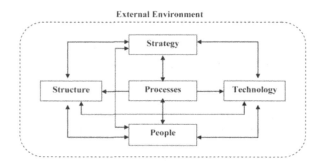

Adapted from Leavitt (1965), and M. Scott-Morton and Allen (1994), and Turban et al. (2002).

implement a business strategy by providing a balance among four controllable areas, viz. customer, financial, business process, and learning and growth (Kaplan and Norton, 1996):

- *Learning and Growth:* In rapid technological advancements, it is becoming necessary for knowledge workers to be in a continuous learning mode. Kaplan and Norton emphasize that 'learning' is more than 'training', and it includes things like mentors and tutors within the organization, as well as corporate culture and ease of communication among workers that allows them to readily get help on a problem when it is needed.
- *Business Processes:* this measure allows the managers to know how well their business is running, and whether its products and services conform to customer requirements (the mission).
- *Customer:* if customers are not satisfied, they will switch to other suppliers that will meet their needs. Customer dissatisfaction is a leading indicator of future decline, even though the current financial picture may look good. In developing metrics for satisfaction, customers should be analyzed in terms of kinds of customers and the kinds of processes for which a business provides a product or service to a customer group.
- *Financial:* Kaplan and Norton did not disregard the traditional need for financial measures. Timely and accurate financial data will always be a priority, and managers will do whatever necessary to provide it.

Organizations are usually involved in a continuous process of alignment (adaptation) with their external environments. Organizational adaptation starts with understanding of PESTIL environments, followed by reaction to these environments, and ends up with putting the organization in its preferred environmental position that secures higher levels of organizational effectiveness or performance. To be responsive to environmental changes does not mean to take a passive reaction to external forces, but to take a proactive response that makes organizations 'fit' with their business conditions.

There are four perspectives that help us to understand the concept of organizational effectiveness: the systems resource approach, the internal process approach, the goal approach, and the constituencies approach.

- *The Systems Resource Approach* focuses on the ability of an organization to acquire the resources it needs, such as getting raw materials during a shortage (Yuchtman and Seashore, 1967).
- *The Internal Process Approach* focuses on the internal mechanism of the organization such as minimizing strain, integrating individuals and the organization, and conducting smooth and efficient operations (Georgopoules and Tannenbaum, 1957).
- *The Goal Approach* focuses on the degree to which an organization achieves its goals, such as increasing market share in the next year by 20%. (Jones, 2001).
- *The Constituencies Approach* focuses on the satisfaction of demands and expectations of stakeholders who have a strategic interest in the organization, such as customers, stockholders, creditors, suppliers, etc (Atkinson et al., 1997). The concept of social responsibility has been advanced to balance commitment to investors, employees, customers, other businesses, and the communities in which they operate. This concept has been introduced as a counterpart to business ethics. One area of social responsibility that has received great attention is responsibility toward the environment.

The aforementioned approaches to organizational effectiveness are not mutually exclusive. The systems resource approach focuses on inputs, the internal processes approach focuses on transformation processes, the goal approach focuses on outputs, and the strategic constituencies approach focuses on feedback. Thus, rather than adopting a single approach, one can understand organizational effectiveness through a unifying model. The core of this unifying model is the organizational system, with its inputs, transformations, outputs, and feedback. Surrounding this core are the four basic approaches to organizational effectiveness as well as a combined approach which incorporates each of the other four. The basic premise behind this unifying approach is that in order for an organization to be effective, it needs to satisfy the requirements imposed on it by each of the effectiveness perspectives (Griffin, 2005).

Objective vs. Subjective Environmental Scanning

Some writers try to explain the concept of organizational change based on the notion of the environment as an objective entity *per se* that pressures organizations to change. Organizations in dynamic and complex business environments need to continue to monitor feedback from their environments and make appropriate adjustments in order to avoid decline or even failure. However, the notion of an objective environment has been challenged by a constructivist view that treats the environment as not having an objective existence outside of individual views and perceptions of it (Smirchich and Stubbart, 1985). Inaccurate perceptions of the environment as an objective entity may occur when the environment is *objectively* stable, but managers perceive it as turbulent and take unnecessary actions (Type I error), or when managers threaten the survival of their firms by failing to take actions as they perceive their environment as stable when it is *objectively* turbulent (Type II error) (Boyd et al., 1993).

Forces for and against change, for instance, are not purely contingent upon objective environmental events but upon images of these events held by the chief executive officer (CEO) and senior management. This implies that organizational change actions will take place only when perceived forces for change exceed those against it, and it also implies that 'brainpower' will have a profound impact on setting future directions of organizations, as manifested in the planning, design, and development of change programs.

The purpose of environmental scanning is to develop a complete understanding of the three dimensions of environments, known as the 'environmental scanning trilogy'. Environmental scanning involves a three-dimensional dynamic and creative macro level analysis of opportunities and threats in business environments that include three components (Figure 2.3): dynamism, diversity, and differentiation (3 Ds).

- Dynamism (static versus dynamic) refers to the fact that environmental conditions are relatively dynamic and are subject to constant changes at different degrees of pace, volume, and intensity.
- Diversity (similar versus diversified) refers to the fact that there are multiple diverse or identical PESTIL factors that exist in the environment and challenge business organizations to respond.

- Differentiation (old versus new) relates to the evolving and renewable nature of diverse and dynamic environmental conditions. For instance, new socio-economic or technological conditions could emerge while old ones are subject to decline or even demise.

Haphazard vs. Planned Organizational Change

Change that may take place in an organization is of two types - haphazard and planned change (Brown and Harvey, 2006). The haphazard change is not prepared for, but is created as a reaction to external environmental pressures. This type of change includes downsizing, where significant staff members are laid off. The second type, planned change, results from proactive attempts of organizations to modify their operations in order to promote improvement (Brown and Harvey, 2006).

Two related types of change may be developed based on the response of organizations to environmental conditions, i.e. reactive or proactive change. The major characteristics of the two approaches to managing change in organizations are documented in Table (2.2).

Figure 2.3. Three-dimensional environmental change scanning model

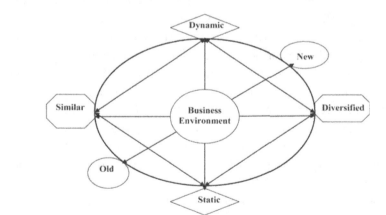

Table 2.2. A summary of characteristics of reactive and proactive change

Dimension	Reactive Change	Proactive Change
Mode	Haphazard	Planned
Driver	Challenges	Opportunities
Orientation	Profit-Satisficing	Profit-Maximizing
Strategy	Risk-Averting	Risk-Taking
Scope	Partial	Total
Focus	Information	Knowledge
Time Range	Short-term	Long-term
Market Position	Follower	Leader

Institutionalized vs. De-Institutionalized Organizational Change

Change is an acceptable fact in life, but its degree and its nature differ from one situation to another. Change is endemic to the practice of organizing and hence is enacted through the situated practice of organizational actors as they improvise, innovate, learn, and adjust their work routines over time (Orlikowski, 1996). Since all organizations are subject to decline (or system entropy), some organizations find it necessary to undergo a program of change.

In the face of environmental pressures, some organizations may be engaged in a responsive change effort, while others may continue to be stable and unresponsive (Palmer et al., 2006). It is argued in the literature that environmental forces of organizational change need to be considered alongside simultaneous forces for stability in order for change to be triggered (Leana and Barry, 2000). Forces for change may include adaptability of organizations to their environment, cost containment (i.e., making human resources a variable rather than fixed cost), impatient capital markets for long-term returns, control (less hierarchy but more empowerment), and competitive advantage. Forces for stability include institutionalization of current practices due to solidity of past practices and power structures, transaction costs (i.e. stability in employment enables firms to invest in human assets), sustained advantage not easily imitated or substituted, and the need for high predictability and certainty (Leana and Barry, 2000).

Organizational learning (OL) theorists (e.g., Senge, 1990) argue that environmental pressures call for innovative adaptation by organization However, some organizational theorists argue that such pressures will inhibit innovative change as managers' cognitive and decision-making processes become restricted when confronted with threatening problems (Mone et al., 1998) or when organizations become trapped by a cognitive frame of success or routines 'institutionalization' that become embedded in the organization as correct ways of operations (Sull, 1999). Such 'learning disability' leads organizations and managers to assume that their market dominance will continue unchallenged in the future and will inhibit them from exploring new business ventures (Palmer, 2006).

The concept of institution in explaining the dynamics of change has a broad sense in institutionalization theory. Institutionalization refers to authoritative, established, rule-like procedures in society with a self-sustaining character. Institutions are broadly defined as 'those social patterns that, when chronically produced, owe their survival to relatively self-activating social process' (Jepperson, 1991). The institutional theory of change argues that it is not possible to explain changes that are happening in organizations only by considering the rational actions of managers due only to environmental drivers. It provides a perspective that takes into account 'irrationality' drivers stemming from the structural and cultural forces in organizations. Institutions are a taken-for-granted standardized sequence of activities in their environment irrespective of their contribution to the process of organizational change (Avgerou, 2000).

Within the prevailing market driven turbulent and complex context, traditional organizational structures have been challenged and new forms of designing organizations started building their own legitimacy. Therefore, it becomes imperative for the design of high-performance organizations to create dynamic stability (equilibrium) and sustainable success (Holbeche, 2005). The quest for and adoption of new organizational forms suitable for their changing environment, constitutes a de-institutionalization process (Avgerou, 2000). However, most organizational change programs are only fashions, contributing to a sense of 'short lived', transient changes rather than to establishing incrementally new organizational norms (Abrahamson, 1991, 1996; Pettigrew, 1998) that replaces the 'cultural persistence' of the old ones (Avgerou, 2000).

Institutionalization is the process through which a particular pattern of change becomes accepted as a social 'fact'. A technological innovation is first adopted and diffused partly for its technical merits (Zucker, 1983) and partly due to the influence of powerful organizational actors (Granovetter and McGuire, 1998). The institutionalist theory probed down into the socio-structural aspects of organizational change and traced the unconscious central values that keep an organization together as an institutional entity, demonstrating that institutional aspects such as the pyramid structure, are maintained and affected by unconscious taking-for-granted 'the way things are done here', which creates institutional inertia (Zucker, 1983). Within organizations, actions follow rule-like patterns, 'norms', which are embedded in formal structures and not tied to particular actors or situations (Zucker, 1987, 1991).

ICT uptake, for instance, has gained unquestionable popularity and validity in contemporary organizations, intertwined with significant changes in the institutionalized structure of power and work practices. Within a period of 30 years, ICT acquired the legitimacy of an 'enabler' for almost anything organizational actors could think as one of the most significant factors justifying and enacting organizational change. The interaction between ICT innovation and organizational change can be conceptualized as a dual process of institutionalization of ICT and de-institutionalization of existing organizational structures and practices (Avgerou, 2000).

ICT innovation often involves a more visible and better-structured area of activities within uncertain and fluid organizational change direction. Through institutionalization, a technological innovation may be adopted and maintained not due to its delivery of promised technical value or its reliance on powerful personalities, but due to its acquired legitimacy (Avgerou, 2000). Therefore, responsiveness to ICT institutionalized change requires organizational change de-institutionalization, i.e., transformation of organizational structure from hierarchical to a more fluid form such as flat pyramid, networked, or even virtual organizations. In horizontal or networked structures, 'process teams' are formed which include specialists representing different business functions, in order to streamline processes and reduce workflow cycle time. In virtual organizations, the boundaries of business organizations are becoming harder to define as more and more companies form a web of autonomous units, partners, contractors, outsourcers, and freelancers. Thus, companies can use ICT to interact with an increasing number of customers, firms, markets, and alliances.

With increasingly rapid, dynamic changes in the business environment, static assumptions embedded in ICTs become vulnerable. Increasing interest is growing in designing ICTs that can take dynamic market changes and diverse interpretations of changing information into account to provide the fast, reliable, and updated information to customers. An example is dynamic and flexible pricing pioneered by websites such as priceline.com and e-bay. However, the challenge remains that ICT solutions often tend to be inflexible and are based upon designers' beliefs that they have already identified the organizational and environmental properties need to be dynamic and flexible.

Gradual vs. Radical Organizational Change

The business world is witnessing more significant changes in the 21st century compared to the 20th century. Many of the changes that take place in the corporate world have a direct impact on business transactions. In today's competitive business world, no organization is immune from changes that are brought by business drivers. Business environments never rest, and organizational responses never stop. Therefore, managers of organizations are called upon to change their organizations, as the success in today's business world cannot be achieved by just following traditional and old business practices and preset rules. Managers need to intervene to stabilize the unstable and destabilize the rigid; adapt to the present and anticipate the future; improve what is and invent what is to be; and lead a renaissance while preserving tradition (Palmer et al., 2006).

There are two major approaches to organizational change, organization development (OD) and organizational transformation (OT) (Brown and Harvey, 2006). OD refers to a deliberate attempt to modify the functioning of the total organization or one of its major parts in order to bring about improvement in performance. It is a planned change that often focuses more on first-order, large-scale changes introduced over a longer time frame and on a more gradual basis such as Total Quality Management (TQM), process improvement, and six sigma. On the other hand, OT may be defined as a drastic, abrupt total redesign of everything such as the corporate structures, processes, and culture (i.e., reengineering, massive downsizing, and business scope redefinition). The difference between OD and OT centers on the magnitude and speed of the change - the difference between revolution and evolution. Moreover, OT tends to use a more top-down directive than participative approach to change. Decisions on parameters of change such as when to initiate change, what the changes will be, how the change is to be implemented, and who is responsible for the change program are usually undertaken in a top-management-driven process (Brown and Harvey, 2006).

In addition, both approaches to change differ in terms of their scale and scope of their products or customer processes. Scale of change may range from incremental and evolutionary to revolutionary and radical change, whereas scope of change relates to who or what will be affected by the change. For instance, radical change programs, such as BPR, may adopt a narrow or a wide definition that focuses on one or more of organizational pillars to which the change applies, i.e., systems, processes, people, and structures. Incremental, gradual, or continuous change involves adjustments in systems, processes, or structures, but does not involve fundamental changes in strategy, core values, or corporate identity (Newman, 2000). Advocates of incremental changes argue that the aim of change is to maintain and develop the organization to support its continuity and order (Boyett and Boyett, 1995). However, incremental changes will not create SCA (Boyett and Boyett, 1995). Examples of gradual change efforts are improving quality, lowering cost, or doing traditional things faster.

Advocates of radical change believe that as incremental changes cannot create nor sustain a competitive advantage, dramatic changes are needed to produce a fundamental reorientation of an organization, or 'creative destruction' (Nolan and Croson, 1995) in order to cope with highly competitive changes in the business environment (Palmer et al., 2006). 'Creative destruction' is a six-stage change process to enable a firm to meet the demands of the business environment. The six stages are concerned with downsizing, seeking a dynamic balance, developing a market access strategy, becoming market driven, developing a market foreclosure strategy, and pursuing a global scope. However, large scale and scope change have often been criticized for their potential chaos, cynicism, and burnout arising from change (Abrahamson, 2000).

Although radical changes may be imperative in turbulent business environments, they need to be undertaken only when the need and readiness for change is well calculated. In large-scale and wide-scope organizational change programs, and instead of undertaking radical changes with higher risks, nor incremental changes with lower returns, a mid-way organizational change approach may be sought. Roger et al. (1994) proposed a 'moderate earthquake' organizational change approach that allows organizations to continue to be responsive and flexible in generating signifi-cant variations in development and delivery of products or services according to customers' preferences. A 'moderate earthquake' is large enough to overcome the inertia that plagues large organizations while avoiding the cataclysmic side effects of massive revolutions'. 'Moderate earthquakes' are important where companies seek to modify the company without destroying the loyalty of employees and other positive company attributes. These mid-range changes are designed 'to destroy outdated aspects of the organization's old identity while simultaneously building on other, still relevant, elements' (Roger et al. 1994:37).

It is beyond doubt that organizational environments may well be changing, but prescriptions for how organizations should be changed in order to meet these new environments need to move beyond ready-made solutions to careful consideration of organizational need and readiness (existing strengths and future requirements). On a broader perspective, to undertake radical or transformational change, organizations need to build in the capability to handle that change in terms of creating a value-adding structure, effective business integration, a market responsiveness leadership, and a learning culture (Carnall, 2003). Thus, managers need to be careful not to rush to remove old organizational practices and replace them with new, more flex-ible practices. Rather than replacing the old with the new, both should be integrated (Palmer et al., 2006).

Partial vs. Total Organizational Change

Organizational change and its management may be analyzed from partial or total change perspectives. A partial change perspective addresses one particular type of intervention, i.e. technology, people, or processes. On the other hand, a total change perspective takes a pluralistic approach to change that is based on simultaneous utilization of multiple sources of intervention. Comprehensive understanding of change and its management will not come from a single discipline (Hughes, 2006). Burnes (1994) suggested that change management is not a distinct discipline with rigid and clearly defined boundaries, but that the theory and practice of change management draws on a number of disciplines.

Many writers advocate the need for total approaches to understanding change. Pettigrew (1990) argued that explanations of change are bound to be holistic and multi-faceted, and the work of Burnes (1996) maintains that there is no one best way to manage change. The previous discussion makes it very logical and practical for this book to adopt a pluralistic, rather than a partial, approach to understanding CKM change management.

RECOMMENDED SOLUTION: A PROPOSED CKM-BASED ORGANIZATION

The 21st century's knowledge-based economy has witnessed a shift from a focus on products to a focus on services for both manufacturing and service organizations. Customer service can be considered as a competitive battlefield, and the process to deliver customer service can be considered as a weapon for competition. Companies recognize that it is more appropriate to concentrate on serving the customer rather than producing the product. Some of the organizational requirements needed for organizations to continue to be competitive are (Burlton, 2001):

- Adopting a customer and product focus, not simply a product focus.
- Designing customizable modules of products that can evolve and change.
- Using adaptable technologies wherein rules and workflows can be changed without getting programmers involved.
- Focusing on the continuous enhancement of the knowledge of workers.
- Building flexible, responsive processes.

One of the most popular business approaches in responding to dynamic and turbulent environmental drivers is to support knowledge-intensive customer processes required for the transformation toward customer-centric organizations. A noteworthy customer-centric business model is the new Permission Marketing model that argues that one doesn't ask an acquaintance to get married when they first meet (Godin, 1999). The model doesn't try to sell too much too soon, rather, a number of steps need to take place in between, each of which requires permission to move to the next step. Finalizing a sale requires building confidence and trust, and then moving up through higher levels of permission to strike a deal. Such a task requires offering knowledge to customers in order to create familiarity and trust, as well as infusion of knowledge into business processes to make it easy for customers to buy and interact with sellers.

The premise of this book is centered on developing a CKM business model. CKM is a totally de-institutionized business model for building a long-term profitable and loyal relationship with customers in order to compete successfully in highly competitive and dynamic business environments. The undertaking of CKM as an integrative business solution requires a complete transformation from a product-centered and hierarchical to a customer-centric knowledge-based organization (CKO). OT reengineers three major infrastructural components of organization: people, processes, and technology.

The major planned change programs that may be undertaken by organizations are: strategic information systems (SIS), TQM, just-in-time (JIT), KM, OL, BPR, CRM, and electronic business (e-biz) (Currie, 2000; Turban, 2002). The proposed CKM-based organization represents a holistic business model that integrates all of the previously mentioned change programs in its response to environmental dynamics (Figure 2.4).

Strategic Information Systems (SIS)

Strategic systems provide organizations with advantages that enable them to increase their market share, better negotiate with suppliers, or to prevent competitors from entering their territory (Callon, 1996). An example of an IT-based strategic system is the overnight delivery system of Federal Express (Fed Ex). This system enables tracking of the status of every individual package. A major challenge with this kind of strategic system is the difficulty of creating SCA, as most of FedEx's competitors duplicated the system. So FedEx moved the system to the Web, but the competitors quickly followed. FedEx is continuously introducing new innovations to keep or expand market share, such as its plan to form a business alliance with the U.S. Postal Service (USPS). The business partnership enables USPS to use FedEx planes to ship mail and packages, and FedEx is able to use post offices as collection centers (Turban, 2002).

Total Quality Management (TQM)

TQM is a corporate-wide quality effort concerned with improving competitiveness, effectiveness, and flexibility. The core of TQM is about improving the relationships with customers and suppliers (Currie, 2000). TQM was developed first in the U.S. by Crosby (1979), Deming (1982), and Juran (1986), and then adapted by Japanese companies (Ishikawa, 1985).

Just-in-Time (JIT)

JIT is a comprehensive production scheduling and inventory control system that attempts to reduce costs and improve workflow by scheduling materials and parts to arrive at a workstation exactly when they are needed. JIT minimizes machine downtime, in-process inventories, wastes, and storage space. Like TQM, JIT was developed in the U.S. (Hall, 1983) and then adapted by Japanese companies to suit their context (Shingo, 1989). JIT is a philosophy that can be applied not only to inventory, but to many business areas such as production management methods and techniques, total quality assurance, total preventive maintenance, customer-supplier relationships, technology/innovation strategies, flexible working practices, and machine performance (Currie, 2000).

Figure 2.4. Business environment, organizational response activities, and the CKO

Source: Influenced by Turban et al. (2002). Information Technology for Management: Transforming Business in the Digital Economy. 3ʳᵈ edition, New York: John Wiley.

Knowledge Management (KM)

KM shows us how to create, store, process, and use knowledge efficiently and effectively. KM is best interpreted as complex, multilayered and multifaceted (Blackler, 1995). Effective KM methods and systems are needed to store, access, navigate, and probably use the vast amount of information to generate knowledge. Examples of KM systems (KMS) are Data Mining (DM), Artificial Intelligence (AI), Neural Networks (NN), Fuzzy logic (FL), Case-Based Reasoning (CBR), and Expert Systems (ES). Recently, many companies have incorporated KM policies and practices into their corporate strategies (Davenport et al., 1998).

Organizational Learning (OL)

The concept of OL became a popular organizational change program from the late 1970s to the early 1990s. OL occurs through shared insights, knowledge, and mental models, and builds on past knowledge and experience. Some writers even emphasize the learning organization and its advantage to business (Senge, 1990).

Business Process Reengineering (BPR)

When continuous improvement efforts fail to deliver in an environment full of strong business pressures, a relatively new approach called BPR is needed. BPR is a 'clean sheet' redesigning or streamlining of work processes to increase efficiency, improve quality, and reduce costs. Technological, human, and structural dimensions of an organization may all be changed in BPR (Hammer and Champy, 1993, Peppard and Rowland, 1995). A somewhat similar approach to BPR, process innovation, was proposed by Davenport (1993). Process innovation encompasses the envisioning of new work strategies, the actual process design activity, and the implementation of change in all complex technological, human, and organizational dimensions (Davenport, 1993).

Customer Relationship Management (CRM)

Due to the increased power of customers and stiff competition, companies are increasingly becoming more customer-oriented. In addition to the traditional activities of customer service, companies are finding it necessary to pay more attention to preferences of customers, so they are redesigning themselves to meet customers' demands (Turban et al., 2002). CRM is a combination of business processes and technology that seeks to understand customers from multiple perspectives to differentiate competitively products and services. The goal of CRM is to 'increase the opportunity by improving the process of communicating with the *right* customer, providing the *right* offer (product or service), through the *right* channel, at the *right* time' (Swift, 2001, p.14). The focus of CRM is to integrate processes in order to build relationships (improve customer satisfaction, loyalty, and revenues) in the face of stiff competition, globalization, high customer turnover, and growing customer acquisition costs (Tiwana, 2001).

Electronic Business (E-biz)

Doing business electronically is the newest and perhaps most promising strategy that many firms can pursue (Turban, 2002). E-biz is another form of organizational response to business pressures. E-biz is an expansion of electronic-commerce by adding computer applications for business transactions such as e-CRM, Enterprise Resource Planning (ERP), Supply Chain Management (SCM), e-procurement (integrates ordering, fulfillment, and payment), and Business Intelligence (BI), applications such as Data Warehousing/Mining and KM technologies (Kalakota and Robinson, 2001).

FUTURE TRENDS

Trends often start slowly but may evolve dramatically and spread like wildfire. Trend spotting is important for managers looking to identify new business opportunities. The smart managers stand at the forefront of trends before they become mainstream ones. Because it takes years to steer large organizations in new directions, company managers must be aware of what lies ahead, or their companies will sink as quickly as the *Titanic* (Kalakota and Robinson, 2001). It is important for CKM not only to understand the current business environment, but it must also gain insights into future trends. The following environmental trends are especially important: a shift from linear to exponential rate of environmental change, a shift from reactive to proactive mode of organizational change, and a shift from product commoditization to intelligent customization.

A Shift from Linear to Exponential Rate of Environmental Change

The hyper intensity of competition, complexity of customer behaviors, proliferation of technological advancements and customer choices, and globalization of marketplaces in the future are likely to make environmental changes highly uncertain. The rate of innovation in products, services, processes, and business solutions is growing rapidly and is expected to accelerate exponentially in the future. For example, newly developed ICTs are becoming integrated with business organizations and are playing an increased role in manufacturing as well as service organizations. Newly developed technologies create or support substitutes for products, alternative service options, and superb quality of service. Some of today's state-of-the-art products or technologies may be obsolete tomorrow (Turban et al., 2002). Future technological advancements will accelerate exponentially and the competitive forces will be expected to follow accordingly.

Gaining insight into a business world full of complex and dynamic turbulence, which creates a higher degree of uncertainty, represents a real challenge for companies in the future. Organizations sometimes fail to see the magnitude and degree of ongoing environmental changes. Like troops on the high ground, the business leader who has the long-sighted and broadest view of what is going on has the advantage. Companies that understand trends and changes in customer needs, preferences, and behaviors will be in a better position than its rivals. Companies of the future are expected to be more concerned with building business intelligence units to gather information on their rivals as well as the whole competitive environment.

For example, geographical dispersion of customers in e-business transactions is likely to carry with it many uncertainties and challenges. The key issue is how to meet customer needs and get the right product at the right time to the right customer in global marketplaces as diverse as the Far East, Europe, the Middle East, or Africa. Diversity of marketplaces requires consideration of many issues related to changes in business logistics, supply chain transactions, facilities, capacity, local government quality standards, and custom tariffs and regulations.

A Shift from Reactive to Proactive Mode of Organizational Change

The ability of organizations to respond quickly to accelerating change and turbulent competitive environmental change is of special importance in future organizations; this requires organizations to adopt a more proactive rather than reactive approach. Proactive change involves opening up new and innovative opportunities and venues for improvement and success instead of responding to challenges when they emerge. Sometimes, organizations fail to see that they are falling prey to organizational inertia, or laziness. Few organizations make significant vision-oriented changes to boost performance unless there is a crisis. The 'boiling frog syndrome' is an appropriate analogy here. When putting a frog into boiling water, it will jump out immediately, but when putting it into cold water and gradually raising the temperature, the frog will boil to death (Peppard, & Ronald, 1995).

Radical changes in organizations may be inevitable in turbulent business environments, and can be evidenced by a radical shift from a traditional vertical structure to virtual existence in cyberspace, or from a half physical-half electronic 'brick and click' business to a fully electronic 'click and click' business. Resistance of employees may challenge organizational response to environmental changes, but it must be handled wisely and carefully by management at all levels. Reasons for resistance to change need to be carefully identified and carefully analyzed. People may resist change due to differences of opinions or uncertainties about the positive and negative impacts of change, lack of awareness of the nature of change and need for change, threat to their 'comfort zone' or 'status quo', threat to job security or sphere of authority, and threat of knowledge and power shifts.

A Shift from Product Commoditization to Intelligent Customization

The days of mass production and mass consumption have passed as companies are moving increasingly from product standardization to make-to-order, knowledge-based customization. As more companies make this shift, make-to-order will inherently become more of a service than merely a manufacturing organization. Customers are becoming more like partners. With advanced manufacturing technologies such as computer integrated manufacturing (CIM), that combines computer-aided design (CAD) and computer aided manufacturing (CAM), important customers will be given greater opportunities to become involved in the product design and manufacturing processes. Customers in the future will be able to order customized products or services according to their own specifications.

In the years ahead, customers will have higher expectations from producers in terms of good or service design flexibility, quality, price, delivery, warranty, and after-sale services. As they have greater access to information due to the proliferation of ICT, such as computers, web, and mobile technologies, customers will become more knowledgeable than before about the quality of products and their uses. Therefore, the importance of customer-based knowledge to business firms is likely to create tough 'rivalries' among competitors over acquiring customers, satisfying customers, and expanding relationships with them by providing customized product design, development, and delivery.

Due to the anticipation of highly turbulent and complex environments in the years ahead, catering for differences in customers' preferences on a 'one-to-one' basis and developing long-term profitable and loyal relationships with customers is likely to be a popular business strategy and almost an imperative for competing companies.

CONCLUSION

History has shown that the business world is in a continuous state of development as it strives to achieve SCA. Organizations operating in the 21st century live in a world of constant dynamic and complex changes in their business environments. In this chapter, changing market dynamics; namely, changing nature and power of customers, increased competition, globalization of business, proliferation of the ICTs, as well as government regulations/deregulations have been discussed. As proposed at the start of the chapter, survival and success in the new wave of business changes depends entirely on the organization's ability to adjust to changing environmental conditions. It is becoming imperative for manufacturers as well as service providers in today's turbulent environments to improve their quality, speed, timeliness of development and delivery in order to satisfy customers and maximize profitability. These environmental forces make organizations respond by change programs such as SIS, TQM, JIT, KM, CRM, OL, BPR, and E-biz.

As the focus of the world's economy changes the rules of competition, as evidenced by a shift from products to services, and shifts power from producers to customers, many companies are looking for internal competencies and distinctive advantages as means to achieve sustainable competitiveness. For organizations that tend to be adaptive and successful in their knowledge-intensive, customer-oriented transformation strategy, identifying and confronting current issues and future trends is very critical. The critical issues that may face organizations in their interactions with their environments are the objective versus subjective scanning of environments, the decision to change or not to change, and if change is selected, is that change institutionalized or de-institutionalized, incremental or radical, and partial or total.

Future business environments are expected to witness accelerating rates of change and uncertainty, with a shift toward a reactive mode of change and knowledge-based customization of products or services. CKM has been introduced as an integrative knowledge-based, customer-centric strategic business model that intends to create value for customers and develop long-term loyalty and profitable relationships.

The second part of the book explores the role of people, ICTs, and customer processes in crafting a successful CKM strategy. The heart of the CKM strategy is the transformation and combination of people, processes, and technology to enable the creation of value for customers. The first chapter in this part addresses the role of people in CKM change.

REFERENCES

Abrahamson, E. (1991). Managerial fads and fashions: The diffusion and rejection of innovations. *Academy of Management Review, 16*, 586-612.

Abrahamson, E. (1996). Management fashion. *Academy of Management Review, 21*, 254-85.

Abrahamson, E. (2000). Change without pain. *Harvard Business Review, 78*(4), 75-9.

Atkinson, A., Waterhouse, J., & Wells, R. (1997). A stakeholder approach to strategic performance. *Sloan Management Review, 38*(3), 25-37.

Awad, E., & Ghaziri, H. (2004). *Knowledge management.* Upper Saddle River, NJ: Prentice-Hall.

Blackler, F. (1995). Knowledge, work and organizations: An overview and interpretation. *Organization Studies, 16*(6), 16-36.

Bontis, N. (2004). National intellectual capital index: A United Nations initiative for the Arab region. *Journal of Intellectual Capital, 5*(1), 13-39.

Boyd, B. K., Dess, G. G., & Rasheed, A. M. A. (1993). Divergence between archival and perceptual measures of the environment: Causes and consequences. *Academy of Management Review, 210*(2), 204-26

Boyett, J. H., & Boyett, J. T. (1995). *Beyond workplace 2000: Essential strategies for the new American corporation.* New York: Dutton.

Brown, D., & Harvey, D. (2006). *An experiential approach to organization development.* 7th edition. Upper Saddle River, New Jersey: Pearson-Prentice Hall.

Burlton, R. T. (2001). *Business process management: Profiting from process.* Indianapolis. Indiana: Sams Publishing.

Burnes, B. (1996). No such thing as a 'one best way' to manage organizational change. *Management Decision, 41*(5), 452-64.

Burnes, B. (2004). *Managing change.* 4th edition, Harlow: FT/Prentice-Hall.

Buttle, F. (2004). *Customer relationship management: Concepts and tools.* Oxford, England: Elsevier Publishing.

Byrne, J. (2000). Management by Web, *Business Week*, August 28, p.8.

Callon, J. (1996). *Competitive advantage through information technology.* New York: McGraw-Hill.

Clifford, M., & Kripalani, M. (2000). Different countries, adjoining cubicles. *Business Week*, August, pp. 182-184.

Crosby, P. B. (1979). *Quality is Free*. New York: McGraw-Hill.

Currie, W. (2000). *The Global information society*. Chichester, England: John Wiley.

Davenport, T. H., & Prusak, L. (2000). *Working knowledge*. 2nd edition, Boston, MA: Harvard Business School Press.

Davenport, T. H. (1993). *Process Innovation: Reengineering Work through Information Technology*. Boston, MA: Harvard Business School Press.

Davenport, T. H., De Long, D. W., & Beers, M. C. (1998). Successful knowledge management projects. *Sloan Management Review*, *39*(2), 43-57.

Davenport, T. H., Harris, J. G., & Kohli, A. K. (2001). How do they know their customers so well. *Sloan Management Review*, *42*(2), 63-73.

Deming, W. E. (1982). Improvement of quality and productivity through action by management. *National Productivity Review*, *1*(1), 12-22.

Edmonson, G. (2000). See the world; erase its borders. *Business Week*, August 28, 113-114.

Gamble, P., & Blackwell, J. (2001). *Knowledge management: A state of art guide*. UK/USA: Kogan Page Limited.

Georgopoules, B. S., & Tannenbaum, A. S. (1957). The study of organizational effectiveness. *American Sociological Review*, *22*, 534-540.

Godin, S. (1999). *Permission marketing: Turning strangers into friends and friends into customers*. New York: Simon & Schuster.

Griffin, R. (2005). *Management*. 8th edition, Boston: Houghton Mifflin Company.

Hall, R. W. (1983). *Zero inventories*. Homewood, IL: Dow-Jones-Irwin.

Hallberg, G. (1995). *All consumers are not created equal*. Hoboken, NJ: John Wiley.

Hammaer, M., & Champy J. (1993). Reengineering the corporation: A manifesto for business revolution. New York: HarperCollins.

Hofstede, G. (2003). Cultural constraints in management theories. In G. Reddding & B. W. Stening (Eds.), *Cross-cultural management*, *2*, 61-74). Cheltenham: Edward Elgar Publishing.

Holbeche, L. (2005). *The high performance organizations: Creating a dynamic stability and sustainable success.* Butterworth-Heinemann, Oxford: U.K.

Hughes, M. (2006). *Change management: A critical perspective.* London: CIPD Publications.

Ishikawa, K. (1985). *What is total quality control? The Japanese way.* Translated by David Lu, London: Prentice-Hall International.

Jacobs, D. (1996). *Het kennisoffensief (The knowledge offensive),* Alphen Aaan den, The Netherlands: Samson.

Jepperson, R. L. (1991). Institutions, institutional effect, and institutionalism. In W.W. Powell, & P.J. DiMaggio (Eds.), *The new institutionalism in organizational analysis* (pp.143-63). Chicago, IL: University of Chicago Press

Jones, G. (2001). *Organization theory and design.* 3rd ed., Upper Saddle River, NJ: Prentice-Hall.

Juran, J. (1986). The Quality trilogy, *Quality Progress, 10*(8), 19-24.

Kalakota, R., & Robinson, M. (2001). *E-Business 2.0: Roadmap for success.* Boston, MA: Addison-Wesley.

Kaplan, R., & Norton, D. (1996). *Translating strategy into action: The balanced scorecard.*

Boston, Harvard Business School Press.

Leana, C. R., & Barry, B. (2000). Stability and change as simultaneous experiences in organizational life. *Academy of Management Review, 25*(4), 753-59.

Leavitt, H. J. (1965). Applied organizational change in industry: Structural, technological, and humanistic approaches. In J. G. March (Ed.), *Handbook of organizations.* Chicago: Rand McNally.

Mone, M. A., McKinley, W., & Barker, V. L. (1998). Organizational decline and innovation: A contingency framework. *Academy of Management Review, 23*(1), 115-32.

Newman, K. (2000). Organizational transformation during Institutional upheaval. *Academy of Management Review, 25*(3), 602-19.

Nolan, R., & Croson, D. (1995). *Creative destruction: A six-stage process for transforming the organization.* Boston, MA: Harvard Business School Press.

Orlikowski, W. J. (1996). Improvising organizational transformation over time: A situated change perspective. *Information Systems Research, 7*(1), 63-92.

Palmer, I., Dunford, R., & Akin, G. (2006). *Managing organizational change: A multiple perspectives approach*. Boston, MA: McGraw-Hill.

Peppard, J., & Ronald, P. (1995). *The essence of business process reengineering*. Upper Saddle River, NJ: Prentice-Hall.

Peppers, D., Rogers, M., & Dorf, B. (1999). *The one-to-one field book*. New York: Doubleday.

Peppers, D., & Rogers, M. (1994). *The one-to-one future*. London: Piaktu.

Peppers, D., & Rogers, M. (2004). *Managing customer relationships: A strategic framework*. Hoboken, NJ: John Wiley.

Pettigrew, A. M. (1998). Success and failure in corporate transformation initiatives. In R.D. Galliers, & W.R.J. Baets, (Eds.), *Informational technology and organizational transformation, innovation for the 21st century organization* (pp.271-90). Chichester, U.K.: John Wiley.

Reger, R., Mullane, J., Gustasfon, L., & DeMarie, S. (1994). Creating earthquakes to change organizational minds. *Academy of Management Executive, 8*(4), 31-43.

Schein, E. H. (1990). Organizational culture. *American Psychologist, 45*, February 109-19.

Schein, E. H. (1999). *The corporate culture survival guide: Sense and nonsense about cultural change*. San Francisco: Jossey-Bass.

Scott-Morton, M., & Allen, T. J. (1994). *Information technology and the corporation of the 1990s*. New York: Oxford University Press.

Senge, P. M. (1990). *The Fifth discipline: The Art and practice of the learning organization*. New York: Doubleday.

Shingo, S. (1989). *A study of the Toyota production system*. Cambridge: MA: Productivity Press.

Smircich, L., & Subbart, C. (1985). Strategic management in an enacted world. *Academy of Management Review, 210*(4), 724-36.

Sull, D.N. (1999). Why good companies go bad. *Harvard Business Review, 77*(4), 42-52.

Swift, R. S. (2001). *Accelerating customer relationships: Using CRM and relationship technologies*. Upper Saddle River, NJ: Prentice-Hall.

Thompson, J. D. (1967). *Organizations in actions*. New York: McGraw-Hill.

Tiwana, A. (2001). *The essential guide to knowledge management: E-business and CRM applications.* Upper Saddle River, NJ: Prentice-Hall.

Turban, E., McLean, E., & Wetherbe, J. (2002). *Information technology for management: transforming business in the digital economy.* 3rd edition, New York: John Wiley.

Usoro, A., & Kuofie, M. H. (2006). Conceptualization of cultural dimensions as a major influence on knowledge sharing. *International Journal of Knowledge Management, 2*(2), 16-25.

Whitting, R. (1999). Myths and Realities. *InformationWeek Online, 22*(11), 1-5.

Wilson, J. (2000). *Consumer welfare and government regulation of telecommunications, CSR Research Paper,* Montreal, Canada (http://www.law.mcgill.ca/institutes/csri/paper-wilson.php3), Retrieved on October 1, 2005.

Wind, J., & Main, J. (1999). *Driving change: How the best companies are preparing for the 21st Century.* London: Kogan Page.

Yuchtman, E., & Seashore, S. (1967). A systems resource approach to organizational effectiveness. *American Sociological Review, 32,* 891-903.

Zucker, L. G. (1991). The role of institutionalization in cultural persistence. In W. W Powell, & P. J. MdiMaggio (Eds.), *The new institutionalism in organizational analysis* (pp. 83-107). Chicago, IL: University of Chicago Press.

Zucker, L. G. (1983). Organizations as institutions. In S.B. Bacharach (Ed.), *Research in the sociology of organizations, 2,* 1-47, JAI Press, Greenwich, CT.

Zucker, L. G. (1987). Institutional theories of organization. *Annual Review of Sociology, 13,* 443-64.

Section II
Reinventing (3Rs)

Chapter III
Reorganizing People

INTRODUCTION

The ability of an organization to compete in rapidly changing business environments is contingent upon its ability to develop competitive strategies that enable
leverage of distinctive core competencies and delivery of value-adding products or
services to customers. Once the competitive strategies have been identified, a plan
is developed to support those strategies. The plan will specify the design and use
or creation of strengths in the organization's resources. The current chapter looks
into the reorganization of people in teams as a major pillar of CKM.

Although this chapter is devoted to discussion of the role of people in CKM,
the role of people as well as ICTs and business processes will continue to play a
significant role in the CKM core value chain activities covered in the remaining
parts of this book.

Setting the stage for CKM strategic change, requires reinvention of the internal
setup of organizations manifested by its three major infrastructural components:
reorganizing people, retooling ICTs, and redesigning processes. This chapter explores
the role of one organizational architectural component, reorganizing people, as it
relates to CKM strategic change. King (1995) introduces the concept of Strategic
Capabilities Architecture wherein the guiding architecture of a firm should be
based on the strategic vision. In other words, this vision bridges the existing status
of the firm ("Where it is") and its projected future status ("Where it wants to be")
related to the firm's current and future capabilities. The guiding rule here is that no
single capability of the firm can provide a SCA to the firm. The firm cannot compete on the basis of "low cost" or "best quality" or "customer service." The SCA
of the firm derives from the "synergy" of the firm's various capabilities. Porter, as

cited in Pastore (1995), proposes a similar concept in his notion of "complementarities". He argues that the various competitive capabilities of the firm should be "complementary" or "synergistic" so that capabilities cannot be easily imitated by rivals. The same argument has been made with reference to different ICT-related innovations, such as BPR (Davenport & Short 1990, Davenport 1993, Davenport & Stoddard 1994).

Organizational reinvention, or transformation, as a concept and an approach has become popular in recent years, largely from its alignment with contemporary trends in corporate strategy, technology, and human resources, rather than from its inherent attractions. It intends to bring about a remarkable shift in one or more of technological, human, process, and/or structural dimensions of organizations (Blumenthal and Haspeslagh, 1994). However, if it is viewed independently of these advantages, the approach promises great benefits but also can be difficult, challenging, and disruptive (Graetz et al., 2006).

CONCEPTUAL FOUNDATIONS

A successful CKM change requires major changes in organizational pillars, i.e. people, processes, and technology (Figure 3.2). Besides high changes in organizational requirements, the development of a CKM strategy requires high organizational alignment *among* and *within* organizational components. Organizational infrastructures need to be mutually supportive and work together to facilitate the achievement of CKM strategic goals, and ultimately a SCA. Strategic alignment is needed when organizational pillars interact among themselves as well as with other organizational components. Organizational changes needed for a successful CKM are covered in this as well as the two subsequent chapters.

On further examination, external business environmental factors as well as internal organizational context, e.g. size, technology, type of industry, strategy, and age, contribute to CKM. Therefore, organizational changes need to 'fit' closely not only with their external environmental dynamics, but also with changes in internal organizational pillars such as technology, people, structure and processes that represent the infrastructure of the CKM value chain. Organizational potentials and DCCs need to be fully utilized in the design and development of infrastructural changes in people, structure, technology, and processes.

The concern of this chapter, 'reorganizing people', is to enable the achievement of the goals of the CKM strategy. Two basic perspectives are used in this section to relate to the process of reorganizing people: structure and culture. It is true that sometimes terminology is used in a vague or contradicting manner. As of the term 'reorganizing', it could mean different things to different people. For instance, Weiss

(2001) explains three approaches to reorganization: restructuring, reengineering, and rethinking. Restructuring involves the reconfiguring of organizational units through initiatives such as downsizing; reengineering refers to attempts to introduce dramatic change in business processes; and rethinking involves the redesign of thinking and mindsets through initiatives such as the learning organization. Further discussion of the learning organization is presented in Chapter XI.

Offering clear working definitions of terminology used in this book is one way to remedy any possible confusion that might surround the use of these terms. In this book, the term 'reinvention' is used in its wider context to refer to overall changes in major organizational pillars: people, technology, and processes. In order to remove any possible confusion or duplication in terminology, the term 'reorganization of people' is used in this book to refer to changes in three people-based aspects: reformation of the structural side of the organization, which in turn affects the design of jobs held by people, 'rehabilitation' of people, and 'reshaping' of the soft side of organizations, i.e. culture and leadership style. It is also to be noted that leadership and learning are directly involved in all of the aforementioned components.

This section provides a discussion of background concepts to the reorganization of people. 'Reorganizing people' is used in this book to refer to transformation of organizations from hierarchical to networked organizations, restructuring of units in which people operate into self-controlled teams and assignment of 'case managers', and changing the corporate culture and leadership style of the newly formed organizations.

Figure 3.2. CKM enabling activities

Types of Organizational Structures

Whenever a group works toward achieving its goals, each person must know exactly what work he or she is expected to do and its level of authority. This is the basic purpose of organizational structure and job design. In its simplest form, the term 'organizing' is deciding how best to group organizational elements (Jones, 2003), which is called sometimes 'departmentalization'. In a static sense, organizing means a formalized structure of a group of individuals who work for achieving stated objectives. In a dynamic sense, organizing is a set of continuous activities of coordinating the efforts of individuals who are working together towards a common goal.

'Organizing' as a dynamic process includes the following activities:

- Designing jobs of individuals' duties and responsibilities (job description).
- Providing a system (organization design) of grouping the activities (departmentalization) of an enterprise that are necessary to achieve its goals (strategy).
- Assigning this group of activities to individuals in the organization.
- Providing individuals with authority and responsibility (or even empowerment) to carry out these activities, and
- Coordinating the efforts of various individuals involved in the activities to eliminate any dysfunctions such as duplication, overlap, and bottlenecks.

Organizational design as a concept refers to the overall set of structural elements and the relationships among these elements (structural configuration) used to manage the whole organization (Griffin, 2005). Thus, organizational design is a means of implementing strategies and plans to achieve organizational goals (Lei and Slocum, 2002).

According to Mintzberg (1979, 1983), an organization's structure is largely determined by the variety one finds in its environment. For Mintzberg, environmental variety is determined by both environmental complexity (simple versus complex) and the pace of change (slowly changing versus fast-changing environment). He identifies five types of organizational forms that are associated with four combinations of complexity and change.

The main characteristics of the five organizational forms are documented in Table 3.1:

- *Simple/Entrepreneurial structure:* young, small firm existing in a simple but dynamic environment. It has a simple structure and is managed by an entrepreneur serving as its single CEO (e.g., small business).

- *Machine bureaucracy:* large-size bureaucracy in a simple and stable environment, producing standard products. It is dominated by a centralized management team and centralized decision making (e.g., midsized manufacturing firm, or support subunits that perform routine functions in universities).
- *Divisionalized structure*: a combination of multiple quasi-autonomous machine bureaucracies produces an additional form, wherein each produces a different product or service, all topped by one central headquarters (e.g., autonomous firms of General Motors such as Cadillac, Pontiac, and Chevrolet).
- *Professional bureaucracy:* knowledge-based organization that exists in a complex but stable environment, where goods and services depend on the expertise and knowledge of professionals. Dominated by department heads with weak centralized authority (e.g., law firms, technocratic subunits in universities, banks, and hospitals may be administered as professional organizations or adhocracies).
- *Adhocracy:* "Task force" organization that must respond to complex and dynamic environments. Consists of large groups of specialists organized into short-lived multi-disciplinary teams with weak central management (e.g., market-based projects, electronics, advertising, consulting, and R&D firms). For Mintzberg, adhocracy is a configuration which substitutes project groups and matrix structures for bureaucracy and is the only organizational structure genuinely responsive to changing industrial environments.

To help explain features of the five forms, Mintzberg define five organizational subunits:

- Strategic Apex: e.g., board of directors and chief executive officers.
- Technostructure: e.g., strategic planning, personnel training, operations research, and systems analysis and design.
- Support Staff: e.g., legal counsel, public relations, payroll, mailroom clerks, and cafeteria workers.
- Middle Line: e.g., VP for operations/marketing, plant managers, and sales managers.
- Operating Core: examples are purchasing agents, machine operators, assemblers, sales people, and shippers.

Turban et al. (1999) provide a classification of basic forms of organizational design based on a continuum of structure that proceeds from the hierarchical to the flattened structure, and ends with the networked design. Additional design options are the matrix organization, mechanistic and organic organization, and the

Table 3.1. Characteristics of organizational structures

	Simple Structure	Machine Bureaucracy	Professional Bureaucracy	Divisionalized Form	Adhocracy
Mechanism of Coordination	Direct control and supervision	Work standards	Standardized norms, skills, and knowledge	Standardized work processes and outputs	Mutual adjustments of ad-hoc teams
Locus of power	Strategic apex	Technostructure	Operating core	Middle line	Support staff
Degree of job specialization	Little specialization	Horizontal and vertical specialization	Much horizontal specialization	Some specialization between divisions and headquarters	Much horizontal specialization
Role of strategic apex	Administrative work	Coordinating fine tuning	External liaison	Performance control	External liaison project monitoring
Role of operating core	Informal work	Routine, formal work	Standardized skilled work with autonomy	Formalized work at division level	Informal project work
Role of middle line	Insignificant	Elaborate and differentiated	Controlled by professionals	Division-level management	Project work management
Role of technostructure	None	Helps to formalize work	Little	Helps headquarters with performance control	Small and blurred
Role of support staff	Small	Elaborate to reduce uncertainties	Elaborate to support professionals	Split between headquarters and divisions	Blurred, part of projects
Flow of informal communications	Significant	Discouraged	Significant in administration	Some between headquarters and divisions	Significant throughout
Flow of decision making	Top down	Top down	Bottom up	Differentiate between headquarters and divisions	Mixed, all levels
Environment	Simple, dynamic	Simple, stable	Complex, stable	Simple, stable	Complex, dynamic
Power	Chief executive control	Technocratic control	Professional control	Mid-line control	Expert control

Source: Adapted from Schultheis et al. (1992). Management Information Systems: the Manager's View. Burr Ridge, IL: Irwin.

Table 3.2. Characteristics of organizational structures

	Hierarchical	**Flat**	**Matrix**	**Networked**
Description	Bureaucratic from within defined levels of management	Decision making pushed down to the lowest level in the organization	Workers assigned to two or more supervisors to make sure organizational functions are integrated	Formal and informal communication networks that connect all parts of the organization
Characteristics	Division of labor, specialization, unity of command, formalization	Informal roles, planning and control; often small and young organizations	Dual reporting relationships. Based on function and purpose	Known for flexibility and adaptability
Type of Environment	Stable Certain	Dynamic Uncertain	Dynamic Uncertain	Dynamic Uncertain
Basis of Structuring	Primarily function	Primarily function	Functions and purpose (i.e., location, product, customer)	Networks
Power of Structure	Centralized	Centralized	Distributed (matrix managers)	Distributed (network)
Type of Technology Used	Mainframe	Personal computers	Networks	Intranets and Internet

Source: Adapted from Pearlson & Saunders (2006).Managing and Using Information Systems: A Strategic Approach. 3rd edition, New York: John Wiley.

strategy-structure linked organization. A summary of characteristics of different design choices is documented in Table 3.2.

Hierarchical Structure

Traditional structures represent the functional tall organizations that emerged following the contributions of the Industrial Revolution godfathers such as Adam Smith and Fredrick Taylor. Vertical structure was followed by an influential structural conceptualization of organizations, viz. bureaucracy, presented by Max Weber (1947). Weber emphasized many aspects related to authority and rationality such as specialization, hierarchy, rules, and unity of command. Many of these Industrial

Revolution and Bureaucracy concepts and practices were replicated later in non-manufacturing contexts.

Key characteristics of hierarchical organizations are division of labor, specialization (functional tasks), unity of command, and formalization. In hierarchical structures, work is divided into a set of cross-functional activities that are fragmented throughout the organization. Work tasks come from the top and are segmented into smaller and smaller pieces until reaching the managerial level in which it should be done. Work tasks, or jobs, are often organized around activities that cut across functions, such as purchasing, production, and marketing. More discussion on cross-functional processes is provided in Chapter 5.

Managers have long seen the advantage of vertical structures for providing managers with strong command and control, clear definitions of roles and lines of authority, providing a mechanism for hierarchically based career development or progression, and enhancing work excellence as a result of accumulation of expertise in a particular area of specialization.

Although functional structures have some advantages, nonetheless, they suffer from several disadvantages, which represent the base for the shift of customer-centric organizations to networked structures:

- Lacking coordination and integration among business functions.
- Getting the right information coordinated, when information is required from several functional units, can be time-consuming and frustrating alike for employees and customers (Turban et al., 1999).
- Lacking a single customer contact point (Peppard and Rowland, 1995) that oversees the whole process.
- Preventing total system synergy when two or more subsystems work together to produce more than the total of what they might produce working alone.
- Making a decision requires climbing up and down the hierarchy. All it takes is one person who does not understand the subject matter to say 'no,' and everything comes to a complete stop (Turban et al., 1999).

Flattened Structure

Midway between vertical and networked organizations comes the flattened organization, which is often found in small and young entrepreneurial organizations. The main characteristics of flat organizations are: centralized power structure, fewer layers of management, and a broader span of control than the hierarchical organization (Turban et al., 1999; and Pearlson and Saunders, 2006).

Networked Structure

Many writers have advocated the concept of the networked organization (e.g., Cash et al., 1994). Unlike the rigid hierarchical structures, networked organizations are flexible structures composed of self-managed teams performing various business tasks, supported with formal and informal distributed ICTs (Figure 3.3). Networked organizations are new forms of organizations that promote creativity, flexibility, empowerment, information sharing, and team contributions while maintaining operational process control (Table 3.3).

Networked organizations are built around three major pillars:

- *Process-based Cross-functional Teams*: In classical organizations, work is done by individuals representing different functional units or groups such as marketing, sales, finance, and logistics, and working separately on a specific task, i.e. fulfillment of customer orders. People organized in functional groups do not have the same level of coordination and collaboration as much as in team-based organizations. In networked organizations, teams are made up of

Figure 3.3. Networked organization structure

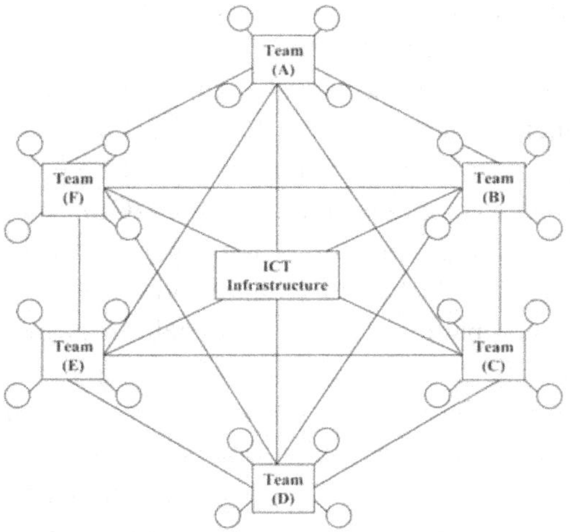

Source: Adapted from Pearlson & Saunders (2006). Managing and Using Information Systems: A Strategic Approach. 3ʳᵈ edition, New York: John Wiley.

Table 3.3. Shift from traditional to new form of organizations

Classical Organization	New Organization
Formal	Informal
Rigid Structure	Flexible Structure
Manage	Facilitate
Control	Participation
Direct	Empower
Employees a Cost	Employees an Asset
Information Management-Owned	Information Shared Ownership
Hierarchical Organization	Manageable Organization
Risk Avoidance	Risk Management
Individual Contributions	Team Contributions

Source: Adapted from Turban et al. (1999). Information Technology for Management: Making Connections for Strategic Advantage, 2nd edition, New York: John Wiley.

small-size, team-minded specialists who come from different functional units of the firm to do the work.

Teams in networked organizations are made up of a small number of people with complementary skills who are committed to a common purpose, performance goals, and mutual accountability. People may float from one team to another as necessitated by their skills and requirements of the task itself. ICTs allow teams to function electronically. Virtual teams may span functional boundaries and may represent relationships with remote collaborators such as contractors, partners, suppliers, and customers (Graetz, 2006). Pfizer and Citigroup are examples of organizations that apply teamwork. Team working is becoming an increasing feature of product and service delivery in service and manufacturing companies. Cross-functional teams are created to carry out inter-departmental activities and enable functional interface and parallel design. A structural enabler for cross-functional teams is the establishment of a single contact 'case manager' point for customers.

Another, even better, alternative to the case manager is a process generalist who may be trained to perform the work of cross-functional specialists or to eliminate the need for them altogether. Given the safeguard against fraud, a one integrated process may seem to be the ultimate solution for efficient integration rather than coordination of cross-functional activities (Grover et al., 1998). A single process generalist at IBM Credit is performing credit checking, pricing, and other activities previously done by four different specialists in processing a loan request. This helped to reduce the application turnaround time from six days to just four hours, and the number of applications to handle increased 100 times (Hammer and Champy, 2003). More discussion on this topic is provided in Chapter 5.

- *Distributed ICT Infrastructure*: Networked organizations resemble computer networks and are supported by inter-organizational information systems. At the heart of the networked organization culture is constant and reliable sharing of information among team members. The primary enabler for information sharing is the utilization of distributed enterprise wide ICT resources (Grover et al., 1998; Pearlson and Saunders, 2006). Networked organizations are increasingly broadening their electronic networks to include suppliers and customers. Key technologies supporting this structure are client-server architecture network, intranets, extranets, Computer Supported Collaborative Work (CSCW) technologies such as Lotus Notes, as well as advanced ICTs that support external contacts with suppliers and customers, i.e. ERP and CRM.

Because networked structures are distributed, many people throughout the organization may share their knowledge and experience and participate in making key organizational decisions. ICTs are fundamental to process design as they improve process efficiency, effectiveness, and flexibility. As part of the execution of these processes, data are collected and stored in centralized databases or DWs for use in analysis and decision-making. Decision-making is more timely and accurate because data are collected and stored instantaneously. The extensive use of ICTs also renders it easier to coordinate across functional business units. Simply put, ICTs tie together people, processes, and organizational units (Pearlson and Saunders, 2006). More discussion on ICTs will be provided in Chapter 4.

- *Employee's Empowerment:* Empowerment is the vesting of decision-making or approval authority in the hands of employees, whereas in traditional structures such authority remains in the hands of managers. Empowerment means allowing self-directed teams and individuals to be in charge of their own career destinies as they meet and exceed company and personal goals through a shared company's vision. Employees are given permission to develop and utilize their skills and knowledge to their fullest potential for the good of the organization (i.e. serving customers in less time, cost, and effort) as well as for themselves (i.e., self actualization and job satisfaction due to their feeling the importance and value of their jobs and its impact on their career development prospects) (Turban et al., 1999). Another practical reason for empowerment in knowledge intensive, customer-centric organizations is that nowadays most people do knowledge work brought about by the evolution of the world's large economies from an industrial-based to an information-based economy. In knowledge-intensive work, the intellectual context of the work increases to the extent where the subordinate may have more expertise than the "hierarchical" supervisor. Therefore, managers have no choice but to empower their staff. If managers knew everything about the work, they could use the hierarchical mechanism to send directives to employees on what to do, how to do it, and when to do it (Turban et al., 1999).

Customer-oriented, self-controlled teams realize greater benefits to customers, employees, as well as to organizations. In terms of customer service and staff productivity, significant improvements in the value-added content of products or services may be achieved through effective leadership, teamwork, empowerment, information sharing, continuous learning, and improvement in co-ordination and co-operation between members who previously operated within autonomous de-partments. As firms migrate to a customer-centric business strategy, it is becoming inevitable to undergo major changes, not only in their structure, but in people's culture, business processes, and ICTs.

Matrix Structure

Matrix organization structure is common for project management organizations. In order to make sure that multiple dimensions of the business are integrated, matrix structure typically assigns workers to two or more supervisors (dual supervision and reporting) and one project manager that runs horizontally and the other is the original functional hierarchy that runs vertically. For example, a member of the marketing matrix team would have a supervisor for marketing decisions and a different supervisor for a specific product line. In some cases, the matrix reflects a third dimension, such as the customer relations segment. ICTs reduce the operating complexity of matrix organizations by allowing information sharing among the different managerial functions. For instance, a salesperson's sales would be entered into the information system and appear in the results of all of the managers to whom he or she reports. This structure is especially suitable to dynamic and uncertain environments (Mantel et al., 2001; Pearlson and Saunders, 2006).

Mechanistic vs. Organic Structure

Burns and Stalker (1961) advanced the conceptualization of organizational structure further by introducing the contingency approach to organization design. They came up with two types of organizations, mechanistic and organic structures, as a response to environments in which the firms operate. Mechanistic structures include a clear definition of jobs, standardized procedures and policies, and rewards determined by supervisory decisions. In contrast, organic structures represent a fluid form of organization with a lesser degree of formality in areas such as operating procedures, job descriptions, and lines of authority. The mechanistic organization structure suggests a 'tall' structure, whereas the organic organization structure suggests a 'flat' one (Hughes, 2006). Hierarchical organizations are the best example of mechanical structures, whereas networked organizations best represent the organic structures.

Strategy-Structure Linked Organization

Miles and Snow (1984) presented a strategic perspective of the fit between organization structures and their environments. They identified four patterns of strategy-structure linkage:

- *Prospectors* are concerned with creativity and flexibility to open up new venues of opportunities (i.e. new products) and are often risk takers and decentralized (e.g., 3M and Amazon.com).
- *Defenders,* rather than seeking new growth opportunities and innovation, are concerned with maintaining stable growth, serving current customers, and protecting its market from new competitors (e.g., BIC and eBay).
- *Analyzers* represent traits of both defenders and prospectors, by seeking to maintain current markets and current customer satisfaction with moderate emphasis on innovation (i.e. customized products) in new markets and somewhat higher customer satisfaction, through both traditional work as well as new opportunities (e.g., IBM and Yahoo).
- *Reactors,* unlike previous forms, are considered inconsistent and unstable in terms of taking inappropriate reactions to changes in their environments (e.g., IH and Kmart). ,

The congruence between CKM organizational design decisions and environmental conditions is a prerequisite to success in the delivery of products or services. For instance, organizations that operate in environments with a relatively low level of environmental uncertainty tend to be defenders in their strategy, and might choose to use the traditional design with rigid rules, regulations, and operating procedures (e.g., mechanistic or hierarchical structure). However, companies that face higher degrees of environmental uncertainty tend to be prospectors in their strategy, and might choose a flexible/organic design with less standardized operating procedures and considerable employee's discretion.

The Virtual Organization

The virtual corporation (VC) is an ICT-based form of organizational design that conducts its business online, and has: a) a very small staff and administrative facilities, b) several business partners, and c) little or no formal physical structure. VCs are structured by electronic networks made up of virtual team members that communicate instantaneously through ICTs. In a VC, the resources of the business partners remain in their original locations but are integrated; whereas major aspects of core processes such as design, production, and delivery are outsourced to the organizations that specialize in these areas. As the needs of the organization change, its managers bring in temporary workers, lease facilities, and outsource basic support services. Global Research Consortium, for example, employs three permanent employees who subcontract the work to an appropriate set of several dozen independent freelance consultants and researchers (Griffin, 2005).

In order to function well, VCs rely on the following ICTs (Turban et al., 1999):

- Communication/collaboration among dispersed business partners, e.g., e-mail, desktop videoconferencing, screen-sharing, etc.
- Electronic Data Interchange (EDI) and Electronic Fund Transfer (EFT)
- Intelligent agents
- Modern database technologies and networking
- Intranet/Internet applications

Virtual organizations exist by agreement of their members and need access to shared interorganizational information systems in order to operate efficiently, such as when a delivery firm takes over the warehousing and distribution of spare parts for a computer manufacturer. Without robust inter-organizational systems, the term 'virtual organization' is no more than a slogan in such situations (Alter, 2002).

A new work arrangement is the 'virtual office' where ICT replaces direct contact with co-workers, customers, and/or physical office location. The benefits of virtual offices are lower cost and worker convenience. However, the problems with virtual offices are (Davenport, 2000):

- Little opportunity to socialize, share tacit knowledge, and learn corporate culture
- Weakened loyalty due to the absence of place to go to work
- Less face-to-face unplanned communications
- Difficult to have access to people when they are not in the office
- Difficult to have access to materials, office equipments, documents, and books

- Difficult to observe performance of subordinates at work

From the above discussion of various organizational structure deigns, one might conclude that the merit of an organization structure design choice is contingent upon its ability to create the best 'match' with its external environmental conditions, its business strategies, and its internal organization infrastructure. Stable and certain business environments are best supported with hierarchical structures. Turbulent and competitive business environments require an ICT-based flexible organization structure design (i.e., networked and virtual structures) to foster creativity, entrepreneurial spirit, and quick response to dynamic uncertain environments.

Types of Corporate Culture

The concept of 'culture' frequently displays a notion of learned, shared, and tacit characteristics (such as language, religion, values, beliefs, traditions, and heritage) that distinguish one group or society from another (Schein, 1999). At the organizational level, culture is commonly conceptualized as dynamic, multi-faceted, and layered and exists at the corporate (macro) or unit (micro) levels (Ogbonna and Wilkinson, 2003).

In terms of level of depth, culture can be defined with reference to three levels of depth of culture: ideologies and beliefs, values, and norms (Kilman et al., 1986; Schein, 1990; Klempa, 1995):

- At the highest level, ideologies or assumptions are a hidden, invisible, coherent set of 'taken-for-granted' beliefs that bind individuals in organizations together and may explain cause-and-effect relationships. Beliefs are understandings that represent credible relationships between credible objects, properties, and ideas. Ideologies and beliefs shape the collection and interpretation of information, underlying all decisions and actions.
- At an intermediate level of depth of culture, values are defined as the overt, espoused internalized normative system about how and why things are done that way (Schein, 1985; Wiener, 1998). The espoused values are antecedents to the formulation of business strategies, organizational learning (or knowledge creation), and individual behaviors (De Long and Fahey, 2000), such as teamwork, customer service, and risk taking. However, it is important to recognize that espoused values may not be the same as values-in-action. For example, senior management may state that risk-taking is encouraged and rewarded. If subordinates have experiences that do not match that statement, they are more likely to believe that those who play it safe and go by the rules are those who are rewarded (Graetz et al., 2006).

- At the lowest level of depth of culture, norms are the unwritten and socially transmitted guides to behavior. Norms may promote creativity (i.e., risk taking, rewards valuing change, and openness), or implementation of creativity (i.e., shared vision, respect and trust, autonomy, and empowerment with focus on quality) (O'Reilly, 1989).

Several writers introduced various understandings of the concept 'organizational culture'. Examples include Handy (1978), Peters and Waterman (1982), Deal and Kennedy (1982), O'Reilly et al. (1991), Kotter and Heskett (1992), Schein (1992), Park et al. (2004), Van den Berg and Wilderom (2004), and Johnson (2005).

Handy (1978) offered a classification based on four types of culture:

- Power cultures may be found in small-sized flat organizations where a person or small group of people at the centre represents a single source of power to influence others. These cultures react quickly to environmental changes.
- Role cultures are characterized by bureaucracies where rules, procedures, and descriptions of different jobs tend to predominate. They are successful in stable environments.
- Task cultures are characterized by project or matrix organizations bringing together the appropriate resources and competences required for effective team functioning. The emphasis is placed on expertise rather than position or charisma. These cultures can be effective for innovative tasks or projects, but are less effective where there is an emphasis on low-cost mass production and economies of scale.
- Person cultures are those which emphasize individual autonomy as part of a collective group action. Examples may be found in academia, creative design, or R & D.

Peters and Waterman (1982), in their famous book 'In Search of Excellence', discussed the relationship between organizational culture and corporate performance of successful U.S. companies. Major attributes of excellence found were bias for action, closeness to the customer, autonomy and entrepreneurship, and productivity through people.

Deal and Kennedy (1982) identified four types of corporate culture based on the degree of risk and speed of feedback characteristics of an organization: a) tough guy culture, e.g. surgeons, b) work-hard, play-hard culture, e.g. McDonald's, c) Net-your-company, e.g., aircraft manufacturers, and d) process-culture, e.g. public sector organizations.

O'Rielly et al. (1991) identified the following seven dimensions of organizational culture, using an instrument called the Organizational Culture Profile (OCP):

- Innovation
- Stability
- Respect for people
- Outcome orientation
- Detail orientation
- Team orientation, and
- Aggressiveness

Kotter and Heskett (1992) and Schein (1992) advocated the notion that culture exists at two levels based on visibility - one is more visible; the other, less visible. At the more visible, espoused, and less difficult to change level, culture represents behavior norms and practices of an organization (what ought to be done) that new employees are encouraged to follow (e.g., employees being quick to respond to customers' requests). At the deeper, less visible, and more difficult to change level, culture refers to basic underlying assumptions and values shared by people in an organization that tend to persist over time (e.g., managers care about customers).

Park et al. (2004) and Van den Berg and Wilderom (2004) have worked on dimensions of organizational culture from a work-practice approach. Once their dimensions are combined, eight dimensions are developed:

- Interdepartmental coordination
- Trust
- External orientation
- Improvement orientation
- Human resource orientation
- Autonomy
- Sharing information freely
- Working closely with others

Johnson (2005) offered the 'culture web' framework for understanding cultures in terms of seven elements: the paradigm, the power structures, organizational structures, control systems, routines, rituals, and stories and myths.

CRITICAL ISSUES

The transition to a customer-centric enterprise is important, but never easy. Reorganizing people is likely to face critical structural and cultural change issues related to people. Addressing these issues is essential for the continued success of customer-value-building services and products. In light of today's competitive business environments and changing power of customers, organizations need to be able to deal with people-based issues in order to secure high-quality customer service and long-life and profitable customer relationships.

People refer to human resources that are involved in CKM activities as front-line staff, support staff, business managers, as well as general managers. Within the general body of employees, there is a group called the 'knowledge workers' who have direct impact on the efficiency and productivity of the work process by capturing, applying, sharing, and disseminating their knowledge within the organization fall into this group (Drucker, 2002; Awad and Ghaziri, 2004).

A knowledge worker is the 'product' of experience, values, processes, education, and the ability to be creative, innovative, and in tune with the culture of the company. He or she is the one who wants a challenge and to be on a winning team. Examples of knowledge workers are managers, lawyers, engineers, system analysts, strategic planners, market analysts, and accountants (Awad and Ghaziri, 2004). Other remaining categories of employees may be considered as support to knowledge workers.

Managing People in CKM

People represent a very important factor in the success of any business project. In CKM, people perform the following activities (Buttle, 2004):

- Develop the change strategy
- Select the ICT solution
- Implement and use the ICT solution
- Coordinate with each other across functions to make change work
- Create and maintain the customer database
- Design the marketing, selling, and service processes
- May need to change established work practices
- Contribute significantly to customer satisfaction and retention when they interact with customers
- Make change work or resist it.

In customer-centric knowledge-based organizations, people are organized in teams. Reorganizing people in teams carries with it a number of issues related to the following aspects:

- Attracting people refers to activities for selecting and recruiting people in the CKM change.
- Developing people refers to training, development, and learning activities of CKM.
- Maintaining people refers to evaluation and compensation activities of people.
- Managing people's resistance to change refers to the leadership role in managing employees' resistance to change.
- Leading people refers to the management and leadership styles needed throughout the CKM.
- Managing knowledge workers refers to the recruitment, selection, evaluation, and compensation of knowledge workers.

Attracting People

Recruitment is the process in human resource planning and development that intends to bridge the gap between current and required levels of skills, capabilities, behaviors, and potentials of human resources required for the delivery of successful customer-centric goods or services. Attracting the 'right' applicant to fill the required skill, knowledge, or behavioral characteristics gap would have a profound impact on the accomplishment of business strategies, goals and objectives, and ultimately on the success of its CKM strategy.

Recruitment of people in customer-centric organizations usually is based, not only on the applicant's qualifications, but also on the extent to which the job applicant's cultural values 'fit' with the required organizational culture, team-based work conditions, and the prospects of the applicants to add value, develop, and grow within the organization (Peppard and Rowland, 1995). But, the challenge that faces CKM is that not all individuals are willing, capable, or ready to work in teams.

In terms of the recruitment process itself, managers alongside other personnel staff usually perform the selection process; yet there are increasing numbers of instances where teams play an important role in 'choosing their colleagues', or even customers choosing their service providers. For example, South West Airlines used its frequent flyers to select cabin crew (Heskett, et al., 1994). However, the remaining challenge that faces customer-centric organizations is how to assess the potential of a person to add value to customers as well as to the company. The degree of 'fitness' with the required organizational culture is very difficult to assess, and remains a rather subjective and illusive quality trait. However, sometimes, motivation and intellectual ability may provide a sound guide for selection (Peppard and Rowland, 1995).

Developing People

Development of people refers here to a set of activities that are initiated by customer-centric companies on-the-job (i.e., job placement and job rotation) or off-the-job (i.e., training workshops and professional seminars, and conferences), with the aim of improving the value-adding contribution of human resources through:

- Acquisition of new customer-centric ICT and job-related skills and knowledge (i.e., marketing, sales, customer service). Examples are:

    ° How to capture customer data? How to survey customers?
    ° How to analyze customer's data?
    ° How to profile or segment customers?
    ° How to design a customized campaign program?
    ° How to create customized product or service?

- Acquisition of customer-focused, team-based behavioral characteristics and decision-making skills (soft skills) refers to values, beliefs, attitudes, and behaviors. Examples are trustworthiness, innovation and creativity, perfection, team spirit, and risk taking.
- Continuous customer-oriented learning and improvement refers to learning how to design a new order fulfillment procedure that requires less time, effort, and money, and ultimately, pleases customers.

Exhibiting the right behavior with customers will, in the end, be reflected in the customer's purchasing behavior and decisions. For example, front-office staff cannot be polite, courteous, and committed to their clients if their own internal organization behaves rudely and indifferently. The behavior of front-office employees will have a direct bearing on perceptions, loyalty and retention of customers. Similarly, the behavior towards suppliers will determine the perception of the company and play a part in motivating partnerships between companies. However, behaving well towards customers and people is not enough. Customers get fed up with the attentiveness of staff if they simply cannot actually do it; so staff skills are also necessary (Peppard and Rowland, 1995).

Planning for training and development needs is based on a gap analysis of current versus desired levels of skills, knowledge, and behavioral characteristics as well as of customer-centric teams. Skills, knowledge capabilities, and behavioral characteristics of customer-centric team members should be carefully planned, designed, and developed in order to help to deliver successful products or services, achieving business goals and objectives, and ultimately business strategies. Current and desired corporate cultural values and the degree of empowerment also will have to be considered when identifying the necessary behaviors, skills, and subsequent training and development needed, expanding a team member's ability to secure a high quality customer service.

Achieving significant changes in a team member's capacity is required for achieving improvement in customer products or services, but is not enough. Self-controlled teams should also be expanded to self-learning teams. Continuous learning is essential to cope with continuous environmental changes. It is not enough for employees to only learn 'how to do things', but they should also learn how to solve business problems, how to add value, and how to develop and maintain interpersonal relationships within and outside the organization. Therefore, customer-oriented development of human resources capacity to provide high quality customer service should take place on an ongoing basis that starts with the introduction of new staff members to a company and its teams, and continues throughout people's professional life.

However, not all people are willing, ready, or capable to work in teams. Team-based work may not be successful all the time, even if we manage to select those who are capable of doing so. Sometimes working in teams may be unfruitful, unharmonious, and may not lead to the desired work synergy (the team's output is greater than that of individuals acting alone). Working in teams may pose a challenge to interpersonal relationships among team members, and may create problems such as personal clashes and conflicts, groupthink, and time consumption (Peppard and Rowland, 1995). The situation will be more aggravated when national cultural values in which organizations operate are intolerant of diversity, but supportive of uniformity that shuns personal differences and sees them as equal to personal hostilities.

The chronic issue that still faces organizations is the viability of the decision to change people's skills, values, beliefs, attitudes, and behaviors. To a large extent, developing team members' hard skills (i.e. structured work-related knowledge and skills) in people is easy. In contrast, developing team-members' soft skills (team-based work values, attitudes, and behaviors) is much harder to implement and reach fruitful results, especially in the short-run time horizon and with contradicting national cultural values. Similar difficulty exists in the attempt to introduce change in the culture of organizations, which are, by nature, enduring and deeply rooted.

Supportive and visionary leadership plays a crucial role in successful structural and cultural change programs.

Maintaining and Retaining People

In CKM, what is important is not only to attract and develop the capacity of team members, but also to be able to keep them loyal, committed, and ultimately retained. Companies need to continue to provide attractive motivation, both intrinsic and extrinsic, in addition to management support. Compensation systems may be viewed by some people as extrinsic motivators, but may be viewed by others as 'hygiene' factors', which do not motivate workers, but rather, may lead to job dissatisfaction if badly designed (Herzberg, 1987).

As of team performance, it is not expected of teams to perform well from day number one of their forming. Usually team working evolves through four stages (Jassawalla & Sahittal, 1999): forming (acquaintance), storming (interactions), norming (acceptance), and performing (goal attainment). However, the challenge that may continue to face such organizations is how to evaluate performance of customer-centric team members' activities, how to align the pay scale with flexi-working hour systems, how to differentiate between high performers and average performers within the same team when applying team-based compensation, and how to improve people's loyalty, job satisfaction, retention, and ultimately job performance.

Traditional productivity measures are frequently inadequate, inaccurate, and may be inapplicable in customer-centric networked organizations. The traditional way of rewarding (e.g. factory floor workers, sales people) was piece rate based, where people are paid according to the number of 'pieces' they process. For example, how could one differentiate between two knowledge workers who provided the same customer service? Is it by time taken? Is it the customer's value of purchase? Is it the customer retention rate? Is it the number of customer complaints? Is it a percentage of new customers acquired? Is it customer satisfaction?

Modern organizations, especially VCs, often face the challenge of supervising and evaluating a workforce that is geographically spread across the world, working in isolation from direct supervision, and working more in teams. Rather than working in a central office, many salespeople work remotely and rely on hand-held pen computers, cellular phones, and pagers to link them to customers and the head office. The nature of team-based work makes it hard to apportion individual-based rewards (Pearlson and Saunders, 2006). Therefore, direct employee supervision may need to be replaced by electronic tracking of employees' activities, such as the number of calls processed, e-mail messages sent, or time spent surfing the Web.

For example, virtual teams cannot be managed in the same way as more traditional teams. The differences in management control of performance activities are particularly pronounced. Monitoring behavior of virtual teams is likely to be more limited than in traditional teams, as the behavior of virtual team members cannot be easily observed. Therefore, performance is more likely to be evaluated in terms of output rather than on displays of behavior (Pearlson and Saunders, 2006). Therefore, evaluation of employees may be partially conducted by using objective compensation systems that reward people for deliverables produced (i.e., a report produced by certain date) or targets achieved (i.e., sales quota), as opposed to subjective systems that emphasize factors such as 'attitude', feel, etc (Pearlson and Saunders, 2006). However, in CKM, subjective performance aspects of the work, such as quality of service and interactions with customers, are considered as important as objective performance measures in creating and maintaining relationships with customers, and cannot be easily skipped.

As organizations migrate from traditional structures to new forms of organizations, so should their compensation systems. In networked organizations, there is no hierarchical and departmental status, but empowerment and an appreciation of the team as a whole, e.g., the name of every team member is shown on business cards and pamphlets (Peppard and Rowland, 1995). People in traditional organizations may consider 'low pay' as a cause of dissatisfaction, but may not consider 'high pay' as a cause of satisfaction. In contrast, members of customer-centric self-managed teams may consider job-related intrinsic factors, such as empowerment, team membership, management recognition, and self-actualization, as replacements to materialistic motivators, viz. a salary increase.

Adopting team-based compensation may be a solution, given that continued membership of the team itself is not automatically guaranteed. Members continue in the team based on their value-adding contribution to the team. As many lower-level service or clerical jobs become partially automated, only those workers that are able to learn new technologies and adapt to changing customer preferences and work practices can anticipate stability in their long-term employment (Pearlson and Saunders, 2006).

Therefore, new forms of customer-centric competitive organizations should encourage:

- Team-based compensation
- Customer and quality focus evaluation: performance evaluation system is based on the contribution of team members to the well being of customers.
- Knowledge-sharing focus evaluation: knowledge-sharing behaviors need to be incorporated in performance appraisal systems and rewarded through recognition, pay raise, and financial incentives.

- Continuous learning and value-adding customer offerings.

Managing People's Resistance to Change

Major organizational change decisions, like downsizing, automation, or process revamping have got an inescapable cost of eliminating some positions such as low-level service or clerical jobs and even middle managers. In collectivist cultures, people openly criticize companies that lay-off people because they cut off their salaries. For instance, in the Arab culture, people frequently repeat this saying 'hanging by the neck is better than cutting-off the means of living'. Whenever companies undertake major transformation programs, people's resistance to change is expected to intensify especially in collectivist societies. Resistance to change is not only culture-sensitive. Besides cultural sensitivity to change, of special interest is the resistance of professional bodies such as computer programmers. Organizations are constantly faced with the issue of how to motivate programmers to increase their productivity by learning new tools and reusing preprogrammed modules (Turban et al., 2008).

In cultures known for their uncertainty avoidance, shunning off risk taking, and high fetish for conformity and passive stability, major change programs such as BPR is viewed as a threat to people's job security. The challenge here is how to handle or cope with such resistance to change. Companies need to offer more educational and awareness programs before and throughout the change itself, and offer job placement advice service and post-termination support programs for 'victims' of the change program. More discussion on people's resistance to CKM implementation will be provided in Chapter 11.

The shift from individual-based to team-based reward systems may be challenged by lack of cooperation among team members (Pearlson and Saunders, 2006). Organizations need also to be aware of the sensitivity of change to people in their organizations. For instance, compensation systems that try to devise new appropriate ways to provide rewards to team members may create negative reactions from employees.

Another challenge is related to culture-sensitivity of some structural change decisions in CKM such as in compensation systems. For example, in national cultures with higher levels of individualism, many workers may prefer reward systems to be linked with the performance of individual employees, whereas same reward system may be counterproductive in a more collectivistic culture (Griffin, 2005).

Leading People

New forms of organizations require a different form of leadership, i.e. transformational leadership (Wentz, 1999). The CKM strategic transformation requires visionary, inspiring, and supportive leadership who can coach not boss. The new leadership role is to provide support and a clear strategic vision of the change program but should not be promising more than can be realistically delivered. New leaders coach and sponsor rather than direct or give orders, and may not be the most senior in the team, but need to possess an admirable work-related knowledge. New leadership also needs to have a total rather than a partial view of the work (holistic that looks at the work as one whole unit), a participative rather than authoritative style, a friendly rather than reserved attitude, and a customer rather than product orientation.

Leadership in CKM transformational change is especially important to decide on the level of the program (i.e., operational, analytical, or strategic), prioritize the CKM strategy and processes over other wide-scale organization processes, provide high-level ownership, support, and oversight of the project, and break down the business functional silo walls because CKM processes are cross functional in nature.

CKM change needs to be championed at the CEO level. However, a lower level of change, i.e. operational CRM projects, needs champions at senior functional management level such as chief marketing officer or sales manager. Analytical CRM needs champions at lower levels yet. In general, CKM champions tend to reside at higher levels or at marketing, sales, or service functional levels. However, it should be noted that if ICT people, with limited business knowledge, champion CKM, there is a danger that it will be seen as an implementation of a pure ICT project, at the expense of its potential business benefits (Buttle, 2004).

Empowerment provides employees with intrinsic rewards and a higher moral status, but not all people have the preference and ability for empowerment. Some people may feel uncomfortable with work that does not follow clear and structures rules and regulations. Such a preference is not purely an individual choice per se; rather, it could relate to national cultures that shun risk taking in favor of uncertainty avoidance. However, the challenge that faces organizations is how to decide on the appropriate level of empowerment provided to employees, and sometimes to customers or suppliers.

Empowerment should be advocated in the same way as technology is advocated; it should be appropriate (Peppard and Rowland, 1995). The appropriate level of empowerment is based on two factors: the extent of organizational empowerment and people's preferences and abilities for empowerment. Organizational empowerment refers to the extent to which the organization defines systems and procedures to which staff must work. On the other hand, people's preferences and abilities for handling empowerment refer to the extent to which people are comfortable, motivated, and able to take the initiative to work without strict procedures (Clutterbuck et al., 1993).

Four patterns of organizations emerge from the combination of different levels (low and high) of the two aforementioned factors (Clutterbuck et al., 1993):

- Adaptive: people with high preference for empowerment, and they exist in an organization that empowers them.
- Compliant: people with low preference for empowerment, and they exist in an organization that does not empower them.
- Anxious: people with low preference for empowerment, but they exist in an organization that empowers them.
- Frustrated: people with high preference for empowerment, but they exist in an organization that does not empower them.

Empowerment should be provided at the right level to the right people at the right time. The 'appropriate' level of organizational empowerment itself usually is contingent upon the situation. For instance, low empowerment is needed in some situations, such as when rigid standards must be adhered to in financial procedures and guidelines, whereas considerable discretion in meeting clients' needs may be needed in others, such as attending to an ad-hoc request of customers. However, the real challenge is how leadership maintains a balance between employees' abilities and preferences for empowerment on one side, and customer satisfaction with the quality of service on the other side. For instance, nothing is more annoying to customers than when the person attending to their needs has to continually refer back up the hierarchy to obtain approval for a particular request. Disempowerment can lead to an extension of lead times, dissatisfied customers, and a general inability to innovate.

Managing Knowledge Workers

Knowledge workers are those employees who can think or work with ideas. The need for these workers, in specific, continues to grow as the importance of knowledge-based competition grows among business firms. However, managing knowledge workers usually poses many challenges to organizations. Knowledge workers often like to work independently, require extensive and highly specialized training, and define performance based on terms recognized by other members of their profession rather than their organization (Griffin, 2005).

A special challenge facing organizations nowadays is the ability of organizations to attract, evaluate, compensate, and retain self-directed knowledge workers. Large companies compete for the attraction of knowledge workers, and work hard to retain them, but not every organization is willing to make the human capital investments necessary to take advantage of these jobs. The challenge to the manager of knowledge workers, according to Drucker (2002), is to treat them more as colleagues and associates than as subordinates.

In recruiting knowledge workers, special importance is paid to their professional and soft skills, and the match with the requirements of the job. The knowledge worker is expected to possess both professional and soft skills. Professional skills relate to technical skills and abilities, whereas soft skills relate to a sense of cultural, political, and personal aspects of knowledge in the business. The personal aspects of knowledge include open, candid, and effective communication skills, a warm and pleasant personality that nurtures knowledge creation, manipulation, sharing, and application in a group setting, and a sensitivity to the political pressures in the department or organization in general (Awad and Ghaziri, 2004).

Measuring productivity of knowledge workers is not as simple as traditional piece-rate performance evaluation (e.g., number of units sold, number of units produced, and number of customers served). Furthermore, performance of knowledge workers may fall below organizations' expectations. Several factors may limit a knowledge worker's performance (Awad and Ghaziri, 2004):

- Time constraint: As there is always more work and less time to do, either quality level or completion time might lag behind targets. Motivation is also affected where urgency supersedes motivation.
- Working smarter and harder but accomplishing little in the short-run: limited time, effort, and manpower are often behind frustrating results.
- Doing work that the firm did not hire them to do.
- Heavy work demands invariably affect a knowledge worker's attention span, motivation, and patience, regardless of pay or benefits.
- Dislike of ideals proposed by management, avoidance.

The role and importance of capable and creative knowledge workers is likely to grow in the new knowledge economy due to the following considerations:

- The role of employees as a key, even central, component in most of companies' strategic design, such as developing a competitive strategy as an organizational response to business drivers.

- The role of employees in planning, analyzing, improving, and redesigning customer processes in knowledge-intensive industries is a key factor in adding value to both business and customers.
- The role of employees, especially in service-based environments that tend to be more people-intensive than capital-intensive, is becoming a more important factor for creating inimitable knowledge-based competition.
- The role of employees in service-based environments, especially which heavily rely on ICT, is still vital because they still need people who are skilled with software, hardware, networks, and can communicate effectively with customers.
- The role of educated, skilled, and experienced employees is important in manufacturing environments that rely on advanced technologies in equipments and machinery.

Although knowledge workers are usually highly paid compared to other people in the same organization, they may monitor the going salary rate in the market; and if they find it higher, it may adversely affect their continuity on the job. Managing knowledge workers with control of corporate knowledge as the core asset of business requires a 'handling with care' approach. Carefully designed and customized systems for selecting, evaluating, and compensating knowledge workers help a lot in reducing their prospective mobility. Sometimes, leadership support and favorable corporate culture may create a noticeable impact on alleviating possible drainage of intellectual assets of organizations.

RECOMMENDED SOLUTION: A PROPOSED PEOPLE REORGANIZATION MODEL

The recommended solution to deal with people change management in competitive business environments is to 'reorganize people' in a customer-centric networked organization. 'Reorganization of people' is operationally defined in Figure 3.4 by three sub-interventions: a) reconfiguring structure, b) rehabilitating people, c) reshaping culture.

Reconfiguring Structure

Fast-moving business environments are creating complex problems for business organizations which cannot be resolved by traditional solutions. One of these solutions is organizational design. It is almost becoming a fact of life that there is no one best way to design organizations, as the best design is contingent upon many

Figure 3.4. A recommended model for the reorganization of people

external as well as internal factors such as the organization's environment, goals, size, strategy, and technology (Bowditch and Buono, 2005).

Customer-centric organizations adopt a flexible organizational design form, i.e. the networked organization, or at another extreme point may even adopt a VC design. In between, some organizations, i.e. banks, may take a mediocre design choice by adopting a hybrid design, which combines the features of both hierarchical and networked organizations, thus creating a mixed balance of centralization and decentralization. In such situations, it may well be appropriate if customer-facing, front-office units such as sales, billing, and customer services follow a networked team-based form, whereas back-office supporting units, such as purchasing, human resources, accounting, and ICT services are kept under the functional and hierarchical structure.

Rehabilitating People

A rehabilitation of staff knowledge and attitude towards customers is essential in the development of a CKM-based organization. A comprehensive and customized staff rehabilitation program is essential to ensure continuation of superior quality in customer products and services and a high level of customer satisfaction and loyalty.

In a addition to the team-based approach to work, effective rehabilitation of staff may be accomplished by changing the mind set of people as well as their paradigms, skills, and capabilities by informing and training them in a customer-centric business environment on how to understand and meet customer requirements. What is needed in CKM based organizations is a complete change, not only in *hard skills* (what they do and how), but in *soft skills* (how they interact with customers) as well, and in the organization's pay and reward systems.

Reshaping Culture

When addressing the role of people in customer-centric knowledge-intensive organizations, it is equally important to address existing corporate culture, the type of
culture that the organization is trying to foster, and bridge the gap between the two
by revamping the existing set of cultural values accordingly. Corporate culture has
been recognized as a pervasive force influencing organizational competitiveness.

Some writers have conceived culture, rather than structure, strategy, or politics,
as the prime mover in organizations (Deal and Kennedy, 1982). Cultural change
programs start with identifying current shared organizational values and norms,
and then proceed to identifying what the culture should be, and end with identifying the gap between the two and developing a plan to close it.

However, changes in culture rather than structure or technology, are the most
difficult to undertake among various pillars of organizations. This difficulty is due
to several factors such as:

- The enormous amount of effort and time that is required to create noticeable
  changes. Cultural change takes place through an ongoing socialization process
  that may take whole life span of employees.
- The feasibility of organizational change to accomplish lasting and long-term
  change in beliefs, values, and norms of people is questionable.
- The employees' resistance to organizational change, viz. business strategy, job
  design, organizational structure, business processes, and technology, which
  works in the opposite direction of the change program.

Although considered essential and having an influential impact on the success of
customer-centric business transformation; organizational culture has been viewed
as intellectually faulty and practically impossible (Ogbonna and Wilkinson, 2003).
Furthermore, the feasibility of changing people's culture, beliefs, values, and norms
to cope with the transformation to customer-centric knowledge-based organizations
may be questioned as opposed to the concept of 'climate' that can be changed (Al-
Shammari, 1992). Nevertheless, cultural change aspirations were very evident in
core principles of famous change programs such as TQM, i.e. customer orientation
and continuous improvement (Hughes, 2006). Corporate culture continues to be
useful as an explanation of organizational dynamics than as a prescription on how
to change in an organization happens.

It is now increasingly recognized that changes in technology and work processes
are fundamentally culture changes, and preparing organizational members for such
culture changes is an important undertaking that cannot be avoided (Turban et al.,
2008). Customer-centric OT requires not only changes in structure, but also nurtur-

ing knowledge-sharing customer-oriented culture. Knowledge sharing culture helps employees in handling customer complaints and converting these complaints from being a challenge to being an opportunity. The ability of employees to excel in handling customer complaints as opposed to their competitors would give them a SCA in terms of creating customer satisfaction and ultimately customer profitability.

The knowledge-sharing culture may be fostered through incorporating it as an element in both performance evaluation and pay and rewards systems, mentoring programs to senior members to transfer their knowledge, training programs in knowledge-sharing methods, and informal organizational gatherings and to improve interpersonal relationships among employees.

The structural and cultural changes would be more effective once they were compatible with the national cultural fabric in which an organization operates. National socio-cultural settings do have various profound impacts on product or service delivery, standards of business conduct, and ethics that the society considers appropriate or inappropriate. For instance, consumer preferences for color, style, taste, and so on may change from one place to another.

As culture represents an integral part of customer-centric organizational transformation, therefore, management of changes in culture becomes very crucial for customer-oriented organizations in order to:

- enable maintenance, innovation and development of the existing customer-oriented value-adding cultural values.
- foster a new customer-oriented, value-adding corporate culture that prevails throughout the organization and emphasizes values such as excellence, trust, respect, teamwork, and focus on achievement.
- resolve or minimize conflicts between subcultures within different teams or units, especially in the case of a merger between or acquisition of two companies with distinct cultures.

Non-conventional business solutions are not expected to flourish in conventional business contexts, and vice versa. Using Hofstede's classification of national cultures, the CKM-based organization is likely to flourish more in the national cultural settings that are characterized by the following:

- *High Individualism*: where people consider it acceptable to cater for individualized preferences of customers, and let these preferences take premium over those of masses of customers in the market. Providing a customized product or service may be seen as unacceptable favoritism treatment of a somewhat discriminatory nature that is based on purchasing power of customers. That is why it is quite possible to find consumers in some countries; for instance, who are willing to pay premium prices for tailor-made clothes, whereas consumers in other countries may be unwilling to pay that premium, and in turn, prefer to purchase ready-made ones.

- *High Power Tolerance*: socio-cultural values also affect the way workers in a society feel about the importance of their jobs and organizations (Griffin, 2005). The role of superiors is changing from directing to sponsoring, coaching, guiding, and mentoring. The role of employees is also changing from receiving orders to being fully entrusted with the power to do the job. Employees' empowerment enables the delivery of higher value to customers, but it works well in power tolerance social contexts, where less significance is attached to a person's position in the hierarchy, and control of power is no longer resides in the hands of superiors, but is distributed and shared by all staff members.

- *Low Uncertainty Avoidance*: where people prefer formalized structure and consistent standard operating procedures, whereas in low uncertainty cultures, people take positive stands and respond to change and creation of new opportunities. As a result of the need for empowerment, employees in networked customer-centric organizations will have to be willing, capable, and ready to accept higher degrees of authority, responsibility, and ambiguity.

- *Aggressive Goal-Orientation*: where people in this culture place a high value on the purchasing power and financial worth of customers, but this is done through building, maintaining, and expanding relationships with customers, and being concerned with their welfare.

- *Long-Term Time-Orientation*: organizations are supposed to be concerned with customers throughout their life cycle time. The suitable cultures for CKM are those that carry a mixture of short-term and long-term time orientations. In a hybrid time outlook, people prefer delivery of products or services that provide more immediate rewards from customers at the early stage of the customer's life cycle (acquisition), maintain customer relationships at the mid-term horizon in order to cast intermediate rewards, and work hard for many years to get more rewards on the long-run (expansion of profitability from customers).

FUTURE TRENDS

The future trends in business reorganization will witness a shift from human assets to intellectual assets, from mechanistic to holistic organizations, from vertical to virtual organizations, from domestically-centralized to globally dispersed business, and from localized unicultural to multicultural organizations.

A Shift from Human Assets to Intellectual Assets

Adaptive organizations of the future will not depend on the mere existence of human resources, but on the ability to nourish and leverage intellectual capacity of human assets. This can be done for example by hiring the right people with the right skills needed to create SCA. Knowledge workers are different from the bosses and the workers of industrial capitalism. It is expected that knowledge workers will operate increasingly in task-focused teams, where the traditional division of labor is replaced by a synchronicity of effort, and 'doing' the work is replaced with 'thinking' about how to design a new and better way to add value to customers and, in turn, to the company itself.

More cooperative modes of collaboration among multiple knowledge workers, working not only in different units within and across organizations, are likely to prevail. Knowledge working teams will last as long as the task requires and may involve participants from different external parties, e.g. suppliers or distributors located all over the world. Corporate cultures of visionary and forward-looking businesses are needed to nurture intellectual entrepreneurism that would reward taking risks and tolerate making mistakes.

A Shift from Mechanistic to Holistic Organizations

Traditional organization designs are internally focused, product-centered, functional, and hierarchical in nature; whereas new forms of organizations are flexible, customer-centric, networked structures. Commentators are in agreement that a new form of organization is emerging which replaces its classical predecessors, but what shape (or shapes) the new form will take is still not clear (Buchanan and Huczynski, 2004). Despite calls to flatten hierarchies, downsize, empower, and form alliances and networks, we are yet to witness the demise of traditional forms of organizing in the short-run. New work design arrangements appear to be supplementing rather than supplanting existing work practices. Surprisingly, advancements in ICT have sometimes facilitated the development of more flexible, adaptive work practices that complement and support rather than replace traditional, yet ever relevant, forms and work practices (Graetz, 2006).

More businesses are likely to shift their organizations from mechanistic (the whole of the business equals the sum of its parts) to holistic (any part of the business reflects the whole organization and its culture). In the context of CKM holistic change, organizations facilitate sharing of beliefs, attitudes, and values wherever the company chooses to do business. Real-time global communication among employees to share ideas and activities fosters employees' commitment to the holistic culture. The holistic culture results in the consistency with which the company treats customers, vendors, distributors, and other business partners.

A Shift from Vertical to Virtual Organizations

Reorganization decisions are affected by many external as well as internal factors. Tough future competition and economic conditions are likely to force companies to opt for reorganization decisions, not only for survival, but also for performance improvement. Managers may opt for different choices of organizational structure: a centralized versus decentralized, rigid versus flexible, tall versus flat, physical versus virtual, or a hybrid structure. Due to the accelerating rates of competition, technological advancements, as well as other business environmental conditions, more future organizations are likely to opt for full utilization of the potentials of ICTs in order to enable various organizational change options.

As a result of transforming into a customer-centric organization, the setting up of self-managed teams, and empowerment of team members, middle managers tend to play a different, but shrinking, role. Middle managers are likely to be the first victims of organizational reinvention, as self-managed teams will soon replace them. The reason is that middle managers usually do the information processing and communication task, telling their subordinates what to do and telling senior managers the outcome of what was done (Pearlson and Saunders, 2006). Self-managed teams that are fully empowered, knowledgeable, and equipped with ICTs, and require no management to make their own decisions will easily replace the job of middle managers. Therefore, the need for middle management positions will start to decline noticeably. Such a future trend may lead to more and more employees, especially middle managers, being cynical and skeptical of the merits of the new organizational change program.

The issues that will continue to face new forms of organizations in the future is how to handle such trends among employees, and how to create an OT program that is a friendly rather than hostile to employees. At the same time, organizations need to face another related challenge of how to continue to enable employees to provide a higher level of performance in the delivery of products or services during major reorganizational change initiatives. Employees' performances are directly related to the experiences of customers, and ultimately, upon customer satisfaction, intimacy, relationship, and profitability.

Organizations may opt for revolutionary changes such as virtuality, downsizing, as well as empowerment. In the short-term, some business organizations (prospectors) may continue to stick for some time to hybridity in their organizational forms by keeping both physical and e-business organizational forms (click-and-brick) till the situation clears up in terms of gains as well as risks. Even at one extreme, some firms may opt for a radical shift from vertical to virtual (cyberspace-based) structures. In the long run, more firms, especially analyzers, are likely to go for a complete migration to a full-fledged e-biz solution (click-and-click).

A Shift from Domestically-Centralized to Globally-Dispersed Business

Companies are moving away from functions *centralization or decentralization* to conducting business *'anywhere'*. Globalization is the ability to do business, e-commerce, e-learning, or e-banking anywhere, anytime using video-conferencing via ICT infrastructures such as satellite, the Internet, intranets, and extranets.

In CKM, organizations may shift from domestic production and marketing to a global structure where financial control is centralized in the home country while production, sales, and marketing units are dispersed in other countries. On the other hand, they may opt for a truly stateless, transnational structure that has no national headquarters or borders and optimizes sources of supply and demand and exploits any local competitive advantages through coordinated global supply chain management. In between the options to locally centralize or globally decentralize is the decision to franchise where a firm coordinates production, marketing, and logistics with foreign franchisers, but centralizes financial control.

A Shift from Unicultural to International Cross-Cultural Organizations

As a result of globalization of business induced by ICT advancements, many companies are becoming increasingly multinational in their operations. Nowadays, most companies interact with customers, suppliers, or competitors from different national cultures. Business organizations are no longer able to face the wave of globalization with their 'localized' cultural value. Companies have already started making their international business operations an autonomous division, and built cross-cultural values for cross-cultural organizations (Al-Shammari, 1994).

More companies are likely to operate in a multicultural corporate culture model that considers the interactions between the PESTIL environmental conditions, discussed in Chapter 1, of the home and host countries. For example, a corporate cultural manifestation of an individualistic society is the existence of heterogeneous cultural values within organizations. In a pluralistic society, organizational members are thought to possess a unified rather than diverse cultural value system. Similar examples can be also found with respect to problem-solving styles (conventional versus innovative), strategic orientation (internally-focused versus externally-focused), risk orientation (risk-taking versus risk-averting), response orientation (proactive versus reactive), and authority style (participative versus directive).

The accelerating pace of business globalization urges companies to develop an understanding and analysis of strategies for a successful management of cross-cultural dissimilarities among organizations and their customers in host countries. The challenge that is facing management of multinational firms is how to reconcile differences between the parent company and the host country's cultural value systems. The challenge here is how to design, develop, nurture, and manage a new set of multicultural, customer-centric values that take into consideration cultural diversity in the background of customers as well as employees. What pleases customers in one country may not be the same in other cultures. Customers may judge a particular customer service as satisfactory in one cultural setting, but the same service may be judged unsatisfactory in another.

Management's choice of the set of cultural values that need to be nurtured in CKM is not a kind of inevitable 'either/or' choice of dominant versus recessive cultural values between organizational and host cultural values. Management needs to seek to find the 'optimal' blend of organizational cultural value systems with those of their customers. Management needs to analyze the emerged customer values and assess the ability of their organizations to make the experience of customers match their expectations.

CONCLUSION

A natural byproduct of customer-orientation is the emergence of process orientation and cross-functional and self-managed teams. Creating customer-centric SCA from organizational changes requires a flexible structure, outsourcing of non-core activities, empowerment of employees, a constant and reliable knowledge-sharing culture, and process-based teamwork.

To be able to function effectively in rapidly dynamic and complex business environments, it is inevitable for forward-looking organizations to adapt to change, add value to customers, reward and capitalize on creative ideas and distinct capabilities, create new business opportunities, and develop an atmosphere that is conducive to continuous life-long systemic-based learning. Today's fast-changing business world is witnessing aggressive fluctuations, higher degrees of uncertainty, and fierce competition. The changing nature of business environments requires dynamic rather than static organizational forms.

Business organizations can no longer be effective in facing rising competition with their traditional structures. The people component of organizations represents a major organizational pillar in facing today's changing business environment through creating distinctive core competencies. In terms of people-based structural changes, the evolution of the world's economy from industrial-based to information-based enabled the trend to shift from the functional and hierarchical to the flexible and networked organizations.

In today's business world, there is a clear trend to shift away from functional organizations based on individuals performing individual tasks to networked structures. Traditional, multilevel, functional hierarchies are rigid structures that depend heavily on rules, procedures, and vertical and lateral referral, which make these organizations intrinsically inflexible, inefficient, ineffective, and unfit for competition. The hierarchical structure must be adjusted to ensure flexibility, speed of service, and the integration among business functions.

Networked structures are flexible designs that are made up of small-sized teams. Small size allows teams to change direction, explore new ideas, and try new ways of doing things without a rigid bureaucratic organizational structure. Although few organizations have actually reached higher levels of customer-centric organizational design flexibility, many customer-centric companies are expected to move toward it. Networked organizations apply team-based incentives and a well-designed reward and recognition system that helps reinforce the desired behavior of being customer-focused. Besides, networked organizations distribute authority and power to people through empowerment. Empowerment helps boosting employee's morale and improves customer satisfaction.

Structural changes in customer-centric organizations also require changes in corporate culture and leadership style. The corporate culture needs to be supportive of knowledge sharing, not knowledge hoarding, and distinction in customer service, not execution of customer service. Leaders of customer-centric OT need to be visionary, inspirational, and supportive, and need to coach, not boss.

Although many customer-oriented organizations have gone through comprehensive and enormous change programs with the aim of maximizing the value-added content of teams in the delivery of products or services, not all of these efforts have succeeded. There is a wide range of challenges that face organizations in their moves toward instituting and reinforcing new forms of customer-centric organizations, such as attracting, developing, and maintaining, and managing people. In CKM, workplace relations are based upon collegiality and consensus, rather than hierarchical command and control.

Several issues may emerge while transforming to a customer-focused organization. Reorganizing people in teams requires reviewing and upgrading in people skills, values, attitudes, behaviors, and performance in order to secure provision of value-adding customer products or services. The product of mismatch between people's skills and requirements of the job is poor performance. The challenge here is how to enhance people's skills, knowledge, motivation, and commitment throughout an ongoing learning program.

The future is expected to witness more migration from the concern with human assets to the concern of intellectual assets, from rigid and internally focused towards flexible and externally oriented structures, and from unicultural to multicultural global organizations. In addition, new forms of organizations are likely to emerge in the future. In moving from a unicultural to multicultural global businesses, managers must be able to draw a fine line between maintaining a culture that is functioning well and changing a culture that has become dysfunctional.

In the next chapter, the role of ICT retooling in CKM value chain will be examined.

REFERENCES

Al-Shammari, M. (1994). On the corporate culture of cross-cultural organizations: A proposed model. *Cross Cultural Management: An International Journal, 1*(1), 28-31.

Al-Shammari, M. (1992). Organizational climate: Differentiates organizational climate from other associated concepts. *Leadership and Organization Development Journal, 13*(6), 30-32.

Alter, S. (2002). *Information systems: Foundation of E-Business.* 4th edition, Upper Saddle River, NJ: Prentice Hall.

Awad, E., & Ghaziri, H. (2004). *Knowledge management.* Upper Saddle River, NJ: Prentice Hall.

Blumnethal, B., & Haspeslagh, P. (1994). Toward a definition of corporate transformation. *Sloan Management Review, 35*(3), 101-106.

Bowditch J. L., & Buono, A. F. (2005). *A primer on organizational behavior.* 6th edition, Hoboken: John Willey & Sons.

Buchanan, D., & Huczynski, A. (2004). *Organizational behavior: An introductory text.* 5th edition, Harlow: FT/Prentice Hall.

Burns, T., & Stalker, G. M. (1961). *The management of innovation.* London: Kogan Page.

Buttle, F. (2004). *Customer relationship management: Concepts and tools.* Oxford, England: Elsevier Publishing.

Cash, J. I., Ecclles, R., Nohria, N., & Nolan, R. (1994). *Building the information age organization structures, control, and Information technologies.* Burr Ridge, IL: Irwin.

Cohen, W. M., & Leventhal, D. A. (1990). Absorptive capacity: A new perspective on learning and innovation. *Administrative Science Quarterly, 35,* 128-152.

Davenport, T. H. (2000). One cheer for the virtual office. In D. Marchand, & T. Davenport (Eds.), *Mastering information management: Your single source guide to becoming a master of Information Management* (pp.238-243). London: FT Prentice Hall.

Davenport, T. H. (1993). *Process innovation: Reengineering work through information technology.* Boston, MA: Harvard Business School Press.

Davenport, T. H., & Short, J. E. (1990). The new industrial engineering: information technology and business process redesign. *Sloan Management Review,* Summer, 11-27.

Davenport, T. H., & Stoddard, D. B. (1994). Reengineering: business change of mythic proportions? MIS *Quarterly, 18*(2), 121-127.

Deal T. E., & Kennedy A. A. (1982). *Corporate cultures: The rights and rituals of corporate life.* Reading, MA: Addison-Wesley.

Deal T. E., & Kennedy, A. A. (1999). *The new corporate cultures: Revitalizing the workplace after downsizing, mergers and reengineering.* London: Orion Business.

De Long, D. W., & Fahey, L. (2000). Diagnosing cultural barriers to knowledge management. *The Academy of Management Executive, 14*(4), 113-27.

Drucker, P. (2002). *Who is the Knowledge worker?* www.pbsilink.com/knowledge-workers.htm, Retrieved on August 12, 2006.

Fiol, C. M., & Lyles, M. A. (1985). Organizational learning. *Academy of Management Review, 10*(4), 803-813.

Graetz, F., Rimmer, M., Lawrence, A., & Smith, A. (2006). *Managing organizational change.* 2nd Edition, Milton, Australia: John Wiley.

Griffin, R. (2005). *Management.* 8th edition, Boston: Houghton Mifflin Company.

Grover, V, Teng, J., & Fiedler, K (1995). The implementation of business process re-engineering. *Journal of Management Information Systems, 12*(1), 109-44.

Hammer, M., & Champy J. (2003). *Reengineering the corporation: A manifesto for business revolution*. New York: HarperCollins.

Handy, C. B. (1978). *The Gods of management*. London: Penguin.

Herzberg, F. (1987). One more time: How do you motivate employees? *Harvard Business Review*, January-February, 109-120.

Heskett, J., Jones, T., Earl, L., & Schlesinger, L. (1994). Putting the service-profit chain to work. *Harvard Business Review*, March-April, 164-174.

Hughes, M. (2006). *Change management: A critical perspective*. London: CIPD Publications.

Jassawalla, A. R., & Sahittal, H. C. (1999). Building collaborative new product teams. *Academy of Management Review*, *13*(3), 50-60.

Jones, G. (2003). *Organization theory*. 4th ed., Upper Saddle River, NJ: Prentice-Hall.

Kanter, R. M. (1989). *When giants learn to dance*. New York: Simon & Schuster.

Keidel, K. (1994). Rethinking organizational design. *Academy of Management Executive*, *8*(4), 12-27.

King, W. R. (1995). Creating a strategic capabilities architecture. *Information Systems Management*, *12*(1), 67-69.

Kilmann, R., Saxton, M., & Serpa, R. (1986). Issues in understanding and changing culture. *California Management Review*, *28*(2), 87-94.

Klempa, M. (1995). Understanding business process reengineering: A sociocognitive contingency model. In V. Grover & W. Kettinger (Eds). *Business process change: reengineering concepts, methods and technologies* (pp.78-122). Pershey, PA: Idea Group Publishing.

Kotter, J. P., & Heskett, J. L. (1992). *Corporate culture and performance*. New York: The Free Press.

Lei, D., & Slocum, J. (2002). Organization designs to renew competitive advantage. *Organizational Dynamics*, *31*(1), 1-18.

Liebowitz, J. (2004). Conceptualizing and implementing knowledge management. In P. Love, P. Fong, & Z. Irani (Eds.). *Management of knowledge in project environment, (*pp. 1-18). Amsterdam: Elsevier Butterworth-Heinemann.

Mantel, S., Meredith, J., Shafer, S., & Sutton, M. (2001). *Project management in practice*. New York: John Wiley.

Miles, R. E., & Snow C. C. (1984). Fit, failure and the hall of fame. *California Management Review, 26*(3), 36-52.

Mintzberg, H. (1979). *The structuring of organizations*. Englewood Cliffs, NJ: Prentice-Hall.

Prentice-Hall.

Mintzberg, H. (1983). *Structure in fives: Designing effective organizations*. Englewood Cliffs, NJ: Prentice-Hall.

Nonaka, I., & Takeuchi, H. (1995). *The knowledge creating company*. Oxford: Oxford University Press.

Ogbonna, E., & Wilkinson B. (2003). The false promise of organizational culture change: a case study of middle managers in grocery retailing. *Journal of Management Studies, 40*(5), 1151-78.

O'Reilly, C., Chatman, J. A., & Caldwell, D. (1991). People and organizational culture: A Q-sort approach to assessing person-organization fit. *Academy of Management Journal, 34*, 487-516.

O'Reilly, C. (1989). Corporations, culture, and commitment: Motivation and social control in organizations. *California Management Review, 31*(3), 9-25.

Park, H., Ribiere, V., & Schulte, W. (2004). Critical attributes of organizational culture that promote knowledge management technology implementation success. *Journal of Knowledge Management, 8*(3), 106-117.

Pastore, R. (1995). Competing interests: An interview with Michael Porter. *CIO, 9*(1), 63-68.

Pearlson, K., & Saunders, C. (2006). *Managing and using information systems: A strategic approach*. 3rd edition, New York: John Wiley.

Peppard, J., & Ronald, P. (1995). *The essence of business process re-engineering*. Upper Saddle River, NJ: Prentice-Hall.

Pettigrew, A. (1999). Organizing to improve company performance. Warwick Business School. Hot *Topics, 1*(5), 1-7

Schein, E. H. (1985). *Organizational culture and leadership*. San Francisco, CA: Jossey-Bass.

Schein, E. H. (1990). Organizational culture. *American Psychologist, 45*(February), 109-19.

Schein, E. H. (1992). *Organizational Culture and Leadership*. San Fransisco, Jossey Bass

Schultheis, R., & Sumner, M. (1992). *Management information systems: the manger's view*. Burr Ridge, IL: Irwin.

Senge, P. (1990a). *The Fifth Discipline: The art and practice of the learning organization*. New York: Doubleday Currency.

Senge, P. (1990b). The leader's new work: Building learning organizations. *Sloan Management Review, 32*, 7-23.

Turban, E., McLean, E., & Wetherbe, J. (1999). *Information technology for management: Making connection for strategic advantage*. 2nd ed., New York: John Wiley.

Turban, E., McLean, E., & Wetherbe, J. (2002). *Information technology for management: transforming business in the digital economy*. 3rd ed., New York: John Wiley.

Turban, E., Leidner, D. E., Mclean, E., & Wetherbe, J. (2008). *Information technology for management: Transforming organizations in the digital economy*. 6th ed., NY: John Wiley.

Van den Berge, P. T., & Wilderom, C. P. M. (2004). Defining, measuring, and comparing organizational cultures. *Applied Psychology: an International Review, 53*(4), 570-82.

Weber, M. (1947). The theory of social and economic organization. Glencoe, IL: Free Press.

Weiss, J. W. (2001). *Organizational behavior and change: Managing diversity, cross-cultural dynamics, and ethics*. Cincinnati, Ohio: South-Western.

Wentz, T. (1999). *Transformational change*. Boston, MA: Corporate Performance Systems

Chapter IV
Retooling ICT Systems

INTRODUCTION

Regardless of the type of organization or operation, the evolving nature of organizational ICT systems helps organizations to live up to changing market dynamics. Although CKM itself is not a technological solution, ICTs are required to enable the integration of its customer-facing processes and, to build knowledge-based endurable and profitable customer relationships. The previous chapter explored the role of people in enabling CKM; whereas the current chapter is devoted to examining the role of ICTs retooling. Retooling ICTs is used in this chapter to refer to the replacement of old legacy systems with new systems in enabling a successful CKM change. The main focus of the chapter is on the hardware, software, and network components of ICTs in the context of CKM.

CONCEPTUAL FOUNDATINS

ICT is a major infrastructural enabler of the implementation of a CKM. Computerized ICTs collect, process, store, analyze, and disseminate information for a specific business application. The retail banking industry is a very common example of an industry constantly searching for ICT-based solutions in order to provide more and better products and/or services to customers and to increase internal productivity. Examples are automated teller machines (ATMs), tele-banking, e-banking, and m-banking used by customers to process account transactions. In the marketing function, ICTs can be used to develop sales information to target customers and identify the market niches. ICTs can also be used to create attractive products and/or services through innovatively redesigning business practices and organizational structures, re-engineering ICT to maintain competitive advantage, and providing superior internal efficiency.

Components of computerized ICTs include hardware, software, data, network, procedures, and people. This section describes the rapidly evolving ICT systems landscape and its role in CKM. It examines the following elements: doing business in the digital economy, ICTs and the CKM strategy, retooling ICTs infrastructure, emerging computing platforms, and classification of ICT systems. The role of ICTs will continue to be discussed throughout the CKM value chain in the remainder of this book.

Doing Business in the Digital Economy

ICTs have brought significant changes to the business world. They have paved the way for the transformation of global economies from the old traditional economy to the new digital economy, and provided the impetus for business organizations to move from standard ways of doing things to new and innovative ways of doing business. The aim of e-business is to add value to customers as well as to business firms. Web-based systems are considered a major infrastructural component of a business change model such as CKM.

The digital economy is characterized by the following (Turban et al., 2008):

- E-Business (e-biz): buying and selling goods and services (e-commerce), servicing customers, and conducting electronic transactions within an organization.
- E-Collaboration: people and organizations interact, communicate, and collaborate..
- Information Exchange: storing, processing and transmission of information.

E-commerce can take several forms depending on the degree of digitization involved. It can relate to: (1) the product or service being sold, (2) the process by which the product or service is produced, or (3) the intermediary or delivery agent (Rainer et al., 2007):

- Pure physical business (brick-and-mortar): all three dimensions are physical
- Pure e-commerce (click-and-click): companies engage only in e-commerce transactions.
- Partial e-commerce (click-and-brick): a mix of digital and physical dimensions.

E-commerce can take various shapes (Rainer et al., 2007):

- Business-to-business (B2B): both buyers and sellers are business organizations (e.g., Commerceone.com).
- Business-to-consumer (B2C): the sellers are organizations, whereas the buyers are individuals (e. g., Amazon.com).
- Consumer-to-business (C2B): customers place orders for what they want and businesses accept or reject their offers, such as when passengers bid on airline seats (e.g., Priceline.com).
- Consumer-to-consumer (C2C): consumers sell or auction second hand items to each other with the help of an online market maker (e.g., eBay.com).
- Mobile commerce (m-commerce): e-commerce that is conducted entirely in a wireless environment (e.g., WAP transmission protocol).

ICTs and the CKM Strategy

Retooling ICTs represents an integral component of organizational enablers of CKM. In ICTs acquisition decisions, managers start out by outlining a business strategy that serves as a 'compass' in guiding the development of more specific business goals and functional objectives. Zinledin (2000) suggests that IT tools should be used not only to provide relationship building credibility and opportunities with customers but also to enable marketers to keep their fingers on the customer's pulse and respond to changing needs.

Earl (1989) proposed a three-pronged approach to ICTs strategy: 'top-down', 'bottom-up', and 'inside-out' approaches. The top-down approach focuses on business strategy objectives and responsibilities; the bottom-up approach emphasizes current ICTs infrastructures and applications as well as future demands and requirements of users; whereas the inside-out approach focuses on ICTs developments that respond to marketplace pressures and/or opportunities. However, in the context of CKM, an 'outside-in' approach might be a more appropriate strategy to incorporate environmental scanning as a trigger of the current as well as future requirements of ICTs. The development of an ICT infrastructure needs to take a strategic perspective and be a balanced process that incorporates both business environmental factors and the internal situation for competitive positioning of organizations.

Retooling ICTs Infrastructure

In the process of retooling an ICT infrastructure, detailed business requirements are derived from all business goals and functional objectives. Business requirements are, then, translated into a more-detailed view of the systems requirements, standards, and processes that shape the ICT architecture, as documented in Table 4.1. The next step is to translate the ICT architecture plan into an ICT infrastructure as shown in Table 4.2 (Pearlson and Saunders, 2006).

An ICT infrastructure refers to four components: hardware, software, network, and data. Hardware includes components such as desktop units, monitors, and servers. Software includes the programs used to do business, to manage the computer itself, and to communicate between systems. The third part of an ICT infrastructure is the network, which is the physical means by which information is exchanged among hardware components, such as through a modem and dial-up network, or through a private digital network. The fourth element of the infrastructure is the data storage, which refer to the facts, the bits and bytes stored in the system.

The ICT architecture represents a conceptual planning of the information and knowledge requirements of the core business of the organization. A common way to classify ICT architecture in the context of CKM is according to the following four computing paradigms (Turban et al., 2008):

- A standalone PC environment that operates in total isolation from other computers.
- A centralized computing environment: all processing is accomplished by one large central mainframe or supercomputer, with many dumb terminals connected to it.

Table 4.1. ICT requirement analysis framework

Component	What?	Who?	Where?
Hardware	What hardware does the organization have?	Who manages it? Who uses it? Who owns it?	Where is it located? Where is it used?
Software	What software does the organization have?	Who manages it? Who uses it? Who owns it?	Where is it located? Where is it used?
Network	What networking does the organization have?	Who manages it? Who uses it? Who owns it?	Where is it located? Where is it used?
Data	What data does the organization have?	Who manages it? Who uses it? Who owns it?	Where is it located? Where is it used?

Source: Adapted from Pearlson, K. & Saunders, C. (2006). Managing and Using Information Systems: A Strategic Approach. 3rd edition, New York: John Wiley.

Table 4.2. ICT architecture and infrastructure analysis framework

Component	What?		Who?		Where?	
	Architecture	Infrastructure	Architecture	Infrastructure	Architecture	Infrastructure
Hardware	Does fulfillment of our strategy require thick or thin clients?	With what size hard drives do we equip our thick clients?	Who knows the most about servers in our organization?	Who will operate the server?	Does our architecture require centralized or distributed servers?	Must we hire a server administrator for the Tokyo office?
Software	Does fulfillment of our strategy require ERP software?	Shall we go with a SAP or Oracle applications?	Who is affected by a move to SAP?	Who will need SAP training?	Does our geographical organization require multiple database instances?	Does Oracle provide the multiple-database functionality we need?
Network	What kind of bandwidth do we need to fulfill our strategy?	Will 10base T Ethernet suffice?	Who needs a connection to the network?	Who needs an ISDN line to his or her home?	Does our WAN need to span the Atlantic?	Shall we lease a cable or use satellite?
Data	Do our vendors all use the same EDI format?	Which VAN provides all the translation services we need?	Who needs access to sensitive data?	Who needs encryption software?	Will backups be stored on-site or off-site?	Which storage service shall we select?

Source: Adapted from Pearlson, K. & Saunders, C. (2006). Managing and Using Information Systems: A Strategic Approach. 3rd edition, New York: John Wiley.

- A distributed or a networked computing environment (client-server network): distributes the processing work among PCs, minicomputers, and mainframes. There are a number of local area network (LAN) or wide area network (WAN) technologies known as topologies or 'general shapes', e.g., star, ring, or bus topologies. One form of distributed processing is the client-server paradigm that splits processing between 'clients' and 'servers' on LAN/WAN and assigns processing functions to the machine most able to perform the function (server). The server provides the client with services and might range from a supercomputer or a mainframe to another desktop computer. Servers store and process shared data and also perform back-end functions not visible to users, such as managing network activities. Clients are normally a desktop computer, workstation, or laptop (Laudon and Laudon, 2002). This type of ICT architecture fits well with customer-centric, process-based networked organizations adopting CKM.

- A Web-based computing environment: refers to those applications or services that are resident on a server that is accessible using a Web browser. The only client-side software needed to access and execute these applications is a Web browser environment. This type of ICT architecture fits well with customer-centric, process-based networked organizations adopting CKM. It includes the following components:

  ° The Internet
  ° Intranets (Laudon and Laudon, 2002):

    ➢ Are private networks for a specific business process or function (e.g., marketing, sales, and finance), that are protected from public visits by firewalls.
    ➢ Provide a universal e-mail system, remote access, group collaboration tools, electronic library, application-sharing systems, and a communication network.
    ➢ Are inexpensive, scalable to expand or contract as needs change, and accessible from most computing platforms.
    ➢ Provide instant connectivity, uniting all computers into a single virtual network system.
    ➢ Can be used to simplify and integrate business processes spanning more than one functional area.
    ➢ Connect well to a corporate database, data mart, or a DW, just as with the Web, enabling employees to execute customer-facing as well as other supporting business transactions.
    ➢ Can help organizations create a richer and more responsive customer-centric information environment, such as on-line repositories of product or customer information that can be updated as often as required.

  ° Extranets (Turban et al., 2008):

    ➢ Private networks accessible only to selected outsiders.

> ➤ Connect several intranets via the Internet by adding a security mechanism and some additional functionalities.
> ➤ Form a larger virtual network that allows remote users, such as customers or business partners, to connect securely over the Internet to the enterprise's main intranet.
> ➤ Employed by two or more enterprises (suppliers and buyers) to share information in a controlled fashion, and therefore play a major role in the development of business-to-business electronic commerce and supply chain systems.
> ➤ Facilitate electronic coordination of supply chain, cross-functional processes, increasing organizational efficiency and responsiveness to customers.

○ Corporate portals: a Web-based personalized gateway to information and knowledge that provides information from different ICTs and the Internet using advanced search and indexing techniques. Portals support and enable virtual communities of practice (COPs), informal and semi-informal networks, and organizational learning based on shared concerns and interests of internal employees with external suppliers and customers. Developing virtual communities of consumers and users is among the key priorities of portals in CKM.

○ E-commerce, or m-commerce, systems: a type of inter-organizational ICT that enables organizations to conduct business transactions with other businesses and/or with customers.

○ E-storefronts: On-line catalogs of products made available to the general public by a single seller.

○ E-markets: Suppliers and buyers conduct electronic business activities in a single virtual market space.

In the context of CKM, organizations need to understand the role of their existing ICT infrastructure, to understand the limitations of implemented ICTs, and to identify gaps in the existing ICT infrastructure when it is linked to the adopted customer-centric business strategy. In the quest for building an effective CKM, organizations need to analyze, leverage and build upon networks, intranets, extranets, as well as systems needed for the generation of CK such as DM, DW, project management, and decision support systems (DSS) tools that are already in place. Intranets, extranets and GroupWare systems need also to integrate well into an organization-wide CKM. E-biz solutions need also to be integrated with backend legacy and enterprise systems, as well as organizational databases. Such integration requires substantial reengineering (Kalakota and Robinson, 2001).

Emerging Computing Platforms

In the first decade of the new millennium several computing platforms have emerged, i.e. Service-Oriented Architecture (SOA), and Web 2.0. Implementing SOA and Web-based services require a set of standards for the flow of information among the participants. These are related to the concept of 'open source' that allows easy flow of information and integration in different computing environments (Turban et al., 2008).

Service-Oriented Architecture

The rise of web-based Application Service Providers (ASP) as the preferred platform for enterprise applications has enabled and, in some ways, driven the rise of SOA. Rather than software components being developed and bundled together to form a monolithic, rigid solution, Applications are increasingly being developed as a 'federation' of services, or composite applications that are tied together only at the point of execution. Instead of buying and installing expensive software applications, users can access applications over a network, with a Web browser being the only need. Usually there is no hardware and software to buy since the applications used over the Web and paid for through a fixed flat subscription fee, or payable per usage volume fee (Turban et al., 2008). In many cases, firms do not have the time, knowledge, or infrastructure to build an effective CRM program, so they decide to concentrate their resources on DCCs and use Internet on-demand outsourced CRM services provided by an ASP. Customers today have no way of knowing who is answering their call centre calls, maintaining their personal data, or designing marketing campaigns aimed at them (Wisner et al., 2008).

Business firms are realizing that SOA provides potential for their companies. SOA views everything as a service provider, from applications, to databases, companies, and devices. Microsoft, Apple, Google, SAP, and IBM all have the strategy to both open and offer their applications as services delivered via the Web and paid for by advertisement and subscriptions. The change to loosely coupled, standards-based integration opens up the opportunity to use many pre-built services and to integrate with business applications on the market, such as ERP systems, CRM systems, accounts systems, billing systems, and web systems (Granebring and Revay, 2007).

SOA has become the platform of choice for a wide variety of applications, and has made it difficult for previous-generation architectures to integrate functionality and systems, and to respond quickly to changing business needs. As CRM applications typically require extensive customization and integration, inflexible application architectures, SOA promises to foster a new, and a more agile, and efficient generation of application systems. SOA is based on open platform application services, such as Enterprise Java Beans (EJBs), implemented by Java 2 Enterprise Edition (J2EE) applications, NET components, or web-based SOA applications. SOA breaks through the barriers of business integration and help enterprises get their information resources in better order. To meet the needs of the agile and flexible enterprise, the practice of SOA adopts the following core principles (Granebring and Revay, 2007):

- The business drives the services, and the services drive the technology. In essence, services act as layer of abstraction between the business and the technology.
- Business agility is a fundamental business requirement. The requirements from business must reach the next level of abstraction 'meta-requirement.'

SOA also facilitates the design, the implementation, and re-use of multi-dimensional OLAP, and increases the availability by presenting services to new categories of BI applications. BI gives CRM information on how customers really act and forecasts how they will act in the future. Major software vendors like IBM, SAP, Oracle, and Microsoft are re-developing their monolithic products into autonomous services accessible over the Internet. SOA serves well as an OLAP decision support driver due to the increasing importance of DWs. SOA encapsulation, high abstract formality, and re-use of components are helpful in the business decision support and data transformation world of BI. BI solutions are tightly coupled to the data sources that feed the DW. A Service-Oriented Business Intelligence (SOBI) architectural framework solves problems of integration in an enterprise of disparate 'stove piped' systems, and provides a common data transformation mechanism for both operational and management information (Granebring and Revay, 2007).

Web 2.0

Web 2.0 can be described broadly as the current generation of web-based social networking applications and services designed around participation and communal collaboration. As social networking is an increasing feature of our daily life, our professional and social lives are increasingly reported, researched, shared and learned through social networks largely unbounded by space and time. Web 2.0 authoring tools easily enable users to collaboratively create, share and distribute knowledge from multiple sources, leverage collective intelligence, and organize action (Eijkman, 2008).

The exponential growth and use of blogs, wikis, pod and vodcasting (the delivery of on-demand video content as in YouTube and FaceBook), make the Web no longer represent a distinct cyber space, separated from people's everyday life, work and learning. Web 2.0 authoring tools and applications, i.e. Wikis, blogs, and multimedia sharing services, exploit and extend the building blocks of existing web-based technologies (Eijkman, 2008) to the point that when compared to Web 1.0, Web 2.0 has the potential to helping businesses better manage their relationships with customers. If online customer communities are in place, Web 2.0 enables networking and collaborative CK construction through access to a vast range and in-depth knowledge from these communities.

Classifications of ICT Systems

ICT application systems represent an integral infrastructural component of the CKM value chain. Classifying ICTs help business leaders to understand which systems they must invest in as well as what these systems should do, besides the role of people and processes, in order to maximize returns and achieve an SCA. Executives need to stop looking at ICT projects as technology installations and start viewing them as periods of organizational change that they have a responsibility to manage (McAfee, 2006).

This section addresses various types of ICTs. Prior to the attempt to classify ICTs, it is important to emphasize that classifications of ICTs are not mutually exclusive, as one way of classifying a system may overlap with other ways of classifying the same systems and, thus, one system may fall under more than one category. ICTs may be classified into seven non-mutually exclusive categories according to: a) organizational level, b) functional area, c) type of support, d) activity supported, e) business processes, and g) basis of system.

Organizational Level

All organizational structure components, e.g., departments, teams, and work units participate in the data collection and generation of CK. Such components form an organization that may report to a higher organizational level, such as a division or a headquarters, in a traditional hierarchical structure. Although nowadays many organizations are migrating towards more innovative forms of organizations, i.e. process-based teams, this classification is still common in many organizations that adopt traditional hierarchical structures. The types of ICTs that follow the organizational structure lines are: departmental, enterprise-wide, and inter-organizational (Turban et al., 2002).

- *Departmental ICT Systems*: It is common for an organization to use several application systems in one functional area or department, i.e. the collection of application subsystems in the sales and marketing department in a single system.
- *Enterprise-wide ICT Systems (EIS)*: The collection of all departmental application systems comprises the enterprise-wide system. Examples are CRM, SCM, and ERP systems. These systems integrate and capture data from major business functions such as procurement, production, marketing, sales, and finance. Commercial application systems include SAP R3, Oracle, and People Soft.

  Nowadays, most enterprise wide systems, e.g. ERP systems, include a workflow management systems (WFMS) that can be used as an aid to manage documents and forms routing. WFMS support a customer-driven and group work-oriented perspective on organizations as well as BPR initiatives; the customer-oriented view of workflows enables new ways of business process analysis and design. WFMS also lead to powerful new combinations of information and cooperation technologies, known as CSCW. WFMS prove to be effective in a wide range of process domains where coordinated teamwork is required, i.e. fulfilling customer orders or customer service processes.
- *Inter-Organizational ICT Systems (IOS)*: This type of system connects several organizations or partners together through B2B and B2C solutions. For instance, external contacts with suppliers may be established via SAPP R3, ORACLE, or extranets which are used in e-commerce as well as global supply chain management. Its major objective is efficient transaction processing, such as transmitting orders, invoicing, billing, and payment using EDI. IOS are used exclusively for business-to-business and business-to-consumer transactions and may include the following systems:

  ◦ Reporting Systems
  ◦ Analytical Systems
  ◦ Prediction Systems

Similar to this line of classification, McAfee (2006) offers a work-changing ICT tools classification based on three types:

- *Function ICT Systems:* assist with the execution of discrete tasks and make the execution of standalone tasks more efficient (e.g. simulators, word processors, spreadsheets, CAD, and statistical analysis packages).
- *Network ICT Systems:* optional systems facilitate interactions and communication between people without specifying their parameters (e.g., e-mail, instant messaging, wikis, blogs, and mashups).
- *Enterprise ICT Systems*: mandatory systems are applicable to specific business processes (e.g., software for ERP, CRM, and SCM).

Functional Area

ICTs used at departmental levels may also support traditional business functions. The major functional ICT systems are (Turban et al., 2002):

- The accounting system
- The finance system
- The operations/production system
- The marketing system
- The human resource system

Type of Support

Once ICT systems are classified according to the type of support they provide, regardless of business function, the following types emerge (Turban et al., 2002):

- *Transaction processing systems (TPS):* supports repetitive, mission-critical activities and clerical staff, such as order processing, invoicing and billing, and shipping.
- *Management ICT systems (MIS):* supports control of functional activities and managers.
- *Decision support systems (DSS):* supports decision making and analysis, such as mathematical modeling, what-if analysis (OLAP-cube slicing and dicing), goal seek analysis, and simulation.
- *Artificial intelligence (AI) support systems:* perform intelligent problem solving, such as NN, FL, DM, and ES.
- *Executive support systems (ESS):* supports executives and senior management.
- *Office automation systems (OAS):* supports office workers.
- *Group support systems (GSS):* supports team work and work group collaboration.

Activity Supported

The fourth way to classify ICT systems is by the nature of activity supported: operational, managerial, and strategic (Turban et al., 2002). The major characteristics of systems classified by the nature of activity supported (operational, managerial, and strategic) are as follow (Turban et al., 2002):

- *Operational Systems:* deal with capturing day-to-day short-term operations of the business, such as fulfillment of customer orders or placing a purchase order, and are used by supervisors (first-line managers), operators, and clerical employees. The ICTs that normally support these activities are TPS and MIS.
- *Tactical or Managerial Systems:* deal with control of middle management activities such as mid-range planning, organizing, and control. These systems are broader in scope than operational systems, and are designed to summarize data, prepare reports, and provide quick answers to queries. They provide several types of support:

  ○ Statistical summaries
  ○ Exception reports
  ○ Periodic and ad hoc reports
  ○ Comparative analysis
  ○ Projections
  ○ Early detection of problems

- *Strategic Systems:* deal with strategic planning activities that significantly change the manner in which business is being done. Relative to time-frame, strategic systems are involved only in long-range (five years or more) strategic planning as a major innovative response to competitors, i.e. systems that allow introduction of a new product or process (FedEx's package tracing system, CAD/CAM, and CRM).

Business Processes

ICT classifications would seem to be more suitable for CKM had they been based on the integrated value chain activities of networked organizations instead of business functions associated with hierarchical organizations. The value chain activities are as follow (Porter, 1985):

- Inbound logistics
- Operations

- Outbound logistics
- Marketing & Sales
- After-sale services

Basis of System

Another way to classify ICT systems is to consider the following four hierarchically-arranged bases, i.e. data, information, model, and knowledge (Table 4.3):

- *Data-based systems (DBS):* refer to online transactional processing (OLTP) systems that record and process daily business transactions (e.g., sales/marketing system).
- *Information-based systems (IBS):* are online analytical processing (OLAP) systems that serve business planning and control by providing routine summary and exception reports that are created from data-based systems.
- *Model-based systems (MBS):* combine data-based systems and quantitative models to support middle managers or professional staff (the level of staff support that exists between top and middle management and acts as advisors and assistants to both levels, such as financial and marketing analysts) in the decision making process.
- *Knowledge-based systems (KBS):* systems that support both content-based (rule-based) or contact-based (people-based) knowledge created by knowledge workers or professional staff. KBS are created from data, information, and model-based systems as well as the human component. Contact-based tools deal with textual (non-numeric) knowledge through systems such as GSS and OAS, whereas content-based ones refer to intelligent support systems that rely on numeric data (e.g., Intelligent Agents, NN, ES, and DM). For example, DM software tools find patterns in large pools of data stored in the DW and infer rules from them that can be used in unstructured decision making situations. DM supports the decision of product differentiation and mass customization (large volume product differentiation where ICT is creating customized products while retaining the cost efficiencies of mass production systems).

CRITICAL ISSUES

Several ICTs issues are discussed; they include: impact of ICTs in organizations, ICTs and value creation, ICTs and business globalization, economics of ICTs, performance of ICTs, security of ICTs, ethics of ICTs, reliability of ICTs, interoperability of ICTs, and scalability of ICTs.

Table 4.3. Characteristics of ICT according to basis of system

Dimension	Data-based Systems	Information-based Systems	Model-based Systems	Knowledge-based Systems
Environment	Certain	Uncertain	Uncertain	Uncertain
Situation	Structured	Structured	Semi-structured	Unstructured
Frequency	Recurrent	Mostly Recurrent	Often Ad Hoc	Often Ad Hoc
Inputs	Data	Information	Data and Model	Rule/People
Processing	Numerical	Numerical	Numerical	Numerical/ Textual
Nature of Outputs	Normative	Normative	Prescriptive	Prescriptive
Sources of Inputs	Internal/External	Internal/External	Mostly External	Mostly External
Number of Users	Many	Many	One or a Few	One or a Few
Types of Users	Supervisors	Middle Managers	Specialists and Managers	Specialists and Managers
Time Orientation	Past/Present	Past/Present	Future	Future
Nature of Domain	General/Specific	General/Specific	General	General
Value-added	Low	Low to Medium	Medium to High	High
Driver	Survival	Growth	Competitive Adv.	Sust. Comp. Adv.
Examples	OLTP	OLAP	DSS	CKM

Impact of ICTs in Organizations

CKM requires not only retooling of ICTs, but also using ICTs strategically in the OT process by aligning it with the business strategy as well as with other organizational components. ICT applications must be designed to have a value-adding impact on individuals, functional units, customer processes, and the organization as a whole. The objectives of ICT retooling are to improve efficiency, improve effectiveness (Schultheis and Sumner, 1992), facilitate achievement of business transformation, create customer loyalty, and achieve an SCA. A summary of ICT impacts in organizations is included in Table 4.4.

Transformation refers to the creative generation of ICT-based knowledge and the innovative application of knowledge in order to change the way organizations do business. This may mean changing the nature of a product or service being delivered to make it information-intensive. ICTs could make it possible for a functional unit or for an entire organization to transform the way business is done. For example, Dell's flexible manufacturing system (FMS) when integrated with a Web-based

Table 4.4. A framework for the impact of ICT in organizations

	People	Functions/Processes	Organization
Efficiency	Task mechanization	Functional/process automation	Boundary extension
Example	*Using a spreadsheet to do a budget plan*	*Purchase order fulfillment, credit checking*	*On-line order entry linking customers and suppliers*
Effectiveness	Work improvement	Functional enhancement	Service enhancement
Example	*Using a prospect database to generate sales letters*	*CAD/CAM*	*On-line diagnostic databases for electric appliances*
Transformation	Role expansion	Functional/process redefinition	Product/process innovation
Example	*Conducting a "what if" analysis*	*CD-ROM disks for business research*	*Dell's mass customization system*

Source: Adapted from Schultheis, R. A., & Sumner, M. (1992). Management Information Systems: the Manager's Perspective, Burr Ridge, IL: Irwin.

ordering system enables transformation of the business model. Dell transforms the way it does business from an intermediary-based-business model into a direct-sale-business model that provides service excellence through compression of time, overcoming geographic restrictions and developing new markets, offering new assemble-to-order computers, and building networks of customer relationships.

Organizations are facing the reconfiguration of the role of ICTs in business. ICTs are of strategic importance only if they are compatible with, and leverage upon, the company's existing characteristics and advantages (Beath and Ives 1986; and Ives and Vitale 1988). In particular, ICT strategies and policies need to be strategically aligned with the business strategy and the directions set by the corporation's senior executives (Earl 1989, Broadbent & Weill 1990). Scott Morton and Allen (1994) proposed five levels of complexity at which ICTs can be applied to organizational re-configuration. Revolutionary changes are ICT-enabled strategic transformations that aim at adding value to customers as well as to organizations, whereas evolutionary ones are only directed at ICT-supported internal integration and control.

The following are details of the ICT-supported evolutionary and revolutionary change levels Scott-Morton and Allen (1994):

- Evolutionary levels:

  ○ *Localized exploitation* within individual business functions. The primary objectives addressed here are local efficiency and effectiveness.
  ○ *Internal integration* between different systems and applications, generally involving not just automation, but also rationalization, and using a common ICT platform. Efficiency and effectiveness are enhanced by coordination and cooperation within the enterprise.

- Revolutionary levels:

  ○ *Business process reinvention* involves more thorough re-evaluation of the enterprise value-chain and the production process, and more far-reaching change.
  ○ *Business network redesign* refers to the reconfiguration of the scope and tasks of the business network involved in the creation and delivery of products and services. Coordination and cooperation extend, selectively, beyond the enterprise's boundaries.
  ○ *Business scope redefinition* involves changing the organization's conception of its existing business.

ICTs and Globalization of Business

ICTs are playing a growing and significant role in the global business environment. Business managers in every industry are now challenged to understand the impact of ICT retooling on their businesses. For example, to keep connected with suppliers and customers all over the world, it is necessary for firms adopting CKM to have international ICTs (e.g., EDI or Extranet). Managing global supply chain business transactions with ICTs involves understanding the implications for increasing the company's sphere of activity in the global market place. Global changes to business are accelerating and destroying traditional concepts of time, geography, competition, and strategic advantage. The Internet provides a radical new global distribution channel. It may complement or destroy companies' existing retailing systems, core competencies, and distribution network assets (e.g., Dell and Compaq PCs industry).

Retooling ICTs enable global companies to move from stovepipe (vertical) communications to networked (integrated) communications at all levels and from replication of resources to economies of scale through coordinating business knowledge. Global IT investments in integrated ICTs make business knowledge and experiences accessible around the world for partners, clients, employees, etc.

Managers of ICTs in knowledge-based global businesses change their roles from being central controllers to core connectors. Managers act as network nodes, amplifiers, and interpreters of the communication system.

Global companies move from the mere geographical presence in a country to a local cultural fit in that country. Business managers, whether a company is expanding into the global arena or protecting domestic markets from global competitors, are more and more concerned with customer-centric, knowledge-based differentiation of their products and/or services on a global basis. Global companies use CK to differentiate their products and services to reflect local culture and tastes of their customers (e.g., producing keyboards and software packages that adapt to local languages).

No industry can match the ICT-based transformation created by business globalization like financial services. Financial managers use ICT to track investment portfolios, foreign exchange rates, and cash flow of corporate divisions located around the globe. The convergence of global competition, customized products, and accessible ICT has redefined financial management practices. It is important for managers to keep abreast of how companies are using ICT around the world and its impact on the new market place. The biggest challenge to management's understanding of how to use ICT is the perception that technology is an alien force to business.

In order to become a truly global, customer-centric business, companies should be organized around processes rather than functions, products, or geographic location. Their spheres of activities need to stretch from beyond where they operate to where they earn revenue, carry out activities, or have a relationship with outside partners or customers. Global business leverages relationships with suppliers, distributors and customers cross-functionally and cross-geographically. An example is Canon, of Japan, that supplies products to many companies around the world (cross-geographic); it also acts as a distributor (cross-functional) to many of these companies within Japan.

Developed and underdeveloped nations alike use communication networks to link data, information, and knowledge of global business transactions. However, success in managing global business is contingent upon the dynamics of national and global ICT policies. Countries have different approaches (encouraged vs. reserved) towards building IT and communications infrastructures. For developing countries, communications infrastructure means access to world markets and a way to keep in touch with developing world resources. Although a communications infrastructure, the electronic highway of the information age takes a significant time to build, but gives companies an unrivalled advantage in global business. The Asian tigers (South Korea, Hong Kong, Taiwan, and Singapore) are enjoying the fastest economic growths in the area and have long recognized the value of an international communications infrastructure to economic growth. For example, Singapore has developed a robust National Information Superhighway, IT Plan, and has several projects underway that will provide it with economic advantages.

Economics of ICTs

In CKM, the decision to retool ICTs should be need- rather than fashion-driven. In a business context, the use of ICTs makes an important difference only when it is part of a work system. ICTs success isn't just about ICTs, it is about how to retool ICTs to help people work more effectively (Alter, 2006).

ICTs 'Black Hole'

The success of ICT-based CKM is not only a technical success, but one which creates or adds value to customers and ultimately to business. When deciding on the ICT infrastructure, the emphasis should not be limited to questions such as What?, Who?, and Where?, but should include critical questions such as Why? and How?

Spending on ICTs could end up in a 'black hole' or productivity paradox, wherein companies spend too much, but get too little, and fail to realize benefits promised from massive investments of money, time, and effort. Several factors contribute to this phenomenon (Peppard and Roland, 1995):

- Major re-writes to existing ICT 'legacy systems' can endanger redesign efforts by becoming too large to contain.
- ICTs have been used for supporting, rather than transforming, traditional business processes (e.g., traditional clerical and operational tasks).
- ICTs could be a source of inflexibility. Automation of existing, but wasteful, tasks may lock those tasks into the process. Therefore, ICTs have been applied to old and existing ways of doing things.
- Data Analysis problems hide productivity gains. Many ICT benefits are intangible. Examples of ICT *intangible* benefits are:

  - facing competitive pressures
  - speeding up business processes
  - providing more accurate information
  - improving communication
  - improving collaboration
  - improving customer satisfaction and goodwill

- In service industries, it is difficult to define the value of improvements to quality of service (i.e., ATMs).
- There is a time lag between ICT introduction and harvesting ICT benefits due to the time needed. Productivity decreases during the initial learning period and then increases afterwards.
- ICT productivity gains are offset by losses in other areas. At the macro level, one company's ICT usage could increase its share of the market at the expense of other companies.
- ICT productivity gains are offset by costs or losses. Direct/indirect costs may include:

  ○ Support costs: PCs hardware, software, and network.
  ○ Wasted time: PCs make it possible to work productively on some tasks, but may result in nonproductive activities in others (down times, loading times, etc.).
  ○ Software development problems: some projects fail, others are cancelled, abandoned (runaway projects), or completed but never used.
  ○ Software maintenance: expenses of fixing bugs and modifying or enhancing systems functionality.
  ○ Incompatible systems and workarounds.
  ○ Junk computing: using ICTs in a way that does not directly advance organizational goals (junk reporting, excessive details, excessive attention to presentation, e-mail, etc.).

Cost/Benefit Analysis of ICTs

ICTs should be used strategically in ways that enable businesses to utilize inimitable DCCs to create value and, ultimately, achieve an SCA. Benefits of ICTs are often difficult to measure (intangible). Occasionally ICT benefits, especially cost savings, are quite measurable. However, the relationship between intangible ICT benefits and business performance may not always be clear. For example, it is not possible to claim that business communication is getting better because employees are receiving more e-mail messages.

Businesses should also recognize that ICTs can create opportunities and options in the future. The value of additional value in the future (projection of future customer purchase) should be added to other benefits of the ICT investment. The expected value approach can be used to estimate possible future benefits by multiplying the size of the benefit by the probability of its occurrence.

In addition to identifying and evaluating ICT benefits, business organizations also need to account for its costs. Accounting systems usually deal with the issue of how to measure ICT costs for management control purposes, and how to charge users for shared (usually infrastructure) ICT investments and services. A behavior-oriented chargeback (chargeout) method is based on two primary objectives: efficiency and effectiveness.

Although there are various methods of ICT chargeback, it is still very difficult to approximate costs of ICTs, especially in companies where multiple independent operating units are sharing a centralized system. For this and other reasons, the difficulties of chargeback may be one driver of ICT outsourcing.

Outsourcing of ICTs

ICTs are not the primary business or core competence of many organizations (things they do best which represent their competitive strengths such as manufacturing, retailing, or services). As ICTs are becoming more complex, expensive, changing, and difficult to manage, using outside vendors rather than internal units as a principal source of their ICT services is becoming a visible trend. Strategic decisions such as outsourcing have been possible through the web technology. Companies may outsource customer e-call centers or ICT infrastructure through shared ASP systems deployed over the Web to subscribers all over the world. Other examples of outsourcing in the CKM context include telecommunication services, e-commerce solutions, network management, extranets, contract programmers, and computer timesharing.

Advantages to outsourcers include the following (Reid and Sanders, 2005):

- Financial (avoid heavy capital investment, enjoy economies of scale - getting discounts on large purchases, and consolidate multiple data centers into one location)
- Technical (i.e., achieve technological improvements as a result of getting up-to-date state of the art technologies)
- Management (concentrate on managing core processes and DCCs to create SCA)
- Human Resources (get skills from a large pool of expertise)
- Quality (clearly define service-level agreements), and
- Flexibility (better ability to handle ICT peaks)

By contrast, outsourcers may be subject to these disadvantages (Reid and Sanders, 2005):

- Limited economies of scale - the advantage of economies of scale is not large over hardware or software lifetime.

- Staffing - vendor's staff are not highly skilled.
- Lack of business expertise - the remaining staff of outsourcers may have more technical knowledge and less business knowledge.
- Contract problems

However, based on the advantages and disadvantages of ICT outsourcing, it is recommended for outsourcers to adopt short-period contracts, subcontract, and selectively outsource to reliable and reputable service providers (Reid and Sanders, 2005). Regardless of the decision to 'build or buy', the challenge of walking the tightrope between adoption of the latest ICTs and remaining up to speed with ongoing business and technology developments is becoming more acute in the e-world of business.

Performance of ICTs

Evaluation of ICT systems focuses on key business objectives (critical success factors), and links a benefit of ICT (i.e., quicker decision making) with a specific business objective (i.e., faster product development and delivery). A performance/importance quantitative scoring methodology, that incorporates both tangible and intangible benefits, may be applied. The methodology identifies key performance issues or factors (criteria), assigns a weight to each issue (criterion), multiplies the scores by the weights which are then totaled, and then chooses the item with the highest score.

Figure 4.1 illustrates an example of using the performance/importance methodology to evaluate three vendors' ICTs based on the importance and performance of five factors (speed, reporting, documentation, support, queries). System 2 was found to be the recommended decision alternative based on its total importance-performance score.

Figure 4.1. A hypothetical example of the performance/importance analysis of ICTs

Importance (Weights)						
	0.3	**0.3**	**0.2**	**0.1**	**0.1**	
Performance	**Reporting**	**Queries**	**Documentation**	**Support**	**Speed**	**Total**
System 1	4	8	7	8	5	**6.3**
	1.2	2.4	1.4	0.8	0.5	
System 2	9	5	8	6	6	**8**
	2.7	1.5	1.6	0.6	1.6	
System 3	8	2	7	4	7	**6.5**
	2.4	0.6	1.4	0.4	1.7	

Security of ICTs

Computer Crime and Intrusion

The term computer crime encompasses any unauthorized use of a computer system (including software piracy) or theft of system resources for personal use to take any actions intended to alter data and programs or to damage or destroy data. *Intrusion* refers to the forced and unauthorized entry into a computer system when hackers break into a system, or when software viruses are inserted into a system to destroy programs and data (Laudon and Laudon, 2002).

Preventing unauthorized access to a system requires excellent physical security as well as some tactics and tips for deterring intrusion by hackers. These might include hanging access passwords, restructuring ICT system use, limiting access to data, setting up physical access controls, encrypting data, establishing procedural controls, auditing system activities, and logging all transaction and user activities (Laudon and Laudon, 2002).

Computer Viruses

A virus is a hidden program that alters, without the user's knowledge, the way a computer operates, or modifies the data and programs stored in the computer. The virus is written by an individual's intent on causing damage (or wreaking havoc) in a system. It is called a "virus" because it reproduces itself passing from computer to computer when diskettes are shuttled from one computer to another. A virus can also enter a computer when a file to which it has attached itself is downloaded from a remote computer over a communications network (Laudon and Laudon, 2002).

Although computer viruses are a fairly recent phenomenon, the majority of them are already known - some bearing such exotic names as Michelangelo virus and Christmas virus. To protect their systems against viruses, companies must buy virus detection software programs that scan the computer's disks and main memory to detect the virus. The three main methods of virus detection are scanning, interception, and digital signature encryption (Laudon and Laudon, 2002).

Cookies

Cookies are bits of data and information that some web servers store on your computer's hard drive during your visit to a web site. You provide this information unknowingly. Net browsers have a section listing your name, internet address (IP address), and organization. As you enter a site, the server software may request your browser to transmit your identity.

Ethics of ICTs

Ethics of ICTs refer to the standards of conduct and moral behavior that people are expected to follow. Ethics include personal ethics – which pertain to people's day-to-day activities in private life, as well as business ethics – which pertain to their actions in the world of business, including how they deal with colleagues or customers. A distinction needs to be made here between ethical behavior and legal behavior. Ethical behavior refers to expected actions, while legal behavior refers to required actions. An action may be legal but unethical, or ethical but illegal.

Many companies have created a general code of ethics to guide the behavior of their employees for issues such as electronic mail privacy, software licenses, and hardware access. Informed consent calls for taking consent before proceeding into an action when in doubt about the ethics, or taking the "higher ethical action" that achieves the greater good for the business and its customers.

Reliability of ICTs

As companies become more dependent on ICTs, they also become dependent on the continued availability of their computers and communications systems. Reliability is the assurance that the system will do what it should, when it should. Currently, there are no laws that explicitly govern services reliability. However, because of the importance of ICTs to business operations, society generally treats services loss as a breach of trust (Laudon and Laudon, 2002).

Interoperability of ICTs

Interoperability refers to the capability of two or more software and hardware systems to communicate, execute programs, or transfer data on different machines from different vendors' *units in a manner that requires the user to have little or no knowledge of the unique characteristics of those units.* The lack of interoperability strongly implies that the described product or products were not designed with standardization in mind. Indeed, interoperability is not taken for granted in the non-standards-based portion of the computing world (Inseparability, 2007).

Interoperability is often more than a technological issue. It frequently has a major impact on the organization concerned, including issues of ownership (do people want to share their data?), staff (are people prepared to undergo training?) and usability. Interoperability can have important economic consequences to a business's competitive position (Inseparability, 2007). Interoperability can be achieved through retooling ICTs.

Scalability of ICTs

Scalability is a desirable property of a system, a network that indicates its ability to either handle growing amounts of work in a graceful manner, or to be readily enlarged (Scalability, 2007). System's scalability positively affects the workload of the system. Scalability helps to reduce cost and effort, and to speed up customer service, and ultimately to achieve higher customer satisfaction.

Scalability can be measured in various dimensions, such as:

- Load scalability: The capability of a distributed system and the ease with which a system or component can be modified, added, or removed, to accommodate a heavier or lighter g load. For example, in an e-biz solution, a scalable online TPS or database management system is one that can be upgraded to process more transactions by adding new processors, devices and storage, and which can be upgraded easily and transparently without shutting it down.
- Geographic scalability: The ability to maintain performance, usefulness, or usability of a system regardless of expansion from concentration in a local area to a more distributed geographic pattern.
- Administrative scalability: The capability of an increasing number of organizations to share easily a single distributed system.

RECOMMENDED SOLUTION: A PROPOSED ICTS CLASSIFICATION SYSTEM

The aforementioned classifications of ICT systems are not mutually exclusive. For example, once one ICT classification is adopted and combined with business value chain and activities supported, a three-dimensional classification, as shown in Figure 4.2 may be developed.

FUTURE TRENDS

The future of ICTs may hold several changes: a) a shift from a supportive to a transformational role of ICTs, b) a shift from function-based to process-based ICTs, c) a shift from station-based to mobile-based computing, and d) a shift from monolithic to service-oriented applications.

Figure 4.2. A three-way classification of ICTs in a manufacturing firm: Integrating type of support, business value chain, and activity supported

	Inbound Logistics	Operations	Marketing & Sales	Outbound Logistics	Services	
ERP/ SCM/ CKM	Customized call center service	Customized product design	Up-selling	Minimum transportation cost	Customized after-sale service	*Strategic Level*
DSS/ ES/AI	Customer call analysis & forecasting	Capacity decision	Sales analysis & forecasting	Transportation network analysis	Service analysis & forecasting	*Analytical Level*
TPS/ MIS/ DW	Call center staff assignment	Aggregate planning	Marketing & sales planning	Delivery scheduling	Service planning	*Operational Level*

A Shift from a Supportive to a Transformational Role of ICTs

A variety of ICTs is anticipated to disrupt many of today's companies and create opportunities for tomorrow's great companies to emerge. As a result, organizations in the future are expected to be more driven by need rather than by technological developments. The future of ICTs is expected to witness a shift from the traditional emphasis on transaction processing, integrated logistics, and work flows to systems that support business transformation and leveraging of competencies for building people networks, customer relationships, and organizational learning. The underlying theme that constantly is adhered to is to link strategy, business models, business processes, and implementation for knowledge-based flexible customization of product and process design, development, packaging, and delivery.

A Shift from Function-based to Process-Based ICTs

Conventional system development and ICT planning methodologies (e.g. matrix mapping techniques, data and process modeling) are based on top-down decomposition of functional transactions and information needs and, inadvertently, serve to institutionalize existing functional boundaries, work practices, and information flows. Such top-down corporate architectures are even more difficult to implement when systems are required to support many organizations in a 'value -chain constellation' (Norman & Ramirez, 1993).

Future trends are likely to shift ICTs from business functions to business processes. Process-oriented software technologies (e.g., workflow management systems, enterprise application integration platforms, business process intelligence tools, and XML standards) are likely to be utilized intensively in the future. In fact, projects implying the use of process-oriented software technologies are usually justified by referring to technical feasibility and assumed benefits (e.g., improved business process performance).

Process-based ICTs are likely to dominate future organizational life. Yet in automating, or shaping business and customer processes, ICTs are making subtle but profound changes in culture as well as development and management of CK. However, the process of acquiring, creating, sharing, and applying CK itself also requires a dynamic inter-departmental and intra-departmental learning process needed to reflect on the created CK. Such dynamic knowledge can be used not only to deliver better products and/or services, but to improve the organizational ICTs, structure, and culture in order to improve the means by which customized products/services are planned, designed, developed, and delivered.

A Shift from a Station-Based to a Mobile-Based Computing Environment

As centralized computing continues to be pervasive throughout organizations, a strong push and pull toward decentralization has emerged (Wysocki and DeMichiell, 1997). However, in line with the shift from centralized to networked structure, many firms are migrating from centralized computing to a client server paradigm (downsizing). However, the future trend is to transfer more ICT architecture from distributed computing towards wireless mobile computing (m-computing) which enables real-time connections between mobile devices and other computing paradigms. Virtual computing in the e-business and e-commerce world is likely to shift towards m-commerce and m-business models in the future.

Mobile computing represents a natural extension of e-business and e-commerce that is likely to be pervasive in the future (both B2B and B2C) in several business areas such as financial services, shopping, and advertising. Although mobile computing involves a set of complex processes and a number of operations and entities (customers, vendors, mobile operators, etc.), it creates new and significant value-adding opportunities for business organizations as well as their customers. M-computing expands the outside reach to customers by breaking the barriers of time and geography and by being available anytime and anywhere (ubiquitous or invisible computing). Mobility in space implies mobility in time and in context (Kakihara & Sorensen, 2002).

A Shift from Monolithic to Service-Oriented Applications

One of the major trends in nowadays business computing is the movement away from large-scale centralized data processing paradigms to distributed client-server computing as well as towards end-user computing (EUC). EUC emphasizes the final user's responsibility and control of his own computing. It emphasizes the systems and tools given directly to staff which allow them to manipulate data, decide when and how to use applications, i.e. DM, or spreadsheet-based analysis, of customer data. In the context of CKM, EUC supports the development of customized knowledge out of stand-alone ICT solutions that nurture one-to-one relationships with customers.

Besides, EUC has coincided with the downsizing trend which has dramatically altered organization structures. Downsizing has also affected the roles and responsibilities of computer professionals. It merged the three traditional categories of task-specific ICT intermediaries into one-person (EUC): the final user of information, the analyst, and the programmer.

In years to come, it is expected to witness more migration of the architecture of CKM applications from monolithic, client/server applications to web-based SOA applications. The reason is that client/server built-in processes can be difficult to customize, whereas SOA applications are more nimble and enable customized processes.

CONCLUSION

The boom years of the late 20th century saw significant developments of ICTs which have changed the way companies perform business, develop services, and interact with customers as well as suppliers. ICTs play a crucial role in an organization's CKM change. The rapid pace of technological advancement offers opportunities to perform work in new and innovative ways. Nonetheless, investment in ICTs has, in many cases, brought disappointment and depleted company reserves without realizing the benefits sought, when used for internal command and control purposes. However, if ICTs are to provide their promised returns, their development needs to be properly aligned with business strategy, integrated inter- and intra-organizationally, and strategically positioning them in their marketplaces.

In CKM context, ICTs enable the leveraging of DCCs to create value to customers as well as to the business. ICTs enable new forms of networked or virtual organizations. They allow increased collaboration, improved management processes, and more customer-focused flexible operations such as product/process redesign, new product development, and faster product delivery. An ICT infrastructure enables customer-centric applications at the level of operations, management, and planning across various functions and processes. At the strategic level, organizations require a clear understanding of how ICTs can transform organizations to make them more efficient and effective and also deliver knowledge-based customer products and services. ICTs may be used to create more attractive products and services, to redesign innovative business processes and organizational structures, and to create SCA.

In a manufacturing context, for example, ICTs can be used to develop knowledge about target customers, identify the market niches, and customize product/process design (via CAD/CAM) as well as delivery options. The retail banking industry is an example of a very competitive business in which banks are constantly looking for ICT-based solutions to provide more customer services and increase internal productivity by using cash dispenser machines (ATMs), tele-banking, e-banking, and mobile banking.

However, ICTs may fail to deliver their potential when they are applied for internal control instead of external strategic positioning. Business firms need to understand why and how ICTs could be better exploited strategically in the delivery of successful knowledge-based, tailor-made products and/or services. It should be remembered always that ICTs alone won't make a knowledge-creating, customer-oriented business organization. Reinventing organizations through behavioral, cultural, process, technology, as well as structural changes is considered a main enabler of CKM.

In the next chapter, the role of business process redesign in the development of CKM change will be examined.

REFERENCES

Alter, S. (2002). *Information systems: Foundation of E-Business*. 4th edition, Upper Saddle River, NJ: Prentice Hall.

Beath, C. M., & Ives, B. (1986). Competitive information systems in support of pricing. *MIS Quarterly, 10*(1), 85-96.

Buttle, F. (2004). *Customer relationship management: concepts and tools*. Oxford, England: Elsevier Publishing.

Comer, D. (2004). *Computer networks and Internets: With Internet applications. 4th edition*, Upper Saddle River, NJ: Prentice Hall.

Davenport, T., & Prusak, L. (2000). *Working knowledge*. 2nd edition, Boston, MA: Harvard Business School Press.

Earl, M. J. (1989). *Management strategies for information technology.* Englewood Cliffs, New Jersey: Prentice-Hall.

Eijkman, H. (2008). Web 2.0 as a non-foundational network-centric learning space. *Campus-Wide Information Systems, 25*(2), 93-104.

Granebring, A., & Revay, P. (2007).   Service-oriented architecture is a driver for daily decision support. *Kybernetes, 36*(5/6), 622-635.

Interoperability. (2007, June 29). In *Wikipedia, The free encyclopedia.* Retrieved July 4, 2007, from http://en.wikipedia.org/wiki/Interoperability.

Ives, B., & Vitale, M. R. (1988) After the sale: Leveraging maintenance with information technology. *MIS Quarterly, 12*(1), 6-21.

Kakihara, M., & Sorensen, C. (2002). Mobility: an extended perspective. *Proceedings of the Hawaii International Conference on System Sciences,* January 7-10, pp. 1-10, Big Island, Hawaii.

Kalakota, R., & Robinson, M. (2001). *E-Business 2.0: Roadmap for success.* Boston, MA: Addison-Wesley.

Knox, S., Maklan, S., Payne, A., Peppard, J., & Ryals, L. (2003). *Customer relationship management: Perspectives from the marketplace.* Oxford, UK: Butterworth-Heinemann.

Kumar, N. (2000). Internet distribution strategies: dilemmas for the incumbent. In Marchand, D., Davenport, T., and Dickson, T. (Eds.). *Mastering information management: Your single source guide to becoming a master of information management* (pp. 205-210). London, U.K: FT-Prentice Hall.

Laudon, K. C., & Laudon, J. P. (2002*). Management information systems: Managing the digital firm.* Upper Saddle River, NJ: Prentice Hall.

McAfee, A. (2006). Mastering the three worlds of information technology. *Harvard Business Review,* November, 141-149.

Normann, R., & Ramirez, R. (1998). *Designing interactive strategy: From value chain to value constellation.* New York: John Wiley.

Pearlson, K., & Saunders, C. (2006). *Managing and using information systems: A strategic approach.* 3rd edition, New York: John Wiley.

Peppard, J., & Ronald, P. (1995). *The essence of business process re-engineering.* Upper Saddle River, NJ: Prentice-Hall.

Reid, R. D., & Sanders, R. (2005). *Operations management.* 2nd edition, New York: John Wiley.

Scalability. (2007, June 6). In *Wikipedia, The free encyclopedia.* Retrieved July 5, 2007, from http://en.wikipedia.org/wiki/Scalability.

Schultheis, R. A., & Sumner, M. (1992). *Management information systems: The Manager's Perspective.* Burr Ridge, IL: Irwin.

Scott-Morton, M., & Allen, T. J. (1994). *Information technology and the corporation of the 1990s.* New York: Oxford University Press.

Senge, P. (1990). *The Fifth Discipline: The art and practice of learning organization.* New York: Doubleday/Currency.

Seybold, P. (2002). *An executive's guide to CRM.* Boston, MA: Patricia Seybold Group.

Turban, E., McLean, E., & Wetherbe, J. (2002). *Information technology for management: Transforming business in the digital economy.* 3rd edition, New York: John Wiley.

Turban, E., Leidner, D., McLean, E., & Wetherbe, J. (2008). *Information Technology for management: Transforming organizations in the Digital Economy.* 6th edition, New York: John Wiley.

Weill P. (1990). Strategic investment in information technology: An empirical study. *Information Age, 12*(3), 141-147.

Wisner, J. D., Tan, K-C., & Leong, G. K. (2008). *Principles of supply chain management: A balanced approach.* Mason, OH: South-Western.

Wysocki, R., & DeMichiell, R. (1997). *Managing information across the enterprise.* New York: John Wiley.

Zineldin, M. (2000). Beyond relationship marketing: technologicalship marketing. *Marketing Intelligence & Planning, 18*(1), 9-23.

Chapter V
Redesigning Processes

INTRODUCTION

In today's turbulent and complex business environments, the focus has shifted from products to services. As a result, services have become a new battleground for competition; and processes, a weapon of war. Organizations wishing to boost their competitiveness need to focus on desired customer outcomes by redesigning business processes through effective use of advanced ICTs and the creativity of their human assets. Organizational *reinvention* of structure, people, and ICTs are driven by the CKM strategic change with a purpose of adding value to both customers and business firms. Reinventing organizations has the potential to create more flexible, team-based and integrated work activities, both internally and externally, to allow customers to be linked intimately to the business, to improve their experiences, and ultimately to develop enduring and profitable relationships with them. This chapter explores the last part in reinvention, viz. the role of business process redesign in CKM.

CONCEPTUAL FOUNDATIONS

Business processes are valuable corporate resources since they directly support corporate business strategies. In the era of highly competitive and dynamic marketplaces, services and managing business processes for optimal performance are essential for the achievement of successful business strategies. Business processes, therefore, need to be managed and reengineered like other business resources in order to achieve typical goals of process design like productivity, quality, efficiency, flexibility and conformance with formal and legal rules such as ISO 2000. Business process redesign, a narrow definition of BPR, is a strategic action that targets business processes, rather than complete transformation of the enterprise, and should be conducted with a clear understanding of the company's vision, strategy, and competitive directions in customer processes and/or services with respect to market opportunities and challenges.

Despite many years of restructuring and downsizing through process automation, many companies have not obtained the improvements needed. This can be attributed to companies leaving the existing processes intact and only using computers to automate and speed them up, without addressing their fundamental performance deficiencies. Many job designs, work flows, control mechanisms, and organizational structures were developed for operational command and control rather than for strategic competitive purposes. Companies need to use the power of the computer not to automate outdated processes, but to radically 'reengineer' business processes (Hammer, 1990). Only through streamlining business processes can companies gain remarkable improvements in operational performance, customer satisfaction, and customer loyalty.

This section provides a theoretical background to BPR. It examines the following elements: the need for business process orientation (BPO), the anatomy of a business process, the concept of BPR, pillars of BPR, principles of BPR, results of BPR, followed by an example of ICT-enabled BPR, integrating KM into BPR, and the context of CKM for BPR.

The Need for Business Process Orientation

BPO is a process thinking view that looks at a business process as a one whole end-to-end entity that spans horizontally throughout the organization. Beyond organizational boundaries, BPO seeks to promote collaboration and knowledge sharing among business network members and enables companies to operate efficiently and satisfy customers at a lower cost and higher speed. BPO entails changes in organizational structure, people's tasks and culture, types of ICTs, and executive leadership in the move from a functional to a process view of the organization. BPO seeks to enhance overall performance and efficiency of organizations through synergizing work processes scattered across functional units. It replaces the rigid hierarchies with structures that are much flatter, more cooperative, more customer-centric, and more process-oriented.

Building an organization with a BPO has led to many reported successes. Texas Instruments, Progressive Insurance, and American Standard have all reported, albeit anecdotally, as receiving improved business performance from building a process orientation within an organization (Hammer, 1996). However, despite several potential benefits, organizations which are moving away from functional- towards a process-based organization structure are relatively rare, but their numbers are growing gradually. It has been estimated that no more than 10 percent of large companies have made a serious and successful effort at it (Hammer, 2004).

Process redesign, which is the concern of this chapter, emphasizes the systemic analysis of value chain business processes and aims for increased operational excellence in the management of business processes. Successful BPR requires a fully integrated and totally automated system that will enable firms to define, track, and manage their work processes. In the CKM context, business process reconfiguration provides an organization-wide view of the end-to-end chain of linked activities which are needed to deliver customer value in terms of products or services.

The Anatomy of a Business Process

A process is a related group of steps or activities in which people use information and other resources to create value for internal or external customers. Business processes consist of steps related in time and place (including cyberspace), have a beginning and an end, and have inputs and outputs (Alter, 2006). The scope (breadth) of a process refers to the number of departments (or organizations) that the process crosses (Peppard & Rowland, 1995) horizontally, or number of subprocesses and activities it includes at the first level, whereas the scale (depth) of a process refers to the number of subactivities that exist (at the vertical level) within each subactivity but at lower levels such as second and third levels.

In competitive business environments, business processes represent a strategic, unique, and difficult-to-imitate DCC. Through business processes, organizations coordinate and organize work activities, information, and knowledge to produce a product or service. Well-designed, value-adding business processes enhance the creation of DCCs and contribute to organizational success and to achievement of SCA. Business processes are typically designed relying on the technology for more mundane, repetitive tasks, and enabling employees to take on more people-oriented and unstructured tasks (Pearlson and Saunders, 2006).

Businesses have traditionally been organized around the functional areas ('the 'silos') of the business. In the CKM context, functional silos hinder the creation of DCCs and, in turn, achievement of SCA. The 'inward' focus of functional areas devotes much attention to what happens within the functional silos while showing little concern for coordinating across the functional areas and maximizing customer value. This explains how a business process is a fundamental idea for understanding how businesses perform work and provide value for customers.

Business processes may be divided into two basic types from a hierarchical perspective (Figure 5.1):

- Core or operational processes to carry day-to-day tasks that aim at 'winning' the customer, satisfying the customer, and supporting the customer.
- Enabling or supporting processes that enable strategic and operational processes to be carried out such as HRM, procurement, management accounting, and security ICTs.

From a cross-sectional perspective, business processes may be divided into three different types with respect to functional areas (Alter, 2006):

- *Processes that cross functional areas:* Business processes that span multiple functional boundaries. Examples of cross-functional processes are product development, order fulfillment, planning, resourcing, and controlling, and customer service that can cut across the functional silos of distribution, purchasing, research and development, manufacturing, and sales. As an example of scope of a business process, the order fulfillment subprocesses include several steps, i.e. take orders, schedule and prioritize orders, procure necessary materials, produce the required service or product, deliver it, obtain payment, and continue to support it.

Figure 5.1. Core and enabling business processes

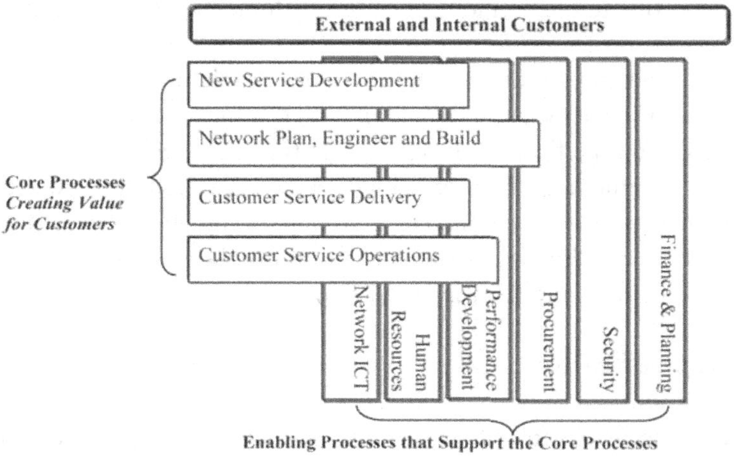

- *Processes typically within a functional area:* Other important processes that belong to a particular functional area, such as identifying manufacturing products, identifying potential customers, and determining hiring requirements.
- *Subprocesses and activities occurring in all functional areas:* These activities are common in every functional area, such as communicating with other people, analyzing data, planning the work that will be done, and providing feedback to employees.

As an illustration of customer-related problems inherited in a fragmented, multi-functional process associated with vertical organizational structures, Hammer and Champy (2003) use an example of retailers who return unsold goods for credit to a consumer products manufacturer. Thirteen separate departments are involved in the process; receiving accepts the goods, the warehouse returns them to stock, inventory management updates records to reflect their return, promotion determines at what price the goods were actually sold, sales accounting adjusts commissions, general accounting updates the financial records, and so on. Yet no single department or particular individual is in charge of handling returns.

For each of the departments involved, returns are a low-priority distraction. As a result, mistakes often occur. Returned goods end up "lost" in the warehouse. The company pays sales commissions on unsold goods. Retailers even do not get the credit that they expect and become angry, which in turn effectively undoes all the efforts of sales and marketing.

Unhappy retailers are less likely to promote the manufacturer's new products. They also delay payment of bills, and often pay only what they think they owe after deducting the value of the returns. This throws the manufacturer's accounts receivable department into turmoil, since the customer's check doesn't match the manufacturer's invoice.

Ultimately, the manufacturer simply gives up, unable to trace what really happened. An estimation of the annual costs and lost revenues from returns and related problems runs into nine figures. From time to time, the company's management has attempted to tighten up the fragmented returns process, but it no sooner gets some departments working well than new problems crop up in others. Even when the work involved could have a significant impact on the bottom line, companies often have no one in charge (Davenport, 1993).

The Concept of BPR

In order for organizations to be lean, flexible, responsive, competitive, innovative, efficient, customer-focused, and profitable, they need to change how they do their work and why they do it that way. Work that requires knowledge-based cooperation and coordination of several different departments within a company is often a source of trouble. Often the efficiency of a company's parts comes at the expense of the efficiency of its whole.

BPR is a radical shift in an organization's strategic thinking and approach towards institutionalization of better and efficient systems and processes. Process redesign involves the breaking of old, traditional ways of doing things and finding new and innovative ways that will have the ability to fulfill their stakeholders' expectations. From the redesigned processes, new rules will emerge that will determine how the processes will operate. The reengineering process is an all-or-nothing proposition, the results of which are often unknown until the completion of its course.

A fundamental notion of the concept of BPR is the obliteration of outdated rules, assumptions, and processes (Hammer, 1990). Processes that are weighing down the company must be challenged and evaluated to see if there is a better option. Traditional rules of work design are mainly based on a model of decentralization (specialization of labor) and economy of scale derived from the Industrial Revolution. This is a breeding ground for tunnel vision where accountability blurs, and critical issues fall between the cracks. No one is able to see the whole picture to be able to respond quickly to new situations.

As a result, it should not be surprising to companies to find their businesses underperforming due to these obsolete processes and structures. Reengineering requires looking at the fundamental processes of the business from a cross-functional perspective. This implies that, by necessity, for reengineering to work, the team assembled to reengineer the process should represent the functional units involved in the process being reengineered and all the units that depend on it. The reengineering effort must break away from conventional wisdom and organizational boundaries, be broad and cross-functional, and use information technology not to automate existing process but to enable a new one.

Pillars of BPR

The ultimate goal for every organization is that all its activities should 'add value' in some way to its customers or to its operational efficiency. When redesigning processes, the emphasis should be on the elimination of all non-value-adding activities, and streamlining of the core value-adding ones. The major pillars of BPR, which are all enabled by ICTs, are as follow (Turban et al., 2002):

• Reducing Flow Time (cycle time, time to market, and waiting time) and operational cost: reducing the business process cycle time and reducing the time from an inception of an idea until its implementation - time to market, are extremely important for increasing productivity, throughput time, and competitiveness. Firms that are first in the market with a product, or that provide customers with a service faster than their competitors, enjoy a distinct SCA. ICTs may be used to expedite the various steps of product or service development, testing, and implementation.

- Empowerment of Employees: empowerment is a strategy that relates to the concept of self-directed teams, and is used by many organizations to give employees the authority to make decisions on their own. Empowerment enables teams to execute the work faster and with fewer delays than un-empowered workers. ICTs, such as the Internet and intranet enable employees to access data, information, and knowledge they need to make quick decisions. 'Expert Systems' can give expert advice to team members whenever human experts are not available. In addition, computer networks allow team members to communicate with each other as well as with other teams in different locations.
- Restructuring: One of the premises of BPR is that organizational structure should fit business processes. One way to achieve this goal is to create an ICT-based 'networked organization' made up of many teams, each responsible for a complete business process 'case team'.

The pillars of BPR seek to remove inefficiencies and to offer answers to the question of "How to get it done?" The pillars of BPR can be summarized by 4 Cs: cancellation, combination, compression, and codification (Figure 5.2).

- Cancellation: omission of duplicate or non-value adding activities.
- Combination: integration of activities.
- Compression: simplification of activities.
- Codification: computerization of activities

Principles of BPR

Hammer (1990) argues that at the heart of reengineering is the notion of discontinuous thinking or recognizing and breaking away from the outdated rules and fundamental assumptions underlying operations. These old rules of work design are based on assumptions about technology, people, and organizational goals that are no longer valid. He suggests the following 'principles of reengineering' (Hammer, 1990):

- Organize around outcomes, not tasks. This principle suggests that a single person performs all the steps in a process and that person's job be designed around the outcome or objective rather than a single task.
- Have those who use the output of the process perform the process. In this

way, there is little need for the overhead cost associated with managing it. Interfaces, liaisons and mechanisms are used to coordinate those who perform the process with those whose use are no longer needed.

- Subsume information-processing work into the real work that produces the information.
- Treat geographically dispersed resources as though they were centralized. Companies can use databases, telecommunications networks, and standardized processing systems to get the benefits of scale and coordination while maintaining the benefits of flexibility and service.
- Link parallel activities instead of integrating their results. Companies need to create links between parallel functions and to coordinate them while their activities are in process rather than after they are completed.
- Put the decision point where the work is performed and build control into the process. Instead of having those who do the work separate from those who monitor it, the people who do the work should also make the decisions and the process itself can have built-in controls.
- Capture information once and at the source. A critical factor for reengineering of the business process to succeed is to have executive leadership with real vision. Only if top-level management back the effort and outlast the cynics will people take reengineering seriously.

Figure 5.2. Process reconfiguration continuum

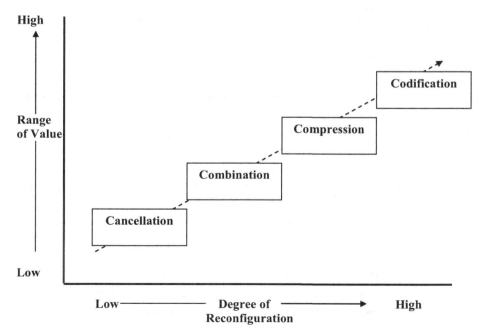

Results of BPR

BPR is a strategy-driven change that is important, potentially effective and often necessary for organizations facing competitive business environments, but its implementation is challenging, complicated, and cumbersome. Not all BPR projects are successful; undertaking BPR projects involves risk. Process changes may not be completed, completed too late, require more resources than planned, or be faced with resistance of people who want to stick to the old and 'sacred' way of doing things. The majority of successful BPR initiatives have had an external drive and a clear strategic vision, ensuring that internal changes deliver perceived improvements to the customers. The starting point for determining what, why, and how to change is an understanding of the value-adding processes in the company or its supply chain.

King (1994) views the primary reason of BPR failures as overemphasizing the tactical aspects and compromising the strategic dimensions. He notes that most failures of BPR are attributable to the process being viewed and applied at a tactical, rather than strategic, level. He identified important strategic dimensions to BPR: notably, Developing and Prioritizing Objectives; Defining the Process Structure and Assumptions; Identifying Trade-Offs Between Processes; Identifying New Product and Market Opportunities; Coordinating the Reengineering Effort; and, Developing a Human Resources Strategy. He concludes that the ultimate success of BPR depends on the people who do it and on how well they can be motivated to be creative and to apply their detailed knowledge to the redesign of business processes (Davenport & Stoddard 1994).

An Example of ICT-Enabled BPR

The following example illustrates an example of retail banking process reengineering (Turban et al., 1999). Banks are historically organized along different types of accounts such as checking or savings accounts, installment loans, mortgage loans, trust accounts, retirement accounts, etc. Over the years, each product division developed a computer-based information system. Each system was developed as an independent subsystem, wherein separate accounts statements were sent to customers.

Customers' accounts in the banking example were integrated through the introduction of a single point of contact for customers (a case manager or an account manager), a master account number. The bank is more customer-oriented and reduces cost. Many ICTs are developed as high-speed, automated versions of existing manual systems. As manual systems were not integrated, nor were the computer systems. The opportunity to integrate the manual systems as they are computerized was not exploited. Lack of planning and automating history caused problems of redundancy and integration. Redundancy relates to the data collected, stored, and processed. One customer can have four account numbers (one in each information system) and data elements (personal information) are identical in many files.

Fragmented ICTs in the bank create the following problems:

- Customers are required to supply duplicate data for each account they open.
- Storage space is wasted (redundancy).
- Processing time is wasted if common data needs update.
- Inconsistencies and/or errors develop in data files.

Difficulties in the integration of information arise for two reasons: a) Account numbers are not logically related and cannot be used for cross-referencing a customer's accounts limiting reporting capabilities, and b) The bank cannot develop mass-customization schemes if it cannot combine information available in different accounts. Example: offering mortgage loans to large depositors.

As bank's ICTs were not designed to integrate information to serve management's needs, information integration has to be planned prior to development. Not all organizational information needs to be integrated. The information architecture illustrates the interconnectedness of all organizational information needs. The cost of integrating non-integrated applications is high. The programming of data relationships that transcend departmental or functional boundaries is complex.

Integrating KM into BPR

KM is a valuable element in customer-centric business processes. KM can contribute significantly to business value in the context of a business process – both as a support to those working in the process and as a means of creating new knowledge. Most knowledge managers are re-evaluating and reassessing what they are doing in their organizations to embed knowledge into business processes, i.e., embedding KM tools, techniques and capabilities into a process, is the second evolutionary stage in KM. Smith and McKeen (2004) identified the following key steps that should be undertaken t to integrate KM into business process design:

- *Focus on Core Business Processes.* Although KM can enhance many processes, its need to demonstrate value to business mean that knowledge managers should pick and choose very carefully where they will maximize value of core processes, i.e. significant improvements in peripheral processes simply won't get the attention of senior executives.

- *Start with Process Redesign.* To ensure that KM is embedded in the process and not vice versa, embedding knowledge in business processes begins with process analysis and design. Both KM and ICTs should both be involved in BPR to determine where and how each can best contribute to business processes through systems analysis and knowledge analysis, i.e. simplifying, streamlining, facilitating and enhancing processes. Knowledge managers should also work not only with business process analysts but also with systems analysts to identify ways in which knowledge can enhance the business process and how technology can facilitate knowledge access and integration.

- *Knowledge Analysis.* The first level of business value KM can add is determining how best to support and facilitate the new business process with knowledge. Several knowledge analysis and design activities are recommended (Figure 4):

  ○ Assess Knowledge Needs
  ○ Organize and package structured knowledge
  ○ Formalize common practices (standardization)
  ○ Analyze & design complex work
  ○ Identify and design links to tacit knowledge

- *Contextual Analysis.* Understanding the context of organizational work is essential to analyzing the higher level knowledge that builds *on* information collected within a process to create, evolve and apply new knowledge in different ways and in different business processes. Contextual knowledge analysis uses a business process as a platform for growing new knowledge that will be useful both within the process and to the organization as a whole. Several types of analysis can be performed on basic process information:

  ○ *Reinforcement Mechanics.* Identify and develop mechanisms that will reinforce the behaviors and values, e.g., knowledge sharing culture, trust, and integrity, the organization desires to instill into the process itself. Ease of use, closing feedback loops, careful attention to expectations and rewards, and good change management practices are all strategies for ensuring a supportive knowledge context in which a process operates.

  ○ *Aggregation and synthesis.* Through analysis of basic transactional process data, valuable new knowledge can be created. For example, Wal-Mart's aggregation and analysis of transaction-level information makes it useful both to the sales process and to other areas of the business such as marketing, supply chain management, store management, and identifies trends and opportunities.

- ○ *Business Intelligence.* KM facilitates higher level decision making by providing "what-if" and "slice-and-dice" analysis tools and intelligent integration with other sources of information, e.g. the Sales System integrates aggregated and synthesized information with external news items and presents it differently for individual sales teams.
- ○ *Relationship Facilitation.* Enhancing informal knowledge transfer and development at higher levels i.e., beyond a single process or function. For instance, it may seek to facilitate building relationships among people doing similar jobs or working with the same clients, e.g., communities of practice, collaborative space, yellow page, or simply make them more visible to each other.
- ○ *Personalization and repurposing.* Revealing knowledge on the habits and preferences of particular users and customers to improve process execution and outcomes and make the process smarter (El Sawy and Josefek, 2003). Knowledge captured for one reason may also be repurposed for another. Thus, the diagnostic tool developed for the service team may be re-presented as a customer service tool.
- ○ *Exception Analysis.* Exception analysis represents a higher level knowledge analysis that promises to be a source of learning about changes in the business environment. Exception processing should be designed as a separate process that captures both identified and non-identified exceptions because they are more knowledge intensive than normal business processes. Exceptions can also be a source of learning about changing customer requirements and uncovering problems and opportunities with current processes (El Sawy and Jacobek, 2003).

- *Verification and Validation.* Embedding knowledge into business processes should be tested for accuracy and evaluated for effectiveness. Ideally, any process changes that include knowledge should make the process easier to use and more intuitive. The quality of outcomes, e.g., accuracy, reliability, customer satisfaction, needs to be measured in whatever ways are important to the organization. Judgments will also need to be made as to whether difficulties are the result of the normal challenges of adapting to new ways of working or design problems that must be corrected.
- *Maintenance and Evolution.* Embedding knowledge in a dynamic process is not a one-time activity. The knowledge embedded in processes or derived from processes must be accurate and timely. KM should put mechanisms in place to detect and correct system, errors, deficiencies, and other problems and to evolve knowledge designs over time.

The Context of CKM for BPR

Marketing, sales, and service are primary customer-centric functions (Porter and Millar, 1986) with a high degree of direct customer contact and knowledge intensity. CKM processes involve the processing of CK to pursue the goals of enduring and profitable customer relationships. Such processes are either triggered by the customer with the aim of receiving information or services or by the enterprise with the aim of delivering information or services to customers. Gebert et al. (2003) introduced a CKM process model that illustrates which KM tools can be applied to the CRM processes to achieve effective CKM. The model identifies six CRM business processes (campaign management, lead management, offer management, contract management, complaint management, and service management), and four aspects of KM (content, competence, collaboration and composition).

Details of the proposed CRM processes are as follows (Gebert et al., 2003):

- *Campaign management* is the core marketing process which fulfills the idea of interactive, individualized, and relational contacts in contrast to traditional transaction. It deals with the planning, control and monitoring of marketing activities towards known recipients. Marketing campaigns are individualized or segment specific and offer communication channels for feedback. Campaign management also generates valuable opportunities or 'leads' as the basis for lead management.
- *Lead management* is the qualification and prioritization of contacts with prospective customers. The objective is to provide sales staff with a qualified and prioritized list of presumably valuable prospects to be precisely addressed by an offer management process.
- *Offer management* is the core sales process. Its objective is the corporate-wide creation and delivery of individualized, binding offers. Offer management activities may be triggered by a customer inquiry, a qualified lead, or a discovered opportunity.
- *Contract management* is the creation and maintenance of contracts for the supply of products and/or services. As such, it supports offer management or service management processes. Contract management also comprises the maintenance and adjustment of long-term contracts.
- *Complaint management* communicates dissatisfaction of customers. The objectives are to improve customer satisfaction by directly addressing problems that led to complaints and to design a continuous improvement process in the future.

- *Service management* is the planning, realization and control of measures for the provision of services. Examples include after-sales maintenance, repair, and support activities.

The knowledge aspects of the CKM model are as follows (Gebert et al., 2003):

- The aspect *content* relates to explicated knowledge in the form of media such as text or images that organizations can only directly manage, and typically requires the use of content management or document management systems.
- The aspect *competence* refers to explicit and implicit knowledge that are not separable from the particular individual possessing it. This aspect makes use of expertise directories or e-learning systems.
- *Collaboration* deals with the creation and dissemination of knowledge among few individuals, e.g. in project teams, through e-mail, group information tools, and instant messaging systems.
- The aspect of *composition* deals with the dissemination and usage of knowledge among a large number of individuals, e.g. helping people find explicated knowledge in enterprise portals. It uses systems such as DM systems, personalization, taxonomy management systems, and knowledge maps.

The knowledge aspects of the CKM model deliver services that support BPR that integrates marketing, sales, and service activities to achieve a common goal. However, in order to integrate marketing, sales, and service activities, CRM requires the strong integration of customer-centric business processes. On a strategic level, companies need to determine how ICTs-enabled CKM can be used to support the redesign of CRM processes. Operational CRM systems directly support all the CRM processes described above, whereas analytical CRM mainly emphasize the processes campaign management, lead management, and offer management (Gebert et al., 2003).

CRITICAL ISSUES

The concept of BPR has been in the literature since the 1990s; however, it is surrounded by many myths, (i.e., is it a need or a fad? Is it radical or a gradual? Is it implemented haphazardly or methodically?). BPR has also been examined in terms of its relationship to TQM, and OT, the role of BPR in value chain, as well as the role of people, ICTs, and modeling in BPR.

Need vs. Fad-Based BPR

BPR has been around for quite some time and a lot has been written about it in both practitioner and academic journals. However, the controversy still remains if BPR is just an appealing label to tag on to whatever your company is doing to suggest that your latest and greatest work is 'in vogue', or it is based on a real need that makes it inevitable to undertake.

Rapid, complex, and turbulent changes in a business environmental context have made businesses not only adopt flexible job designs and corporate structures, but also flexible business processes. In an ever-changing global business environment, organizations seek to be flexible enough to adjust quickly to changing market conditions, lean enough to beat any competitor's price, innovative enough to keep its products and services technologically fresh, and dedicated enough to deliver maximum quality and customer service. This can be achieved directly through reengineering customer products, processes and/or services.

Radical vs. Gradual BPR

Although BPR is inevitable in turbulent and dynamic business environments, the controversy still remains if there is any accurate description of the nature of BPR itself. Two basic approaches to BPR have emerged in the literature: a) continuous improvement of existing processes, and b) complete radical change of existing processes from scratch and re-installment of new ones.

An Old Version of BPR: The Radical View

To some researchers, BPR is an approach for critical analysis and radical redesign of workflows, processes, and structures within and between organizations to achieve dramatic improvement in performance (Hammer, 1990; Davenport & Short 1990; Hammer and Champy, 2001). Teng et al. (1998) define BPR as the critical analysis and radical redesign of business processes to achieve breakthrough improvements in performance measures.

Regardless of Hammer's (1990) buzz word: "Don't automate, obliterate!" the clean sheet approach is rarely found in practice. Davenport and Stoddard (1994) believed that a 'blank sheet of paper' used in design usually requires a 'blank check' for implementation. Therefore, a more affordable approach for most companies is to use a *clean sheet* that entails a detailed vision for a new process without concern for the existing one. However, the implementation is done over several phased projects. The argument of Davenport and Stoddard (1994) ran contrary to the common views of BPR held by Hammer (1990). Hammer (1990) purports that although reengineering can deliver radical designs, it does not necessarily promise a revolutionary approach to change.

Moreover, a revolutionary change process might not be possible given the risk and cost of revolutionary tactics. For instance, if existing processes are totally ignored, new processes that are placed could represent a high risk because of the failure to build on the knowledge and experience which has been developed over time. However, if existing processes are deeply analyzed and followed, this could constrain the thinking of new ways of working. Therefore, both approaches should be analyzed with a balance between gaining knowledge of existing processes and new thoughts on how things ideally could be done (Peppard and Rowland, 1995).

A New Version of BPR: The Gradual View

Unlike several calls for all out 'radical change' (e.g., Hammer, 1990; Davenport and Short, 1990; and Hammer and Champy, 2001), most companies have a portfolio of approaches to organizational change including reengineering, continuous improvement, incremental approaches, and restructuring techniques (Davenport and Stoddard, 1994).

Due to several failures of BPR projects, and the emergence of web-based applications that solve many of the problems that BPR was supposed to solve, the concept of BPR has been revised lately to *business process redesign*, which can include redesign of one individual process, or a few individual processes (e.g., Sarker and Lee, 1999; Turban, et al., 2008), in addition to the redesign of the whole enterprise (El Sawy, 2001).

Another extension of BPR is business process management (BPM) which combines workflow systems and redesign methods. This emerging methodology covers three process categories: people-to-people, systems-to-systems, and systems-to-people interactions. It is a blending of workflow, process management, and applications integration (Turban et al., 2008).

As an attempt to consolidate both views of BPR, a pragmatic approach has been revised based on a continuous, rather than a one-shot, intervention approach. This continuum provides change initiatives, with varying degrees of radicalness supported by ICTs, at the heart of which is to deliver superior performance standards through establishing process sustainable capability (Al-Mashari and Zairi, 2000).

Ad Hoc vs. a Methodic BPR

BPR is a concept, as well as a methodology, for achieving remarkable improvement in performance and customer satisfaction. Implementing BPR is not an ad hoc, free-form exercise. There is a systematic approach with specific steps that needs to be followed to guide the effort and to utilize all organization resources.

There are several approaches to BPR. Davenport and Short (1990) prescribe a five-step approach to BPR:

- Develop the Business Vision and Process Objectives: BPR is driven by a business vision which implies specific business objectives such as Cost Reduction, Time Reduction, Output Quality Improvement, Quality of Work Life, Learning, and Empowerment.
- Identify the Processes to be redesigned: Most companies use the High-Impact approach which focuses on the most important processes or those that conflict most with the business vision. A lesser number of companies use the exhaustive approach that attempts to identify all business processes and then prioritize them in order of redesign urgency.
- Understand and Measure the Existing Processes: This step is needed in order to avoid the repetition of old mistakes and to provide a baseline for future improvements.
- Identify ICT Levers: Awareness of ICT capabilities should influence process redesign.
- Design and Build a Prototype of the New Process: The actual redesign should be viewed as a prototype, with successive iterations to align the approach with quick delivery of results and the involvement and satisfaction of customers.

Successful BPR undertakings are not implemented haphazardly, but usually they follow no 'standard' methodology for effective implementation. Although there is no specific recommended methodology for BPR, the following steps are introduced as a proposed generic BPR approach:

- Derive desired customer outcomes from business strategy: the attributes of products or services that customers value most (customers' needs, requirements, and expectations) through surveys, interviews, complaints, etc.
- Determine the key business processes that affect our customers' value attributes.
- Redesign the key business processes to be aligned with customer requirements.
- Make necessary changes in people, structure, culture, and leadership styles.
- Leverage ICT systems to achieve outcomes in new ways.

- Choose alternative process design.
- Implement the new process design:

  ○ Piloting stage
  ○ Phasing-out stage (gradual introduction of new processes)
  ○ Paralleling (old and new processes are being run concurrently)
  ○ Cutting-over (turning off the old and turning on the new)

- Monitor performance results.

BPR and TQM: An Overlapping vs. a Duplicating Relationship

The increased attention to business processes in recent years is largely due to TQM (Teng et al., 1998) who argue that TQM and BPR share a cross-functional orientation. Davenport (1993) observed that quality specialists tend to focus on gradual change and continuous improvement of processes, while proponents of reengineering often seek radical redesign and drastic improvement.

Davenport (1993) also notes that *Quality Management*, often referred to as TQM, refers to programs and initiatives that emphasize incremental improvement in work processes and outputs over an open-ended period of time. In contrast, *Reengineering*, also sometimes known as business process redesign or business process innovation (BPI), refers to discrete initiatives that are intended to achieve radically redesigned and improved work processes in a bounded time frame. There are several differences, as well as similarities, between TQM and BPR. Once BPR adopts an

Table 5.1. Process improvement (TQM) vs. process innovation (BPI)

Dimension	TQM	BPI
Level of Change	Incremental	Radical
Starting Point	Existing Process	Clean Sheet
Frequency of Change	One-time/Continuous	One-time
Time Required	Short	Long
Participation	Bottom-Up	Top-Down
Typical Scope	Narrow, within functions	Broad, cross-functional
Risk	Moderate	High
Primary Enabler	Statistical Control	ICTs
Type of Change	Cultural	Socio-Technical

Source: Adapted from Davenport, T. (1993). Process Innovation: Reengineering Work through Information Technology. Boston, MA: Harvard Business School Press.

incremental rather than radical approach to process change, then BPR overlaps with TQM. However, with regards to the role of ICTs in the change process, ICTs play a significant role in BPR projects, whereas TQM usually adopts an ICT-free type of methodology. Contrasts between TQM and BPI are provided Table 5.1.

BPR and OT: A Standalone vs. a Stepping-Stone Relationship

BPR is a process that contributes to OT; however it is not synonymous with transformation. OT is generally about the emergence of a new belief system, (e.g. customer-centricity), and necessarily involves reframing that is a discontinuous change in the organizations strategy, leadership style, shared culture, ICTs, structure, and processes. Besides changes in work processes, OT also involves broad changes in other organizational dimensions such as strategy, structure, people, and capabilities (Davenport and Stoddard, 1994). It is considered a post-BPR change strategy that is higher in terms of scope, magnitude, and expected results of the change program. If an OT initiative is undertaken, BPR fits as a stepping-stone towards OT.

Davenport and Stoddard (1994) speculate that BPR has peaked in the U.S and would probably become integrated with much broader organizational phenomena (e.g., its synthesis of ideas that includes the precepts of reengineering; its integration into existing change methods, such as OT; or its combination with quality and other process-oriented improvement approaches into an integrated process management approach).

Role of BPR in Value Chain: A Supporting vs. an Enabling Role

BPR generates, through advanced ICTs, a streamlined business process and an inimitable source for organizations, viz. knowledge. Knowledge generated through ICTs can provide organizations with an SCA over their rivals. ICT-enabled BPR is used as a strategic weapon not only to redesign internal operations, but is extended to the marketplace by revamping supply chain (e.g., disintermediation) to add value to customers.

BPR and the Business Value Chain

In its simplest form, an SCA, either cost or differentiation-based, is a function of a firm's value chain. ICTs are spreading through a firm's value chain activities, transforming the way value activities are performed and the nature of the linkages among them. They enable a firm to better coordinate its activities and thus give it greater flexibility in deciding the breadth of activities that suit its customers.

SCA may be achieved when customers and suppliers are linked successfully to the business external value chain (e-supply) system. The e-supply chain system is used to place orders, check on prices and delivery dates, and manage inventories. The external value chain model helps organizations know where they can add value to their customers or suppliers. The value chain integrates front-office with back-office transactions and improves the efficiency of processing purchase orders by cutting down on product/process cycle time and by enabling retailers to check on available sock before placing orders. The e-supply chain also gives manufacturers a competitive advantage as customers are linked electronically to the order-entry system and find it easier to place orders through the network, (e.g. EDI, of certain manufacturer than with others).

By coordinating and integrating, and reengineering value chain activities through strategic systems, e.g. ERP, an enterprise should be able to reduce transaction costs, reduce cycle time, gather better information for control purposes, and substitute less costly operations in one activity for more costly ones elsewhere. Therefore BPR is becoming increasingly important for gaining SCA. In this situation, ICTs play a crucial role in enabling value chain revamp (removal of business mediators such as wholesalers, distributors and retailers). Manufacturers sell directly to the customer (e.g., Dell Co.). Values achieved include higher efficiency (lower cost due to elimination of non-value adding [NVA] processes), product customization, reduced time, and higher flexibility. Re-intermediation is possible through new intermediaries (e.g., infomediaries, e-retailers, aggregators, and portals) introduced at the downstream supply chain processes related to delivering the products to final customers or consumers.

Nonetheless, Senge (1990) took a contradictory view by arguing that organizations seeking to manage knowledge have placed too much emphasis on ICTs. He emphasized the role of organizational learning more than ICT, information, and even knowledge. According to Senge (1990), the world of organizational learning is the 'fifth discipline' that places too little emphasis on structured knowledge and the use of technology to capture and leverage it.

BPR and the CKM Value Chain

The CKM value chain model seeks to bring workers together, and by their synergies and shared values, produce as a group in excess of their individual capacities. The value chain model may be operationalized through:

- Adoption of a customer-centric, process-based rather than functional-based organization

- Adoption of a customer-centric business strategy
- Development of a networked organization structure
- Development of a networked ICT infrastructure
- Development of a team working spirit that allows knowledge sharing

In CKM, the ultimate aim is achievement of SCA, which in turn is a function of how well a company can manage its entire CKM value chain (Chapters 6-11). An enterprise's value chain for competing in a particular industry is embedded in a larger stream of knowledge-based market activities that may be referred to as the 'external value chain' or 'supply chain' that includes suppliers and distribution channels. Achieving SCA requires that a firm's value chain be managed as a system, rather than as a collection of separate parts.

Retooling ICTs in order to enable reconfiguration of knowledge-based value chain, customer-centric activities, (e.g., order fulfillment, sales, and customer services), is often the key to a major improvement in a firm's competitive position. To gain competitive advantage over competitors through CKM, a firm must either provide comparable value to the customer, but utilize strategic systems to perform activities more efficiently than its rivals (lower cost), or utilize ICTs to perform activities in a unique way that creates greater value for customers and secures a higher price (differentiation).

Role of People in BPR: A Complementary vs. a Substitutional Role

People, structural and technological changes are prerequisites to effective process orientation of work activities. In the process change model, two major catalysts can facilitate the direction of work process flow: changes in ICTs, and changes in organizational structure, such as institution of cross-functional teams, case managers, and process generalists (Grover et al., 1995). Of course, other changes are not less important in the transformation towards customer-centricity, such as changes in people, corporate culture, and leadership style. There are also many strategic decisions in reengineering related to leadership of BPR projects, such as the selection of individuals to lead the BPR project. People would wonder whether such a position is a permanent leadership position for a continuous and ongoing reengineering effort.

The implementation and execution of redesigned processes depend upon those who do the work. Therefore, the participation, and more importantly, acceptance and ownership, at the grass roots level are essential for successful BPR (Davenport and Stoddard, 1994). The idea of 'Process Ownership' needs to be introduced in the move away from functional and hierarchical organizations towards a structure wherein employees have a clear vision and ownership of what they do, and to make a difference to customers.   In customer-centric organizations, the assignment of a 'process owner' makes a significant difference between a functional organization and a process-based organization which addresses the whole of customers' needs rather than partial customers' needs.

Role of ICTs in BPR: A Mutual-Interdependency vs. a Mutual-Independency Role

Business processes, i.e. fulfillment of a customer order, represent a new approach to coordination across the firm; and the ultimate impact of ICTs, workflow management systems, is seen to be the most powerful tool for optimizing coordination among team members.   Generally, function-based, day-to-day business operations exist in older ICTs and consist of fragmented systems with manual application program interfaces (APIs) that link them together.   Hammer (1990) considers ICTs as the key enabler of BPR which he considers as 'radical change.' He prescribes the use of ICTs to challenge the assumptions inherent in the work processes that have existed long before the advent of modern ICTs.

Davenport and Short (1990) argued that ICTs and BPR have a recursive relationship.   ICT should be viewed as fundamentally reshaping the way business is done more than an automating or mechanizing force, and business processes should be viewed in terms of the capabilities ICTs can provide.   This broadened recursive view of ICTs and BPR has been referred to as the 'new industrial engineering'.   Davenport and Short (1990) outline the following capabilities that reflect the roles that ICTs can play in BPR: transactional, geographical, automatical, analytical, informational, sequential, knowledge management, tracking, and disintermediation.

Teng et al. (1998) believe that the way related functions participate in a process (i.e., the functional coupling of a process) can be differentiated along two dimensions: degree of mediation and degree of collaboration.   They define the Degree of Mediation of the process as the extent of sequential flow of input and output among participating functions.   They define the Degree of Collaboration of the process as the extent of information exchange and mutual adjustment among cross-functional team members when participating in the same process.   In their framework, ICTs are instrumental in Reducing the Degree of Mediation and Enhancing the Degree of Collaboration.   Also, innovative uses of ICT would lead inevitably to the development of new, coordination-intensive structures, which enable firms to coordinate their activities in ways that were not possible before.   Such coordination-intensive structures are critical components of DCCs that may improve organizations responsiveness to customers' preferences, leading to high potential of SCA.

The role of ICTs in business-process redesign, in particular, takes three forms, alongside three phases of implementation: before the process is redesigned, while the process is being redesigned, and after the design is complete (Attaran, 2003):

- Phase 1 - Before the process is redesigned, ICTs play the role of an *enabler*. The activities that ICTs may enable in this phase may include the following:

  ○ Utilizing newer and better technology to develop a strategic vision (e.g., Dell's mass customization of products and disintermediation of supply chain).
  ○ Tracking information and breaking geographical and organizational barriers allow organizations to increase the amount and effectiveness of internal and external communication (such as the Internet, Intranet, call centers, e-mails, and shared databases) and collaboration and knowledge transfer within teams in ways that were not possible before.
  ○ Using CSCWs to introduce organizations to the experience, expertise, and creative practices of other organizations with respect to different approaches to manage a process.
  ○ Using ICT capabilities to create flexible infrastructures, such as flexible organization designs, that support evolving organizations and adapt to changing external drivers.
  ○ Facilitating ICTs alliances and inter-organizational coordination by enabling organizations to create linkages between suppliers, distributors, and customers. These cross-functional engagements enable firms to streamline their processes and maximize efficiency.

- Phase 2 - While the process is being designed, ICTs play the role as a *facilitator* as follows:

  ○ Facilitating the reengineering design process through the use of project management and electronic communication tools.
  ○ Gathering and analyzing information on the performance of processes to identify and select processes for redesign through drawing process map/chart models using tools such as computer aided software engineering (CASE).
  ○ Computing technologies such as DWs have facilitated process-oriented approach to system development.
  ○ Using ICTs such as CAD/CAM, LANs, CSCWs, and groupware techogies to improve collaboration among personnel of different functional units to accomplish a common task of designing a process.

   ° Gathering information from customer satisfaction surveys or business data from customers which can be used to create a web-based CRM system, which in turn, enables the creation of 'virtual organization'.

   ° Using ICTs to identify alternative business processes and to replace information poverty with information richness, i.e. through ES and DM.

- Phase 3 - After the design is complete, ICTs are used as an *implementer* as follows:

   ° ICTs can facilitate the implementation of the new process through the use of project management and process analysis tools.

   ° Electronic communication systems facilitate ongoing and real time communication of the reengineering process between users and facilitators.

   ° ICTs can greatly facilitate in evaluating the potential investments and returns of the reengineering effort, and determine how much value the new process contributes to the overall performance.

   ° ICTs allow reengineering by forming cross-functional collaborative teams and flattened organizational structures, and allow synchronous and real-time meetings (e.g., teleconferencing) as well as asynchronous (e.g., message boards) meetings.

   ° ICTs make it possible for a reengineering project to have specific information on a specific definition of success 'Digital Feedback Loop' related to a specific end, e.g. KPIs and CSFs.

Rigidity of ICT systems may pose a real challenge to BPR projects. For example, ready-made, functional-based systems, such as ERP, may inhibit process-based conversion if adopting organizations cannot find a way around it. Nonetheless, ICTs and BPR remain natural partners as the role of ICTs in organizations is not only in automating processes, but in helping organizations to cope with increasingly complex and uncertain business environments. ICTs can change fundamentally and radically organization structures, shape the way work is done, and enable the new processes designs, besides their traditional role in supporting existing processes, with the aim of achieving dramatic improvement in performance.

Role of Modeling in BPR: A Primary vs. a Supplementary Role

There is a growing realization of the importance of modeling as a powerful tool for business analysis and for the facilitation of BPR. A business is a system or a network of interdependent relationships that exist between different components in order to achieve pre-specified goals or objectives. A model is a logical or functional representation, usually graphical or mathematical in nature, of a system's behavior and performance. Usually, a model represents the system from the perspective of what is moving through it, be it a process or data. The purpose of process modeling is to visualize and analyze the actual work flow, identify its potential problem areas or bottlenecks, e.g. indicated by long waiting, and to introduce a new process design that seeks to improve performance of process operation by making it faster, more efficient, less costly, and more responsive.

There exist a number of modeling tools and techniques for business analysis. Examples of these are flow charts, spreadsheets, and simulations. Flow charts are powerful modeling tools that graphically document the flow of processes or data, e.g. a purchase order flow chart describes the series of steps involved and decisions made when a purchase order is being processed. Spreadsheets are also a cost-effective modeling tool for quick and accurate 'what-if' and 'goal-seeking' scenarios. BPR gurus, Hammer and Champy (2003), noted that many of the reengineering projects have often applied flowcharts and spreadsheets in the analysis of performance.

Although flowcharts and spreadsheets are adequate for answering 'what-if' questions, they are inadequate for answering 'how,' 'when' or 'where.' Business processes are too complex and dynamic to be understood and analyzed by flowcharting and spreadsheets alone. A powerful modeling tool, such as visual simulation, can provide both accurate analysis and dynamic representation of business processes. Process simulation allows visualization of processes, people, and technology in a dynamic computer model. However, the interactions of people with processes and technology result in an infinite number of dynamic scenarios and outcomes that are impossible to comprehend and evaluate without the help of a visual simulation tool.

Dynamic models are interactive representations that can show the effects of a decision on other variables, whereas static models cannot show the effects of a decision on availability of staff, increases in work, interruptions, and so on. For example, in the simulation of a purchase order fulfillment process, we imitate the behavior dynamics of all departments involved in processing purchase orders such as sales, inventory, accounting, and shipment. Simple simulation of the work time required to process purchase orders, once combined with other processes, may suggest that there is an opportunity for process reengineering and corporate downsizing.

RECOMMENDED SOLUTION: A PROPOSED ORGANIZATIONAL REINVENTION MODEL

In order to secure an effective CKM change, Table 5.2 introduces a proposed template model that can help to develop an enterprise-wide, high-level, strategic analysis of organizational reinvention requirements, with a sample of three generic questions: What? Who? and How? Additional questions may be added such as: Why? When? and Where?

Table 5.2. High-level organizational transformation analysis framework template with examples of generic questions

	WHAT?	WHO?	HOW?
Strategy	What are our goals and objectives? What is the base of our business strategy? What are the best practices in our industry?	Who envisages our business vision and strategy?	How does process redesign contribute to the achievement of business strategy?
People	What are our customers' needs and requirements? What is the gap between our current situation and customers' needs (Gap Analysis)	Who 'owns' the process? Who leads the BPR initiative? Who are our customers? Who are the members of the BPR team?	How do we select, train, motivate, and reward people?
Technology	What are the required ICTs for the redesign of processes?	Who oversees the ICT retooling decision and process?	How do we use ICTs to enable the redesign of new processes?
Structure	What are the functional units that will be affected by the redesign of processes?	Who oversees the restructuring decision and process?	How do we align structural changes with process redesign?
Processes	What are the business processes that need to be redesigned? What are functional units that will be affected by the redesign? What is the gap between our current situation and customers' needs (Gap Analysis)	Who oversees the process redesign decision and process?	How do we describe the flow of the existing process? (Use flow charts to map the old process). How do we redesign the process? (Use flow charts to map the new process).

FUTURE TRENDS

Several future trends are explored: a shift from BPR to total OT, a shift from process rigidity to process agility, and a shift from in sourcing to outsourcing of processes.

A Shift from Business Process Redesign to Total Organizational Transformation

The BPR concept has evolved from a 'radical change' to account for the contextual realism (Caron et. al 1994, Earl 1994) and to reconcile with more incremental process change methods such as TQM, towards a broader, yet more comprehensive, process management concept (Davenport 1995).

As BPR failures are mainly attributed to tactical, rather than strategic, view and application levels, more organizations in the future are expected to consider reengineering not only their processes, but also transformation of their entire business structure, jobs, processes, and ICTs. The objective is to move from partial change to total change that integrates fragmented silo functions, jobs, processes, and systems into a comprehensive strategic intervention, such as OT and the learning organization (LO). When successfully conducted, redesigning processes and organizations has great potential to improve an organization's competitive position.

A Shift from Process Rigidity to Process Agility

In recent years, business environments have been changing from centralized-and-closed to distributed-and-open. Traditional approaches to process management are often inadequate for complex and dynamic environmental situations due to their lack of flexibility and adaptability to manage dynamic changes, as well as foster flexible interactions within and between organizations. Transition to knowledge-based economies have made establishment of effective and flexible business processes within companies crucial to SCA.

The future trend of business organizations is to witness an increasing move from physical work to virtual work and from rigid processes to dynamic and agile processes. Virtual work and 'virtualization' and their recursive influence on work practices, organizations, and business networks uses simulated images and processes rather than exchanges of physical materials and performance of physical processes. Members of these teams may be located in different countries and have very different cultural backgrounds.

A larger variety of virtual work forms are likely to emerge to differentiate work environments where individuals are physically or temporally dispersed. Such virtual work environments may include individuals working at home (telecommuting) as well as teams of employees from different organizations who manage a supply chain, pulled together based on skills and not location. The accelerating trend of globalization of supply chains urgently requires electronic collaboration and knowledge sharing among organizations and seamless integration of processes to stay competitive in the global market. Many crucial aspects, such as privacy and security, reliability and flexibility, scalability and agility will continue to prevail.

'Virtuality' continues to grow in scale and scope due to the growing number of businesses that are shifting to, or newly establishing, e-biz models. ICTs and virtual work will continue to develop a dual impact on human actions, 'virtual' group dynamics, and social structures in the future, in which ICTs shape human actions and the social context in which the action takes place, while human actions, group dynamics, and social context shape ICTs simultaneously.

A Shift from In-Sourcing to Outsourcing

More rapid, dynamic, and complex changes in the future business environments require dramatic changes in future organizations, (i.e., downsizing, outsourcing, empowerment, entrepreneurial team spirit, innovative culture, flexible structure, integrated process, and learning organizations that are capable of leveraging distinctive core competencies).

The noticeable change in the form of future organizations from vertical to virtual is interlinked with the decision to outsource non-core business processes (e.g., logistics such as distribution, warehousing, packaging, payroll, and transportation) to a third-party service provider. Besides, BPO will be a key strategic decision area for organizations in their move to focus on distinctive core competencies critical to success of the firm, as core competencies should not be outsourced.

Usually, BPO is implemented as part of the downsizing effort in many organizations. It is adopted as a cost-saving mechanism for activities that a company requires, but does not depend upon, to maintain its position in the marketplace. BPO may be contracted outside a company's own country, contracted to a company's neighboring country, or contracted within the company's own country.

CONCLUSION

The organization has to readjust itself according to the demands raised by one or more of its environmental factors. Customers, competition, and other relevant changes that take place in the external environment are factors that drive change in organizations. In addition to the organizational structure and ICTs explained previously, business processes need to be flexible and functional in order to provide faster and better customer services. The concern of this chapter was to discuss the strategic importance of process change and innovation in adapting to complex, dynamic and competitive business environments by leveraging process-based DCCs of organizations. With a well-planned and managed redesign of processes, redundancies are eradicated, inefficiencies eliminated, and processes streamlined.

A functionally aligned hierarchical organization is sub-optimal when viewed from the perspective of the customer because it had delays, was more expensive and less efficient to operate. Successful implementation of CKM requires BPR of the whole organization, i.e. OT. BPR is a concept, methodology, and philosophy that aim at achieving improvements in performance by maximizing the value–added component of business processes, and minimizing non-value-adding ones. This chapter focused on the role of ICTs, organizational restructuring, and innovation of people for streamlining and synthesizing customer-centric business processes in order to achieve breakthrough improvements in performance measures. The role of processes will discussed further as an issue in the CKM value chain covered in Chapters VI-XI.

Customer-centric business strategy requires not only flexible organiza-tional design, but also flexible business process design in order to maximize value provided for customers. Customer process redesign refers to a set of customer-focused activities for aligning business processes with customer requirements and is carried out with the aim of providing higher satisfaction for customers and higher financial performance for companies. In turbulent and competitive market conditions, it is important for organizations to adopt a customer-centric business process orientation BPO, and value-chain driven approach to understanding 'how the business works', and hence how it may be improved via a combination of reengineering of business processes, re-structuring, and new ICTs.

BPR is needed for CKM, knowing that KM itself is a process-based, cross-functional intricate endeavor. Plans to make better use of knowledge as a resource must be built into the structure and culture of the organization in the medium term. KM technology alone is not enough to create a competitive advantage unless it has been coupled with the necessary OT from 'silo-based' to 'process-based' structure. This is true especially in the front-end business operations, and capitalizing on the power of the intellectual assets of people to improve the quality of delivered services while achieving better efficiency and efficacy. In the CKM context, BPR provides an organization-wide view of the end-to-end chain of linked activities which are needed to deliver customer value in terms of products or services. Successful BPR requires a fully integrated and totally automated ICT system that will enable firms to define, track, and manage knowledge embedded in their work processes.

To this point in the book, we have examined the role of external business environments in driving CKM (Part I: Strategizing), and explained reinventions of major organizational pillars: people and structure, ICTs, and business processes (Part II: Reinventing). The next section of the book (Part III: Capitalizing) proceeds to the analysis and blueprinting of the CKM value chain.

REFERENCES

Al-Mashari, M., & Zairi, M. (2000). Revisiting BPR: A holistic review of practice and development. *Business Process Management Journal, 6*(1), 10-42.

Alter, S. (2002). *Information systems: Foundation of e-business.* 4th edition, Upper Saddle River, NJ: Prentice Hall.

Attaran, M. (2003), Information technology and business process redesign. *Business Process Management Journal, 9*(4), 440-458.

Bueren, A., Schierholz, R., Kolbe, L. M., & Brenner, W. (2005). Improving performance of customer-processes with knowledge management. *Business Process Management Journal, 11*(5), 573-588.

Champy, J. A. (2002). *R-Engineering the corporation: Reinventing your business in the digital age.* New York, NY: Warner Books.

Davenport, T. (1993). *Process innovation: Reengineering work through information technology.* Boston, MA: Harvard Business School Press.

Davenport, T. H., & Short, J. E. (1990). The new industrial engineering: Information technology and business process redesign. *Sloan Management Review,* Summer, 11-27.

Davenport, T. H., & Stoddard, D. B. (1994). Reengineering: business change of mythic proportions? *MIS Quarterly, 18*(2), 121-127.

El Sawy, O. (2001). Redesigning enterprise processes for e-business. New York: McGraw-Hill.

El Sawy, O., & Josefek, R. Jr (2003). Business process as nexus of knowledge. *Handbook on Knowledge Management, 1,* 425-438. Berlin: Springer-Verlag.

Gebert, H., Geib, M., Kolbe, L., & Brenner, W. (2003). Knowledge-enabled customer relationship management and knowledge management concepts. *Journal of Knowledge Management, 7*(5), 107-123.

Grover, V., Teng, J., & Fiedler, K. (1995). The implementation of business process re-engineering. *Journal of Management Information Systems, 12*(1), 109-44.

Hammer, M., & Champy, D. (2003). *Reengineering the Corporation: A Manifesto for Business Revolution.* New York: HarperCollins Publishers.

Hammer, M. (1990). Reengineering work: Don't automate, obliterate. *Harvard Business Review*, July-August, 104-112.

Hammer, M. (1996). Beyond Reengineering: How the process-centered organization is changing our lives. New York, NY: Harper Business.

Hammer, M. (2004). Deep Change, *Harvard Business Review, 82*(4), 84-93.

Hammer, M., & Champy, J. (2001). *Reengineering the corporation: A manifesto for business revolution.* NY: HarperCollins.

King, W. R. (1994). Process reengineering: The strategic dimensions. *Information Systems Management, 11*(2), 71-73.

Pearlson, K., & Saunders, C. (2006). *Managing and Using Information Systems: A Strategic Approach.* 3rd edition, New York: John Wiley.

Peppard, J., & Ronald, P. (1995). *The Essence of Business Process Re-Engineering.* Upper Saddle River, NJ: Prentice-Hall.

Porter, M. E., & Millar, V. E. (1986). How information gives you competitive advantage. *Harvard Business Review, 36*(4), 61-78.

Sarker, S., & Lee, A. (1999). IT-enabled organizational transformation: A case study of BPR Failure at TELECO. *Journal of Strategic Information Systems, 8*(1), 83-103.

Scott-Morton, M., & Allen, T. J. (1994). *Information Technology and the Corporation of the 1990s.* New York: Oxford University Press.

Smith, H. A., & McKeen, J. D. (2004). Developments in practice XII: Knowledge-enabling business processes, *Communications of the Association for Information Systems, 13*(25), 25-38.

Stoddard, D. B., & Jarvenpaa, S. L. (1995). Business process redesign: Tactics for managing radical change. *Journal of Management Information Systems, 12*(1), 81-107.

Teng, J. T. C., Jeong, S. R., & Grover, V. (1998). Profiling successful reengineering projects. *Communications of the ACM, 41*(6), 96 – 102.

Turban, E., Leidner, D. E., Mclean, E., & Wetherbe, J. (2008). *Information technology for management: Transforming organizations in the digital economy.* 6th edition, New York: John Wiley.

Turban, E., McLean, E., & Wetherbe, J. (1999). *Information technology for management: making connection for strategic advantage*, 2nd edition, New York: John Wiley.

Turban, E., McLean, E., & Wetherbe, J. (2002). *Information technology for management: Transforming business in the digital economy.* 3rd edition, New York: John Wiley.

Section III
Capitalizing (3Cs)

Chapter VI
Capturing Data from Customers

INTRODUCTION

The customer is a strategic element in a company's downstream supply chain. In the new economy, customers, whether they are individual consumers or businesses, are becoming demanding, powerful, and more knowledgeable than before. The pressure of customers for more improvements (e.g. in quality, cost, and delivery), has been intensified by globalization of marketplaces and the emergence of new business philosophies and models (e.g. click and mortar direct-sale business model). Customer data is the key to successful relationships with customers. Data acquisition is the process to capture, integrate, cleanse, and load customer data, from various customer touchpoints, into the operational data store (ODS) and DW in order to create customer information and knowledge.

This chapter intends to examine the concepts, issues, and trends related to capturing customer data and routing it to, or sharing it with, people in other units within the organization.

CONCEPTUAL FOUNDATIONS

In CKM, interactions with customers are becoming increasingly inevitable to improve quality, cut costs, increase revenues, capture market leadership, and achieve SCA. ICT systems are no longer used for internal command and control purposes, but for adding value to customers through new products and/or procedures. CKM requires organizations to gather data, information, and knowledge needed to:

- Identify target customers and market.
- Determine the needs, requirements, and expectations of customers.
- Develop and produce products, services, and processes that meet these needs.

The importance of customers to business firms has created tough 'rivalries' among competitors over acquiring new customers or retaining/expanding relationships with current ones. In particular, CK has been utilized as a major weapon to gain competitive advantage following the transformation of organizations from 'product-centric' to 'customer-centric' ones. Therefore, CKM is needed to build good customer relations, satisfaction and loyalty, which in turn would be used to achieve SCA.

This section is set to explain the meaning of the concepts of customer, data, customer data, and to discuss various ICT applications used in the data acquisition process.

What is a 'Customer'?

A customer is a party that acquires or uses an offering, be it product and/or service, of an organization. This includes subentities such as Prospect, Using Customer/Consumer, and Buying Customer (Imhoff et al., 2001). The customer in a B2B context is an organization: a profit-oriented-company, or a not-for-profit institution. In a B2C context, the customer is an individual or a household. The word 'customer' historically derives from 'custom,' meaning 'habit; a customer was someone who frequented a particular shop, who made it a habit to purchase goods there, and with whom the shopkeeper had to maintain a relationship to keep his or her 'custom' - expected purchases in the future.

What is 'Data'?

The concepts of data, information, and knowledge are essential elements in the CKM value chain and each one needs to be clearly distinguished from the other. Although sometimes these concepts of data, information, and knowledge may be used interchangeably, several authors draw distinction among them (Gore and Gore, 1999). Data refer to representations of unprocessed or raw facts (e.g., statistics, observations, other objective and quantifiable metrics). They are static sets of facts, numbers, or individual entities without context or purpose, and are preceded by a universe of noise, but subsequenced by 'in-formation' when presented in a form that has meaning. Accumulated information plus analysis, interpretation, synthesis, and evaluation create knowledge.

It has often been pointed out that data, information, and knowledge are not the same; but despite efforts to define them, many researchers frequently use the terms interchangeably. Knowledge and information are thus similar in some aspects, but different in others - while information is more factual, knowledge is about beliefs and commitment. Knowledge and information are both about meaning in the sense that both are context-specific and relational, but knowledge is always about action - the knowledge must be used to some end (Nonaka & Takeuchi, 1995). This book takes the position that the three concepts form a hierarchy that starts with data, continues with information, and ends with knowledge. This view is advocated by Davenport and Prusak (2000), Choo et al. (2000), Bellinger et al. (2004), and Sharma (2005).

Data refer to the individual raw facts that are out of context, have no meaning and are difficult to understand. Facts are numbers, characters, character strings, text, images, voice, video and any other form wherein a fact may be presented. Data, in context, are facts that have meaning and can be easily understood. They are the raw facts in context with meaning and understanding, but are not yet information because they have no particular relevance or time frame (Brackett, 1999).

What is 'Customer Data'?

Customer data supplied directly to CKM consists of data obtained directly from customers, prospects, or suspects to identify future profit opportunities. Directly supplied customer data consists of three types (Peppers and Rogers, 2004):

- *Demographic*: represent personal data, such as age, income, education level, marital status, gender, and home ownership. Customer demographics can be used to segment customers.
- *Attitudinal* data: relate to, or are expressive of, personal attitudes or opinions reflecting attitudes about customer satisfaction, product/service quality, desired features, unmet needs, lifestyles, brand preferences, and social and personal values and dispositions.
- *Behavioral* data: relate to purchase and buying habits data, interactions with the company, communication channels chosen, language used, product consumption, company share of wallet, and the like. Behavioral data are the data type used most extensively in customer-centric intelligence CKM applications. Behavioral data may be used to develop customer purchasing behavior model based on the following customer variables (Reed, K. L. & Berry, J. K., 1999):

recency (time since last visit), frequency (number of visits per unit of time), and monetary (average transaction value).

Customer data may be divided, according to their measurement scale, into four types: nominal, ordinal, interval, and ratio scales.

- *Nominal:* a type of categorical data where there are various characteristics, but no natural ordering, (e.g. yes or no answers, gender, and eye color).
- *Ordinal*: a type of measuring scales using a natural ordering of levels, but the intervals between the categories are inconsistent or undefined. An example is where items are sorted into order of preference, such as customer satisfaction surveys often use a 5-point Likert scale.
- *Interval:* a type of measurement scale with a fixed and defined interval between successive points; however, the zero point does not indicate absence of the characteristic being measured, but is arbitrary or undefined (e.g. temperature and calendar time).
- *Ratio:* the ratio scale is the top level of data measurement scales. Ratio scales are like interval scales except they have true zero points. A good example is the volume of sales, value of sales, net income, and number of recurrent customers. The factor which clearly defines a ratio scale is that it has a true zero point.

Customer-Centric Data Acquisition Systems

In order to maintain customer satisfaction and loyalty, it is necessary for companies to serve each customer in his preferred way, therefore requiring customer data, information, and knowledge, which in turn requires utilization of advanced ICTs. The traditional store of data is the database. CKM is a customer-relationship-based enterprise-wide business strategy that captures and integrates data from order, sales, marketing, and service processes in order to understand customers and establish a profitable and longer relationship with them.

Customer-centric ICT applications may be divided into three types (Seybold, 2002): a) customer-facing applications (Table 6.1), b) customer-touching applications (Table 6.2), and c) customer-centric intelligence applications. Customer-touching applications and customer-facing applications relate to the first part of the CKM value chain, viz. capturing data from customers; whereas the last type, customer-centric intelligence applications, relates to the development of customer information and knowledge.

The CKM system development process starts with acquisition, analysis, and use of data from, information of, and knowledge about customers in order to sell efficiently more goods or services. Development of CKM application systems is built on enterprise-wide systems, such as DWs, intranets/extranets, and on analytical tools such as DM, DSS, and ES.

Customer-Touching CKM Applications

Unlike customer-facing applications, customers in this category *interact directly* with the applications, such as marketing self-service customer support, e-commerce, and campaign management. In order to achieve optimum results, front-office and back-office applications need to be integrated. For example, the system for fulfillment of purchase orders must be integrated with the CRM system so customers can find out when their orders are going to be shipped (Seybold, 2002). However, enterprise-wide systems and e-business are blurring the distinction between front-office and back-office (Knox et al., 2003).

Table 6.1. Description of customer-facing CKM applications

Customer-Facing CKM Applications	
Application	**Description**
Call Center	E-call centers support marketing, sales, and service and implement tele/e-marketing, sales, and service functions. E-marketing is usually an outbound activity- when e-marketing representatives contact customers. E-service is typically an *inbound activity* — when customers contact support centers and communicate with customer support representatives. E-sales may be either an inbound or outbound activity. E-marketing presents offers to leads, prospects, and customers using predefined scripts. E-sales present product information and quotes to prospects and customers or respond to customer requests with product information and quotes. E-service responds to requests with service instructions found in a knowledge base or with incidents that represent requests for service that cannot be handled through the contact/call center.
Sales Force Automation (SFA)	SFA applications support the selling efforts of sales force, managing leads, prospects, and customers through the sales pipeline.
Field Service Automation (FSA)	FSA applications support the customer service efforts of field service representatives and service managers. These applications manage customer service requests, service orders, service contracts, service schedules, and service calls. They provide planning, scheduling, dispatching, and reporting of field service representatives for service calls.

Source: Adapted from Seybold, P. (2002). An Executive Guide to CRM. Boston, MA: Patricia Seybold Group.

Table 6.2. Description of customer-touching CKM applications

Customer-Touching CKM Applications	
Application	**Description**
Self-Service Customer Support	Self-service customer support applications enable customers to get product support information, create service requests, manage information about them, and manage their orders.
E-Commerce	E-commerce applications implement marketing, sales, and service functions through online touch-points, most typically the Web. These applications enable sellers to market products through online catalogs and associated Web content. They let customers shop for products through a virtual shopping cart metaphor and purchase the products in their shopping carts through a virtual check-out metaphor. Customers may also perform self-service support tasks such as order status and history inquiry, return processing, and customer information management.
Campaign Management	Campaign management applications automate marketing campaigns. They present offers to targeted leads, prospects, and customers on demand, on a schedule, or in response to business events through direct mail, e-mail, contact centers, field sales, and Web touch-points. Ideally, these applications are able to record responses to offers.

Source: Adapted from Seybold, P. (2002). An Executive Guide to CRM. Boston, MA: Patricia Seybold Group.

Customer data are gathered and analyzed through interactions with customer-facing processes, i.e. contact/call center, sales force automation (SFA), and field service automation. These interactions take place through a variety of customer-touching applications, i.e. campaign management, e-commerce, and self-service customer support. In order to create a truly customer-focused enterprise, and avoid creating a partial view of customers, a corporate-wide DW is needed.

Customer-Centric Intelligence Applications - Data Warehousing

Customer-intelligence applications include three parts that represent three levels: a) data warehousing, b) reporting, and c) analytics. The DW is discussed in this section as it directly feeds customer data into customer-centric intelligence applications, viz. customer reporting and analytics that will be discussed in Chapters VII and VIII respectively.

The DW is the engine of CKM. DW is a subject oriented, time-variant, nonvolatile collection of data that provide the input to customer-centric intelligence applications (*reporting* and *analytics*) and support management decision processes (Inmon, 1996; Seybold, 2002). The objective of DW (Turban et al., 2006) is, specifically, to create a *repository* of historical data, subject-oriented and organized, summarized, and integrated from various sources so as to be easily accessed and manipulated for decision support. DW holds aggregated, tiny, and historical data for management separate from the databases used for On-Line Transaction Processing (OLTP). A data mart represents a scaled down version of the DW in terms of the volume of data stored and the number of users. It is customized and/or summarized data that is derived from the DW and tailored to the specific analytical requirements of a specific business function or process (Imhoff et al., 2001).

DWs have become an important strategic system in organizations to enable on-line analytical processing (OLAP). Their development is a consequence of the observation that operational-level OLTP and decision support applications OLAP cannot coexist efficiently in the same database environment, mostly due to their very different transaction characteristics. Many of the OLAP applications have standard queries that run periodically, (e.g. total product sales by market segment, by sales channel or by sales representative). These "ready-made" reports are easily created ahead of time and run on a regular schedule so that the user simply can view the results rather than having to repeatedly create and run the report every time it is needed.

CRITICAL ISSUES

This section addresses various issues related to the following design choices: type of customer data to be captured, method of data acquisition, data measurement scale, quality of customer data, customer data model, adoption of operational/analytical processing, integration of customer data, and protection of privacy of customer data.

Which Type of Customer Data to Capture?

Following the identification of target customers, CKM may then proceed to the identification of the *right* data that need to be captured from the *right* customers and to address the various issues. Operational and analytical needs typically define the contents of customer data. The content of customer data relates to, and may include, numbers, text, images, audio, and video.

Success in CKM requires choosing the right data that best represent the customer behavior or situation that needs to be analyzed. The best people to decide on the best type of data that are needed are those who interact with customers and those who have to make strategic decisions. A marketing manager might have a particular offer in mind and wants to identify and profile prospective customers that are most likely to respond. He or she might want to know response rates to previous mailings broken down by customer group, the content of those offers, and sales achieved by these mailings. He or she would also want to know the names and addresses of the selected target, their preferred means of communication (Mail, E-mail, Phone), their preferred form of greeting (First Name, Mr., Ms), and the types of successful offers in the past (Buttle, 2004).

In categorizing data contained in a customer database, it is important to recognize that some data - *stable data*, such as birth date or gender - will only need to be gathered once. Following verification, these data can survive in a database over long periods and in many programs. Updates of stable data should be undertaken to correct errors; otherwise, stable data will not need much alteration. In contrast, there are other data-*adaptive data*, such as a person's intended purchase- that will need constant updating. However, in reality, this is not a dichotomous classification, as some data are *relatively* more stable or adaptive than others (Peppers and Rogers, 2004).

Once demographic profiles are combined with recent changes in customer behavior, they can tell a service provider *which* customers are likely to defect to a competitor in the next couple of months; but once demographic profiles are combined with attitudinal data, they can tell *why* customers are likely to defect to other competitors, or *what* might motivate them to stay. However, attitudinal data may not be as useful for analyzing customer acquisition prospects as it is for analyzing existing customer profiles. Attitudes and trends can be inferred from identifying purchasing patterns in order to provide insights into the buyer's possible motives and attitudes.

How to Capture Data from Customers?

Data about customer needs and expectations may be determined through selection of the *right* data collection method. Customer data can be sourced internally or externally. External data may be acquired from suppliers, business partners, franchisees, and other external sources. A significant amount of customer data is captured through internal databases or warehouses, e.g. CKM online operational systems (Figure 6.1). Internal data are the foundation for the DW that represents a "snapshot" or a single consistent state that integrates heterogeneous information sources (databases) and is physically separated from operational systems and usually accessed by a limited number of users. When companies sell through mediators such as distributors and retailers, they may have little information about the demand chain unless they share an online database with their partners.

Customer data may be captured through interviews, surveys, conversations, and DM. As well, customer data may be captured from customer surveys, warranty registration cards, customer service interactions, website responses, focus-group interviews, or other direct interactions with individuals.

For more accurate customer data, it is advisable to include a balanced combination of non-traditional types of data, such as survey data and data about online business activities. Data collected from online activity can improve the quality and accuracy of customer information. A Web mining tool may be used to add a deeper level of insight to customer data analysis. Survey data can add critical attitudinal insights to customer information. Combining multiple types of data gives a more complete picture of customers. Besides, a combination of behavioral and attitudinal data is best for a 360-degree, comprehensive insight of customers. As a lot of customer data may be hidden in text documents, using a text mining tool allows efficient search of these sources and discovery of valuable customer information.

Which Measurement Scale of Customer Data to Adopt?

In acquiring data from customers, it is essential to decide on the *right* scale of data measurement to be used. Customer data measurement refers to the assignment of numbers to objects or events in a systematic manner.

There is a relationship between the level of measurement and the appropriateness of the data analysis method. In choosing a particular data measurement scale in the data acquisition stage, it is important to remember that such a decision should fit the subsequent data analysis stage. The data measuring scale determines the amount of information that is captured, and the way it can be manipulated. Some customer data analysis techniques are appropriate only for certain data measurement scales. When selecting a data analysis method, it is essential to understand how the data to be analyzed were measured, as certain data measurement scales may influence the choice of data acquisition method (e.g. observation, interview, survey).

For example, it is not possible to compute the mean of nominal measurements. However, the appropriateness of statistical analyses involving means for ordinal level data has been controversial. One position is that data must be measured on an interval or a ratio scale for the computation of means and other analytical statistics to be valid. Otherwise, the median can serve as a measure of central tendency when data are ordinal (non-parametric.

How to Decide on Essential Data Quality Characteristics?

Maintaining high quality data about customers is an imperative for today enterprises. Organizations require access to the most current, accurate, and complete view of their customers. The difference between a good query and a bad one is the amount of thought and prior analysis done by the person posing the question, whereas the difference between a good answer and a bad one basically comes from the quality of the data being queried.

Enterprises may posses a substantial amount of customer data, but much of it is locked in functional silos distributed throughout the enterprise. Because there are so many operational systems - each doing its own bit of processing for the corporation, each with its own narrow slice of its corporate data, each with its own way of doing business – it is no wonder that the quality of customer data has become a major point of concern for CKM (Imhoff et al., 2001).

The success or failure of CKM depends heavily on operational systems that supply the required quality characteristics of data to enable firms to understand customers and to design offerings that suit customers. The data that support CKM decision making should satisfy a number of criteria. They should be shareable, transportable, accurate, relevant, timely and secure, and can be remembered through the acronym STARTS. The details of the STARTS desirable data characteristics are as follow (Imhoff et al., 2001):

- *Shareable*: data need to be sharable because several users may require access to the same data at the same time. For example, a profile of customers who have bought annual travel insurance might need to be made available to customer service agents in several geographical locations, simultaneously, as they deal with customer enquiries in response to an advertising campaign.
- *Transportable*: data need to move from storage location to user and need to be made available wherever and whenever users require them. The user might be a customer service representative, a delivery driver en route to pick-up, an independent mortgage consultant, or a salesperson in front of a prospect. Corporations with global supply chain and globally distributed customers face particularly challenging data transportation problems. Electronic customer databases are essential for today's businesses, together with enabling technologies such as data synchronization, wireless communications and web browsers to make the data fully transportable.
- *Accurate*: in the business world it would be very idealistic to have 100 percent data accuracy. However, data accuracy carries a high level of cost. Data are captured, entered, integrated, and analyzed at various stages. Any, or all, of these stages may be a source of inaccuracy. Keystroke mistakes can cause errors at the data entry stage. Inappropriate analytical processes can lead to wrong conclusions. In CKM, data inaccuracy can lead to undue waste in marketing campaigns, inappropriate prospecting by salespeople and generally suboptimal customer experiences. It also erodes trust in the CRM system, thus reducing its prospective use. Therefore, data need to be entered at source rather than second hand; user buy-in needs to be managed; and data-quality processes such as de-duplicating need to be introduced. News agency and book retailer WH Smith attributes high response rates of CRM-enabled direct

marketing to the accuracy of its database. Data accuracy needs to be checked in order to prevent future problems such as the following:

- ° Attribute names and the values they contain do not fit together
- ° Some attributes are missing
- ° Some fields are blanks
- ° Duplicate data
- ° Data errors (e.g., customers shown to have churned?? before they even became customers)
- ° Invalid data

- *Relevant*: data need to be pertinent for a given purpose. To check customers' credit worthiness, their transaction and payment histories are needed, as well as current employment and income status. To flag customers who are hot prospects for a cross-selling campaign, their propensity-to-buy scores are needed. In designing a data management system to support a CRM strategy, it is necessary to know what decisions will be made and what information is needed to enable them to be made well.
- *Timely:* data are timely when they are available as and when needed. Data that are retrieved after decisions have been made are unhelpful. Besides, decision-makers do not want to be burdened with data before the need is felt. For example, bank tellers need to have propensity-to-buy information of a customer available to them at the time a customer is being served.
- S*ecure:* data security is a hugely important issue for most companies as data about customers is a major resource and a source of competitive advantage. Companies need to protect their data against loss, sabotage, and theft. Many companies regularly back up their data. Security is enhanced through physical and electronic barriers such as firewalls. Managing data security in a partner- or supply-chain environment is particularly challenging.

How to Design a Suitable Customer Data Model?

In CKM, the goal of CRM is to provide the best possible experiences for customers whenever and wherever they interact with the firm different contact points, e.g. call center, the Web, e-mail, etc. The best customer experiences result in the most satisfied and loyal customers, which in turn result in repeated and expanded purchases. It is essential absolutely to know customers in order to provide better products and/or services and create better and more profitable relationships with them. For such a purpose, it is becoming inevitable to develop better customer data models for better CRM systems to create better knowledge about customers.

After developing a plan to gather customer data and addressing various issues related to data acquisition, the enterprise then decides how to design a customer database model. A relational database management system (RDBMS) model presents a logical representation of the information that an application processes. Data models for CRM, ERP, and supply chain applications represent the business entities involved in the processing that these applications perform. For example, a data model of a supply chain application may represent entities such as catalogs, products, purchase orders, invoices, and shipping notices.

Most significantly, the data models for CRM, ERP, and supply chain applications represent customers. The customer data model is the architectural key to customer-centric organizations driven primarily by customers, not by internal processes and requirements (Seybold, 2002). The customer database model is subject to normalization process, which includes creating tables and establishing relationships between those tables according to rules designed both to protect the data and to make the database more flexible by eliminating data redundancy and inconsistency.

With the advancement of CRM applications, much of this design work has been done by the software vendors. Although it is likely that a generic CRM application will have all the information required for a specific company's CRM efforts, the availability of industry-specific applications, with their corresponding industry-specific data models, allows for a much closer fit. The database design process for both operational and analytical CRM applications becomes one of the implementing exceptions that have been overlooked by the generic industry model. Some CRM vendors have also designed the extract, transform and load processes to move metadata from OLTP to OLAP databases. In designing CRM systems, metadata describes customer data in each table, index, and view and their relationships with firms. All the metadata needed to get the data into a data staging area should be listed and prepared for loading into one or more data marts.

To use customer data effectively, it is usually necessary to assign unique and reliable customer identifiers to each individual, (e.g. customer ID number, phone number, or a "username"). There are four key features of a customer data model that are believed to make a "better" customer data model: richness, openness, flexibility, and consistency (Seybold, 2002):

- *Richness:* Richness refers to the breadth and depth of that information in representing every possible aspect of customers' identities, their business relationships and transactions, and the marketing, sales, and service interactions. The richness of a customer data model is mirrored by equivalently rich functionality, and functional richness is one of the major reasons that a particular CRM product or suite is selected. Also, the more that is predefined, the less that has to be modified or extended, and the easier it may be to integrate and synchronize customer information with existing applications. Details of the important characteristics of customer data model richness are provided in Table 6.3.

- *Openness:* The customer data model should be made available to CRM power users. CRM managers and developers may study its design in order to facilitate customization and integration (Seybold, 2002).

- *Flexibility:* Firms need to be able to modify and extend the customer data model in order to address their business requirements. They should reflect the customer data models of other operational applications as they are integrated

Table 6.3. Key characteristics of richness of customer data model

Identification	Identification data/information may include name, address, company, company organization person contact for B2B, household and household relationships for B2C, preferences, and demographics for B2C.
Relationship	Relationship data/information represents the terms and conditions of any ongoing business between a company and its customers. For B2B relationships, this information represents the contracts between companies and customers. Contracts have product, price, quality of service, and payment terms. They are associated with a customer's organizational entity, and they have identification, role, and authority information for contacts and administrators (different than identification contacts). For B2C relationships, this information might represent warranties or service contracts that include product, price, and quality-of-service terms, as well as contact identification information.
Marketing	Marketing data/information should include customer value, customer profitability, the segments to which a customer belongs, and scores and indicators for loyalty, satisfaction, recency, frequency, and wallet share. It should also include a history of all the campaign offers that have been made to the customer and the customer's responses to those offers.
Sales	Sales data/information should include the quotes and proposals that have been made to customers and the orders that customers have placed. It may include complete quote, proposal, and order histories, all quote, proposal, and order details, and an indication of the touchpoint with relevant touchpoint information such as the sales representative through which each quote, proposal, and order was placed.
Service	Service data/information represents customers' requests and the firm's responses for product support and service, order management actions such as returns and complaints, and customer management actions such as identification information changes. This data/information may include outstanding requests and their priority, the histories and details of these interactions, the touchpoints through which they occurred, and identification information of relevant personnel.

Source: Adapted from Seybold, P. (2002). An Executive's Guide to CRM. Boston, MA: Patricia Seybold Group.

with new CRM products, in order to provide a consistent customer experience across all touchpoints and business processes (Seybold, 2002).

•   *Consistency:* For operational CRM applications, the customer data model and the values of its attributes must be accessible consistently across all the customer touchpoints and across all CRM applications. The aim here is to treat customers the same way no matter how they decide to interact with a firm (Seybold, 2002).

How to Much of Operational vs. Analytical Processing to Adopt?

Xu & Walton (2005) conducted a four-year survey of CRM applications in the UK and an evaluation of CRM analytical functions provided by 20 leading software vendors. They found out that some 40 per cent of the CRM systems offer analytical functions, and Forty-five per cent of the CRM vendors evaluated provide e-CRM solutions. The e-CRM systems allow internal and external users to access customer-related information via the internet or intranet, and also to enable e-commerce functionality.

The main driving force of the implementation of CRM systems appears to be improving operational efficiency, rather than acquiring strategic customer information from the systems. Many implemented CRM systems are aimed at improving operational, rather than analytical, functions of CRM systems. The operational efficiency in dealing with customer enquiries could result in improved customer satisfaction. However, gaining CK from CRM systems and providing strategically important customer information to other departments are not perceived as important as improving operational efficiency (Xu & Walton, 2005).

The operational CRM applications, e.g. contact management, call centre, sales, and service support applications, implemented by many companies outnumber analytical applications with limited CK gained from the current CRM application. Even analytical CRM in most cases are made up of a number of discrete pieces of technologies that need to work together to provide actionable information about customers (Xu & Walton, 2005). The analytical power of CRM needs to be adequately utilized by companies and need not to be limited to some large organizations. There is a need also to have "pure play" analytics vendors to provide analytical CRM solutions.

How to Integrate Data from Customers?

One of the most important challenges that face CKM nowadays and in the future is the managing integrated channel across various customer touchpoints and databases. A front office in needs to integrate sales, marketing, and service processes and data across media (call centers, people, stores, Web). Customer data integration across corporate databases is the prerequisite for developing a single view of the customer regardless of data source or format. As corporations typically have older mainframe legacy systems (e.g., production, sales, marketing, and service) - each doing its own bit of processing, each with its own narrow slice of customer data, each with its own way of doing business - it is not unusual that data-quality problems exist. Integration of customer data from legacy systems that are typically batch processing systems, with newer real-time systems that are real-time, is cumbersome, time-consuming, expensive, and is creating many challenges in data cleansing and loading into operational data stores and the DW.

Merging available information about customers into a single coherent view is the domain of technology. There are a number of approaches to deliver Customer Data Integration (CDI), ranging from Enterprise Application Integration (EAI), which delivers process level integration, to Enterprise Information Integration (EII) or virtual data federation which leaves customer data in place, but distributes queries across all the data sources.

Customer-centric firms treat the integration process of channel and media as a strategic issue in building endurable relationships with customers. Customer-centric businesses establish a channel and media framework that manages the customer's experience at each point of contact. They improve media quality within the existing channel structure, extend media to improve the customer experience, reduce costs, and attract new customers, and design a well-integrated multi-channel, multi-media strategy to innovate in the marketplace and create a new customer value offering (Knox et al., 2003).

Although integration of customer data is a complex and time-consuming task, it is critical to information extraction. Integration is one of the most difficult tasks that companies face in implementing CRM systems. There are many integration technologies and products available. Integration is becoming easier as more companies recognize the business benefits of responsive customer service and supply chain management.

In addition, customer data models need to interface well with other tools. Users of the operational CRM, as an example, need to interface easily with business intelligence tools or desktop tools such as word processing, spreadsheet, and presentation tools.

How to Protect Privacy of Customer Data?

Privacy refers to how personal information of customers is being collected, used, and protected. The enormous capabilities of ICT to store and retrieve data have amplified the need to protect privacy. Customer data privacy is one of the sensitive issues that need to be addressed by businesses. Access to customer data should be controlled very carefully. Firms may design schemes that provide role-based access with privilege levels that control the operations that can be performed within roles.

The electronic world is introducing a new dimension to the problem of privacy. Prior to e-commerce, computer systems mimicked business practices in the physical world. With or without computers, businesses have been able to sell their lists of customers to a third party. Computers make the process more efficient. In web-based advertising, for example, it is possible to track messages and content of messages that have been seen, or responded to by a particular individual, as well as purchases made (Berry and Linoff, 2000).

Customers should have the appropriate roles and privileges to access the data that firms manage about them. They should even be able to update and delete some of their data. Potential privacy challenges require organizations to define precisely privacy data elements for the retail industry. To protect individual privacy, several important pieces of legislation have been passed dealing with the following issues:

- There must be no personal-data recordkeeping system which is a secret.
- There must be a way for people to prevent access to information about themselves.
- People must be able to correct or amend information.
- There should be no misuse of data.

RECOMMENDED SOLUTION: A PROPOSED CUSTOMER-CENTRIC INTELLIGENCE ARCHITECTURE

Proposed DW-based customer-centric intelligence architecture, customized for telecommunications industry, is shown in Figure 6.1. The architecture is enabled by three solutions: operational CRM, DW, and analytical CRM (Al-Shammari, 2005). Collaborative CRM solutions may be used to generate non-transactional human-based tacit CK from business-customer interactions (e.g., through customer discussion groups or forums).

The operational CRM is composed of three layers: a) customer contact/interaction channels such as Integrated Voice Recognition (IVR) and e-commerce (EC), b) customer-facing departments, i.e., marketing, sales, and services, and c) front-office operational data store (FODS) systems.

The FODSs are as follows:

Figure 6.1. A proposed customer-centric intelligence architecture

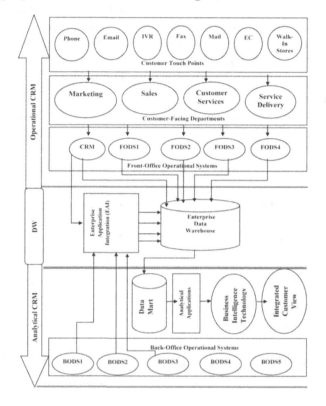

- CRM: Fixed telephone line service provisioning system.
- FODS1: Fixed telephone line billing
- FODS2: Internet protocol billing
- FODS3: Pre-paid mobile telephone line service provisioning
- FODS4: Post-paid mobile telephone line provisioning and billing

The second part of the customer-centric intelligence architecture is the DW. Incoming transactional data from all FODS systems as well as many BODS systems feed into the DW. The DW extracts data from operational databases, viz. sales, service, and marketing systems, transforms the data into a form acceptable for the DW, cleans the data to remove errors, inconsistencies, and redundancies, and loads the data into the DW.

The third part in the proposed architecture is the analytical CRM (the business intelligence technology). The analytical tools are the back office applications for CRM as they operate behind the scene are completely invisible to users and customers. In addition, there is an EAI layer to address the problem of diverse customer data sources and platforms. It integrates the front office CRM provisioning system with the three back-office operational data store (BODS) billing systems, viz. BODS1, BODS2, and BODS3, which then feed into the DW. While all FODS applications feed data into the DW, only three out of five major BODS applications feed into the DW.

The main BODSs are as follows:

- BODS1: GIS (a billing system integrated with the DW)
- BODS2: Mediated billing for fixed telephone lines (integrated with the DW)
- BODS3: BO billing gateway for mobile telephone lines (integrated with the DW)
- BODS4: ERP system
- BODS5: Human Resource Management System (HRMS)

FUTURE TRENDS

Future trends in customer data acquisition include a shift from static to dynamic customer data management, a shift from functional to integrated data management, and a shift from relational databases to data marts and DWs.

A Shift from Static to Dynamic Customer Data Management

More and more business drivers will depend on accurate, consistent and accessible information to understand customers through dynamic enterprise-wide, integrated systems - the days of static information are over. To compete effectively in a rapidly changing, regulatory, competitive and internal business landscape, management increasingly will demand near real-time views of their organizations, no longer willing to rely on inflexible reports that force them to view their businesses in the context of their data rather than in the context of their businesses. Companies that rely on rigid information infrastructures will need to develop a more active information environment, or they will find themselves quickly overtaken by competitors. Cost competitive and flexible data acquisition systems, supported by "point-and-click" systems, are expected to flourish in the near future.

A Shift from Functional to Integrated Data Management

Companies are demanding enterprise-wide, integrated solutions, i.e., ERP, and these demands are expected to continue to grow in the future. They look for hardware and software solutions that are built on standard and open architecture, and that speed up data collection, analysis, reporting and archiving while reducing the cost. The trend in the future is to have a greater demand for such superior customer data management hardware and software solutions coupled with well-designed customer services. Customer call centers will undergo a great change and move away from the factory sweatshop image to a more service-oriented culture. There will be an accelerated convergence of structured and unstructured data management software tools into more flexible, service-oriented environments.

A Shift from Relational Databases to Data Marts and Warehouses

Relational databases are used by businesses on computer systems of all sizes and types. However, more companies are expected to add the DW as a repository of data coming from operational legacy systems as well as other newer online systems. At a lower level of use, a small scale version of DW, known as a data mart, is likely to flourish in small and medium-sized enterprises.

CONCLUSION

Consumer's power, knowledge, and changing preferences are increasingly becoming major drivers for organizational transformation in today's turbulent business environments. Old-fashioned, command-and-control companies have no place in today's competitive business world. A critical prerequisite for success in a digital economy is the implementation of an integrated, knowledge-based, customer-led value chain that extends across - and beyond - the enterprise. Knowledge has been recently utilized by leading organizations as the main tool to face globalization, competitive environments, and changing customers' preferences. Increasingly, CK, in particular, is becoming a principal resource for organizational customer-centricity.

In CKM strategic change, CK is used as a DCC base for achieving SCA. Although there is a blurred line that distinguishes the concepts of data, information, and knowledge from each other, however, data is viewed here as the raw material for information which is the raw material for the knowledge environment. The data may be hard facts or soft opinions, history of past events, situational evaluations, situations to avoid, alternatives to pursue, and so on, but they are still stored as data in context. Information is data in context that is being stored to support information sharing. While formal definitions of 'information' and 'knowledge' remain messy, many observers make the distinction that information is data that has been given structure and knowledge is information that has been given meaning.

DW is used to collect, clean, and store customer data for later analysis. Customer data are the most private and sensitive data that a firm gathers and manages in order to draw conclusions about historical customer behavior patterns to segment customers, and to make predictions about future purchase trends. Therefore, having good data is the number one prerequisite for CKM.

This section of the book discussed the process of capitalizing CKM value chains through acquisition of customer data, composition of customer profiles, and the creation of CK. The data acquisition process involves extracting data from the operational environment, integrating it with data from other systems, and transforming it into information and knowledge. These activities are also part of a longer set of primary value chain activities, i.e. maximizing value for customers, measuring value of customers, and managing and learning from change.

The CKM initiative is a combination of business processes, strategies, and technological solutions used to understand the "customer's lifetime value" in order to differentiate competitively products and services.

The objective of the CKM systems is to enable the exploitation of CK at both operational and analytical levels. The operational day-to-day level includes capturing of customer interactions by the front-end's units such as call centers and customer care, and allowing identification of customers and creating customer segmentation. CKM intends to respond to customers' priorities and to be able to answer customers promptly and efficiently, giving the agent dealing with them on-line information about their identity, spending, products and services requested, and needs. Everything that customers ask about on-line is captured into the analytical side straight away and is used for customer segmentation and profiling.

Additionally, companies need to address the various issues related to several design choices throughout the customer data acquisition process, viz. types of customer data, methods of data acquisition, data measurement scales, volume of customer data, characteristics of customer data, customer data model, customer data integration, and protection of data privacy.

REFERENCES

Al-Shammari, M. (2005). Implementing a knowledge-enabled CRM strategy in a large company: A case study from a developing country. In M. E. Jennex (Ed.), *Case studies in knowledge management* (pp. 249-278). Hershey, PA: Idea Group Publishing.

Awad, E., & Ghaziri, H. (2004). *Knowledge management*. Upper Saddle River, NJ: Prentice-Hall.

Bellinger, G., Castro, D., & Mills, A. (2004). Data, information, knowledge, and wisdom. Available at *http://www.systems-thinking.org/dikw/dikw.ht* (Retrieved on November 14, 2007).

Berry, M., & Linoff, G. (2000). *Mastering data mining: The art and science of customer relationship management*. New York: Wiley.

Brackett, M. H. (1999). Business intelligence value chain. *DM Review Magazine*, March. http://www.dmreview.com/issues/19990301/115-1.html (retrieved on 17 January 2008).

Camerer, C. F., & Johnson, E. J. (1991). The process-performance paradox in expert judgment. In K. A. Ericson, & J. Smith, J. (Eds). *Toward a general theory of expertise* (pp. 195-217), Cambridge, U.K: Cambridge University Press.

Choo, C. W., Detlor, B., & Turnbull, D. (2000). *Webwork: Information seeking and knowledge work on the World Wide Web*. Kluwer Academic Publishers, Dordrecht.

Customer. (2007). In *Wikipedia, The Free Encyclopedia*. Retrieved October 6, 2007, from http://en.wikipedia.org/wiki/Customer.

Davenport, T., & Prusak, L. (2000). *Working knowledge*. 2nd edition, Boston, MA: Harvard Business School Press.

Dubin, R. (1978). Theory building in applied areas. In M. D. Dunnette (Ed.), *Handbook of industrial and organizational psychology* (pp. 17-39). New York, NY: Wiley.

Gebert, H., Geib, M., Kolbe, L., & Brenner, W. (2003). Knowledge-enabled customer relationship management and knowledge management concepts. *Journal of Knowledge Management*, 7(5), 107-123.

Gore, C., & Gore, E. (1999). Knowledge management: the way forward. *Total Quality Management*, 10(4/5), 554-60.

Gray, P., & Watson, H. J. (1998). *Decision support in the data warehouse*. Upper Saddle River, NJ: Prentice Hall.

Imhoff, C., Loftis, L., & Geiger, J. (2001). *Building the customer-centric enterprise: Data warehousing techniques for supporting customer relationship management.* New York: Wiley.

Inmon, W. H. (1996). *Building the data warehouse.* 2nd ed., New York: Wiley.

Knox, S., Maklan, S., Payne, A., Peppard, J., & Ryals, L. (2003). *Customer relationship management: Perspectives from the marketplace.* Oxford, UK: Butterworth-Heinemann.

Love, B. (1996). Strategic DSS/data warehouse: A case study in failure. *Journal of Data Warehousing, 1*(1), 36-40.

Nonaka, I., & Takeuchi, H. (1995). *The knowledge-creating company: How Japanese companies create the dynamics of innovation.* Oxford University Press, New York, NY.

Park, C., & Kim, Y. (2003). A framework of dynamic CRM: Linking marketing with information strategy. *Business Process Management Journal, 9*(5), 652-671.

Pearlson, K., & Saunders, C. (2006). *Managing and using information systems: A strategic approach.* New Jersey: John Wiley.

Peppers, D., & Rogers, M. (2004). *Managing customer relationships: A strategic framework.* Hoboken, NJ: John Wiley.

Reed, K. L., & Berry, J. K. (1999). Customer loyalty, competition analysis, propensity to defect and ad media selection. Presented at the *GIS'99 Conference*, Vancouver, British Columbia, March 1-4. *http://www.innovativegis.com/basis/Papers/Other/Retail/Where.htm* (retrieved on November 12, 2007).

Rowley, J. (2002). Eight questions for customer knowledge management in E-Business. *Journal of Knowledge Management, 6*(5), 500-511.

Seybold, P. (2002). *An Executive guide to CRM.* Boston, MA: Patricia Seybold Group.

Sharma, N. (2005). The origin of the "data information knowledge wisdom" hierarchy. http://www-personal.si.umich.edu/~nsharma/dikw_origin.htm.

Turban, E., Leidner, D., McLean, E., & Wetherbe, J. (2006). *Information technology for Management: Transforming organizations in the digital economy.* 5th edition, New York: John Wiley.

Xu, M., & Walton, J. (2005). Gaining customer knowledge through analytical CRM. *Industrial Management & Data Systems, 105*(7), 955-971.

Chapter VII
Compiling Profiles of Customers

INTRODUCTION

Whether companies are engaged in B2B or B2C transactions, they need to understand their customers. Once customer data are captured and stored in ODSs or DWs, they are then subject to further customer-centric intelligence processing in a manner that facilitates the execution of complex query performance and the competition on 'analytics' (Davenport, 2006). It is certainly not true that companies with the most data always win; the success lies in processing the existing data to learn about trends and attitudes of customers. This chapter, as well as the coming chapter, discusses the strategic, or analytical, side of CKM. The term 'analytical CKM' is used in this book to refer to both information and knowledge discovery tools. The views presented in this chapter are from the 'information management' perspective, whereas the coming chapter adopts a 'knowledge management' perspective.

CONCEPTUAL FOUNDATIONS

The new millennium has witnessed several turbulent and discontinuous environmental changes on one hand, and a proliferation of information/knowledge seeking organizations on the other, in the search for achieving SCA. This section provides discussion of the role of customers in the new economy, the concept of 'customer information', customer-centric information discovery process and systems, and an example of setting customer profiling and up-selling rules.

The Information Age: All Power to the Customer

National economies are engaged in a competition for a larger share of global markets and economic wealth. In the 21st century, the information age, the wealth of nations depends on how well a society can organize information and knowledge. The national wealth of an information-based economy will depend upon the *efficiency* and *effectiveness* of information workers and strategic utilization of ICT systems.

The increasing demand of customers for higher quality, innovative, and customized products and services puts companies under pressure. Effective design and development of CKM enable organizations to 'do right things right' by leveraging DCCs, investing heavily in CK to understand customers better, and by adding value for specific segments of customers in the search for achieving SCA. Discovering best-target customers requires extensive, comprehensive, and reliable customer-profile information to customize effectively marketing programs. Planning and implementing a particular campaign for one segment of customers, or a specific customer, requires understanding of the demographic characteristics, lifestyle behaviors, product preferences, and channel preferences that drive their buying decisions. Customer-profile information helps companies find new customers for their businesses by extracting prospective customers that match the profile for current customers, and who are more inclined to buy certain products or services.

The Concept of 'Customer Information'

Compiling profiles for customers takes place by converting customer data into customer information. Information is a descriptive entity that relates to past and present events (Camerer and Johnson, 1991; Dubin, 1996). It is a set of data in context that is relevant to one or more entities at a particular point in time or for a period of time. Information is data in context with respect to giving meaning to facts. It is data filled with meaning, relevance and purpose. A set of data in context is a message that only becomes information when one or more persons are ready to accept that message as relevant to their needs (Brackett, 1999).

Customer information may represent the number of residential or business customers (age groups, living areas, etc.); products which may represent the number of mobile or fixed telephone lines; traffic that may relate to the usage behavior of customers (in terms of volume, duration, and time of calls per each category of customers, products, age groups, or living areas); or revenue that may refer to the amount of money generated per category by customers, products, age groups, or living areas.

Information refers to data, plus meaning and understanding of patterns and relationships that take place through the following five major functions (5Cs) identified by Awad and Ghaziri (2004):

- Condensation: summarizing in more concise form and unnecessary depth is eliminated.
- Contextualization: knowing why the data were collected.
- Calculation: analyzing data.
- Categorization: grouping of data; the unit of analysis is known, such as customer value.
- Correction: errors have been removed.

Customer-Centric Information Discovery Process and Systems

Customer-centric data analysis techniques involve a set of predetermined activities that are performed to capture data *from* customers, profile customers, and predict behavior of customers (knowledge). In Chapter 6, the ICT applications for capturing customer data (i.e. customer-facing applications, customer-touching applications, and the first component of the customer-centric intelligence application, viz. data warehousing), have been discussed. In this chapter, the customer-centric, information/reporting applications will be discussed, whereas the customer-centric, knowledge-based applications will be discussed in Chapter 8. Information discovery is viewed in this chapter as a step in information management process. Information management is responsible for managing activities related to collection, processing, storing, and analyzing data and disseminating information to achieve business goals.

CRM implements the marketing, sales, and service business processes - the customer-facing and customer-touching business processes through which companies interact with their customers. Customer-facing and customer-touching applications are operational CRM applications responsible for acquisition of data from customers. Operational CRM automates horizontally integrated business processes and involves interactions with customers via multiple, interconnected delivery channels of scattered front-office customer touch points across sales, marketing, and customer service. Also, it focuses on the software installations, and the changes in process affecting the day-to-day operations of a firm (Peppers and Rogers, 2004). The *operational* day-to-day side activities involve online capturing of customer interactions by the front-end units such as call centers and customer care.

Typically, operational CRM has the potential to respond to customers' priorities in terms of their value and to be able to answer customers promptly and efficiently and to feed at the in-bound and outbound directions into the DW (bi-directional).

To do so, the agent dealing with them would have online information about their identities, spending, products and/or services, and needs. On the other hand, anything customers ask online would be captured into the marketing side straight away by the front-end units such as call centers and customer care, and would be used for customer segmentation and profiling by the reporting CKM.

Customer-centric, analytic applications aim at the discovery of customer information and knowledge. Customer-centric, reporting applications aim at the generating customer information, whereas the customer-centric intelligent applications generate knowledge when they receive data from DW or ERP, and generate knowledge through analytical and collaborative activities (Buttle, 2004; Peppers and Rogers, 2004; and Turban et al., 2008). Both information and knowledge discovery applications depend on DWs for input about marketing, sales, and service initiatives. In fact, information discovery tools often use several different types of data from several types of sources, each of which give additional insight (e.g. transactional databases, web data, survey data, textual documents, and online activity). Therefore, in order to secure successful and accurate results, information discovery tools need to integrate well with different types of data from multiple sources without costly, time-consuming customization.

The major types of DW techniques that support analytical CRM are ad hoc querying and reporting (AQR), online analytical processing (OLAP), and data mining (DM) (Imhoff, 2001; Seybold, 2002; Buttle, 2004; and Turban et al., 2004):

- *AQR:* The AQR represents an *ad hoc* exploration data mart whose purpose is to provide information for an exploratory report based on specified characteristics or properties. Analysts can develop hypotheses quickly from their ad hoc processing. Reports provide a range of tabular and graphical presentation formats and allow analysts to interact with the report presentation, changing its visual format, drilling up into summary information and/or drilling down into detail (Seybold, 2002).
- *OLAP:* The OLAP data mart contains data that are customized and reformatted to support *predetermined*, multi-dimensional analytic requirements of a given business unit or function. Multi-dimensional requirements include the ability to "slice and dice" data to drill up, down, and around predefined cubes of data (Babcock, 1995). OLAP marts can also be used for managed or repetitive queries.
- *DM:* DM analyzes large quantities of data and discovers hidden patterns and relationships in order to help managers make decisions related to their customers, and uses tools such as NN and CBR. The DM is a third type of data mart created so analysts can test or prove their hypotheses, assertions, and assumptions developed in the exploration warehouse.

DM is a high level analytical process that differs from data management. Data management is viewed in this book as a low level operational process responsible for collection and organization of stored data items for easy access, retrieval, and manipulation for information and knowledge management support. DM performs both information and knowledge discovery analytics and can be used for market segmentation and customer valuation purposes. DM is used in this book as a step in both information and knowledge discovery processes.

Two new technologies of mining, text mining and web mining, represent a new layer of 'qualitative' mining of 'unstructured' data rather than 'numerical' or 'quantitative' mining of 'structured' data. Text mining is concerned with data in a text or other non-numerical format. Web mining is the process of analyzing data from online activities - including pay-per-click advertising and other marketing campaigns - to discover relevant patterns and important behavioral insights. Both types of 'unstructured' or 'non-numerical' DM provide valuable breadth and depth about opinions and preferences of customers that could help to explain customer behaviors and actions. Combining unstructured and structured data in DM projects can help business produce more accurate valuable CK.

The process of DM is concerned with extracting patterns from the data by using techniques such as classification, segmentation, regression, and association (Turban et al., 2004).

- Classification. Infers the defining characteristics of a certain group and identifies the group to which an object belongs based on examining characteristics of the object. The groups are defined by an external criterion (contrast with clustering).
- Clustering. Identifies groups of items that share a particular characteristic. It groups records based on similarity. For example, an insurance company might use clustering to group customers according to income, age, type of policy purchased, or prior claims' history. Clustering divides a dataset so that records with similar content are in the same group, and groups are as different as possible from each other (contrast with classification). Clustering differs from classification in that no predefining characteristic is given.

  ○ Forecasting. Estimates future values based on patterns within large sets of data.
  ○ Regression. Maps a data item to a prediction variable.
  ○ Time Series analysis examines a value as it varies over time.

Though AQR and OLAP enables managers to learn about what is happening and what happened previously with past data, they cannot predict what will happen in the future as much as DM. DM allows users to feed certain business rules for certain customer groups into the operational side of CRM applications, as well as predict future trends and behaviors and discover previously unknown patterns. OLAP of DW data for back-end marketing management activities, such as campaign management, churn analysis, propensity analysis, and customer profitability analysis provides power users with sales cube view of their past records of customers through pivot tables, drilling down, *slicing,* and *dicing* (Babcock, 1995).

Churn analysis evaluates the attrition or turnover behavior of customers when they defect to a competitor, whereas propensity analysis assesses the degree to which a particular customer is likely to buy a product, repay a loan, or display any particular behavior with a commercial value. A customer profitability analysis identifies valuable existing customers that disproportionately contribute to business profitability and deserve to receive focused attention. Identification of this group may help to expand profitability through cross-selling and up-selling. Companies may obtain demographics of profitable customers from ODS, DWs, and OLAP to identify other customers with similar characteristics that are not contributing equally to their profitability. That information can be used to tailor a marketing campaign to this segment of customers as well as to manage that campaign.

An Example of Setting Customer Profiling and Up-Selling Rules

In order to illustrate some of the concepts discussed in this chapter as well as the previous one, this section provides a simple example of setting customer profile and up-selling rules (Figures 7.1, 7.2, 7.3, and 7.4) from the Open Source Business Rules Management System (OpenRules, Inc.).

CRITICAL ISSUES

In turbulent, global, and competitive customer-centric business environments, companies seek to leverage their knowledge-based DCCs, e.g. customer profiling, in order to provide offerings that maximize the experience of customers and value of companies, and to achieve SCA. The customer profiling process faces several issues, challenges, and decision points that need to be addressed: deciding on strategic competition based on information versus knowledge, deciding on information volume versus information value, deciding on information richness

Figure 7.1. Initial customer data

First Name	John	Mary
Middle Initial	D.	K.
Last Name	Smith	Smith
Age	28	25
Customer From Date	10/15/1998	3/10/2002
State	NJ	NJ
Products	Checking Account	Checking Account
	Saving Account	
Combined Balance	$12,000.0	$10,000.0
Customer Profile	?	?

Source: http://openrules.com/examples.htm, retrieved on July 26th, 2008.

Figure 7.2. Set new customer profile

Combined Balance Min	$0.00	$500.0	$2,000.0	$5,000.0	$15,000.0
Combined Balance Max	$500.00	$2,000.0	$5,000.0	$15,000.0	$10,000,000.0
Set Profile	New	Bronze	Silver	Gold	Platinum

Source: http://openrules.com/examples.htm, retrieved on July 26th, 2008.

Figure 7.3. Upgrade old customer profile

IF a Customer from this Date or Earlier	1/1/2000	1/1/2000	1/1/2000	1/1/2000	1/1/2000
AND Customer Profile is	New	Bronze	Silver	Gold	New
THEN Set Profile	Bronze	Silver	Gold	Platinum	Bronze

Source: http://openrules.com/examples.htm, retrieved on July 26th, 2008.

Figure 7.4. Set up-selling rules

If Customer Profile is	New	New	New	Gold	Platinum
	Bronze	Bronze	Bronze		
	Silver	Silver	Silver		
And Customer Already has Products	Checking Account	Checking Account	Checking Account	Checking Account	Checking Account
		Overdraft Protection	Saving Account		Saving Account
But Does NOT have Products	Saving Account	CD with 25 basis point increase	CD with 25 basis point increase	CD with 50 basis point increase	CD with 50 basis point increase
		Money Market Mutual Fund	Money Market Mutual Fund	Money Market Mutual Fund	Money Market Mutual Fund
		Credit Card	Credit Card	Web Banking	Web Banking
Offered Products	Saving Account	CD with 25 basis point increase	CD with 50 basis point increase	CD with 50 basis point increase	CD with 50 basis point increase
	Debit/ATM Card	Money Market Mutual Fund	Money Market Mutual Fund	Money Market Mutual Fund	Money Market Mutual Fund
	Web Banking	Credit Card	Credit Card	Credit Card	Credit Card with no annual fee
			Debit/ATM Card	Debit/ATM Card	Debit/ATM Card
			Web Banking	Web Banking	Web Banking with no charge
				Brokerage Account	Brokerage Account
Set Comment				Gold Package	Platinum Package

Source: http://openrules.com/examples.htm, accessed on July 26th, 2008.

versus information reach, selecting data analysis technique(s), and selecting the data analysis application, report, and format.

Strategically Competing on Information vs. Knowledge

Though literature on strategic usage of information and knowledge resources is extensive, there is much confusion concerning the meaning of the terms 'information' and 'knowledge' management.   Davenport (1997) presents an approach that encompasses the company's entire information environment, the management of which he calls information ecology. Information ecology is a revolutionary way to look at information management, one that takes into account the total information environment within an organization. He argues that the information that comes from computer systems may be considerably less valuable to managers than information that flows in from a variety of other sources, such as human information processing.

Davenport (1997) sheds light on the critical components of information ecology, discusses the importance of developing an overall strategy for information use, and explores the political battles and professional jealousy that can hinder sharing of information. To Davenport (1997), the ideal information staff, not only store and retrieve information, but also provide context, enhance style, and choose the right presentation medium, examine how information management should be done on a day-to-day basis and present several alternatives to the structured 'machine-engineering' approach to modeling information.

The information ecology approach does not only consider information handling and/or information behavior of individuals, but also includes an information culture that results from the total information behavior of the organization as a whole. This approach makes synonymous use of information and knowledge assets, as it emphasizes the management of work practices that aim at improving the generation of new, and the sharing of existing, knowledge. Though information can be made tangible and represented as objects outside of the human mind, knowledge, on the other hand, is a much more elusive entity. In particular, the terms knowledge and information are often used interchangeably, even though the two entities are far from identical. The information ecology approach may be expanded to knowledge ecology to make it fit dynamic business environments.

As explained in Chapter 6, this book adopts a hierarchical view, wherein the concepts of data, information, and knowledge are represented by a continuum line with varying degrees. The idea of the continuum line reflects the fact those concepts differ not in terms of their type but in terms of the degree of understanding and connectedness.

Deciding on Volume vs. Value of Information

Companies require data and information to profile customers, create knowledge needed to maximize value of offerings provided to customers, develop long-term relationships with them, and ultimately to expand customer loyalty and profitability. At the ideal level, companies seek to achieve a complete, 360-degree view of the customer. However, in reality, that level is difficult to attain, and therefore companies need to decide on the best available data analysis source, technique, application, and tool that they consider most likely to provide the right information for understanding the right customers.

Relevant, usable, and helpful customer information models, profiles, and formats are needed for profiling the target customers - what are they like, what do they buy, and where and how to conduct business with them. Customer information models are based on connecting various customer segmentation variables. For example, to produce a richer picture of customers, customer purchasing patterns can be combined with customer demographic characteristics to produce a customer behavioral model, e.g. propensity analysis model. By analyzing customers' demographic characteristics (income or age group), lifestyle behaviors, and purchasing preferences, companies can tailor successful offerings to the preferences of customers, with the aim of acquiring new customers, retaining existing customers, and increasing value for existing customers.

In their quest to develop a 360-degree view of customers, business organizations are challenged constantly by the question of how much is the *right* amount of information about customers, products, and contacts for profiling customers. It is not certain that customers universally are willing to provide unlimited amounts of their personal information. Some customers may feel that holding more personal information about them is an invasion of their privacy, which could aggravate negative consequences such as dissatisfaction, churn, or defection to a competitor. The challenge that lies ahead for business organizations is to decide on the 'critical mass' of customer information needed to compete successfully in dynamic business environments, and at the same time, not to violate the privacy of customers.

Given that there is always a trade-off between time, money, and the amount of information, it is worth developing some guidelines for the question of "how much is enough?" Companies need to avoid analyzing a pile of data with no clear business goals in order not to fall into the trap of being 'data rich but information poor.' The business goals, rather than the volume of information, should be the prime factor that drives customer profiling. Having a relevant and sufficient amount of real-time customer information is more important than a large volume of information that does not guarantee the 'critical mass' of information for the right profiling of the right customers.

For some companies, the answer to the question on how much data should be acquired and processed is always 'None.' They choose to operate solely on the basis of qualitative value judgment - i.e., SWOT and PESTIL analyses (Buttle, 2004) or past experience, with no deliberate learning activity. At the other extreme end of the spectrum are companies that want perfect customer information that is too idealistic to be achieved given discontinuous business conditions and dynamic consumer purchasing patterns. The quest for perfect information demands the highest investment of time and money and ignores the law of diminishing returns.

Somewhere in the middle are successful companies whose leaders combine superior business judgment with some measure of information and analysis to create a state of informed intuition (Anderson, 2004).

On a pragmatic level, the 'more is better' or the 'need-to-have', rather than 'nice-to-have', information seems to be a very realistic answer. The more an enterprise knows about a customer than its competitors do not know, the better such an enterprise can personalize customer relationships as well as goods or services. However, it is becoming inevitable to distinguish between 'need-to-have' and 'nice-to-have' customer information; that is, between customer information needed for customer-centric decisions in the short run, and information that might or might not be used for some future point of time.

Deciding on Richness vs. Reach of Information

Informational is the glue that ties elements of the business value chain together. Information transactions have two properties: reach richness and reach. Reach refers to the number of people who share particular information, whereas richness is defined as a complex concept that combines: bandwidth (amount of information transferred in a given time), customization, interactivity (dialogue between the sender and recipient), reliability (when it is circulated among a small group of trusted individuals), security, and currency (up-to-date) (Evans and Wurster, 2000).

Traditionally, organizations have a choice to focus on 'rich' information - customized products and services tailored to a niche audience - or on a 'reach' out to a larger market, but with watered-down information that sacrifices richness in favor of a broad, general appeal. Much of business strategy rests on this fundamental trade-off between richness and reach, e.g. increasing the information reach of consumers, or products/services requires a compromise in the information richness - in general the greater the reach, the less the richness, and vice-versa.

However, Evans and Wurster (2000) argued that with the advent of powerful ICTs, this historic trade-off between richness and reach may no longer be applicable. It is now possible for organizations in the new economy to compete on the benefits of both reach and richness. This change in strategic possibilities has come through greater connectivity through electronic networks and, increasingly, the adherence to standards for transmitting and receiving information in a digital format. Connectivity and standards have led to blowing apart 'deconstruction' of the foundations of traditional business strategy and the 'disintermediation' of traditional intermediaries (Evans and Wurster, 2000).

Increasingly, customers will have rich access to a universe of alternatives, suppliers will exploit direct access to customers, and competitors will pick off the most profitable parts of the value chain. The spread of electronic connectivity and common standards is redefining the information channels that link businesses with their customers, suppliers, and employees. For example, the marketing mix of media channels through which sellers persuade buyers includes newspapers, direct mail or telemarketing, and salespeople. Newspaper advertisements reach a wide range of prospective customers but have a limited, static content. Direct mail or telemarketing are a bit richer in personalization and interactivity but are much more expensive, and therefore have to be targeted. Unlike advertisers, direct marketers give up reach in order to add richness. A salesman offers the highest level of customization, dialogue, and empathy but with only one customer at a time. Therefore, the marketing mix results in the distribution of information channels across a tradeoff between richness and reach. Buyers live with, and adapt to, the same tradeoff. It forces them to search hierarchically and to navigate their way from high reach/low richness media, e.g. the yellow pages, towards high richness/low reach information channels, e.g. the salesman (Evans and Wurster, 2000).

Organizations support richer information exchange among a small number of insiders, whereas markets trade thin information in a wider universe. The boundary of the corporation is thus a point on the tradeoff. Within the organization, hierarchy is shaped by span of control, which reflects a tradeoff between richness and reach in how people collaborate. 'Relationships' among corporations of a particular industry's supply chain or a particular corporation's value chain, as well as with retail customers, 'loyalty' to a product or an employer, and trust of a person or a brand are all the products of rich exchanges of information among people, who by doing so, have narrowed the reach of their options. Financial services businesses, for example, are largely defined by three sets of forces that bundle product offerings together and lock in customer relationships: the economics of common physical delivery, cross-selling on the basis of superior understanding of the customer, and the customer's preference for one-stop shopping and established relationships (because of the high cost of searching, switching and complexity). In short, these businesses are defined by 'department store' economics (Evans and Wurster, 2000).

But the three forces that define financial services are weakened significantly when the richness/reach tradeoff is blown up. Physical delivery of goods becomes irrelevant in a world of home electronic banking. What remains, such as cash dispensing, is done more economically by grocery shops. As the cost of gathering, packaging and reselling information comes closer to zero, the most advantaged owner of information about an individual is the individual. That is, customers can assemble more valuable information about themselves than any other third party, and can profit accordingly.

As well, the costs of searching, switching, and complexity are reduced massively, and are eliminated even for higher value products. As the informational glue melts, competitive advantage in delivering the bundle comes to matter less than the advantage in each of the constituent products and/or services. Advantage rolls down towards the focused player. Navigators, advisors and mono-line product providers are the winners: category killers, not department stores (Evans and Wurster, 2000).

As the digital age entails changes in the way companies are used to doing business, this will make no business model safe from changes. The e-biz model provides new business opportunities as it provides companies tremendous "reach" for customers without sacrificing "richness" or the quality of the information about products and services. Therefore, it is becoming unavoidable for companies to prepare their executives and analysts for a fundamental change in business competition, to show them how to design and build new strategies that reflect a world in which information richness and reach go hand in hand, and initiate processes to make the most of the new forces shaping competitive advantage.

Selecting Data Analysis Technique(s)

Each customer data analysis technique has pros and cons. DM, for example, denotes a targeted-push information discovery strategy that can yield powerful results but without explanatory power. In DM, the company develops a range of products and/or services and tries to infer which customers are likely to find them attractive and which of those would actually purchase. After it defines its segment customers, it pushes the offerings out to customers, and hopes that the targeted customers will accept. Machine-based profiling techniques may be combined with human-based information processing strategy, wherein DM is used to identify prospect customers and try to bring them in, and then try to elicit a signal from them to determine what terms they should be offered. This approach may not be used in large companies that adopt mass customization strategy as the costs of designing customized offerings are simply too high to allow much customization (Clemons, 2000).

As of the interpretive power of data analysis techniques, a complete CRM solution includes collaborative CRM that, once added to operational and analytical CRM techniques, help identify the target customers, differentiate among them and identify the high value, or strategically significant, customers, interact with them, and customize right products and/or services for them, at the right time and through the right channel. More discussion on the collaborative CRM will be provided in Chapter VIII.

One of the simplest ways of segmenting the data is basic cross-tabulation analysis. Respondents can be divided into, say, age or income groups and their differences studied across a variety of questions. This approach of pre-defining the respondent is often referred to as a priori segmentation. Use of a priori segments, while attractive, often is not sufficient, given the need to obtain complex segments based on multiple variables.

One of the simplest ways of segmenting the data is basic cross-tabulation analysis. Respondents can be divided into, say, age or income groups and their differences studied across a variety of questions. This approach of pre-defining the respondent is often referred to as a priori segmentation. Use of a priori segments, while attractive, often is not sufficient, given the need to obtain complex segments based on multiple variables.

While different types of approaches to segmentation analysis have been discussed here, it is not clear that there is one approach that is best in every situation. Segmentation analysis often involves trying more than one method to obtain the best result. The main reason for this is that unlike key driver analysis, segmentation analysis is quite unstructured. The final solution depends on the number and nature of variables included in the analysis. Changing even one variable can have a strong impact on the results. Without seeing the results, however, it is hard to identify the variables that can be useful in the analysis. This type of circular problem implies that the most important step in a segmentation analysis is the choice of variables to use. The more thought we put into selecting the variables, the more likely it is that the results will be useful.

In analyzing customer data, business firms need to decide on the issue of the *right* analysis level, i.e. descriptive or analytical statistics. Descriptive statistics, e.g. frequencies, measures of central tendency (such as mean, median, and mode), and measures of dispersion (such as standard deviation and variance), or analytical statistics such as correlation analysis (e.g., Pearson and Spearman correlations), and trend statistics (e.g., regression analysis) may be considered. Advanced data analysis includes OLAP, NN, and FL.

The most important criterion in choosing the data analysis technique is to ensure a match between the capability sought and the proper technology to support it. For example, if the capability is to simply report on campaign progress, then perhaps a simple reporting and querying tool is sufficient. However, if the goal is to develop sophisticated and complicated models for predicting purchasing behavior, then the use of more advanced, and possibly more difficult-to-use, tools appropriate for DM or exploration may be required. In all cases, the tools should be able to handle massive amounts of data with ease and to display this information in a comprehensible and manageable format.

Analytical CRM tools deliver accurate, consistent, and high-quality profiles for customers. However, standalone tools may be used instead, especially by small and medium-sized enterprises. Standalone software programs need to work with existing data sources and formats and integrate well with databases, DWs, or data marts, as well as with other application tools. In order to maximize their chances for reliable results, companies need to choose a tool that can fulfill their business requirements for CK by pulling, combining, and analyzing customer data from multiple sources and formats. Companies usually choose a tool that they know to be useful for solving their business problems and that has a successful track record in the industry.

The selected data analysis tool needs to provide efficient and effective extraction of data, interactive exploration, model building and testing, and visual presentation. Data analysis tools need to allow users to quickly gain insights by slicing and dicing (Babcock, 1995), and making changes within graphs to create multi-dimensional, new graphs.

To ensure the best results, the data analysis tool needs to be flexible in addressing business problems or requirements. An adaptable tool performs well in a variety of analyses, rather than one designed for a specific type of data or analysis situation. For example, a flexible data analysis tool offers a wide range of techniques or algorithms for visualization, classification, clustering, and association. In flexible data analysis tools, users may try one technique or combine a number of techniques to get accurate, effective results for the data set on hand.

It is critical to choose a tool capable of integrating data analysis results into operational applications now and in the future, and one whose integration will be cost effective if it will require additional time and money. Additionally, companies need to consider the extent to which the data analysis tool can be customized for users of varying expertise and for various business needs, while saving existing business processes and automating tasks without additional investments.

Selecting Data Analysis Application, Report, and/or Format

Data analysis is performed with tasks that vary from one model to another. No rule of thumb exists that explains which application is the best. The selection of the model depends heavily on the type of problem, the objective of an organization, the data structure, and the data format and scale. Therefore, it is critical to examine thoroughly the aforementioned variables, as well as others, before choosing the analytical application.

However, since each application looks at customers, channels, offerings, and relationships differently, it is wise to try a variety (such as campaign management, churn analysis) to find all of the relevant patterns to the creation of a 360-view of customers, and to maximize value for customers. From a pragmatic perspective, trying several application models may be necessary to get the right understanding of customers. To improve understanding of the customer, adding or removing new applications may be required.

Descriptive statistical models are good for initial data analysis, especially in the early stages of a DM project to gain an overview of the structure of the data. Developing a concise description of the characteristics of the data can help to develop hypotheses and plan further analysis. Propensity models are good for predicting customer behavior, e.g. who is most likely to purchase, most likely to churn, and most likely to default on loans. This information is used commonly to determine which customers or prospective customers offer the highest profitability.

Data analysis results are distributed in a report and format that is favored by the recipient (e.g., graphical or table format), and can be used as a way to identify customer segments for analysis or a new sales campaign. Consequently, team members, counterparts in other business areas, or business partners may have their own favorites. However, these differences and different approaches to analysis may no longer be applicable when the business becomes customer-centric. Businesses must have a single view of customers to provide a consistent experience to all of them. Thus, a consistent set of information reports must be generated and reviewed by customer-centric organizations (Seybold, 2002).

However, Davenport (2007) urged for engagement of senior executives in discussions about what information should be defined and managed at the enterprise level, versus information that can vary in definition and format across the organization. He called this a 'federalist' approach to information management, rather than the feudalism or anarchy that many organizations have. As it is extremely difficult for information reports and formats to fall into the 'one size fits all', a balanced approach between the standardized/customized approaches to information reports and formats may be more practical for CKM.

RECOMMENDED SOLUTION: A PROPOSED INFORMATION REQUIREMENT ANALYSIS MODEL

Getting appropriate level of information requires an investment of time, money, and training. In order to identify customer information requirements, a strategic analysis model is introduced. Four quadrants emerge from intersection between two levels of each of 'need' and 'have' dimensions (Figure 7.5):

- Quadrant I: *Nurture* (Don't Need but Have): nurture customer relationships as customers have valuable information for a business that may need to be used at a later stage. It is much *better to have* and do not *need*, than *need* and do not *have*.

Figure 7.5. A proposed information requirement analysis model

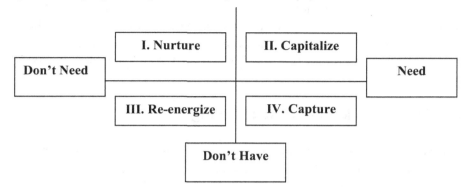

- Quadrant II: *Capitalize* (Need and Have): leverage and harvest the relationship with customers in order to create SCA. Capitalizing requires a firm to deliver customer value that enables it to anchor/expand relationship and loyalty with existing customers and/or win new prospective customers.
- Quadrant III: *Re-energize* (Don't Need and Don't Have): re-energize a business to focus on 'difficult-to-imitate' DCCs, viz. knowledge-based customer relationships, and to be repositioned into a customer-centric strategy in order to outperform rivals.
- Quadrant IV: *Capture* (Don't Have but Need): shortage of customer information may be a result of lack of data captured, or of over-emphasizing customer touchpoints automation but under-emphasizing customer data processing to effectively use it to enrich customer experience (data rich, but information poor).

FUTURE TRENDS

Future business environments are likely to witness a shift from one-dimensional to multi-dimensional data analysis, a shift from DM to text and web mining, a shift from human addition to human attention.

A Shift from Uni-Dimensional to Multi-Dimensional Data Analysis

Relational databases are the current standard for the storage of customer data in businesses. They function well for certain DWs in data marts, but they were not designed specifically to handle multi-dimensional data views of customers. CKM users often engage in an analysis of only a few data dimensions. One- and two-dimensional analysis can be viewed as tables and graphs, or cubes, like MOLAB; but usage of hypercubes in customer data analysis to describe data arrayed by three or more dimensions will increase in the future. Greater use of multi-dimensional database management systems (MDBMs) is expected to be a notable trend in the future.

A Shift from Data Mining to Text Mining

Text mining allows companies to develop a more complete view of the customer and to get a combination of better insight and an increase in predictive accuracy through collection of non-numerical knowledge from customer contacts through systems such as collaborative CRM.

Ignoring free-text expressions of customers can be costly. In fact, one of the most common uses of text mining is to identify customer concerns in an unstructured way before discontented customers start switching their loyalties. But the real value is almost achieved when numerical data is combined with text data. In the future, we will see greater use of textual and even web-based DM.

A Shift from Competing with Informatics to Competing on Analytics

Information systems, or 'informatics', may play several strategic roles in business. A business may use IT to help it become an agile company that responds quickly to changes in its environment. The Internet, intranets, extranets, and other Internet-based technologies may be used strategically for e-business and e-commerce, as well as for reengineering business operations that improve their efficiency and effectiveness dramatically and provide an SCA.

Many companies use advanced informatics that capture, accumulate, and store large amounts of data and reports, but with no real benefit to the business (data rich but information poor). In the future, businesses are expected to shift from competing with ICTs that enable low costs of doing business, for example, to competing in creating unique value and innovation through analytics. The mere existence of ICTs cannot provide companies with an SCA unless the potential of these technologies has been utilized strategically. An SCA in the global, competitive, and turbulent business environments of the future can only come from innovative use and management of organizational information and knowledge by CKM-based companies and learning organizations. Davenport (2007) forecasts the future as witnessing a merging of analytics and reporting systems into 'predictive reporting' capabilities.

A Shift from Information Accumulation to Information Attention

With the emergence of the Internet, the information marketplace has become more dynamic and volatile. The exchange in the information economy today is built on the exchange of information which is not a scarce resource. The truly scarce resource of the new economy is no longer just 'capital, labor, information and knowledge,' but human attention. Information is now plentiful but human attention is scarce. Attention refers to the focused mental engagement on a particular piece of information, and interest has now been focused on how both people and the organizations in which they work get attention, keep attention, and allocate attention.

Once the DW is built, the next step is to data mine and to try to discover previously unknown patterns. DM comprises a range of data analysis techniques, including cluster analysis and neural networks. Patterns uncovered in the data may be used to develop new marketing strategies or revise existing ones. Data analysis tools solve a common analysis paradox: the more customer data one has the more difficult and time-consuming it is to analyze effectively and draw meaning from them. Information discovery tools, such as OLAP and DM, use a clear business orientation and powerful analytic technologies to explore quickly and thoroughly mountains of data, pulling out the valuable and usable customer information that meets business needs.

In traditional businesses, the marketing mix, customers' searching and switching behavior, branding, retail franchises, organizations and even the boundaries of the corporation are built universally on the tradeoff between information richness and reach. The new economics of information attacks a pervasive and fundamental aspect of the old economics: the tradeoff between richness and reach. The web technologies can break the historical trade-offs between richness and reach and provide an important strategic tool to companies adopting the e-biz model. Therefore, the tradeoff is becoming rapidly obsolete and inapplicable.

Customer data processing may involve tactical actions and issues such as contacting the customer for a cross-selling opportunity, or deciding on a customer demographic profiling technique, application, report, or format. To ensure that a particular business has the right technique for each model and situation, it should choose a DM tool that offers a wide range of techniques and modeling options. Data analysis results also need to be evaluated to determine whether and how well the results delivered by a given model will help achieve business goals. Is there any business reason why the model is deficient?

CKM seeks to provide users with an easy-to-use and simple tool to distill information from data. It enables analytical activities and provides the flexibility to match the tool to the task. Customer-centric CKM reporting application presents the information that has been loaded into the DW in order for managers and analysts to view and analyze it. The reporting side of the CKM feeds the transactional processing data captured from different customer touch-points into the DW and then conducts analytical processing of these data to develop profiles for customers and CK. Typically, customer profiling includes reporting and on-line analytical processing (OLAP). CKM leveraging activities end up with the generation of CK and prediction of customer behavior which will be discussed in Chapter 8.

CONCLUSION

The actual implementation of the CKM value chain leveraging activities begins with the gathering of customer data, followed by customer segmentation, and profiling activities to score customers and prospect customers who fit the selected target profile via the optimal channel for each target. Analysis of customer profiles can go a long way in providing new knowledge, e.g. predicting and prospecting, that companies can use to improve their businesses. Targeting customers should focus only on those prospects that represent profitable and sustainable opportunities. Customers may be categorized based on their prospect value/loyalty into yellow, green, and red colors.

Once the DW is built, the next step is to data mine and to try to discover previously unknown patterns. DM comprises a range of data analysis techniques, including cluster analysis and neural networks. Patterns uncovered in the data may be used to develop new marketing strategies or revise existing ones. Data analysis tools solve a common analysis paradox: the more customer data one has the more difficult and time-consuming it is to analyze effectively and draw meaning from them. Information discovery tools, such as OLAP and DM, use a clear business orientation and powerful analytic technologies to explore quickly and thoroughly mountains of data, pulling out the valuable and usable customer information that meets business needs.

In traditional businesses, the marketing mix, customers' searching and switching behavior, branding, retail franchises, organizations and even the boundaries of the corporation are built universally on the tradeoff between information richness and reach. The new economics of information attacks a pervasive and fundamental aspect of the old economics: the tradeoff between richness and reach. The web technologies can break the historical trade-offs between richness and reach and provide an important strategic tool to companies adopting the e-biz model. Therefore, the tradeoff is becoming rapidly obsolete and inapplicable.

Customer data processing may involve tactical actions and issues such as contacting the customer for a cross-selling opportunity, or deciding on a customer demographic profiling technique, application, report, or format. To ensure that a particular business has the right technique for each model and situation, it should choose a DM tool that offers a wide range of techniques and modeling options. Data analysis results also need to be evaluated to determine whether and how well the results delivered by a given model will help achieve business goals. Is there any business reason why the model is deficient?

CKM seeks to provide users with an easy-to-use and simple tool to distill information from data. It enables analytical activities and provides the flexibility to match the tool to the task. Customer-centric CKM reporting application presents the information that has been loaded into the DW in order for managers and analysts to view and analyze it. The reporting side of the CKM feeds the transactional processing data captured from different customer touch-points into the DW and then conducts analytical processing of these data to develop profiles for customers and CK. Typically, customer profiling includes reporting and on-line analytical processing (OLAP). CKM leveraging activities end up with the generation of CK and prediction of customer behavior which will be discussed in Chapter 8.

REFERENCES

Anderson, M. (2004). Making decisions: how much info is enough? *Automotive Design & Production*, May, p.1.

Awad, E., & Ghaziri, H. (2004). *Knowledge management*. Upper Saddle River, NJ: Prentice-Hall.

Babcock, C. (1995). Slice, dice, and deliver. *Computerworld, 29*(46), 129-32.

Brackett, M. H. (1999). Business intelligence value chain. *DM Review Magazine*, March. http://www.dmreview.com/issues/19990301/115-1.html (retrieved on 17 January 2008).

Buttle, F. (2004). *Customer relationship management: Concepts and tools*. Oxford, England: Elsevier Publishing.

Clemons, E. (2000). In search of the ideal customer. In D. Marchand, T. Davenport, and T. Dickson (Eds.). *Mastering information management: Your single source guide to becoming a master of information management* (pp. 59-63). FT-Prentice Hall, London: U.K.

Davenport, T. H. (1997). *Information ecology: Mastering the information and knowledge environment*. Oxford, U.K.: Oxford University Press.

Davenport, T. H. (2000). Attention: The next information frontier. In D. Marchand, T. Davenport, and T. Dickson (Eds.). *Mastering information management: Your single source guide to becoming a master of information management* (pp. 46-49). FT-Prentice Hall, London: U.K.

Davenport, T. H. (2006). Competing on Analytics. *Harvard Business Review*, January, 99-107.

Davenport, T. (2007). *Competing on Analytics*. Interviewed by Power, D. posted at www.dssresources.com/interviews/davenport/davenport05272007.html, retrieved on 2 December 2007.

Evans, P. (2000). Strategy and the new economy of information. In D. Marchand, T. Davenport, and T. Dickson (Eds.). *Mastering information management: Your single source guide to becoming a master of information management* (pp. 37-42). FT-Prentice Hall, London: U.K.

Evans, P., & Wurster, T. (2000). *Blown to Bits: How the New Economics of Information Transforms Strategy*, Harvard Business School Press. Boston: U.S.A.

Imhoff, C., Loftis, L., & Geiger, J. (2001). *Building the Customer-Centric Enterprise: Data Warehousing Techniques for Supporting Customer Relationship Management*, New York: Wiley.

Seybold, P. (2002). *An Executive Guide to CRM*. Boston, MA: Patricia Seybold Group.

Turban, E., Leidner, D., McLean, E., & Wetherbe, J. (2008). *Information Technology for Management: Transforming Organizations in the Digital Economy*. 5th edition, New York: John Wiley.

Turban, E., McLean, E., & Wetherbe, J. (2004). *Information Technology for Management: Transforming Organizations in the Digital Economy*. 4th edition, New York: John Wiley.

Chapter VIII
Creating Knowledge about Customers

INTRODUCTION

Increasingly, knowledge is becoming a primary engine of growth in the globalized business world and is making nations more competitive as they shift from information-based to knowledge-based economies. In business contexts, knowing customers better is expected to help companies gain an SCA over others. This chapter represents the last activity in leveraging CKM value-chain. It seeks to discuss various concepts, issues, and trends concerning composition of knowledge about customers.

CONCEPTUAL FOUNDATIONS

Following the aggregation and dissemination of customer information comes the generation and sharing of CK. This section addresses the importance of knowledge as a corporate asset, the concept of knowledge, the concept of CK, CK discovery process, CK discovery systems, the concept of CKM, and a CKM case study.

Knowledge as a Corporate Asset

Change is becoming increasingly inevitable when operating in constantly dynamic and complex business environments, manifested by acceleration in the pace of change and transformation in the base of competition. In today's global economy, the customer has more and better choices than ever before, bringing on one of the biggest challenges the business community faces today - customer satisfaction, retention, and loyalty. The days of push-based production of goods and services without knowing customers have gone. The days of selling products rather than remaining resilient and vibrant to customer needs, wants, and preferences have passed. Knowledge is becoming a strategic asset of organizations in designing and developing products or services, and in building and maintaining customer relationships.

Since the early 1990s, knowledge has captured a great deal of attention in the literature as a non-depleting and strategic organizational resource to create and sustain competitive advantage. The need here is to deliver knowledge a) at the *right* time, b) at the *right* place, and c) in the *right* shape/format. The end result is to use knowledge to create value to customers and companies (Awad and Ghaziri, 2004).

The beauty of using knowledge as a base of SCA is that it is a non-depleting resource that. Unlike other business resources that diminish once shared, knowledge development follows the law of increasing returns - the more knowledge is used, the more value it creates. Furthermore, the more knowledge is shared, the more new knowledge is generated. Knowledge sharing, therefore, is becoming a successful way to increase the value of 'intellectual assets' in improving knowledge-intensive customer processes and adding value to customers and profitability to the business. Knowledge sharing takes place while people work internally within different units, departments, or the organization as a whole.

As competition in the marketplace accelerates rapidly, CK must be created and utilized in new business areas. As a response to business environmental drivers, CKM is introduced as an ICT-based organizational change model that leverages corporate DCCs by managing interactions among organizational main pillars of people, technology, and processes, for the collection, development, and application of CK. The basic theme behind CKM is to utilize DCCs of organizations, i.e. knowledge, to add value to customers as well as to companies by delivering the *right* product and/or service, at the *right* price, to the *right* customer, at the *right* time and location, and through the *right* distribution channel. The aim of CKM is to add value to customers from one side and to secure enduring and profitable relationships with customers and achievement of SCA for companies from the other side. CKM represents a shift from product-focused, hierarchical, and function-based data-oriented organizations to customer-centric, networked, and process-based learning organizations.

The aim of CKM is to help organizations succeed in identifying strategically significant customers and to develop durable and profitable relationships with them, based on information provided by customers about themselves, what products they want, and what they think of those products. CKM can generate valuable intelligence on customer desires and purchasing plans. By integrating this knowledge into the supply chain, the organization can better anticipate its needs for products and parts. Business Intelligence (BI) is the raw material that supports business strategies. The active and dynamic role of knowledge is critical in enabling customer-centric problem solving, decision-making, and organizational learning.

The Concept of Knowledge

Knowledge is richer, deeper, and more valuable than information (Pearlson, and Saunders, 2006). It is a mix of contextual information, experiences, rules, and values that relate to different domains of the business, such as products, customers, markets, operations, logistics, finance, and human resources.

Compared to the concepts of data and information, the concept of knowledge is more fluid and illusive. While information is descriptive - as it relates to the past and the present, (e.g. categorizing customers based on their value) - knowledge is predictive eminently as it provides the basis for the prediction of the future, with a degree of certainty based on information about the past and the present (Camerer and Johnson, 1991; Dubin, 1996). Besides, knowledge is actionable information and bound to people (or in a few cases by intelligent computer systems such as AI) after a process that involves comparison, consequences, connections and conversation (Alter, 2002; Topin, 1996; Davenport and Prusak, 2000, and Awad and Ghaziri, 2004).

However, information alone, lacking qualitative richness and being aggregated (possibly missing important details), provides, at most, just half of the true picture about customers. Information helps companies to recognize patterns, but fails to interpret these patterns, or to predict future trends. Information also often tends to assume linear relationships between independent and dependent variables and extrapolate current trends to future events; such extrapolation can prove dead wrong (Awad and Ghaziri, 2004). Therefore, the need arises here for a higher-level concept than information, viz., knowledge to interpret and predict situations or events related to customer behavior and actions.

Knowledge is cognizance, cognition, the fact or condition of knowing something. It is the acquaintance with or the understanding of something, the fact or condition of being aware of something, of apprehending truth or facts. It is information combined with experience, context, reflection, and synthesis, and has relevance, value, and the ability to meet business performance goals. The key to unlocking the value of knowledge is 'action'; it must be dynamic. Tacit knowledge is all the knowledge that is in people's heads or the heads of a group of people, such as an organization. It is what makes people smart and act intelligently. Explicit knowledge is knowledge that has been rendered explicitly to a community of people, and is what they deem to know (Brackett, 1999; Awad and Ghaziri, 2004).

Knowledge is information plus analysis, interpretation, synthesis, and evaluation. It is built around ground truth/common sense, expertise, experience-based insights, intuition, compressed expertise, creativity and innovation, judgment, values, assumptions, and beliefs. Knowledge is processed through the 4 Cs (Awad and Ghaziri, 2004):

- Comparison: compare information about this situation to other situations known.
- Consequences: find implications of the information for decision/actions.
- Connections: relate this bit of knowledge to other bits of knowledge.
- Conversation: interact with other people to learn the way they think about this information.

The concept of knowledge may be apprehended through the following: knowledge forms, knowledge categories, knowledge levels, and knowledge characteristics.

Forms of Knowledge

Knowledge may have two forms, *tacit* that is subjective and difficult to transmit, and *explicit* that is objective and easy to communicate (Nonaka, 1994). Tacit knowledge represents the subtle, human-based, subjective, cognitive, and experiential learning knowledge that is either localized 'sticky' in the brain of an individual or embedded in the group interactions that take place within a department or unit. This form of knowledge stores experiences, mental maps, insights, expertise, tips, skill sets, understanding, and learning that an organization has, as well as the organizational culture that has embedded in it the past and present experiences of the organization's people, processes, and values (Nonaka and Takeuchi, 1995). Especially difficult is the capture of 'tacit' knowledge, as it is subtle and sticky and resides primarily in the heads of experienced employees.

In contrast to tacit knowledge, explicit knowledge is the computer-based, codified knowledge that deals with more objective and technical knowledge (data, procedures, documents, software, etc.). Explicit knowledge has also been called 'leaky' knowledge because of the ease with which it can be acquired from an individual, document, or the organization (Turban et al., 2002), but it is limited in depth and serendipity

Among many other business initiatives such as BPR and TQM, KM can also extend outside organizational domains to suppliers and distributors, via alliance knowledge; cultural alignment and trust are key pre-requisites for such transfers.

KM is a strategic management approach that is used to catalyze strategic choices and improve organizational effectiveness and efficiency. Additionally, KM is more organic and humanistic as compared to the various business strategy paradigms such as BPR and TQM. In BPR, for example, the human factor is underemphasized, whereas process improvement is overemphasized, which often ignores opportunities for knowledge exchange among employees and with customers (Gamble and Blackwell, 2001).

Nonaka and Takeuchi (1995) propose four modes (processes) of knowledge creation and transfer 'knowledge spiral': socialization (originating- tacit to tacit knowledge), externalization (dialoguing- tacit to explicit), combination (systematizing- explicit to explicit knowledge), and internalization (exercising- explicit to tacit knowledge). These four modes of conversion processes show that the transfer of knowledge is dependent upon the transfer of a common context of understanding from the knower to the user of the knowledge. In turn, the common context of understanding consists of the context (the story behind the knowledge, the conditions and situations which make the knowledge understandable) and the experience (those activities which produce mental models of how the knowledge should be used) expressed in a culturally understood framework (Jennex, 2006).

Knowledge creation appears in two forms: tacit knowledge that is subjective and difficult to transmit and explicit knowledge that is objective and easy to communicate. Organizations nowadays recognize the need to integrate both types of knowledge into corporate-wide systems (Turban et al., 2002).

In the understanding the KM world, two distinct factions may be observed. The first faction believes that organizational behavior and individual socialization determine how much knowledge passes between individuals, and that technology is not the answer, but rather a distraction from issues such as change management, culture, and leadership. At the other end of the spectrum are ICT advocates who see technology as the solution to the KM question (Offsey, 1997).

Categories of Knowledge

Knowledge, as a corporate resource, may be divided into three major categories (Edvisson and Malone, 1997):

- Human capital *(people-based)* - All the brainpower that "leaves at 5:00 p.m.". It represents the knowledge inherent in employees and contactors, and it is difficult to calculate. The best way to do this is to assess the potential inherent in human knowledge - the value that has not yet manifested itself.
- Structural capital *(process- and technology-based)* - All the brainpower that "stays after 5:00 p.m.". It includes policies and operating procedures, cus-

tomized software applications, training courses, patents, and the like. The value of structural capital can be calculated easily because it has physical properties.

- Customer/market capital (*customer data/transaction-based*) - It refers to corporate knowledge about future customer and market prospects. The value of customer relationships (except future relationships and lapsed contacts) can be calculated in terms of business results they have provided and the trend in those relationships.

Levels of Knowledge

Knowledge can be possessed by a wide variety and diversity of bearers, viz. individuals (e.g., concepts or skills), groups (e.g., stories and metaphors), and the enterprise (best practices and patents). Knowledge can be arranged in different levels (Ackoff, 1989; Blackler, 1995; and Zack, 1999b) ranging from lowest (level 1) to highest (level 5) as follows:

- Level 1: Know-What/That (Cognitive). Shallow conceptual skills and cognitive knowledge (general rule) of what should be done in a particular situation (e.g., operating procedures).
- Level 2: Know-When (Conditional). Understanding when to apply a particular procedure or solution.
- Level 3: Know-With (Relational). Understanding how the procedure interacts with other units.
- Level 4: Know-How (Applied). The ability to translate bookish knowledge (general rules) into action-oriented results that are developed through repeated exposure to real-world, complex problems rooted in a specific context (e.g., best-work practices).
- Level 5: Know-Why (Rule-of-Thumb). Synthesization of the 'know-what' and 'know-how' through the reasoning (cause-and-effect) process enables knowledge workers to move away from general rules in their practice into rule-of-thumb (e.g., a stockbroker intuitively knowing when to sell or buy).

Characteristics of Knowledge

There are several key attributes of knowledge, which must be factored into KM practices (Kluge, et al, 2002; and Davenport and Prusak, 2000):

- Subjectivity: context and individual background shape the interpretation of knowledge.

- Transferability: knowledge can be extracted and transferred to other contexts.
- Embeddedness: knowledge is often in static and buried form that makes it difficult to extract.
- Self-reinforcement: knowledge is the only unlimited resource, the one asset that its marginal utility increases and does not decrease once used or shared.
- Perishability: knowledge can become outdated.
- Serendipity (spontaneity): knowledge can develop unexpectedly in a spontaneous or incidental process (e.g., water cooler knowledge exchanges).
- Velocity: *speed* with which knowledge moves through an organization (e.g., computers and networks excel at enhancing the velocity of knowledge).
- Viscosity: *richness* or *stickiness* of detailed or subtle knowledge transferred (e.g., apprenticeship or mentoring relationship).

The Concept of CK

CKM seeks to develop "customer's lifetime value" by conducting customer profiling, behavioral segmentation, products portfolio analysis, revenue analysis, and traffic analysis. Through CKM, companies understand customer needs and form relationships with customers not only by pushing products and services. Companies need to capture knowledge to enable them to predict buying behaviors and to do market research.

Companies need a wide variety of knowledge about customers, such as (Hanvanach et al., 2003; Rowley, 2002a):

- Who are our customers?
- How can we use knowledge to retain and support them?
- How can knowledge help us acquire new customers?
- How can we use CK to improve continuously our products and services?
- How can we use CK to create new products and services?
- How can we use CK to better understand our markets?

CK refers to understanding customers' needs, wants, and aims when a business is aligning its processes, products and services to create real customer relationships management (CRM). Sometimes, CK can be confused with CRM. Although there could be some overlap, CK works at both a micro and a macro level and includes a wider variety of less-structured information that will help build insight into customer relationships. CK should include information about individuals (micro) that helps explain who those individuals are, what they do, and what they are looking for; and it should also enable broader analysis of the customer base as a whole (macro). Similarly, CK should include both quantitative insights (i.e., numbers of orders placed and value of business), and qualitative insights ('tacit' or unstructured knowledge that resides in people's heads).

The aim of building a strong body of CK is to enable the company to build and manage customer relationships now and over the longer term. CRM is an interactive business-customer process that seeks to share or create CK in order to generate the maximum value to both parties. CRM emerged as an amalgamation of different management and ICT approaches, and entails the following processes (Gebert et al., 2003):

- Measuring inputs across all functions - including marketing, sales, and service costs - as well as outputs in terms of customer revenue, profit, and value.
- Acquiring and updating constantly knowledge on customer needs, motivation, and behavior over the lifetime of the relationship.
- Applying CK to constant improvement of performance through a process of learning from successes and failures.
- Integrating marketing, sales, and service activities to achieve a common goal.
- Continuously contrasting the balance between marketing, sales, and service inputs with changing customer needs in order to maximize profit.

CK should determine what to offer, when to offer it and for how much. In the long term, the company has to design new products, offer new services, and compete in new markets. However, even in the short term, a top salesman could become ill or be headhunted. Would the business know enough to keep its accounts? What companies currently know about their customers may not be sufficient in order to build and sustain stronger relationships with customers. Companies may need to build in processes and systems to gather more information and data about who their customers are, what they do, and how they think in terms of future purchasing decisions. Therefore, analytical, or deduced, CK such as prediction of customers' expectations and future-purchasing patterns using advanced computer models and BI technologies, is becoming a prerequisite to the establishment of strong customer relationships.

CK Categories

In the interaction between organizations and their customers, four CK categories have been distinguished (Davenport et al., 2001; Garcia-Murillo and Annabi, 2002; Gibbert et al., 2002; Desouza and Awazu, 2005; and Smith and McKeen, 2005):

- Knowledge *for* customers is a continuous flow of knowledge (also data or information which can be analyzed, interpreted, and converted into knowledge) directed from the company to its customers in order to support customers in their buying cycle (i.e.) is a prerequisite. Knowledge for customers comprises information about products, markets and suppliers and is primarily addressed by CRM service processes.

- Knowledge *from* customers (also data or information which can be analyzed, interpreted, and converted into knowledge) refer to customers' needs or consumption patterns of products and/or services that have to be incorporated by the company for product and/or service innovation, idea generation as well as for the continuous enhancement of its products and/or services.
- Knowledge *about* customers (also data or information which can be analyzed, interpreted, and converted into knowledge) encompasses the customer's past transactions, present needs and requirements, and future desires. The collection and analysis of knowledge *about* customers is certainly one of the most important activities in CKM.
- Knowledge *co-creation (with customers)* refers to a two-way business-customer relationship for the development of new knowledge or a new product, e.g. Microsoft shares its 'beta-ware' version with customers in order to learn with them and debug the software. KM Front line tools and communities of customers may be used to gain knowledge about how customers view the company and its products.

CK Discovery Process

Knowledge discovery is a higher level process than information discovery as it extracts patterns and makes prediction from volumes of data stored in DWs. Knowledge discovery/generation is a step in KM process. KM activities includes knowledge capture and/or generation, knowledge sharing and dissemination, and application (Dalkir, 2005) of explicit knowledge, expertise (tacit knowledge) that are part of organizational memory and that may reside in unstructured forms in organizations (Turban et al., 2008).

Several authors have made contribution to the delineation of CK discovery process. Notable among them are the works of Rowley (2002b), Chen and Su (2006), Su et al. (2006), Lopez-Nicolas and Molina-Castillo (2008). Rowley (2002b) presented a set of reflections on CKM in e-business as compared to traditional marketplace. She identified four levels of CK that organizations in e-business require as follows:

- Cognition: customer behavior in relation to Web sites and marketing/delivery channels, as the basis for assessing the effectiveness of Web sites and marketing/delivery channels

- Customization: development of customer profiles a basis for developing 1-to-customer relationships
- Cumulation: trends in customer behavior and other aspects of market research and analysis that inform the product marketing strategy of the e-business
- Context: the relationship between consumer behavior in the traditional and e-marketplaces, and the impact of online consumer behavior on other channels, and vice versa

Chen and Su (2006) introduced a Kano-CKM model for managing attractive quality creation in new product development projects. They propose the following four stages of CK discovery for innovative product development: product benefits/preference identification (knowledge for customers), customers' satisfaction categorization (knowledge about customers), market segmentation (tacit knowledge codification), and customers' usage pattern extraction (knowledge from customers).

Su et al. (2006) proposed an E-CKM model for delineating the process of CKM for innovative product development using web-based surveys and DM to extract CK from different market segments. In the E-CKM model, the CKM process comprises the following four stages: product features/benefit identification (knowledge for customers), customers' needs categorization (knowledge about customers), market segmentation implementation (tacit knowledge codification), and customers' needs pattern extraction (knowledge from customers).

Lopez-Nicolas and Molina-Castillo (2008) studied the role of customer perceived risk in using CKM and e-commerce tools and its impact on customer's purchase intention. They grouped different dimensions comprising the perceived risk construct as follows:

- Product-based risk dimensions

  ○ Technical risk: the probability that a product fails to function as expected.
  ○ Service risk: the probability that the firm will not offer a good service in the future
  ○ Social risk: the probability that a product results in disapproval of friends or family.
  ○ Psychological risk: the probability that a product results in inconsistent self-image

- Place-based risk dimensions

- ○ Performance risk: the probability that the purchase process does not perform as expected
- ○ Financial risk: the probability that a purchase decision results in loss of money
- ○ Time risk: the probability that the buying results in loss of time
- ○ Delivery risk: the probability that the purchase results in delivery problems

CK Discovery Systems

Knowledge about customers is generated through interactions with customers through processing of customer orders, as well as through different customer interaction channels such as phone, e-mail, interactive voice recognition (IVR), fax, mail, electronic commerce, and front-office stores. Knowledge about customers is developed from customer information (e.g., customer's personal information and purchasing history that are held in computerized ODS, i.e., billing and provisioning data stores) and accessed by staff of these units. Each time a customer makes contact with the company, the customer's needs, as well as the actions taken to satisfy these needs, represent information that may be processed further to generate knowledge that ultimately would benefit future customer interactions.

Knowledge-based systems, i.e. analytical CRM, are shaping the next generation of ICT tools and influencing how businesses cope with unusually advanced capabilities. Davenport and Prusak (2000) discussed specific types of knowledge discovery systems that may be used as stand-alone systems or part of CRM analytical systems: broad knowledge repositories, focused knowledge systems, real-time systems, and long-term analysis systems.

Broad Knowledge Repositories (BKR)

BKR are a giant collection of databases that are used in order to locate knowledge. A few organizations have used external online services to store internal knowledge repositories. The best example of BKR is the Internet (the hypertext of the World Wide Web allows related content to be linked regardless of its physical location). However, the majority of Internet search *hits* are irrelevant and worthless (time wasted sorting through trash to find a treasure). Future Internet technological innovations (e.g., increased speed and search sophistication) will make it a better knowledge source.

Repositories were largely external to any organization attempting to obtain external market, economic, legal, or financial knowledge. Lotus Notes and Intranet-based Webs are two leading tools for managing knowledge repositories. Lotus

Notes (used by professional services and consulting firms such as Anderson and Ernst & Young) excel at the following:

- Database management
- Applications development
- E-Bulletin board announcements
- Discussion-groups (cc mail)
- Search facilities (GrapeVINE & Hoover)

The Intranets grow faster than the Notes, and excel at the following:

- Publishing/producing web documents with the HTML and Java
- Displaying knowledge that is linked to other knowledge
- Discussion groups
- Search facilities
- Multimedia features (audio, graphic, and visual)

Focused Knowledge Systems

Focused knowledge systems are constraint-based systems (e.g., ES) which are suited for narrow problem domains or situations with high levels of data, but normally are less quantitative than that required by NN. The knowledge of one or two experts can be shared by a much broader group of workers (insurance salespeople who need to do financial planning for their customers but know little about it). ES typically are structured in a set of rules and can perform very complex reasoning (e.g., financial planning in insurance, approval of credit facilities or loans by banks).

Real-Time Knowledge Systems

Real-time knowledge systems are used in solving real-time customer support or 'help desk" problems (e.g., *Magic* Call Help Desk system adopted by some banks). *Solution-Builder* is another example of a KM solution for customer support based on breaking down a problem into its knowledge components. If users are somewhat expert - understand problems but cannot solve or classify them - then CBR is the solution. CBR requires someone to input a series of 'cases', customer analysts to receive calls, and experts to construct the cases and maintain them over time.

Longer-Term Analysis Systems

Using data to classify cases into one category or another (e.g., a default or a pay back loan) evolves through learning from long-term historical cases (i.e., DM). Customer-centric BI applications are ICT-based analytic applications that analyze the results of operational processing systems. Their results can be used to improve the efficiency and effectiveness of operational CRM applications. For example, analytic applications may be designed to provide insight into customer behavior, requests, and transactions, as well as into customer responses to marketing, sales, and service initiatives. Analytic applications also create statistical models of customer behavior, values of customer relationships over time, and forecasts of customer acquisition, retention, and desertion. Analytic systems are the same applications as BI, DSS, DM, or analytic CRM applications.

DM uncovers patterns in data, using predictive analytics and modeling. Predictive analytics combines advanced analytic techniques with decision optimization. It uses historical information to make predictions about future behavior, and then delivers recommended actions; whereas predictive modeling creates models to predict future activity, behavior, or characteristics (e.g., showing which customers are most likely to churn in the future based on profiles of previous churners).

DM can be defined as the *automated* extraction of *hidden predictive* information from online transactional databases, DWs, survey data, and textual documents. DM refers to powerful analytic techniques that help companies to extract quickly and thoroughly information from mountains of customer data, and can incorporate data from a wide range of sources and types.

DM supports RDBMS and DWs through data analysis algorithms for classification, prediction, regression, clustering, associations, feature selection, anomaly detection, feature extraction, and specialized analytics. While OLAP is concerned only with analysis of present and past events, DM is a process for analyzing present and past, as well as understanding what will happen in the future. DM uses predictive modeling, including statistics and machine-learning techniques such as NN to predict what will happen. For example, queries and reports show the total sales for last month, whereas OLAP goes a layer deeper to report sales by product for last month. DM, however, identifies who is likely to buy the company's products *next* month. For the best business results, these insights should be incorporated into the marketing campaign strategy to determine, for example, how to make personalized offers that have the best likelihood of leading to sales.

The development of DM models or algorithms is expanding to fulfill a wide variety of real world problems and applications. Various models have been employed commonly to solve business and non-business problems. There are three major techniques of DM (Berry and Linoff, 2000): clustering, decision analysis, and NN.

As for NN, they represent a recent addition to advanced data analysis techniques. There are two basic types of NN: supervised learning and unsupervised learning networks. Supervised learning networks can be used in place of traditional methods like regression and discriminant analysis, whereas unsupervised learning networks generally are used when there are no clear distinctions between dependent and independent variables in the data and when pattern or structure recognition is required. Since pattern recognition is really what is needed in segmentation analysis, unsupervised NN can be used for this purpose. NN are known for the following:

- Requiring a lot of quantitative data and a powerful computer.
- Operating as a 'black box' in terms of the processing mechanism.
- Classifying cases according to nodes (inputs and outputs) and variable weightings in the hidden layers.
- Eliminating the need for human intervention due to the use of pattern identification and matching capabilities.
- Relying on human beings only to structure data, interpret results, and make decisions.

Customer-Centric Collaborative Applications

In addition to operational and analytical CRM systems, collaborative CRM may be used to generate CK. Unlike operational and CRM applications that enable development of transactional content-based CK, collaborative applications provide the opportunity to build personal relationships with a wide range of people to generate non-transactional contact-based CK. Collaborative CRM systems, or online networking applications, deal with all the communication, coordination, and collaboration between vendors and customers. They include examples such as forums, chat rooms, e-mail newsletters, and discussion lists (Turban, et al., 2008). A collaborative CRM can be extended to include employees, suppliers, or partners. A collaborative selling CRM can offer knowledge to everyone in the extended enterprise, and to help drive sales through every channel from call centre to the Web (Xu and Walton, 2005).

The Concept of CKM

The concept of KM encompasses three major parts: knowledge capture and/or creation, knowledge sharing and dissemination, and knowledge application (Dalkir, 2005). Since the business environment usually is dynamic, so is the need to create a holistic business strategy that seeks to develop knowledge-intensive, cross-functional capabilities and add value to customers based on pluralistic perspectives to change. Since knowledge, and in particular CK, is the heart of newly emerging KM and CRM business strategies, the term CKM is thought to be a more accurate representation of the merge between CRM and KM.

CKM is not just about customer data nor is it just about customer relationships, viz. social (people-based) or transactional (technology-based); rather, CKM is a knowledge-based business strategy enabled by a holistic organizational reinvention manifested by changes in people, structure, processes, and technology. Research specifically on the concept of CKM has shown growing appearance in the literature. Major CKM contributions include Garcia-Murillo and Annabi, (2002), Gibbert, et al. (2002), Rowley (2002 a,b), Kolbe, et al. (2003), Bueren, et al. (2005), Desouza and Awazu (2005), Paquette (2005), Smith and McKen (2005), Chen and Su (2006), Su and Chen (2006), and Lopez-Nicolas and Molina-Castillo (2008).

CKM may seem to be just another duplicate name of CRM or KM, to the extent that some researchers have called for it to replace the term CRM (Roscoe, 2003). Although CKM incorporates the principles of both KM, and CRM, but it differs from these along a number of key variables as follows (Gibbert et al., 2002):

- *KM*

  - Scope: Involves employees and company networks.
  - Objective: The sharing of information held (intellectual capital) about customers among employees.
  - Customers: Products and services are developed without the direct involvement of customers.
  - Driver: Customer retention.

- *CRM*

  - Scope: Focuses on customer database information.
  - Objective: Mining and using customer information to benefit long term relationships.
  - Customers: Sought and retained using loyalty and incentive schemes.
  - Drivers: Customer satisfaction and loyalty.

- *CKM*

  - Scope: Focuses on customer creativity and experiences.
  - Objectives: Gaining, sharing, and developing customer insights.
  - Customers: Collaboration and joint value creation sought.

° Drivers: Performance against competitors, customer success, innovation, growth, and organizational learning are key business drivers.

Gibbert et al. (2002) discussed five basic styles of CKM, which originate from a relationship between the business firm and its customers: prosumerism, team based co-learning, mutual innovation, communities of creation, and joint intellectual property development.

- *Prosumerism.* It describes a customer filling the dual role of consumer and producer. In this form, knowledge co-production is generated from role patterns and interactivity. For example, Bosch develops engine management systems with Mercedes-Benz who then creates and assembles the finished car. Bosch's customer, Mercedes-Benz, is allowed to share value-adding ideas and facilitates the development of new initiatives and products.
- *Team-based co-learning.* Whereas the Prosumerism CKM style focuses more on co-production of products and services, team-based co-learning focuses on reconfiguring entire organizations and systems of value. This involves intense interactions with the customer to gain their knowledge on processes and systems to facilitate systematic change. A prominent example of this style is Amazon.com. By restructuring their structure from being an online book retailer to a seller of many varieties of goods, they accomplished many co-learning interactions with their customers, i.e., suppliers, to design a new value chain. Amazon.com uses this value chain as a competitive advantage against other online retailers, as it allows for quick movement of goods at competitive prices. This strategy has the added value of creating closer relationship with their suppliers that other online retailers will not be able to duplicate. Through co-learning interactions Amazon.com's original identity has been transformed, which in turn implies new value chain systems relationships. A second illustration is the transformation process in Xerox Corporation from being a 'copying machine company' to becoming the 'document company' is similarly based on organizational learning resulting from CKM. CK was the key to reconfigure the entire system of document management and its infrastructure, spanning resources and processes much broader than its own traditional realm of activities.
- *Mutual innovation.* This form was initially identified by von Hippel (1988), who discussed that most product innovations come from the end-users of the product. Mutual innovation is more than just asking for future requirements, but constructing knowledge that comes from closely integrated innovation practices. Rider Logistics developed complex and extensive logistical solutions for its customers through close examination of their manufacturing operations

and supply chain strategies, then designed services that fit and added value to these processes.

- *Communities of creation.* In this style companies organize their customers into groups holding similar expert knowledge and encourage interaction in order to generate new knowledge. These groups are characterized by working together over a long period of time, sharing a common interest, and wanting to create and share valuable knowledge. Unlike traditional Communities of Practice (COPs) advocated by (Wenger, 1998), these groups span organizational boundaries and develop value for multiple organizations. Microsoft beta testing with customers is an example where groups of targeted customers test products together with the Microsoft product development engineers to jointly create a product that provides value for Microsoft and its participating customer organizations. These communities also form through informal relationships which are capable of producing valuable knowledge.

- *Joint intellectual property.* This style probably involves the most intense form of cooperation between a company and its customers. Intellectual property of CK does not reside in the company, but is "owned" partly by the customers. Thus, the company takes the view that it is owned by its customers and they have ownership in future product development projects. Skandia Insurance is an example where a company and its valued consumers created new businesses owned by both. They have proven this strategy especially successful in emerging markets where the company initially lacks CK, yet gains a great deal from its local customers. Customer success in fact becomes corporate success, and vice versa.

A CKM Case Study

Gibbert et al., (2002) presented a case study that shows how an international cement manufacturer, Holcim Inc., manages CK (Table 8.1). Holcim's companies in the U.S. conducted analysis how to deliver e-commerce solutions to their customers. But Holcim's aspiration was more ambitious than simply conducting e-commerce transactions. The idea was to create a knowledge sharing platform, where any member of the community of cement and aggregates consumers (concrete producers, distributors, engineers, and architects) would be able not only to transact business (place orders, pay online), but also share and exchange knowledge (e.g. share cement order forecast and share good and bad experiences).

In order to test and further develop this aspiration, Holcim's CK managers conducted meetings with selected customer mix that was intentionally varied, comprising selected large multi nationals, medium domestic, and small family owned companies in the U.S. The objective of the meeting was to discuss current and emerging trends in the cement industry and the potential impact of these developments on creating value for their customers. The discussion was open and free flowing, although Holcim had developed a set of value added services that were thought appropriate, but it did not implement these until after the customers had given their views.

Holcim has also built and implemented the knowledge sharing platform in Canada, Belgium and France, Spain and the U.S. During the platform 'build' phase, the company kept close contact with the customers and permanently validated with them what it did, which was much-appreciated by its customers.

Table 8.1. Holcim's CKM approach

Area	CKM Process	Business Results
Trouble-shooting	Online solutions to customer inquiries	Reduced time to solve problems Savings in labor and materials Increased satisfaction of customers Enhanced reputation of manufacturer
Quality Control and Product optimization.	Collection of test data, document submittal and approvals, and mix design.	Reduction in usage of cement. Optimization of setting times Optimization of raw materials Reduction of customer claims
Inventory and supply management	Automation of the inventory and supply processes	Elimination of costly plant shut-downs for lack of cement.
Purchasing	Enable customer to access the purchasing platform	Price reduction in raw materials, trucks, and equipment
Technical library	Comprehensive data warehouse on core products.	Easy access to rich resources of information of the cement manufacture's knowledge base
Engineering consulting	Provide business services and expertise	Educating concrete manufactures in business management will improve their efficiency
Promotions and testimonials	Access to tools and information to 'grow the pie,'	Educating specifiers (surveyors) in concrete lifecycle costs will increase the adoption of concrete vs. other materials
Market information	Consolidation of micro and macro analysis of market information.	Exposure of the concrete manufacturer to business opportunities and market tracking information

Source: Adapted from Gibbert, M., Leibold, M., & Probst, G. (2002). Five styles of customer knowledge management and how smart companies use them to create value. European Management Journal, 20(5), 459-469.

CRITICAL ISSUES

This section discusses specific issues related to the creation of knowledge about customers: adopting a traditional versus emergent knowledge views, selecting a KM framework, adopting a KM strategy, facing challenges in KM implementation, deciding on analytics versus human base of competition, deciding on who hold versus who should hold CK, adopting relationship-based versus intellectual-based CK generation, adopting market-based versus community-based CK generation, sharing versus hoarding culture in CK generation, recognizing the for-profit versus not-for-profit context in CK generation, and integrated versus fragmented customer touchpoints in CK generation.

Adopting Traditional vs. Emergent Knowledge Views

The current KM research has made significant contributions to understanding the concept of knowledge in various organizational contexts, in general, and effective management and coordination of organizational knowledge as pivotal corporate assets, in particular. In the late 1990s, many researchers and practitioners further energized KM research by linking the management of knowledge to various ICT applications such as groupware and management information systems (Davenport et al., 1996; Davenport and Prusak, 1997). However, KM researchers have not addressed sufficiently the *emergent* nature of knowledge (Nonaka and Nishiguchi, 2001).

Intrinsically, the concept of knowledge involves emergent properties and systemic characteristics that cannot be analyzed or even perceived *a priori*, because knowledge, unlike data or information, emerges from subjective human interpretation and complex interaction between human beings (Stacey, 2000). Most of the current KM research has been predicated upon reductionistic and functionalist assumptions about the nature of knowledge focusing on conceptualizing knowledge as being static, decomposable and transferable. Knowledge encompasses emergent characteristics resulting from situated and largely unplanned decision-making and activities (Suchman, 1987).

Kakihara and Sorensen (2002) reconsidered multiple, competing definitions of knowledge in the literature. Based on a synthesis of several epistemologies, they outlined four distinct knowledge discourses; namely, knowledge as object, knowledge as interpretation, knowledge as process, and knowledge as relationship. The first perspective can be characterized as representationistic (structured); and the three others are interrelated, anti-representationistic perspectives on knowledge.

Knowledge as Object

Although this paper aims to address the emergent nature of knowledge, it is still important to grasp the traditional, dominant strand of discourse on the concept of knowledge. This debate is associated closely with the problem of *representation*. From a representationistic perspective, *a* reality is always an imperfect "mirror image" of *the* perfect, 'positivistic' objective world. According to Aadne et al. (1996), a representationistic view on knowledge is based on several general assumptions about knowledge.

- First, it presupposes that knowledge is seen as a representation of a pre-given world. This indicates that social reality is totally outside the observing actor.
- Second, in this view, human intelligence can be seen as information processing and rule-based manipulation of symbols. Behind this assumption is the traditional view of cognitive science; that is, human intelligence is to a large extent tantamount to the characteristics and functionality of computation.
- Third, knowledge is seen as objectified and transferable. Based on the cognitivistic point of view, knowledge is perceived as a billiard-ball-like entity that can be transferred stably within and between human brains.
- Fourth, learning is thought of as creation of the most accurate or "truthful" representations of the objective world. In this view, learning implies improving representation through acquiring information from the outside world and assimilating it to former experiences.

In management and organization studies, the discourse of knowledge as object is closely linked with the 'mechanistic', information-processing paradigm (Galbraith, 1973; Simon, 1981). Based on the information-processing view of the organization, conventional KM research has seen knowledge as objectified and codified – similar to data – and sought an effective utilization of ICTs for coordinating such object-like knowledge. Although it has been subject to strong criticism (e.g. Winograd and Flores, 1986; von Krogh and Roos, 1995; Hodgson, 2000; Stacey, 2000), it is clear that the discourse of knowledge as object has contributed in clarifying the explicit and relatively static aspects of organizational knowledge.

Knowledge as Interpretation

Many philosophical scholars have argued that knowledge is associated inherently with human-based, 'ontological', inter-subjective interpretations and that the process of interpretation simultaneously shapes and is shaped by social reality (e.g. Berger and Luckmann, 1966; Schutz and Luckmann, 1974). In the traditional 'objective', representationistic view of the world, the fundamental assumption is that the world is pre-given, and its aim is to create the most accurate or 'truthful' representations of this objective world. This view is challenged by the view that knowledge, in managerial and organizational contexts, is not just as a representation of the pre-given world but also as the creative act of human cognition and interpretation (Kakihara and Sorensen, 2002).

Although the representationistic view of knowledge has contributed to the development of a functional analysis of organizational behavior concerned with knowledge, it could be argued that the concept of knowledge cannot be grasped fully and dealt with without taking human interpretative behavior into account.

Knowledge as Process

The static and objectified view of knowledge which has been pervasive in the literature has emerged mainly because knowledge, more or less, has been equated with physical resources in organizations such as money, labor, and land, and fits very well with the mechanistic and functional understanding of organizations. However, this static, 'mechanistic' view of knowledge has been subject to criticism from the *process* view of knowledge by the work of Whitehead (1929), who proposes that reality is no longer viewed as a superficial, accidental changing of its static structure, but as a continuous process and an active alteration in the fabric of reality itself. Whitehead (1929) insists that there exists neither subject nor object that can be isolated from reality itself and both subject and object are bound intrinsically to ongoing processes of transition of reality. From a process-oriented view, knowledge is not a static entity but the manifestation of a dynamic *process* of 'knowing' by which human beings make sense of the reality (Varela et al., 1991; Blackler, 1995).

It seems that this process-view of knowledge, or knowing, has gradually permeated the research of scholars. Senge (1990), for example, applied systems-thinking approaches to the study of the learning organization. He stressed that, in order to apprehend an organization's reality, it is becoming crucial to see processes of change rather than snapshots. Senge warned that the static and cause-effect based view toward an organization is dangerous for understanding the complex problems organizations face. Nonaka and Tekeuchi (1995) argued that knowledge should be viewed as a dynamic human process of justifying beliefs toward the 'truth'. Spender (1998), focused, not on the static framework dictated by positivism's epistemology, but on the processes that generate, distribute, and apply the firm's intangible knowledge assets.

It may be concluded here that the concept of knowledge does encompass dynamic and fluid as well as static aspects. Knowledge emerges out of dynamic processes between objectivity, which relates to what we know ('truth or real world') and how we know from one side, and socially constructed, subjective meanings we give to what we know based on the perspective or point of observation from the other side.

Knowledge as Relationship

As explained earlier, knowledge is a result of human mental acts, and those acts are dependent on various socio-cultural contexts. Besides being interpretive and process-oriented, knowledge is, by nature, *relational* to its surrounding world. At the same time, mental acts, along with linguistic acts, continuously shape social reality and can induce new contextual meanings of the world (Maturana and Varela, 1992). Knowledge does not exist in an isolated state in the objective world, but rather resides within a variety of contextual factors that are connected inseparably with the body of knowledge (Kakihara and Sorensen, 2002). Therefore, knowledge can be seen as an interconnected web of *relationships* in which human interpretative acts eternally shape and maintain, both intentionally and unintentionally, the relational setting of the web and contextual disposition of the social reality (Stacey, 2000).

In recent studies, the idea of knowledge as relationship has acquired significance, since there is a strong resonance between this idea and an emerging social reality. Largely helped by the development and diffusion of ICTs, particularly the Internet, organizations are becoming relatively freed from geographical constraints and institutional rigidity and incompatibilities across various geographic boundaries, and are directly reaching and connecting with a variety of players in the market such as customers, business partners, and suppliers of raw materials and parts (Rochart and Short, 1991; Jarvenpaa and Ives, 1994). Thus, in such a new reality, organizational knowledge should be viewed in terms of, not only possession and storing, but also, or more importantly, relationship and connectedness with other social actors and structures (Kakihara and Sorensen, 2002).

In order to characterize emergent properties of knowledge, it is important to emphasize the notion of interaction - a primal source of knowledge emergence - not as a discrete unit of human activities but as an *ongoing, nonlinear, fluid process* of interaction of participating actors oriented towards other actors and/or systems (Stacey, 2000; Kakihara et al., 2002). Cook and Brown (1999) pointed out the importance of interaction by proposing the distinction of the *epistemology of possession* and *epistemology of practice*. They argued that the traditional understanding of the nature of knowledge is predicated on the epistemology of possession whereby the forms of "what is known" typically are treated as something people possess. Because this epistemology cannot account for the dynamic interplay between human action and a body of knowledge, they propose the *epistemology of practice,* whereby knowing, rather than knowledge, plays an active role of interaction with other actors and the world as part of human practice.

Hence, it is important to understand the role of human-based interaction, not only in terms of the relationship among human actors, but also in terms of the reciprocal interplay between the actors' actions and the world in which they live. Thus, it is through such interaction that knowledge, be it explicit or tacit, individual or collective, can hold its relation to actual social reality, rather than being separated from it. Further, it is by interaction that knowledge is enacted and mobilized in an organization's KM practices. Based on the results of one case study, it is argued by Kakihara and Sorensen (2002) that human interaction is the source of knowledge emergence. In the CKM context, companies maximize their earnings from collaborative relationships and interactions with customers.

Although the fundamental nature of the emergence of knowledge is human-based, the weak, external validity of case analysis makes it extremely hard to generalize results of one case study to others. Therefore, and in order to take a more balanced view, KM may be considered as a socio-technical process initiative when it comes to enhancing, sharing, and utilizing knowledge and information in corporate settings. A socio-technical KM approach connects KM theory to KM practice in more than one situation and allows KM issues to be approached in a holistic and systematic manner. This provides a better understanding of the benefits and limitations of KM initiatives, especially in the sphere of social-oriented knowledge culture, communities, initiatives and rewards, measurement, ICT-based knowledge repositories, modeling, and discovery systems.

Selecting a KM Framework

There are four fundamental approaches to KM: the process, the practice, the integrated, and the contingency approaches. Most KM process frameworks stress three major stages: knowledge capture and/or creation, knowledge sharing and dissemination, and knowledge application (Dalkir, 2005), and three major components of a KM strategy: people, process/culture, and technology. In the KM field, 80 percent are people and process/culture oriented, and the other 20 percent are technology oriented (Liebowitz, 1999).

From an internal organizational perspective, Nonaka and Takeuchi (1995) introduced their famous 'spiral' KM development approach, where corporate knowledge is developed, shared, and used through four conversion processes: socialization (originating - tacit to tacit knowledge), externalization (dialoguing

- tacit to explicit), combination (systematizing - explicit to explicit knowledge), and internalization (exercising - explicit to tacit knowledge). Their model can be included as part of the traditional life-cycle-based KM strategy composed of knowledge identification and capture, knowledge sharing, knowledge application, and knowledge creation. Once knowledge has been identified and captured, a human socialization effect occurs, which results in knowledge sharing among employees. Knowledge resulting from knowledge sharing becomes externalized, which results in knowledge application. This knowledge is then combined with other knowledge that the individual possesses, as well as externalized along with the individual's value hierarchy. This should result in new knowledge being created, which needs to be preserved as it becomes captured and the cycle continues (Liebowitz, 2004).

There are a number of KM process frameworks worthy of mention, including those that have incorporated models for the KM process: Wiig (1993), Wiig (1997), Holsapple and Joshi (1997), Beckman (1999), Probst et al. (1999), Davenport and Prusak (2000), Rubenstein-Montano et al. (2001a,b), Tiwana (2001), Jashapara (2004), and Liebowitz (2004). In addition to these KM process frameworks, there are several KM successful implementation frameworks presented by Lindsey (2002), Massey et al. (2002), and Jenex and Olfman (2003). The following represents a sample of contributions introduced by notable researchers in the field:

- Wiig (1993): creation, sourcing, compilation, transformation, dissemination, application, and value realization.
- Holsapple and Joshi (1997): KM resources (employee/computer, culture, artifact, infrastructure, strategy, and purpose), KM activities (acquiring, selecting, internalizing, using, generating, and externalizing knowledge), and KM influence (managerial, resource, and environmental).
- Zack (1999b): acquisition, refinement, store/retrieve, distribution, and presentation.
- Bukowitz & Williams (2000): get, use, learn, contribute, assess, build/sustain, and divest.
- Probst et al. (1999): knowledge goals, knowledge identification, knowledge acquisition, knowledge development, knowledge sharing, knowledge use, and knowledge preservation.
- Davenport and Prusak (2000): access, generate, embed (codification and coordination), and transfer.
- Rubenstein-Montano et al. (2001): strategize (perform strategic planning of business needs), perform conceptual modelling (knowledge audit, planning, sharing-culture, etc.) in addition to physical modelling (architectural design), act (capture, represent, organize and store, combine, create, share, and learn

knowledge), revise (pilot operational use of the KM system, conduct knowledge review, and perform KM system review), and transfer (publish knowledge, coordinate KM activities, use knowledge to create value, monitor KM activities, conduct post-audit, expand KM initiatives, and continue to learn and loop back through the phases).

- Tiwana (2001): analyze existing infrastructure, align KM and business strategy, design the knowledge infrastructure, audit existing knowledge assets and systems, design the KM team, create the KM blueprint, develop the KM system, deploy, using the result-driven incremental methodology, manage change, culture, and reward structures, evaluate performance, measure ROI, and refine the KM system.
- Jashapara (2004): discover knowledge, generate knowledge, evaluate knowledge, share knowledge, and leverage knowledge.
- Liebowitz (2004): knowledge identification and capture, sharing, application, and creation.

In contrast to the process approach, the practice approach to KM assumes that a great deal of organizational knowledge is tacit in nature that is difficult to capture through formal KM systems, processes, and ICTs. Therefore, organizations focus on socialization and collaboration by building COPs to facilitate the sharing of tacit knowledge. COPs are groups of people who share a concern or a passion for something they do and learn how to do it better as they interact regularly. Three characteristics are crucial for COPs (Wenger, 1998; and Wenger et al., 2002):

- *The domain:* A community of practice is not merely a club of friends or a network of connections between people. It has an identity defined by a shared domain of interest. Membership therefore implies a commitment to the domain, and therefore a shared competence that distinguishes members from other people.
- *The community:* In pursuing their interest in their domain, members engage in joint activities and discussions, help each other, and share information. They build relationships that enable them to learn from each other. A website in itself is not a community of practice. Having the same job or the same title does not make for a community of practice unless members interact and learn together.
- *The practice:* A community of practice is not merely a community of interest - people who like certain kinds of movies, for instance. Members of a community of practice are practitioners. They develop a shared practice of resources: experiences, stories, tools, and ways of addressing recurring problems. The

development of a shared practice may be more or less self-conscious. The 'windshield wipers' engineers at an automobile factory make a concerted effort to collect and document the tricks and lessons they have learned into a knowledge base. By contrast, nurses who meet regularly for lunch in a hospital cafeteria may not realize that their lunch discussions are one of their main sources of knowledge about how to care for patients.

Besides the above frameworks, the literature also contains some more recent 'integrated' and 'contingent' frameworks of KM. Handzic and Zhou (2005) introduced am integrated approach that brings together different perspectives on knowledge management and provides a unifying view that depicts the concepts of working knowledge, knowledge processes, and knowledge enablers. The core of the framework is a two-by-two matrix with 'explicit' and 'tacit' 'know-that' and 'know-how' dimensions of working knowledge. Working knowledge is affected by processes that generate, transfer and apply knowledge. Technological and organizational factors act as enablers that influence knowledge processes.

The aforementioned research that examined several KM process frameworks, consider each process as universally applicable. However, Becerra-Fernandez and Sabherwal (2001) propose that the context influences the suitability of a KM process. They developed a contingency framework, including two attributes of the organizational subunit's tasks: process or content orientation, and focused or broad domain, and links of KM processes to them: internalization for focused, process-oriented tasks; externalization for focused, content-oriented tasks; combination for broad, content-oriented tasks; and socialization for broad, process-oriented tasks. Zhu (2004) questioned the claim that KM is a universal concept and, instead, proposed KM in cross-cultural contexts that clearly reveal the unique associated problematics of different KM styles. Al-Shammari (2008) added a new KM profile for the Arab region. The Arab KM profile was compared with other styles: the American, the Japanese, the European, and the Chinese in line with the dimensions set by Zhu (2004): motto, mentality, ideal-type, embodiment, mechanism, aim, focus, strategy, process, means, and metaphor.

Although KM is a young discipline for which no universally accepted framework has been established, some authors were concerned with creating KM frameworks. The role of KM frameworks is to oversee, or provide guidance for, the discipline (Rubenstein-Montano et al., 2001a). The KM frameworks, with their very general approach to KM, provide an excellent starting point for developing a business-specific KM process model. KM process models are approaches or methodologies that are more specific than frameworks, detailing how to carry out KM in a manner consistent with a particular framework.

Adopting a KM Strategy

In the context of KM, emphasis is put on management of data, information, and knowledge in the search for SCA. The concepts of KM have captured a great deal of importance in the literature since the early 1990s. However, in the literature, there has been a great deal of debate on the meaning of KM and its difference from other related concepts of data management and information management. In data management, as well as information management, the role of computer-based systems in business operations is being emphasized, but the role of people is being deemphasized. In KM, the role of people is being emphasized, but role of technology is being deemphasized. KM involves a set of systematic processes introduced to help companies effectively create, capture, share, and leverage knowledge (Davenport et al., 1998; and Rumizen, 2001), and to aid in decision making and creating a sustainable distinctive advantage. According to Davenport et al. (1998), the objectives of KM projects were the creation of knowledge repositories, improvement of knowledge access and transfer, enhanced knowledge environment, and management of knowledge as an asset.

However, the current state of the field reveals competing research paradigms, raging definitional debates, elusive value of knowledge management, evangelism, technology-focused initiatives, early wins difficult to replicate, motherhood status, and foreboding questions beginning to emanate from the ranks of senior executives looking for returns on investments. Moreover, there is a lack of objectivity, as those involved in KM initiatives are often relying on anecdotal (narration vs. codification) evidence emanating from their experience; and a lack of generality, as KM methods are usually context dependent and not transferred easily from one organization to another.

Therefore, KM may be approached in two ways (Hansen et al., 1999; Turban et al., 2002):

- Personalization: human-based information processing activities such as brainstorming sessions periodically to identify and share knowledge. Personalization strategy is more focused on connecting knowledge workers through networks, and is better suited to companies that face *one-off* and unique problems that depend more on tacit knowledge and expertise than on explicit, codified knowledge. Institutional memory, business knowledge and business experience all reside in the human resource of an organization. Unlike data and information, knowledge is a resource only with respect to the human resource, not with respect to computer storage and retrieval.
- Codification: systematic processes for regularly capturing and distributing knowledge. The codification strategy is more focused on technology that

enables storage, indexing, retrieval, and reuse of knowledge after it has been extracted from a person, made independent of that person, and reused.

According to KPMG consulting company, KM adoption stages fall into five types of maturity (Gamble and Blackwell, 2001): knowledge-chaotic (no structured KM approach), knowledge-aware (basic cataloguing available), knowledge-enabled (standardized processes implemented), knowledge-managed (integrated KM culture, chief knowledge officer), and knowledge-centric (daily assessment and improvement of knowledge environment).

The development of an effective KM strategy begins with a vision of what knowledge is strategically critical for a firm, and how to capitalize on a firm's intellectual resources and capabilities that have a profound impact on the business key performance (Zack, 1999a; Hofer-Alfeis, 2003). Once business strategy is made final, the next step is to establish a link between business strategy and knowledge strategy. Business strategy formulation entails setting goals and objectives (what a firm must do) and conducting strategic gap auditing (what a firm must do versus what a firm can do). Knowledge strategy, in turn, should specify knowledge requirements (what a firm must know) and audit knowledge gaps (what a firm must know versus what a firm already knows) as related to business strategy. Alternatively, business and knowledge strategies may be converged into a one-off knowledge-based strategy that integrates knowledge-strategic gap auditing into one rather than two separate stages.

Concerning types of knowledge strategies, two major factions are observed - exploration versus exploitation (March, 1991). The knowledge exploration strategy represents the supply side in which emphasis is placed on generation of new knowledge; whereas the emphasis of the exploitation strategy is on exploitation of existing knowledge. Most firms balance their use of both knowledge strategies to be successful, by focusing on one and using the other supportively. Combining a firm's knowledge exploitation versus exploration orientation provides a more complete picture of a firm's knowledge strategy. Firms oriented toward exploiting internal knowledge exhibit the most conservative knowledge strategy, while unbounded innovators (those that integrate knowledge exploration with knowledge exploitation without regard to organizational boundaries) represent the most aggressive knowledge strategy (Zack, 1999a). However, it is not logical for firms to be an explorer before becoming an exploiter.

Once knowledge strategies are developed, they need to be followed by a KM strategy. KM strategy is a high-level approach to outlining the processes, tools, as well as organizational and technological infrastructure needed to manage knowledge gaps or surpluses and to permit knowledge to flow effectively (Zack, 2002). Some researchers argue that KM strategy may replace the firm's business strategy, or, a business strategy may evolve to become a KM strategy, or, the two strategies may complement one another (Civi, 2000; Vera, 2001).

KM can be approached in two ways - personalization and codification (Hansen et al., 1999; Turban et al., 2002). Recently a process-oriented KM approach was suggested as a step to bridge the gap between human- and technology-oriented KM. Examples are knowledge maps, lesson learned, and best practices (Davenport et al., 1996, and Maier and Remus, 2003). Firms may focus on one, but do not have to choose from personalization, codification, or process-based KM approaches.

At one end of the spectrum comes the personalization approach, which is rooted deeply in organizational behavior and individual socialization through COPs, to determine how much knowledge passes between individuals. This approach is a practice approach that assumes that a great deal of the firm's knowledge is tacit in nature and those formal controls, processes, and technologies are not suitable for this type of understanding. Rather than building formal systems to manage knowledge, the focus is to build the social environments or COPs necessary to facilitate the sharing of tacit knowledge (Leidner, et al., 2006).

In this approach, technology is not the answer, but rather a distraction from issues such as change management, culture, and leadership. This approach is more focused on connecting knowledge workers through networks, and is better suited to companies that face *one-off* and unique customized solutions to unique problems that depend more on tacit knowledge and expertise than on codified knowledge. It includes activities such as brainstorming sessions periodically to identify and share knowledge. For these firms, collaborative computing tools (for example, Lotus Notes, videoconferencing, and e-mail) help people communicate (Turban et al., 2008).

At the other end of the spectrum are ICT advocates who see technology as the solution to the KM question (Offsey, 1997). ICT enables a systematic capture, storage, indexing, retrieval, distribution, and reuse of knowledge after it has been extracted from a person, made independent of that person, and reused.

From another viewpoint, Apostolou and Mentzas (2003) developed an integrative KM approach that includes interactions among strategy, assets, process, systems, structure, individuals, and teams, across and within organizations. Along the same line, Sveiby (2001) introduced the following nine questions to guide KM strategy formulation of a firm:

- How can we improve the transfer of competence between people in our organization?
- How can the organization's employees improve the competence of customers, suppliers and other stakeholders?

•

- How can the organization's customers, suppliers and stakeholders improve the competence of employees?
- How can we improve the conversion of individually held competence to systems, tools and templates?
- How can we improve individual competence by using systems, tools and templates?
- How can we enable conversations among the customers, suppliers and stakeholders so they improve their competence?
- How can competence from the customers, suppliers and other stakeholders improve the organization's systems, tools, processes and products?
- How can the organization's systems, tools, processes and products improve the competence of the customers, suppliers and other stakeholders?
- How can the organization's systems, tools, processes and products be integrated effectively?

It is beyond doubt that knowledge will continue to be a primal component of business strategies in dynamic business environments. As competition intensifies in today's marketplace, and as the competitive advantage may not be sustained over a long period of time, it is imperative for business organizations to create knowledge-based competitive strategies. A KM strategy may entail a choice of one or more knowledge and KM alternative strategies, or a combination of strategies but with different levels of emphasis, i.e. personalization versus codification and creation versus acquisition strategies. In the end, KM should reflect the strength of the organization, nature of its business, and inclinations and expertise of its personnel (Wiig, 1997).

Facing Challenges in KM Implementation

Several studies have been conducted to identify the challenges in KM implementation, and have come up with various findings that are significant for theory, research, and practice. The following contributions are note-worthy:

- Davenport, et al. (1998) identified eight factors that were common in successful KM projects: senior management support, clearly communicated KMS purpose/goals, linkages to economic performance, multiple channels for knowledge transfer, motivational incentives for KM users, a knowledge friendly culture, a solid technical and organizational infrastructure, and a standard, flexible knowledge structure.
- Alavi and Leidner (1999) found organizational and cultural issues associated with user motivation to share and use knowledge to be the most significant.

- Ginsberg and Kambil (1999) explored issues in the design and implementation of an effective KM System (KMS) and found knowledge representation, storage, search, retrieval, visualization, and quality control to be key technical issues and incentives to share and use knowledge to be the key organizational issues.

- Sage and Rouse (1999), reflecting on the history of innovation and technology, identified the following issues: modeling processes to identify knowledge needs and sources of KMS strategy for the identification of knowledge to capture and use and who will use it , provide incentives and motivation to use the KMS, infrastructure for capturing, searching, retrieving, and displaying knowledge, an understood enterprise knowledge structure, clear goals for the KMS, and measuring and evaluating the effectiveness of the KMS.

- Holsapple and Joshi (2000) found leadership and top management commitment/support to be crucial. Resource influences such as having sufficient financial support, skill levels of employees, and identified knowledge sources are also important.

- Jennex and Olfman (2001) identified these design recommendations for building a successful KMS: developing a good technical infrastructure by using a common network structure, adding KM skills to the technology support skill set, using high end PCs; integrated databases; and standardizing hardware and software across the organization, incorporating the KMS into everyday processes and IS by automating knowledge capture, having an enterprise-wide knowledge structure, having Senior Management support, allocating maintenance resources for organizational memory systems (OMS), training users on use and content of the OMS, creating and implementing a KM Strategy/Process for identifying/maintaining the knowledge base, expanding system models/life cycles to include the KMS and assessing system/process changes for impact on the KMS, designing security into the KMS, building motivation and commitment by incorporating KMS usage into personnel evaluation processes; implementing KMS use/satisfaction metrics; and identifying organizational culture concerns that could inhibit KMS usage.

- Koskinen (2001) found the key to the success of a KMS was the ability to identify, capture, and transfer critical tacit knowledge; and that since new members take a long time to learn critical tacit knowledge, a good KMS facilitates the transference of this tacit knowledge to new members.

- Lindsey (2002): proposed a KM successful implementation framework that defines effectiveness in terms of two main constructs: Knowledge Infrastructure Capacity and Knowledge Process Capability. The knowledge intrastate capacity is operationalized by technology, structure, and culture, whereas knowledge process capability represents the acquisition, conversion, application, and protection of knowledge.

- Massey et al. (2002): presented a KM success framework developed from a case study. The framework recognizes that KM is an organizational change process and KM success cannot be separated from organizational change success. The key components of the framework include KM strategy, key managerial influences, key resources influences, and key environmental influences.
- Barna (2003) found that the main managerial success factor in KM projects is creating and promoting a culture of knowledge sharing within the organization by articulating a corporate KM vision, rewarding employees for knowledge sharing, creating COPs, and creating a 'best practices' repository. Other managerial success factors include obtaining senior management support, creating an LO, providing KMS training, and defining precisely KMS project objectives.
- Malhotra and Galletta (2003) identified the critical importance of user commitment and motivation and found that using incentives did not guarantee a successful KMS.
- Yu, et al. (2004) explored the linkage of organizational culture to KM success and found that KM drivers such as a learning culture, knowledge sharing intention, KMS quality, rewards, and KM team activity significantly affected KM performance.

Selecting Analytics vs. Human Base of Competition

Companies have long used BI for specific applications, but these initiatives were too narrow to affect corporate performance. Leading firms are building broad capabilities for enterprise-level business analytics and intelligence, instead of a single application. Their capability goes well beyond data and technology to address the processes, human skills, and cultures of their organizations. Davenport (2006) argued that companies compete on analytics when:

- They apply sophisticated information systems and rigorous analysis, not only to their core capabilities, but also to a range of functions as varied as marketing and human resources.
- Their senior executive team not only recognizes the importance of analytics capabilities but also makes their development and maintenance a primary focus.
- They treat fact-based decision making, not only as a best practice, but also as a part of the culture that is emphasized constantly and communicated by senior executives.
- They hire not only people with analytical skills, but a lot of people with the very best analytical skills and consider them a key to their success.

- They not only employ analytics in almost every function and department, but also consider it so important strategically that they manage it at the enterprise level.
- They not only are expert at number crunching, but also invent proprietary metrics for use in key business processes.
- They not only use plentiful data and in-house analysis, but also share them with customers and suppliers.
- They not only avidly consume data, but also seize every opportunity to generate information, creating a "test and learn' culture based on numerous small experiments.
- They not only have committed to competing on analytics, but also have been building capabilities for several years.
- They not only emphasize the importance of analytics internally, but also make quantitative capabilities part of their company's story, to be shared in the annual report and in discussions with financial analysts.

However, Davenport (2007) himself viewed findings or results generated from analytical systems (analytics) as simply a form of knowledge derived from data. Analytical systems, and even reporting systems, usually involve some sort of data reduction, so they allow firms to use less human attention to find out what is going on. Whereas in knowledge management there is a fairly high degree of orientation to the human role, there is not much in analytics or data mining.

Deciding on Who Hold vs. Who Should Hold CK

CK is created though acquisition and processing of fragmented information found in files and databases specific to the particular application which was designed to process whatever transactions were being handled by the application, e.g., billing, sales, accounting, etc. In GTCOM's case study (Al-Shammari, 2005), customer contact/delivery channels (e.g., phone, e-mail, fax, store) as well as front-office departments (marketing, sales, and customer services) were operating as 'silos' with their own island of automation; information from each customer contact/delivery channel was owned as a separate entity within that unit. However, with each unit having its own information, leveraging information across the myriad of customer contact channels did not carry out, nor was it possible to provide a consistent customer service experience. For example, a customer may make a telephone call to a call centre to enquire about a transaction conducted through the website only to be told to 'call the Internet department'.

Although GTCOM does have knowledge about its customers, frequently this knowledge is in a fragmented form, difficult to share or analyze, sometimes incomplete, and often unused for business decisions. Advances in ICTs increasingly are providing GTCOM with opportunities to support customer service operations and to integrate CK through several contact/delivery channels.

Direct users of CK are power users at customer-facing departments, viz. sales, marketing, and customer services. Managers of these departments currently hold CK, but that knowledge is often fragmented and incomplete and should have an analytical 360-degree view of customers. In addition to power users, there are other users with authorized access to GTCOM's CK. These users are

- Basic users: operational staff at the clerical level
- Administrative users: IT people
- Executives: senior managers, general managers, and chief executives.

The organizational structure of GTCOM does not reflect the needs for effective utilization of knowledge resources. No special unit was found in charge of promoting KM activities and programs where knowledge ideas could be computerized and shared across different departments. In addition, no one was found to be in charge of the generation, storage, sharing, distribution, and usage of CK, i.e. chief knowledge officer.

Deciding on Relationship-Based vs. Intellectual-Based CK Generation

Although customers traditionally are considered the main business assets of organizations, it is becoming imperative for customer-based businesses to care for the well being of their intellectual assets, or 'brainware', as much as they do for customers. The traditional view of human resources was not so much as a valuable resource, but as an organizational resource that can be replaced easily. Launching E-business initiatives has aggravated the situation as they normally lead to loss of productive and capable staff as a result of downsizing, outsourcing, and automation.

Acquisition and retention of customers may not be possible without attracting, retaining, and satisfying competent, knowledgeable, innovative staff members with appropriate learning capabilities and attitudes towards customers. Loyalty of skilled staff members with appropriate customer-centric skills and capabilities increasingly is becoming the key difference between successfully competing and failing companies. When the brainpower of organizations becomes loyal, more propensities towards fostering learning communities to share CK and minimize knowledge walkouts would be secured. Highly marketable employees with unique knowledge can create severe damage to their employers. Brain drain that goes to the rivals is probably the worst thing that can happen to a company struggling for survival and success in the new knowledge economy (Awad and Ghaziri, 2004).

Adopting Market-Based vs. Community-Based CK Generation

The idea of a 'knowledge market' was advocated by Davenport and Prusak (2000). The knowledge market includes knowledge sellers, buyers and brokers. In addition, it includes price mechanisms based on reciprocity. Alternatively, the concept of collaborative 'knowledge community' was introduced by Miles and Snow (2006) to emphasize connection and commitment. When most individuals care about their colleagues, a working knowledge market is developed based on relationship and trust.

Knowledge communities function because a few important 'behavioral protocols' are in place, understood and agreed to by the community and agreed to. This new organizational form can be replicated or repurposed to form communities capable of new strategies unavailable to classical organizations.

Companies can create and orchestrate online customer communities in order to get valuable feedback about their products-in-use. Information from manufacturers may be discounted by customers in favor of information and assessments from peers and other groups. As online customer communities form, power shifts from manufacturers to customers and peer-level information dissemination replaces mass advertising to communicate with distinctive features of brands. Companies taking this approach include Intel, Harley-Davidson, Egghead Software, Travelocity, Toyota and Apple Computers (Venkatraman and Henderson, 2000).

At the same time, some customer communities are formed but remain independent of major sellers. Areas include photography (www.photoshopper.com), cars (www.autoweb.com, www.edmunds.com), general goods (www.netmarket.com), and water utilities (www.wateronline.com). The credibility of such sites is largely due to their lack of ownership links to product and service providers. The major challenge that faces these communities is to maintain the trust of the consumers as they collect information about them and provide value-added services (Venkatraman and Henderson, 2000).

The 'knowledge market' approach emphasizes the role rendered to individuals versus the role rendered to group in knowledge generation. It also emphasizes the role of financial incentives in contrast to the 'knowledge community' approach which focuses on nurturing connections among group members. The case study documented in Appendix (B) clearly shows how a CK market approach led to a limited success in the implementation of CKM.

Sharing vs. Hoarding Culture in CK Generation

Although considered important tools for disseminating information or knowledge within an organization, ICTs alone cannot secure efficient flow of information or knowledge, if corporate culture is not conducive to knowledge sharing among employees. People in the organization need to be capable, willing, and ready to share knowledge or provide a high quality product or service. Although the design of robust ICT systems, e.g. CSCW, significantly contribute to the facilitation of CK transfer and sharing, the final decision to share or not to share lies within the hands of people.

The prevailing corporate culture may hinder or foster CK development. Corporate culture plays an integral role in CK sharing among people and in successful development of CKM and in promoting distinction in offering customer products or services. Salespeople, for instance, may like to hoard their customer CK because they have unfounded fears of internal sabotage. In this case, the answer is to explain to the salespersons why you need the information and what exactly will be done wit it (Anderson and Kerr, 2002). Organizations may also provide attractive economic incentive structure for knowledge sharing and use, and they even may make knowledge sharing one element of performance appraisal systems.

Here comes the need for organizations to transform to a customer-centric cooperative and knowledge sharing rather than competitive and knowledge hoarding culture. An effective customer-centric corporate culture is the one that (Buttle, 2004):

- Identifies which customers to serve.
- Understands customers' current and future requirements.
- Obtains and shares CK across the enterprise.
- Measures customer results: satisfaction, retention, future re-calls, and referral behaviors (word-of-mouth).
- Designs products and services that meet customers' requirements better than competitors.
- Acquires and deploys resources (information, materials, people, and technology) that create the products and services that satisfy and meet customers' requirements.
- Develops the strategies, processes, and structure that enable the company to satisfy customers' needs.

Recognizing the For-Profit vs. Not-for-Profit Context in CK Generation

Developing customer-centric organizations and managing relationships with customers is found in the for-profit and not-for-profit contexts. Although the majority of customer-relationship applications are found in the for-profit organizations, not-for-profit organizations, as well, develop learning relationships with customers. Governments care about becoming more citizen-centric. State-run traffic licensing departments are streamlining and customizing the task of drivers' licenses renewal. Municipalities and city councils allow residents to pay parking tickets and municipal bills online and to develop learning relationships with their individual citizens (Peppers & Rogers, 2004). Municipalities use customer-citizen relationship management technologies such as call centers and web sites to maintain effective communication with citizens, to respond to requests for information, queries or complaints, and to track the progress of citizens' requests for service. Charity funds and social organizations such as the Salvation Army use CRM to assess the value of different donor segments, and work at retaining them. Universities also manage relationships with students, alumni, and second-generation alumni (Buttle, 2004).

Addressing Integrated vs. Fragmented Customer Touch-Points in CK Generation

Analytic applications typically are not linked into computerized business processes. Rather, most of them are conducted in separate, offline DW environments. However, analytics are used frequently in line with operational applications to implement real-time analysis in areas such as cross-sell, up–sell, and retention. Real-time analytic applications are effective only if they can be integrated with operational applications and integration approaches, requirements, and issues such as those discussed above (Seybold, 2002). Integration of internal and external business systems aims at maximizing customer value along the business value chain and across customer touchpoints by connecting end-to-end processes starting from the supplier-centric, upper-bound logistics, such as purchasing, handling, and inventory warehousing, passing through several internal operations, and ending with lower-bound customer-centric logistics such as packaging, warehousing, transportation, and distribution.

Internal business systems refer to operational CRM applications and back-office systems, as well as DW and analytic applications. External business systems refer to the CRM systems of sales and marketing business partners and the back-office systems of business suppliers. For example, an e-commerce application should provide integration with inventory systems in order to present real-time information to online shoppers. A customer service call centre system should provide integration with order management systems so that customer service representatives can answer questions about current order status or historical order details.

Besides, it is becoming important to integrate with the external business systems of customers and suppliers - a seller should be able to receive and process customer purchase orders, send back a purchase-order acknowledgement; similarly, a seller should be able to have the same exchange with its suppliers. Most significantly, CRM products should provide an integrated, 360-degree view of customers, collect customer information from numerous and heterogeneous sources, and provide consistent access across all applications. CRM suites can address this requirement more easily than standalone products that implement individual applications because suites 'own' more of the customer profile and are likely to have roots in ERP and supply chain applications which own even more (Seybold, 2002).

Although extremely essential to develop complete customer view, integrating CRM systems is one of the most difficult tasks that a business may face. To address this issue, there exist many emerging integration technologies and products, standards in messaging protocols, and business process specifications. Integration is becoming easier as more companies recognize the business returns of responsive customer service and supply-chain management, but do not underestimate its complexity and the time and effort needed to do it effectively. Selecting a CRM product from one of the leading suppliers can have a significant, positive impact on the success of integration (Seybold, 2002).

Figure 8.1. A preliminary CKM development model

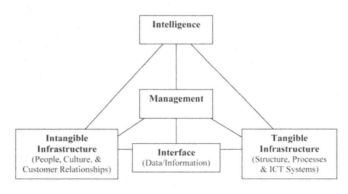

RECOMMENDED SOLUTION: A PROPOSED CKM BUSINESS MODEL

As an attempt to simplify the dynamics-knowledge generation in customer-centric organizations, a higher-level model might be suggested to enact and promote CKM composed of five organizational aspects: tangible infrastructure, intangible infrastructure, interfaces between tangible and intangible infrastructures, management, and intelligence (Figure 8.1). CKM outlines the kinds of customers that the organization wants to target, together with their personal and purchasing profiles.

CKM focuses on the automation of horizontally integrated, customer-facing business processes involving touch points across sales, marketing, and customer service via multiple interconnected delivery channels. Also, it focuses on the software installations and the changes in process affecting the day-to-day operations of a firm (Buttle, 2004; Peppers and Rogers, 2004). This level includes CKM activities that represent the major types of corporate knowledge resources, viz. human knowledge capital, structural knowledge capital, and CK capital (Edvisson and Malone, 1997).

CKM collects large amounts of data about customers and their transactions to help companies understand the behavior of their customers through Advocates of CRM argue that that it improves customer retention and satisfaction by providing customer-tailored services (McKeen and Smith, 2003). KM enables CRM to expand from its current 'mechanistic, technology-driven, data-oriented approach' towards more 'holistic, complex, and insightful ways of developing and using CK (Gebert et al., 2003).

The literature introduces several frameworks for building knowledge-enabled CRM strategy. The term CRM is used commonly in the literature to refer to the customer-centric business strategy that seeks to establish and nourish relationships with customers. CRM's goal is to satisfy customer need or desire, in order to improve customer acquisition, customer retention, customer loyalty, and customer profitability by improving the process of meaningful communications with a) the *right* customer, b) providing the *right* offer (product or service), c) at the *right* price, d) at the *right* time, and e) through the *right* channel (Swift, 2001). However, the emphasis on knowledge for building long-term and profitable CRM strategy has been introduced only recently in building a knowledge-enabled CRM strategy (i.e. Gebert, et al., 2003; Bueren, et al. 2005; and Al-Shammari, 2005).

The major CRM perspectives cited in the literature are as follow:

*   CRM Implementation and Management (Peppers and Rogers; 1999; Peppers et al., 2004): The model is based on four tasks: identify customers, differentiate

them, interact with them, and customize treatment. Building customer value requires process, organization, technology, and culture management.

- CRM Strategy Implementation Model (Brown, 2000): This suggested implementation approach focuses on three areas that affect customer care: customer strategy, channel and product management strategy, and infra-structure strategy.

- The CRM Process Cycle Model (Swift, 2001): It includes four groups of actions: knowledge discovery, market planning, customer interaction, and analysis and refinement. Tactical strategies for the CRM process include four elements: *interact* (with a customer to collect THE data from all contact points), *connect* (management of customer interaction points), *know* (insights gained through capture and analysis of detailed information to create continuous learning - about customer, products, channels, markets, and competitors - from the DW and/or knowledge bases created, interrogated, and analyzed), *and relate* (application of insight to create relevant interactions or communications with consumers, customers, channels, suppliers, and partners that builds value relationship).

- Knowledge-enabled CRM (KCRM) Process Model of Gebert, et al. (2003), and Bueren, et al. (2005): This model combines both approaches of CRM and KM into one KCRM model. It identifies core processes of CRM and the KM building blocks that support them. The model suggests six CRM business processes: campaign management, lead management, offer management, contract management, service management, and complaint management. The model suggests four KM components: content, competence, collaboration, and composition.

- CRM Functional Model (Chaudhury and Kuiboer, 2002). The CRM perspective adopted here is rather technical. Four functions of CRM software were identified: operational, analytical, collaborative, and web-based CRM (e-CRM).

- CRM Implementation Model (Chen and Popovich, 2003). The model looks at CRM as an integrative approach that combines people, process and technology, and seeks to manage relationships by focusing on customer retention and relationship development.

- CRM Processes Model (Knowx, et al., 2003): A strategic model was suggested based on five major processes: strategy development process (business strategy and customer strategy), value creation process (value customer receives and value organization receives), channel and media integration process (sales force, outlets, customer call center, direct mail, and the Internet), information management process (data repository, IT systems, analysis tools, front office applications, and back office applications), and performance assessment process (shareholder results and performance monitoring).

- Dynamic CRM model (Park and Kim, 2003). It integrates customer information types, viz. transaction, relationship, and feedback data (of-the-customer, for-the-customer, and by-the-customer information) along with relationship evolution phases, viz. acquisition, retention, and acquisition.
- CRM Value Chain Model (Buttle, 2004): This model identifies five primary stages of the value chain: customer portfolio analysis, customer intimacy, network development, value proposition development, and management of the customer lifecycle. These stages represent the three main phases of CRM strategy: analysis, resource development, and implementation. The development and implementation of the CRM strategy is supported by four conditions: leadership and culture, data and information technology, people, and processes.
- CRM Levels Model (Buttle, 2004). This perspective views CRM at three levels: operational, analytical, and strategic. The operational CRM focuses on major automation projects such as service automation, sales force automation, or marketing automation. The analytical CRM perspective focuses on the intelligent mining of customer data for tactical or strategic purposes. The strategic perspective views CRM as a core customer-oriented business strategy that aims at winning and keeping profitable customers.
- CRM Implementation Model (Lindgreen, 2004). The model is organized around eight areas: commitment of senior management, situation report, analysis, strategy formulation, implementation, management development, employee involvement, and evaluation of loyalty-building processes.
- CRM Types (Turban, 2002). Identifies operational, analytical, and collaborative CRM types. The Operational CRM is related to data capture through processes such as customer services, order management, and invoice/billing; whereas analytical CRM involves analysis of customer data, and collaborative CRM deals with all the communication, coordination, and collaboration between sellers and customers.

In this book, CKM is used to refer to a knowledge-enabled, transformational change strategy that focuses on building enduring and profitable relationships with customers in dynamic and fast-paced environments. CRM itself demonstrates a change from weak to strong customer relationships based on changing marketing strategies of mass marketing, target marketing, and customer-relationship marketing (Chen and Popovich, 2003). Many companies realize that customers are not alike, not only in terms of their preferences but also in their profitability. Research has shown that, in most industries, a minority of customers generate the majority

Figure 8.2. A proposed CKM model: Linking competitiveness, reinvention, knowledge, KM, and CRM strategies

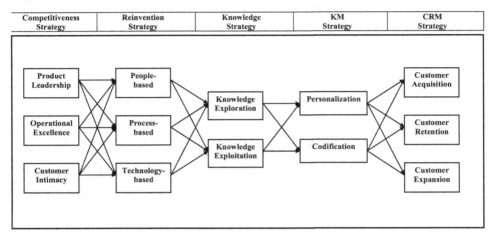

of profits (Hallberg, 1995). CKM change adopts a 'less for more' rather than a 'more for less' strategy, e.g. 20-80 percent rule, in which 20 percent of customers are most profitable, whereas the rest of customers, 80 percent, are least profitable. Therefore, development of knowledge about customers becomes the cornerstone in the DCC-based strategy for the achievement of SCA.

However, establishing an effective CKM initiative is a challenge for most organizations. Achievement of SCA requires a whole-system approach that captures and builds on the unique range of customer-centric knowledge, skills, and resources of organizations. Knowledge originates in human beings and is created by them, not by computers. So, CKM is not just about data, although data are analyzed, and not just about relationships, be they social (people-based) or transactional (technology-based), although they are sought. The heart of CKM is knowledge to add value to customers.

The proposed CKM model relates to a set of decisions regarding strategies of competitiveness, reinvention (e.g., BPR), knowledge, KM, and CRM. CKM is used in this book as a knowledge-intensive, customer-oriented, holistic business strategy that seeks to reengineer organizations through people, processes, and technology reinvention, and to utilize CK embedded in people, processes and technology to create value that enables firms to acquire and retain customers, expand relationships with them, and ultimately attain a sustainable customer, intimacy-based competitive advantage (Figure 8.2).

FUTURE TRENDS

The future trends discussed in this section are as follow: a shift from information-based to knowledge-based strategic competencies, a shift from technology-based to 'tech-knowledgy' based strategies, and a shift from machine intelligent tools to Web intelligent agents.

A Shift from Information-Based to Knowledge-Based Strategic Competencies

With progressive changes in the business world, the value of a business enterprise increasingly lies within the acquisition of CK and its accessibility. Harvesting and protecting this 'intellectual capital' will continue to be brought into the center-stage of organizations in the future. Over time, to remain competitive it will be essential to be customer-oriented and knowledge-enabled to be able to act quickly and effectively. Therefore, more adoption of customer-centric, knowledge-based business models will continue to grow to face turbulent environments and unexpected pressures.

In the future, organizations will continue their quest to establish links between strategic competencies, KM, organizational learning and innovation, specifically, how an organization identifies, assesses and exploits its knowledge-based strategic competencies, rather than information-based operational competencies and translates these into new processes, products and/or services.

These future trends are expected to be in line with the move towards virtual and knowledge-based learning organizations, enhancing the absorptive capacity of organizations, valuing knowledge on the balance sheet of organizations, providing greater rewards for leveraging knowledge, and reducing significant restrictions on knowledge workers.

A Shift from Technology-Based to 'Tech-knowledgy' Based Strategies

Technology is acquired usually to improve customer processes and quality, reduce costs, improve product delivery, and provide an advantage over other competitors. However, the competitive advantage of products, services, and technologies is short-lived and can be emulated easily by others. Therefore, technology alone should not be considered as a core competency for customer-centric business competition, but a knowledge-based core competency as a competitive differentiator.

Although technology can move information or knowledge at light speed, it is people who turn knowledge into timely and creative decisions (Awad and Ghaziri,

2004). Furthermore, information generated by technology cannot be used to make decisions without the correct knowledge to interpret it. Over 80 percent of all technology-centered, knowledge-based business initiatives have been known to fail because of the lack of attention to people (Whiting, 1999).

As a consequence of fast-changing, complex business processes, the availability of knowledge about customer business processes and their interdependencies has become a key success factor for businesses. Therefore, the ability to utilize the skills and creativity of people to develop, share, and utilize business knowledge is the key to success in this new economy. This is true, not only in traditional knowledge intensive areas such as customer service, consulting, training, and research and development, but also in production, facility management, and maintenance easily available knowledge makes the difference between efficient and inefficient business processes.

Knowledge management is much more than technology, but 'tech-knowledgy' is clearly a part of KM (Davenport and Prusak, 2000). Therefore, knowledge-based, customer-centric strategies are much more than technology, and the real danger is not when computers begin to think like people, but when people begin to think like computers. Businesses should focus on customer-centric 'tech-knolwedgy', not customer-centric technology, when facing competitive environments. The concern for customer 'tech-knowledgy' is a concern for both technology and humanity (human thinking and learning). This requires complete knowledge-based transformation from product-centric to customer-focused organizations.

A Shift from Machine Intelligent Tools to Web Intelligent Agents

Machine intelligent tools represent a set of methods that enables a computer to learn a specific task — such as decision making, estimation, classification, or prediction — without manual programming. Once the DW brings together data from several sources, the process of DM, e.g. classification of customers, may start scanning the data to find information that can be used to take actions related to customers, such as ways to increase sales or keep customers who are considering defecting.

DM agents can be used to detect major shifts in customer purchasing trends and to alert companies to the presence of a new trend. Advanced DM tools contain special types of artificial intelligent programs known as intelligent agents to perform these tasks. More use of customer-centric web intelligence and DM agents is expected to prevail over customer-centric intelligent tools that operate in a DW-discovering information environment.

CONCLUSION

Business firms are becoming increasingly aware of the need to collect, organize, mobilize, increase, and manage, the knowledge essential for their ability to survive, adapt and evolve in a turbulent business context. KM is a keyword, with different organizational and technological approaches to answer this need of the 21st century's organizations. Nonetheless, the current state of the field reveals a great deal of debate on the definition of the concept of knowledge and the value of KM for business organization measured by return on investment, and reveals the existence of competing KM research paradigms.

Knowledge is an intellectual capital resource for many organizations as it is combined with experience and understanding and is retained. CKM *content* technology (e.g., Analytical CRM) enables a company to integrate a large volume of customer information and to efficiently transform this information into useful knowledge. CKM *contact* technology (e.g., Collaborative CRM) enables a company to interact with its customers in ways that provide value to the customer as well as to make it easier for the customer to do business with the company.

CK may be viewed as analysis and human-based reflection and synthesis about what information means to the business and how it can be used. It is the raw material for BI that supports KM and is the core of an intelligent learning organization that must be accumulated, cultivated and managed to achieve SCA. Therefore, knowledge as a valuable corporate resource needs to be delivered at the right time, available at the right place, presented in the right shape, satisfying the quality requirements, and obtained at the lowest possible costs. In addition to quality of the data source, knowledge quality is a function of the quality of the environment for sharing information and the quality of the human resource that discovers, develops and retains the knowledge.

CK cannot be managed in the sense that data and information are managed. Unlike data and information, knowledge is retained by both 'brain-ware' and hardware systems. CKM is really the management of an environment in which people generate tacit knowledge and render it into explicit knowledge, then feed it back to the organization. This process forms the base for more tacit knowledge development which keeps the cycle going in an intelligent, learning organization. It is the process of creating, institutionalizing and distributing knowledge among people. Therefore, CKM initiatives need to be considered as socio-technical initiatives in order to provide a better understanding of the benefits and limitations of CKM initiatives, especially in the realm of social-oriented knowledge culture, communities, initiatives and rewards, measurement, technology-oriented knowledge repositories, modeling, and discovery systems.

Establishing an effective CKM initiative is a challenge for most organizations. Especially difficult is the capture of tacit knowledge that resides primarily in the heads of experienced employees. CK involves three overlapping factors, viz. people, organizational processes (content), and technology (ICT). However, those involved in KM initiatives often are relying on technology-focused initiatives or anecdotal (personalization vs. codification) evidence originating from their experiences; and a lack of generality, as CKM methods are usually context dependent and not easily transferred from one organization to another.

Personalization strategy refers to human-based, information processing activities such as brainstorming sessions periodically to identify and share knowledge. Codification is the systematic process for regularly capturing and distributing knowledge. Personalization strategy is more focused on connecting knowledge workers through networks, and is better suited to companies that face *one-off* and unique problems that depend more on tacit knowledge and expertise than on codified knowledge.

On the other side, the codification strategy is more focused on technology that enables storage, indexing, retrieval, and reuse of knowledge after it has been extracted from a person, made independent of that person, and reused. Personalized knowledge refers to implicit knowledge that is usually *sticky* and difficult to exchange, whereas codified knowledge refers to explicit knowledge that is usually *leaky* and easy to transfer, but limited in its depth and serendipity.

With respect to the role of ICTs in generating CK, they include both operational and analytical parts. The analytical part of the CKM includes BI technology for back-end marketing management activities, such as campaign management and sales management; it allows users to feed on certain business rules for customer groups into the operational side, as to predict future trends and behaviors and discover previously unknown patterns. It also facilitates marketing campaigns and surveys. Finally, the new generated knowledge feeds into the DW.

In CKM, CK creation is a spiral process of interaction between explicit knowledge and tacit knowledge so as to achieve SCA. CK may be generated through data mining of corporate databases and warehouses, creating knowledge from the expertise, creativity, and insights of people, or knowledge sharing among people across and around the organization. Especially difficult to capture is tacit CK that resides primarily in the heads of experienced employees. A knowledge-intensive customer-led business interacts directly with an individual customer, or group of customers to, in order to know about customer preferences for products and/or services. Based on knowledge developed from customer interactions, offerings are designed in a way that adds value to customers as well as to organizations.

The best use of customer data is, not only to look at the past but to forecast the future through using predictive analytics to generate knowledge. Although knowledge is a dynamic concept that is defined quite loosely, it is still evolving as a main source of wealth for many national economies as well as companies. The creation of SCA lies in resource creation rather than resource allocation, and in strategic management of CK to thrive rather than operational dependence on information to survive.

In CKM strategy, organizations utilize their DCCs in people, processes, and technology to secure the provision of knowledge-based products and/or services for customers. The CKM strategy is devised and implemented in real time through access to an organizational information base, authority to take decisive action, and the requisite skills that are embedded at the front-line offices where real customer-centric processes take place. Operational customer data are used to profile customers, and the knowledge from which is used to develop from operational data leads to an understanding about customers.

Successful development of CKM strategy depends on specificities of knowledge captured by an organization or shared among partners or suppliers (knowledge type, level, form, and characteristics), knowledge strategy, KM strategy, as well as CKM strategy adopted. Further, it is expected that inter-organizational CK generation will be influenced by the absorptive capacity of organizations as well as the type and level of interactive activities conducted.

CKM integrates knowledge in a way that enriches the quality of decision-making throughout the organization. The aim of CKM strategy is to produce a positive return on investment in people, processes, and technology, as well as efficient production, marketing, sales, customer services, and improved morale of employees. The implications of the customer-centric knowledge-based shift in organizational responses towards today's changing environments are evidenced in a faster cycle of knowledge-creation and its application not only in products or services but also in long-term relationships with customers.

The next part of the book is the forth and last part. It includes three chapters that address successful harvesting and mastering of CKM value chain.

REFERENCES

Aadne, J. H., Krogh, G. & Roos, J. (1996). Representationism: the traditional approach to cooperative strategies. In: G., Krogh, & J., Roos (Eds.). *Managing knowledge - perspectives on cooperation and competition*, SAGE Publications, UK: London.

Alavi, M., & Leidner, D.E. (1999). Knowledge Management Systems: Emerging Views and Practices from the Field. *32nd Hawaii International Conference on System Sciences*, IEEE Computer Society.

Al-Shammari, M. (2005). Implementing a knowledge-enabled CRM strategy in a large company: A case study from a developing country. In M. E. Jennex (Ed.), *Case studies in knowledge management* (pp. 249-278). Hershey, PA: Idea Group Publishing.

Al-Shammari, M. (2008). Toward a knowledge management strategic framework in the Arab region. *International Journal of Knowledge Management*, *4*(3), 44-63.

Ackoff, R. L. (1989). From data to wisdom: Presidential address to ISGSR. *Journal of Applied Systems Analysis*, *16*, 3-9.

Anderson, K., & Kerr, C. (2002). *Customer relationship management*. New York: McGraw-Hill.

Apostolou, D., & Mentzas, G. (2003). Experiences from knowledge management implementation in companies of the software sector. *Business Process Management Journal*, *9*(3), 354-381.

Awad, E., & Ghaziri, H. (2004). *Knowledge management*. Upper Saddle River, NJ: Prentice-Hall.

Barna, Z. (2003). Knowledge management: A critical e-business strategic factor. Unpublished Masters Thesis, San Diego State University.

Berger, P. L., & Luckmann, T. (1966). *The social construction of reality*. Garden City, NY: Anchor Books.

Berry, M., & Linoff, G. (2000). *Mastering data mining: The art and science of customer relationship management*. New York: Wiley.

Blackler, F. (1995). Knowledge, knowledge work and organizations: An overview and interpretation. *Organization Studies*, *16*, 1021-46.

Becerra-Fernandez, I., & Sabherwal, R. (2001). Organizational knowledge management: A contingency perspective. *Journal of Management Information Systems*, *18*(1), 23-55.

Brackett, M. H. (1999). Business intelligence value vhain. *DM Review Magazine*, March. http://www.dmreview.com/issues/19990301/115-1.html (retrieved on 17 January 2008).

Bueren, A., Schierholz, R., Kolbe, L. M., & Brenner, W. (2005). Improving performance of customer-processes with knowledge management. *Business Process Management Journal, 11*(5), 573-588.

Bukowitz, W., & Williams, R. (2000). *The knowledge management Fieldbook.* London: Prentice Hall.

Buttle, F. (2004). *Customer relationship management: Concepts and tools.* Oxford, England: Elsevier Publishing.

Chaudhury, A., & Kuiboer, J. (2002). *E-business and e-commerce infrastructure.* New York: McGraw-Hill.

Chen, I., & Popovich, K. (2003). Understanding customer relationship management (CRM): People, process and technology. *Business Process Management Journal, 9*(5), 672-688.

Chen, Y-H., & Su, C-T. (2006). A Kano-CKM model for customer knowledge discovery. *Total Quality Management, 17*(5), 589-608.

Civi, E. (2000). Knowledge management as a competitive asset: a review. *Marketing Intelligence & Planning, 18*(4), 166-174.

Cook, S. D., & Brown, J. S. (1999). Bridging epistemologies: The generative dance between organizational knowledge and organizational knowing. *Organization Science, 10*(4), 381-400.

Dalkir, K. (2005). *Knowledge management in theory and practice.* Amsterdam: Elsevier Butterworth-Heinemann.

Davenport, T. H., DeLong, D. W., & Beers, M. C. (1998). Successful knowledge management projects. Sloan Management Review, *39*(2), 43-57.

Davenport, T., & Prusak, L. (2000). *Working knowledge.* 2nd edition, Boston, MA: Harvard Business School Press.

Davenport, T. H., Javenpaa, S. L., & Beers, M. C. (1996). Improving knowledge processes. *Sloan Management Review, 37*(4), 53-65.

Davenport, T. H., Harris, J. G., & Kohli, A. K. (2001). How do they know their customers so well? *Sloan Management Review, 42*(2), 63-73.

Davenport, T. (2006). Competing on Analytics. *Harvard Business Review,* January, 99-107.

Davenport, T. (2007). *Competing on analytics*. Interviewed by Power, D. posted at www.dssresources.com/interviews/davenport/davenport05272007.html, retrieved on 2 December 2007.

Desouza, K. C., & Awazu, Y. (2005). What do they Know? *Business Strategy Review, 16*(1), 41-.45.

Galbraith, J. (1973). *Designing complex organizations*. Reading, MA: Addison-Wesley.

Garcia-Murilo, M., & Annabi, H. (2002). Customer knowledge management. *Journal of the Operational Research Society, 53*, 875-884.

Gebert, H., Geib, M., Kolbe, L., & Brenner, W. (2003). Knowledge-enabled customer relationship management and knowledge management concepts. *Journal of Knowledge Management, 7*(5), 107-123.

Gibbert, M., Leibold, M., & Probst, G. (2002). Five styles of customer knowledge management and how smart companies use them to create value. *European Management Journal, 20*(5), 459-469.

Ginsberg, M., & Kambil, A. (1999). Annotate: A Web-based knowledge management support system for document collections. *The 32nd Hawaii International Conference on System Sciences*, IEEE Computer Society Press.

Hallberg, G. (1995). *All consumers are not created equal*. New York, NY: John Wiley.

Handzic, M., & Zhou, Z. (2005). *Knowledge management: An integrative approach*. Oxford: Chandos Publishing.

Hansen M. T., Nohria, N., & Tierney, T. (1999). What's your strategy for managing knowledge? *Harvard Business Review, 77*(2), 106-116.

Hodgson, G. M. (2000). The concept of emergence in social science: its history and importance. *Emergence, 2*(4), 65-77.

Hofer-Alfeis, J. (2003). Effective integration of KM into the business starts with a top-down knowledge strategy. *Journal of Universal Computer Science, 9*(7), 719-728.

Holsapple, C. W., & Joshi, K.D. (2000). An investigation of factors that influence the management of knowledge in organizations. *Journal of Strategic Information Systems, 9*, 235-261.

Jarvenpaa, S. L., & Ives, B. (1994). The global network organization of the future: information management opportunities and challenges. *Journal of Management Information Systems, 10*(4,) 25-57.

Jashapara, A. (2004). *Knowledge management: An integrated approach.* Harlow, England: Prentice-Hall.

Jennex, M. E., & Olfman, L. (2001). Development recommendations for knowledge management/organizational memory systems. Contemporary trends in IS development (pp. 209-222). Norewll, MA: Kluwer Publishing.

Jennex, M. E., (2006). Culture, context, and knowledge management, *International Journal of Knowledge Management, 2*(2), i-v.

Kakihara, M., & Sorensen, C. (2002). Exploring knowledge emergence. From chaos to organizational knowledge. *Journal of Global Information Technology Management, 15*(3), 48-66.

Kolbe, L., et al. (Eds). (2003). *Customer knowledge management.* Berlin: Springer.

Koskinen, K. U. (2001). Tacit knowledge as a promoter of success in technology firms. *The 34th Hawaii International Conference on System Sciences,* IEEE Computer Society.

Maier, R., & Remus, U. (2003). Implementing process-oriented knowledge management strategies. *Journal of Knowledge Management, 7*(4), 62-74.

Liebowitz, J. (1999). *The Knowledge management handbook.* Boca Raton, FL: CRC Press.

Leidner, D. E., (2006). The ongoing challenge of knowledge management initiatives. *Cutter Benchmark Review, 6*(3), March.

Liebowitz, J. (2004). Conceptualizing and implementing knowledge Management, In P. Love, P. Fong, and Z. Irani (Eds.). *Management of knowledge in project environment* (pp. 1-18), Amsterdam: Elsevier Butterworth-Heinemann.

Lindgree, A. (2004). The design, implementation, and monitoring of a CRM programme: A case study. *Marketing Intelligence & Planning, 22*(2), 160-186.

Lindsey, K. (2002). *Measuring Knowledge Management Effectiveness: A Task-Contingent Organizational Capabilities Perspective.* Eighth Americas Conference on Information Systems, (pp. 2085-2090).

Lopez-Nicolas, C., & Molina-Castillo F. J. (2008). Customer Knowledge Management and E-commerce: The role of customer perceived risk. *International Journal of Information Management, 28*(2), 102-113.

Maier, R., & Remus, U. (2003). Implementing process-oriented knowledge management strategies. *Journal of Knowledge Management, 7*(4), 62-74.

Malhotra, Y., & Galletta, D. (2003). Role of commitment and motivation as antecedents of knowledge management systems implementation. *36th Hawaii International Conference on System Sciences*, IEEE Computer Society.

March, J. G. (1991). Exploration and exploitation in organizational learning. *Organization Science, 2*(1), 71-87.

Massey, A. P., Montoya-Weiss, M. M., & O'Driscoll, T. M. (2002). Knowledge Management in Pursuit of Performance: Insights from Nortel Networks. MIS Quarterly, *26*(3), 269-289.

Maturana, H. R., & Varela, F. J. (1992). *The Tree of Knowledge: The Biological Roots of Human Understanding.* Boston, MA: Shambhala.

McKeen, J., & Smith, H. (2003*). Making IT Happen: Critical Issues in IT Management.* Chichester, UK: John Wiley.

Miles, R., Miles, G., & Snow, C. (2006). *Collaborative entrepreneurship: How communities of networked firms use continuous innovation to create economic wealth*, Stanford, California: Stanford University Press.

Nonaka, I. (1994). A dynamic theory of organizational knowledge creation. *Organizational Science, 5*(1), 14-37.

Nonaka, I., & T. Nishiguchi, ed. (2001). *Knowledge emergence: social, technical, and evolutionary dimensions of knowledge creation.* Oxford: Oxford University Press.

Nonaka, I., & Takeuchi, H. (1995). *The knowledge-creating company: How Japanese companies create the dynamics of innovation.* New York: Oxford University Press.

North, D. C. (1986). The new institutional economics. *Journal of Institutional and Theoretical Economics, 142*, 230-37.

Offsey, S. (1997). Knowledge management: Linking people to knowledge for bottom line results. *Journal of Knowledge Management, 1*(2), 113-122.

Paquette, S. (2005). Customer knowledge management. In D. Schwartz (Ed.), The *Encyclopedia of knowledge management* (pp. 90-96), Hershey, PA: Idea Group.

Park, C., & Kim, Y. (2003). A framework of dynamic CRM: Linking marketing with information strategy, *Business Process Management Journal, 9*(5), 652-671.

Peppers, D., & Rogers, M. (2004). *Managing customer relationships: A strategic framework*. Hoboken, NJ: John Wiley.

Peppers, D., Rogers, M., & Dorf, B. (1999). *The one-to-one field book*. New York: Doubleday.

Probst, G. et al. (1999). *Managing knowledge: Building blocks for success*. New York: John Wiley & Sons.

Rochart, J., & Short, J. (1991). The networked organization and the management of interdependence. In *The corporations of the 1990s: IT and organizational transformation* (pp. 189-216). In M. S. Scott-Morton (Eds.). Oxford: Oxford University Press.

Roscoe, D. (2003). So what is the future for CRM? *Journal of Customer Management*, *11*(2), 42-3.

Rowley, J. (2002a). Eight questions for customer knowledge management in E-Business, *Journal of Knowledge Management*, *6*(5), 500-511.

Rowley, J. (2002b). Reflections on customer knowledge management in E-Business. *Qualitative Market Research*, *5*(4), 268-280.

Rubenstein-Montano, B., Liebwowitz, J., Buchwalter, J., McCaw, D., Newman, B., & Rebeck, K. (2001). SMARTvision: A knowledge-management methodology. *Journal of Knowledge Management*, *5*(4), 300-310.

Sage, A. P., & Rouse, W.B. (1999). Information systems frontiers in knowledge management. Information Systems Frontiers, *1*(3), 205-219.

Schutz, A., & Luckmann, T. (1974). *The structure of the life world, 1*(1). London: Heinemann.

Senge, P. M. (1990). *The fifth discipline: The art and practice of the learning organization*. London: Random House.

Seybold, P. (2002). *An executive guide to CRM*. Boston, MA: Patricia Seybold Group.

Smith, H. A., & McKeen, J. D. (2005). Developments in Practice XVIII - Customer Knowledge Management: Adding Value for Our Customers. *Communications of the Association for Information Systems*, *16*, 744-755.

Spender, J. (1998). Pluralist epistemology and the knowledge-based theory of the firm. *Organization*, *5*(2), 233-56.

Stacey, R. D. (2000). The emergence of knowledge in organizations. *Emergence, 2*(4), 23-39.

Su, C-T., Chen, Y-H., & Sha, D. Y. (2006) Linking innovative product development with customer knowledge: a data-mining approach. *Technovation, 26*(7), 784-795.

Suchman, L. A. (1987). *Plans and situated actions: The problem of human-machine communication.* Cambridge: Cambridge University Press.

Swift, R. (2001). *Accelerating customer relationships: Using CRM and relationship technologies.* Upper Saddle River, NJ: Prentice-Hall.

Sveiby, K. E. (2001). A knowledge-based theory of the firm to guide in strategy formulation. *Journal of Intellectual Capital, 2*(4), 344-358.

Tiwana, A. (2001). *The essential guide to knowledge management: E-business and CRM applications.* Upper Saddle River, NJ: Prentice-Hall.

Turban, E., Leidner, D., McLean, E., & Wetherbe, J. (2008). *Information technology for management: Transforming organizations in the digital economy.* 5th edition, New York: John Wiley.

Turban, E., McLean, E., & Wetherbe, J. (2002). *Information technology for management: transforming business in the digital economy.* 3rd edition, New York: John Wiley.

Varela, F., Thompson, E., & Rosch, E. (1991). *The embodied mind: Cognitive science and human experience.* Cambridge, MA: MIT Press.

von Hippel, E.A. (1977). Has a customer already developed your next product? *Sloan Management Review, 18*(2), 63-74.

von Krogh, G., & Roos, J. (1995). *Organizational epistemology.* New York: St. Martin's Press.

Wenger, E. (1998). *Communities of practice: Learning, meaning, and identity.* Cambridge: Cambridge University Press.

Wenger, R., McDermot, R., & Snyder, W. (2002). *Cultivating communities of practice: A guide to managing knowledge.* Boston, MA: Harvard Business School Press.

Whitehead, A. N. (1929). Process *and reality.* New York: Macmillan.

Wiig, K. (1993). *Knowledge management foundations.* Arlington, TX: Schema Press.

Wiig, K. M. (1997). KM: where did it come from and where will it go? *Expert Systems with Applications, 13*(1), 1-14.

Winograd, T., & Flores, F. (1986). *Understanding computers and cognition: A new foundation for design.* Norwood, NJ: Ablex Publishing.

Yu, S., Kim, Y., & Kim, M., (2004). Linking organizational knowledge management Drivers to knowledge management performance: An exploratory study. *The 37th Hawaii International Conference on System Sciences*, HICSS36, IEEE Computer Society.

Zack, M. H. (1999a). Developing a knowledge strategy. *California Management Review, 41*(3), 125-145.

Zack, M. H. (1999b). Managing codified knowledge, *Sloan Management Review, 40*(4), 45-58.

Zack, M. H. (2002). A strategic pretext for knowledge management. *Proceedings of the Third European Conference on Organizational Knowledge, Learning and Capabilities,* Athens, Greece, April 5.

Zhu, Z. (2004). Knowledge management: Towards a universal concept or cross-cultural contexts? *Knowledge Management Research & Practice*, (2), 67-79.

Section IV
Mastering (3Ms)

Chapter IX
Maximizing Value for Customers

INTRODUCTION

Efforts to improve the experience of customers do little to boost customer satisfaction and loyalty if they fail to connect with customers and anticipate their needs. The first chapter of this last part of the book deals with the CKM harvesting phase. A process-oriented customer-centric enterprise needs to know its customers and to be resilient and vibrant towards them and their preferences by creating and delivering superior value offerings that suit their desired needs and/or preferences. Doing good things for customers reciprocates good things for business.

As the long-term objective of a competitive business strategy is to build SCA, focus should be on 'difficult-to-imitate' resource-based capabilities (Salck et al., 2006). The CKM strategy is adopted in order to leverage business DCCs, i.e. CK, to deliver highest value-adding (VA) products and/or services to customers, and achievement of SCA for organizations.

CONCEPTUAL FOUNDATIONS

The business environment of the 21st century is characterized by extremely tight competition between companies. Companies are forced constantly to reduce costs and outperform their rivals. However, as customers increasingly are becoming demanding and pressuring organizations for higher quality products and/or services, competing only with price is becoming very risky. Although efficient and cost-based operations have been traditionally adopted, other bases of competition need to be put in place.

Business organizations strive to satisfy the minimum expectations of their stakeholder groups, including customers. Businesses aim to deliver satisfaction levels above the minimum for different stakeholders: companies might aim to delight their customers, perform well for their employees, and deliver a threshold level of satisfaction to their suppliers (Kotler, 2006). For convenience only, the view of consumers in the B2C context may have been emphasized in this as well as the subsequent chapter. However, the adopted definition of customers in this book is much broader and includes more than individual consumers; it encompasses groups such as business customers, civilians in the Government, patients in healthcare, etc.

This section of the chapter covers the following parts: customer segmentation, customization, mass customization (MC), MC examples, and ICT requirements for MC.

Customer Segmentation

In recent years, the role of marketing has changed radically. Instead of interacting with large simultaneously numbers of customers, the new role is to interact with individual customers, focusing on the specific needs of that customer through customer segmentation.

Customer segmentation and analysis is the process that seeks to understand customers better, and increase revenue and retention by dividing a customer base into groups that share similar characteristics, based on demographics such as attitude and psychological profiles (e.g., age, gender, interests, and spending habits). Value-based customer segmentation, on the other hand, looks at groups of customers in terms of the revenue they generate and the costs of establishing and maintaining relationships with them.

Usually, only a few broad segments would be defined based on overall demographic information, such as older users and young users. However, with utilization of advanced data storage and analysis systems, it is possible to define many more segments at a much finer and finer level of precision. It is now possible to define the segments based on their value and volume of interactions with the company (rather than general demographic information) and to automate different responses to each segment. However, CKM needs to address the issue of segment granularity- how small the customer segments may be before they become too many for the organization to handle (Knox et al., 2003)

Market segmentation follows three approaches (Hill and Jones, 2007):

- No market segmentation, wherein a product is targeted at the 'average customer',

- High market segmentation, in which a different product is offered to each market segment, and
- Focused market segmentation that offers one product to one or a few market segments.

Customer-centric services include three types:

- Customization for customers (e.g., DELL)
- Modularization
- Bundling (cross-selling and up-selling)

Customer Experience on the Internet

Customer experience refers to a target customer's perception and interpretation of all the stimuli encountered while interacting with a firm. On the Internet, customer experience can be defined as the interpretation of one's complete encounter with the site, from the initial look at the homepage through the purchase experience, including decisions such as abandoning a shopping cart (Mohammed et al., 2003).

Seven key facets of the customer experience are observed (Mohammed et al., 2003):

- *The Objective Experience:* Certain level of functionality must exist for the site to work. Examples of objective experience problems include complex checkout, poor site reliability and accessibility, poorly designed or implemented search software, missing information and incorrect prices.
- *The Perceived Experience*: Relates to the individual's perception of the encounter with the firm. Every experience needs to be understood in terms of how each customer perceives, or interprets their interactions with the site.
- *The Encounter Experience:* Includes both the process and output measures of the shopping experience. Focus of data collection and assessment must be on both process and output measures throughout the encounter.
- *The Reactions to Stimuli Experience:* In a retail context, reactions to stimuli experience includes a customer's response to the storefront, layout, merchandising, ambiance, as well as the traditional service encounter with the retail sales staff. Also includes reactions to higher-order stimuli such as reactions to brand presentation, other customers in the store, the retail location and product assortment.
- *The Sensory Experience*: Some sites only stimulate one sense – sight through text, photos, and other graphics. Other sites enrich the sensory experience

by including audio files or the option of making direct contact with a service representative.

- *The Cognitive and Emotional Experience:* Customer reactions are both cognitive 'I think the site is easy to navigate' and emotional 'I feel good about this brand'. Cognitive responses are more thoughtful and evaluative in nature whereas emotional responses tend to capture the moods, attitudes and feelings of the customer.
- *The Relative Experience:* Consumers' prior shopping experiences and most have prior experiences on other websites can affect a consumer's reaction to various stimuli during a site visit or a purchase. All consumer experiences are evaluated relative to some other experience, whether offline or online or merely tangentially related. For example, experience of using Barnes&Noble. com is always judged relative to users' experience at both Amazon.com and the Barnes and Noble retail store.

The Internet Experience Hierarchy

Customer Experience develops through four stages (Mohammed et al., 2003):

1. Stage One: Experiencing Functionality

This stage is best described by this statement "The Site Works Well". It includes five characteristics, viz. usability and navigation, speed, reliability, media accessibility, and security, which are considered the price of entry:

- Usability and Navigation: Usability is the ease with which a site can achieve a user's goals, e.g. search inventory, check prices or make a purchase. Usability is affected by many elements of a site, e.g. site's loading speed, structure of its pages and its graphic design.
- Speed: Refers to the time required to display a site page on the user's screen. Since most consumers still use dialup models, every bit of information needs to count
- Reliability: Extent to which a website experiences periods of downtime or times when users cannot access its pages, typically due to planned maintenance or unplanned system crashes. Reliability also defines the extent to which the site correctly downloads to the user.
- Media Accessibility: With the proliferation of Internet-enabled devices, or Web appliances, media accessibility (i.e. the ability of a site to download to various media platforms) is becoming increasingly important. Websites therefore have to be simplified and specifically designed for multiple plat-

forms until standards are established and accepted universally across al l platforms.

- Security: Consumers will attempt to determine if they can trust a site by asking basic questions such as whether the site is secure, will their privacy be protected, whether the site can be trusted with credit card information, etc.

These five characteristics can be considered the price of entry. Firms, however, often violate these basic tenets by designing graphics-heavy sites, overloading the customer with information or creating complex navigation.

2. Stage Two: Experiencing Intimacy

This stage is best represented by the statement "They Understood Me", and includes four elements: Customization, Communication, Consistency, and Trustworthiness.

- Customization: The site's ability to tailor itself or to be tailored by each user. Customization initiated or managed by the firm is tailoring while customization initiated or managed by the user is called personalization. For example, Yahoo offers both tailoring and personalization. Yahoo can use the personal-profile data entered when users register at the site to tailor email messages, banner ads and content to the individual. On the personalization end, users can create personalized My Yahoo! pages by features such as stock quotes, weather conditions, and local television programming schedules.
- Communication: Refers to the dialogue that unfolds between the site and its users. Communication can be in three forms:

  - Firm-to-user (e.g. email notification)
  - User-to-firm (e.g. customer service request)
  - Two-way communication (e.g. instant messaging)

- Consistency: Refers to the degree to which the site experience or retail store experience is replicable over time. Expectations are established during the user experience, and that deviation from these expectations is what ultimately matters, not the objective experience per se.
- Trustworthiness: Trait that is established over time, after users have the chance to evaluate the site's services. Four characteristics that reflect the intimacy of the customer experience:

  - The degree of customization (both personalization and tailoring)

- ° Deeper levels of personal communication
- ° The consistency of the experience over time
- ° The degree of trustworthiness that the site (or store) has earned over time.

3. Stage Three: Experiencing Internalization

This stage is best represented by the statement "It's Part of Me". Having internalized the experience, the user re-creates and replays it when they are no longer directly engaged with the site or retail store. This stage includes four elements: Exceptional Value, Shift from Consumption to Leisure Activity, Active Community Membership, and "The Company Cannot Manage without Me".

- Exceptional Value: User is convinced that the firm offers exceptional value and cannot be persuaded otherwise.
- Shift from Consumption to Leisure Activity: Instead of thinking about a visit to the firm's website as a task that needs to be done, users begin to think about such visits as something they do for pleasure.
- Active Community Membership: While not all customers will engage in community activity, those who reach this stage often want to participate with other like-minded folk who share the same passion for the experience.
- "The Company Cannot Manage without Me": Customer perceives that the firm is either incapable of managing the experience without the user.

4. Stage Four: Experiencing Evangelism

This stage is best described by the statement "I Love to Share the Story". This stage includes two substages: Taking the Word to the Market and Defending the Experience.

- Taking the Word to the Market: Individuals often tell stories about products that their wonderful and exceptional experiences. There is a clear emotional connection and passion about telling the story.
- Defending the Experience: Much like staunch Republicans or Democrats, customers who reach this stage are ardent defenders of their viewpoints – so much so that they can become visibly angry when others disagree or buy competitive offerings.

Mass Customization

MC is a flexible or agile approach for producing customized goods and services to meet individual customers' needs with near mass production efficiency (Gilmore & Pine, 1997) associated with make-to-stock (MTS) items. Table 9.1 documents a few examples of companies that are adopting the MC approach (Mok et al., 2000).

The requirements of MC must be unified into a cohesive framework. As in ICT systems, many companies are synthesizing a cohesive suite of ICT tools to reach MC. The process of MC is supported by three interdependent pillars (Bourke, 1999): a) product modularization, b) product planning and control, and c) ICT infrastructure support.

Product Modularization

Product modularization, or product definition, involves using the quality function deployment (QFD), design for mass customization (DFMC), CIM, and CAD/CAM software to design products that maximize the interchangeability of standard parts and assemblies. The results should reduce direct product costs, and overhead costs associated with excess and duplicated parts in the product database and inventory. The most recognizable way to accomplish modular design is to modularize components to be able to customize products and services. One criterion for modular design is to provide maximum flexibility by facilitating custom configuration as late in the order fulfillment cycle as possible, e.g. adding the final options in the distribution channel. Modular design is not accomplished only with product definition tools. For instance, CIM data can be supplemented with volume, cost, and quality information from the ERP system, and used for strategic sourcing decisions, including supplier base reduction.

Broad ranges of software tools are required to configure customizable products. The selections of tools include the following:

- *QFD:* A structured methodology to ensure that customer needs are identified and honored. QFD is often referred to as listening to the Voice of the Customer (VOC).
- *CAD:* Software tools for creating and modifying product designs.
- Computer-aided Engineering (CAE): Software tools for conducting analytical evaluation of the product design.
- *CAM*: Software tools for creating and modifying manufacturing methods.

Table 9.1. Examples of companies adopting the MC approach

Companies	MC Approach
Dell Computer	Dell Computer uses the collaborative approach and assembles computers to a customer's exact specifications. Dell sells double-digit million U.S. dollars worth of built-to-order PCs a day. Dell passed IBM in early 1998 to claim the second spot in the PC market share.
British Airways	British Airways (BA) plans to deliver top-notch customer service to its first-class frequent flyers through streamlining its supply-chain process. Understanding passengers' needs beforehand makes it possible for BA to deliver individualized items for passengers on each flight just before takeoff.
Ritz-Carlton	Ritz-Carlton uses software to personalize guests' experiences by linking to a database filled with quirks and preferences of half a million guests. Any desk clerk can find out whether a guest is allergic to feathers, what their favorite newspaper is, or whether they like extra towels. The company stores guest information in a database and uses it to tailor the service to each guest on his/her next visit. This is a transparent way to customize for those customers who do not want to be bothered with direct collaboration.
Planters Company	Planters chose cosmetic customization when it retooled its old plant in Suffolk, Virginia. As an example, Wal-Mart wanted to sell peanuts and mixed nuts in larger quantities than 7-Eleven did. In the past, Planters could produce only long batches of small, medium, and large cans giving customers only these few standard packages which may not meet their requirements. Today, Planters can switch quickly between sizes, labels, and shipping containers, responding to each retailer's desires on an order-to-order basis.
Regent, Hong Kong	In the fine dining restaurant, the hotel cosmetically customizes paper napkins and matchboxes by printing their customers' names on them. Although personalizing a service in this way is cosmetic, it is of value to many customers.
Lutron Electronics	Lutron's customers can adapt its lighting systems to maximize productivity at the office or to create appropriate moods at home without having to experiment with multiple switches each time they desire a new effect. The customers can achieve quickly the desired effect by punching in the programmed settings.
ChemStation	ChemStation produces soap after independently analyzing each customer's needs. It formulates the right mixture of soap for each customer, which goes into a standard tank. The company learns each customer's usage pattern and delivers more soap before the customer has to ask.

Source: Adapted from Mok, C., Alan, S., & Wong, L. (2000). Mass Customization in the Hospitality Industry: Concepts and Applications, Fourth International Conference 'Tourism in Southeast Asia & Indo-China: Development, Marketing and Sustainability', June 24-26.

- *Component Supplier Management (CSM):* Software tools used to classify, store, search, and retrieve parts. CSM generates information for maximizing the reuse of existing parts and to identify quickly new part sources when needed.
- *DFMC:* It is a methodology used to ensure ease of assembly, and to reduce costs by evaluating product complexity early in the definition phase before costs are committed.
- *Visualization:* Animation and communication tools used to facilitate collaborative product definition by providing simplified graphical output from 3D CAD models.
- *Product Data Management (PDM):* Software systems are used to manage all forms of product and process data as well as the product definition activities. Core PDM functions include an electronic vault for document and file storage, workflow management, and product structure management, also known as Bill of Material (BOM) inventory management system.
- *Product Configurator (PC):* Systems that create, maintain, and use electronic product models that allow complete definition of all possible product options and variation combinations. This capability is essential for companies offering unique configurations to satisfy specific customer needs. The issue is how to define options and variations for unique product configurations without creating a massive, bulky database of BOMs for every possible combination of finished items. To address this issue, PCs are often developed as a module in ERP systems. As product configurations became more complex, however, more sophisticated software methods have evolved.

Product Planning and Control

From the perspective of the production, marketing, and delivery phases of the MC value chain, several ICT-based applications are required.

Sales Force Automation (SFA)

SFA is a broad term encompassing the use of advanced ICT to automate the total sales cycle. The overall objective of SFA is to gain an SCA. SFA systems consist of many subsystems, such as Quotation and Proposal Preparation. Of the many subsystems, however, the essential one is the PC module, described above.

Within the range of SFA processes, the PC software module is the most relevant example to emphasize. The capability of this module, and how effectively a company uses it, determines whether a company gains a primary benefit: accurate order entry of a customized product configuration without further validation editing by engineering staff. The product model, represented in the PC software, can be used in the SFA process in these three methods:

- Mobile lap top computers—for use by sales staff in an on-site assisted buying mode; or
- Web-based—for quoting, configuring, and order entry by the buyer—without assistance from an on-site sales personnel; or
- Computers manned by inside sales staff at the manufacturing or headquarters site.

Enterprise Resource Planning (ERP)

ERP systems evolved from Material Requirements Planning (MRP) developed in the 1960s, and Manufacturing Resource Planning (MRP II) in the 1980s to their current state. ERP systems are tools for the plan and control of the product from order entry throughout shipment. As MRP II systems expanded into ERP, more functionality was added, such as accounting and financial capabilities. In addition, ERP systems differ from earlier MRP II systems in the use of some capabilities, such as Graphical User Interfaces (GUIs).

ERP systems are designed to optimize flow of material and manufacturing processes. ERP systems generate successive levels of plans, such as master schedules, material requirements, and capacity plans. Though many companies realize bottom-line benefits with ERP when properly implemented, industry now demands more dynamic planning and scheduling methods needed to compete effectively. Recently, ERP systems are viewed in a fresh perspective since Advanced Planning and Scheduling (APS) systems have delivered on their promise.

Advanced Planning and Scheduling (APS)

Limitations in ERP systems, coupled with recent advances in ICT, have fueled the rapid growth and acceptance of APS systems as production planning and decision support tools.

APS systems take into account demand and resource constraint data, and process the data using intelligent analytical tools to prepare realistic and achievable plans. APS are characterized as modeling and optimization systems. A model defines the demands (e.g., dates, quantities), resources (e.g., personnel, equipment, material), and objectives (e.g., maximize throughput, deliver 99.8 percent on-time delivery). Management can then set priorities as input to the model and analytical routines that are logic rules to determine the optimum plan.

APS systems, unlike ERP systems, provide a fast response using advanced ICT capabilities (e.g. fast, in-memory processing) through which multiple 'what-if' simulation scenarios can be generated quickly for decision support and analysis. What's more, they can develop simultaneously plans and schedules, in contrast to the serial approach of ERP systems. Thus, APS systems downgrade ERP systems to a new role as transaction processing backbones for the decision support capabilities of APS systems. In effect, APS systems do not replace ERP systems; rather, they need to be integrated tightly with ERP systems to leverage the capabilities of each.

Flow Manufacturing (FM)

The ability of the manufacturing organization to be highly flexible and responsive to customer needs and preferences is an essential ingredient for Flow Manufacturing (MC). This ability is known widely as 'agile manufacturing,' and that term also encompasses 'lean' or 'JIT' manufacturing.

The objective of flow manufacturing is to produce a high-quality product in the shortest order fulfillment time at the lowest cost. It is based on 'customer-pull' methods rather than 'producer-push' execution; that is, a customer's order triggers the assembly and manufacturing process, not a master schedule based on the forecast.

ICT Infrastructure Support

Capitalizing on new ICT capabilities may well be a company's competitive differentiator. Currently, among the major ICT support capabilities relevant to MC, are interoperability, componentization, and the Web.

Interoperability

Interoperability is the ability of systems, comprised of a heterogeneous network of computer hardware and software, to share application software in a seamless manner. In essence, interoperability recognizes and addresses the fallaciousness of the 'one size fits all' production strategy of the past. Such strategy has proven unsuccessful in the constantly changing industrial environment.

The objective of interoperability is to facilitate a 'best-of-breed' manufacturing strategy. A class of software known as 'middleware,' or Enterprise Application Integration (EAI) software, provides the necessary capabilities to unify the numerous ICT elements in a 'best-of-breed' strategy.

There are many choices for 'middleware' software, each with a wide range of capabilities. From an executive management viewpoint, the primary consideration is to ensure that the ICT department has selected properly the appropriate middleware package, consistent with company objectives and strategy.

Componentization

Componentization refers to the software development practice used to remedy the difficulty of implementing and maintaining the large, monolithic applications of past programming approaches. ICT departments were often asked by executive steering committee pleas for quick changes in application logic with totally unacceptable and outrageous time and cost implementation plans. With componentization, business logic or technical functionality is encapsulated in small interchangeable software modules, or components, of information with explicit descriptions of procedures and instructions of how to manipulate information. Importantly, the modules can be reused, thus shortening new application development time or modifying existing applications.

The major benefits of componentization include the following:

- Improving application systems agility and flexibility.
- Allowing a company to choose the best fit of software choices.
- Avoiding 'big bang' implementations when systems must be upgraded with new software releases.
- Facilitating gradual, not overnight, systems changes.

The Web

Perhaps the most highly visible of all recent ICT advancements is the explosive use of the Web in its two basic forms, Internet and Intranet, for a host of B2B applications. In the context of MC, an excellent example of the strategic use of the Web is the ability to connect the virtual enterprise of customers and partners, enabling rapid information flow regionally or even globally.

The major benefits of the Web, at the operational level, include the following:

- Reducing the total cost of ownership of PC-based ICT architectures.
- Increasing the use and value of the data in all ICT systems in a virtual environment, by allowing information access to a broader range of users.

Because the Web should play a central role in achieving MC, some essential guidelines to consider are:

- Defining the roles of Web users—power vs. casual—and expectations regarding essential information that adds value to them and to their customers.
- Establishing security policies-especially important when operating in a virtual enterprise mode. Both customers and suppliers must have full confidence about the use of their data.
- Budgeting for adequate hardware and systems software technical support, e.g. the ability of the computer network to transmit large amounts of data, and to respond to user processing needs.

Either of the aforementioned methods, viz. *product definition, and planning and control systems* can be used in the make-to-order (MTO) production model depending on the product complexity and/or the sophistication of the buyer. The first alternative is more appropriate for complex products, or with less sophisticated buyers. The MC is valid for the Web-based method. The MTS method, while still in use, is being replaced rapidly by the first two methods (Bourke, 1999).

CRITICAL ISSUES

The critical issues discussed in maximizing value for customers are as follow: capitalizing on imitable versus difficult-to-imitate competencies, identifying VA versus non-value adding (NVA) processes, creating effective versus ineffective customer segmentations, adopting physical versus electronic markets, offering tangible versus intangible products, customizing product itself versus representation of product, valuing costs versus benefits of MC, influencing customer expectations versus customer experiences, and fostering high-quality versus low-quality corporate culture. .

Capitalizing on Imitable vs. Difficult-to-Imitate Competencies

CKM as a business holistic change model is centered on the creation of DCC based on CK with the aim of achieving SCA. As the long-term objective of business competitive strategies is to build SCA, focus should be on harvesting 'difficult-to-imitate', resource-based capabilities (Salck et al., 2006). The competitive advantage of imitable resources is short-lived; it may soon be imitated rapidly by a capable competitor or made obsolete by an innovation of a rival. Major attributes of difficult-to-imitate SCA are documented in Table 9.2.

The challenge that is facing business firms is, not only to attain competitive advantage, but to sustain it. A competitive advantage of one firm may soon turn into a competitive necessity once it has been imitated by rivals. For example, adoption of ATMs has enabled banks to gain a competitive advantage, but could not to sustain it. Due to their widespread diffusion in the banking industry, ATMs no longer represent a source of competitive advantage; but a source of competitive necessity, as customers nowadays would not think to open an account with a bank not having ATM services. In contrast, Wal-Mart's low-cost competitive strategy was supported with difficult-to-imitate business processes or logistics that are embedded in its operations strategy (low inventory level and short flow times), structure (linked communications between stores and fast transportation system), infrastructural technologies (EDI/Satellite enabling technologies), and infrastructural processes (cross-docking and focused locations).

Table 9.2. Major attributes of difficult-to-imitate SCA

Attribute	Definition
Perception	Customers perceive a consistent difference in one or more key buying factors.
Impact	Differences in customers' perceptions are attributable directly to the SCA.
Durability	Both the customers' perceptions and the impact on SCA are durable.
Transparency	Mechanics/details of the SCA are difficult to understand by competitors.
Accessibility	Competitors have restricted access to the required resources to mimic the SCA.
Replication	Competitors would have extreme difficulty reproducing the SCA.
Coordination	SCA requires difficult and subtle coordination of multiple resources.

Source: Adopted from Swift, R. (2001). Accelerating Customer Relationships: Using CRM and Relationship Technologies. Upper Saddle River, NJ: Prentice-Hall.

Identifying VA vs. NVA Customer Experience

In rapidly changing market conditions, the nature of customer value is prevailing over other factors of competition. A competitive business looks at itself from outside-in as well as inside-out, and uses CK to create value for customers by bridging the gap between its current and future customers' needs and preferences, as well as between its customers' currently fulfilled and unfulfilled needs and preferences. Achieving SCA requires changing innovation capabilities of businesses and introducing new or revised products, and/or services.

However, SCA is not achieved only by inventing new products of services, but by inventing and perfecting new and difficult-to-imitate, knowledge-based, value-adding products and/or services as well as processes. Therefore, it becomes essential to distinguish between VA and NVA activities. To better understand process-based SCA that creates value, Porter's (1985) value chain model is used to separate the business system into a series of value-generating activities.

Porter's value chain is a process-based model that can be used as a framework for identifying opportunities for competitive advantage. The goal of the value chain activities is to offer the customer a level of value that exceeds the cost of activities, thereby resulting in a profit margin. The value chain seeks to bring workers together, and by their synergies and shared values, produce as a group way in excess of their individual capacities. The model provides a systematic method for analyzing the way internal activities interact across departments and hierarchical boundaries to add value for customers as well as to the firm. Competitive advantage grows out of the way an enterprise organizes and performs discrete activities. The processes of any enterprise can be divided into a series of activities such as salespeople making sales calls, service technicians performing repairs, scientists in the laboratory designing products or processes, and treasurers raising capital. M-commerce value chain, for example, is a complex process involving a number of operations and entities (customers, merchants, mobile operators, etc.).

Value chain activities of a business, according to Porter (1985), fall into two broad categories: primary and support. Primary activities are those involved in the physical creation of the product, its marketing and delivery to customers, and its support and servicing after sale. Support activities provide the infrastructure whereby the primary activities can take place. Primary and support activities are linked together to form the enterprise's value chain. The primary value chain activities are as follow:

- Inbound Logistics: the receiving and warehousing of raw materials and their distribution to manufacturing as they are required (e.g., material handling, dependent demand inventory control, and material storage).
- Operations: the machining or assembling processes of transforming inputs into finished goods (e.g., lathing, milling, drilling, grinding, and painting).
- Outbound Logistics: the packaging, warehousing, distributing, and transporting of finished products to customers.
- Marketing and Sales (e.g., the identification of customer needs and generation of sales, advertising, pricing, promotion, and selling the product to buyers).
- Service: the support of customers after the products and services are sold (e.g., installation, repair, parts, and training) that maintain good customer support after the sale.

The primary activities are supported by support activities. Support processes are those that have internal customers (employees) and represent the backbone or 'back-office' of core processes (Earl, 1994). The ultimate aim of business organizations is to maximize their profit margin. Profit margin accumulates when the price increment obtained through various activities exceed the cost of performing it. The support activities are:

- Firm Infrastructure: accounting, finance, general management, organization structure, control systems, company culture, etc.
- Human Resource Management: employee recruiting, hiring, training, developing, and compensating.
- Technology Development: technologies that support value-creating activities (e.g., CAD/CAM).
- Procurement: purchasing inputs such as materials, supplies, and equipment.

A firm may create a value either by reducing the cost of individual activities, or by reconfiguring the internal or external value chain. Internal value chain reconfiguration may include structural changes inside the firm (e.g., new production process), whereas external value chain reconfiguration includes a revamp of the chain extended to suppliers and intermediaries (e.g., a new distribution channel). In addition to the integration of supply chains, an e-business model provides new ways of doing business such as de-intermediation (removal of wholesaler/distributor and retailer between manufacturers and consumers) and re-intermediation in supply chains (e.g., manufacturers, infomediaries, e-retailers, aggregators, portals, and consumers).

A firm may develop a cost advantage by controlling cost drivers related to value chain activities better than competitors. Porter (1985) identified ten value chain cost drivers which include:

- Economies of scale
- Learning
- Capacity utilization
- Linkage among activities
- Interrelationships among business units
- Degree of vertical integration (backward and forward)
- Timing of market entry
- Firm's policy of cost or differentiation (tradeoffs between cost and differentiation)
- Geographic location
- Institutional factors (regulation, union activity, taxes, etc.)

The ultimate aim of any business strategy is not only to achieve competitive advantage, as reflected in such measures as higher profit margin, but to secure an SCA. SCA can be realized through infinite combinations of strategic moves (Swift, 2001). The planning process of competitive advantage extends beyond the organization to encompass its stakeholders. Achievement of SCA is based on the creation, utilization, and sustaining of the firm's DCC. The process of leveraging DCC starts with creation of mission and vision statements of where the firm wants to be in the future. An example of a vision is that of IBM Rochester, which is to become a worldwide leader in customer satisfaction. An example of a mission statement to exceed continually customer's increasing expectations. Following the development of mission and vision statements, goals and objectives are set, which culminates in the development of strategies and action plans to achieve the selected goals and objectives. Finally the strategic planning process ends with an evaluation of performance and adjustment of strategies to exploit new market opportunities. DCC of a firm also play a significant role in the firm's ability to articulate distinct mission and vision, setting goals, and developing strategies and action plans.

Porter (1985) proposed four competitive strategies (i.e., cost leadership, differentiation, cost focus, and focused differentiation) in order to deal with the five competitive forces. Rainer, et al. (2007) introduced five value-adding strategies which can be adopted by businesses to counter Porter's five forces, and to achieve SCA:

- Cost leadership strategy: based on producing products and/or services at lower costs than competitors, such as the Wal-Mart leadership of cost through cross-docking to reduce inventory storage and flow time.
- Operational effectiveness strategy: based on improving internal processes performed by organizations with the aim of improving quality, productivity, and employee and customer satisfaction. An example is the reengineering of Ford Motors' accounts payable/procurement process.
- Differentiation strategy: based on offering different product designs, services, or features, such as MC adopted by Dell computers.
- Innovation strategy: based on introducing new products, services, or features, such as the introduction of ATMs by Citibank as a weapon to create a competitive advantage over competitors, but after so long the competitive weapon turned into a competitive necessity.
- Customer-orientation strategy: based on making customers happy by using the Web to provide customized offerings and to develop 1-to-1 relationship with each customer.

SCA is based on various competitive priorities that have been cited frequently in the literature. However, companies must recognize the need to focus on one base of competition more than others when undertaking business strategies, i.e. companies that compete on flexibility cannot usually compete on low cost, as flexibility is usually costly. Peppard and Rowland (1995), and Slack (2006) cited the following competitive advantage strategies:

- Quality
- Speed in development and delivery
- Dependability (reliability in delivery)
- Flexibility (in product or service design and volume)
- Price
- Relationship

Figure 9.1. The ICTBV matrix

WHAT is the Business Value Added? / WHERE is the Value Added?	Quality	Cost	Speed	Innovation	Relationship
Inbound Logistics					
Operations					
Outbound logistics					
Marketing/Sales					
Customer Service					

Source: Adapted from Mendonca, J. (2003). A Model and Sample Case for Teaching the Business Value of Information Technology, Journal of Information Technology Education.Vol. 2, 61-72.

In dynamic and fast-changing environments, the only way to create SCA over time is to continue to focus on four generic blocks of competitive advantage- efficiency, quality, innovation, and responsiveness to customers- and to develop DCC that contribute to performance in these areas. (Hill and Jones, 2007). Furthermore, competitiveness strategies may be grouped into three major types: cost leadership, differentiation, and focus/customer intimacy (Treacy and Wiersema, 1995; Porter, 1998; and Heizer and Render, 2006).

The three composite priorities that correspond to a fairly representative set of values available for organizations when competing with their rivals are:

- Product Leadership/Differentiation strategy (best product): concentrates on uniqueness by distinguishing the offerings of leading-edge products or new applications of existing products in a way that the customer perceives as adding value, i.e. product customization, convenience of store location, quality, product or service features, and after-sale services (i.e., customer support, repair, or maintenance services). Opportunities for creating uniqueness are not constrained to a particular activity but can arise virtually in every thing that an organization does.
- Operational Excellence/Cost Leadership strategy (best cost): seeks to reduce manufacturing and other costs, or deliver a combination of quality and price (value for money) that no one else can match in the market.
- Customer Intimacy/Focus/Response strategy (faster and reliable offerings): unlike industry-wide differentiation and cost leadership competitive strategies, the focus strategy seeks to limit its scope to a narrow segment of regional market, product line, or group of customers through two variants: cost focus

and differentiation. In today's rapidly changing customers' preferences, an entire range of values may be integrated into one composite, customer-oriented response strategy to develop high customer loyalty, i.e. integrating *rapid* development and delivery with *reliable* delivery.

Mendonca (2003) proposed an ICT-based Business Value (ICTBV) model (Figure 9.1) for explaining value of ICT in enabling organizational processes. The model is comprised of two parts: a) a two-dimensional application matrix, which focuses on *what* business value is and *where* it can be applied in the organization; and b) a set of action 'triggers' that focus on the 'how to' of discovering value opportunities. The horizontal axis of the matrix (the *what*) identifies five value factors, i.e. quality, cost, speed, innovation and relationship. The vertical axis identifies five functional areas where ICT-enabled value propositions can be applied. The action

Table 9.3. The BPR action triggers

ACTION	TARGET
1. Eliminate non-value added processes	1.1 Wait time (perform parallel processing) 1.2 Transporting documents/data 1.3 Inventory 1.4 Duplication 1.5 Inspection 1.6 Reformatting
2. Minimize non value-added processes	(reduce number of activities) 2.1 Handling 2.2 Checks 2.3 Controls 2.4 Verifications
3. Simplify	3.1 Forms 3.2 Procedures 3.3 Communications 3.4 Technology 3.5 Work flows 3.6 Customer contact
4. Integrate	4.1 Jobs 4.2 Teams 4.3 Customers 4.4 Suppliers
5. Automate	5.1 Difficult tasks 5.2 Data capture and transfer 5.3 Error checking

Source: Adapted from Mendonca, J. (2003). A Model and Sample Case for Teaching the Business Value of Information Technology, Journal of Information Technology Education. Vol. 2, 61-72.

Figure 9.2. BPR actions and targets applied to the ICTBV matrix

WHAT is the Business Value Added? WHERE is the Value Added?	Quality	Cost	Speed	Innovation	Relationship
Inbound Logistics	5.2		5.2		
Operations	1.1	2.1	5.2		
Outbound logistics		2.1			
Marketing/Sales	5.2	5.2	5.2		
Customer Service	2.1				1.1 & 2.1

Source: Adapted from Mendonca, J. (2003). A Model and Sample Case for Teaching the Business Value of Information Technology, Journal of Information Technology Education. Vol. 2, 61-72.

triggers presented in Table 9.3 are based BPR principles and seek to activate the process through the discovery of value adding opportunities. Figure 9.2 documents a sample of BPR applied to the ICTBV matrix of a case study that builds and sells homes (Mendonca, 2003).

As business constantly are engaged in creation and utilization of difficult-to-imitate DCCs, a well-crafted strategy for achieving SCA may be based on resources, capabilities, assets, and knowledge-based processes with specific attributes that provide a form with a distinct attraction to its customers and a unique advantage over its rivals. SCA strategy is a statement that identifies a business strategy to compete upon, as well as goals, and the plans and policies that will be required to carry out these goals.

The formulation of an effective SCA strategy requires an analysis of DCCs, which reveals strengths and weaknesses, and the screening of the market environment, which reveals opportunities and challenges. CK gained may help companies to create an SCA by producing data to improve sales, profitability, and market penetration. CKM enable companies to analyze customer purchasing patterns, tastes, and preferences so that marketing campaigns may be launched and customized products or services may be produced for smaller target customers. The benefits of CKM to customers are increased convenience and speed of service, and the benefit to an organization is its ability to develop profitable, customer-focused strategies.

Creating Effective vs. Ineffective Customer Segmentations

The customer profiling phase in the CKM value chain involves precise targeting of customers and prospects precisely by choosing segments that match customer base and media channels that match customer preferences. The CRM automated campaign management software seeks to develop the *right* CK that enables a company to target the *right* customers with the *right* product and/or service at the *right* time via the *right* channel (a means by which the enterprise contacts or provides offerings to customers) in order to enable businesses to acquire new customers, retain the existing customers, and expand relationships with them.

However, once a particular segment of customers (and prospective customers) is defined, customers need to be selected based on certain customer characteristics, and only then the execution process of the marketing campaign starts. For example, if we target customers who are likely to churn because of customer service problems, we need to use DM to mine for customers from the DW with a certain number of unsatisfactorily addressed complaints in the last month.

Therefore, customer segmentation and analysis represents an essential part in leveraging the CKM value chain as it addresses significant issues and challenges. CKM involves a set of processes that strives to deliver highest value added to customers via CK and through empowerment of teams, technology, and processes. CK is used to identify the value potential of each identified customer segment, and then to target the specified segment by providing offerings that will maximize the experience of customers, which in turn, will maximize the profitability of the business.

The challenge for business organizations is to decide on the most effective criteria to segment markets. Kotler (2006) suggested five criteria for an effective segmentation:

- *Measurable*: It has to be possible to determine the values of the variables used for segmentation with justifiable efforts. This is important especially for demographic and geographic variables. For an organization with direct sales (without intermediaries), their own customer database could deliver valuable information on buying behavior (frequency, volume, product groups, mode of payment etc).
- *Relevant*: The size and profit potential of a market segment have to be large enough to economically justify separate marketing activities for this segment.
- *Accessible*: The segment has to be accessible and servable for the organization. That means, for instance, that there are target-group specific advertising media, such as magazines or a website, the target audience likes to use.
- *Distinguishable*: The market segments have to be so diverse that they show different reactions to different marketing mixes.
- *Feasible*: It has to be possible to approach each segment with a particular marketing program and to draw advantages from that.

Adopting Physical vs. Electronic Markets

The products sold over electronic markets can be purely digital goods and services, and/or physical products. Digital goods include information goods and services, such as financial information, news services, reference and learning materials, entertainment and multimedia products, software distribution services, and online advertising, and distributed database services. These products are characterized by being difficult to value and easy to copy; related issues are disputes over copyright, zero marginal costs and uncertainty over quality (Whinston et al., 2000).

In the digital market, companies use different pricing, advertising, and distribution strategies. They include customization, and bundling, bundling valuable content with advertising to provide 'free' goods, introducing different versions of the same product to suit different users, charging subscriptions and, most importantly, using market mechanisms to help set the price.

The potential advantage of the networked environment includes the scope for real-time interaction within a vast networked community, the possibility of using sophisticated market mechanisms, and the illusion of almost infinite inventory (when an intermediary acts for many suppliers). Examples of digital businesses that have exploited these opportunities and achieved enormous success are Amazon.com and eBay (Whinston et al., 2000). Nonetheless, it is quite possible that a particular segment of customers may develop a preference for the physical world over the digital world. For example, senior citizens may favor front-office contacts over e-banking or mobile banking models because of the value-adding personal touch, whereas customers with special physical disabilities may prefer e-business models.

Whinston et al. (2000) argued that the virtual environment makes possible unpredictable customization of products and services. In the physical market, sellers specialize in highly standardized, individual products. Customers try to coordinate purchases across a broad spectrum of products on the bases of posted prices. The digital market, in which information can be acquired and processed with ease, lets sellers tailor their products to individual customers. They added that the ease of customization and the ability to cater to variations in consumer preferences has led to the possibility of bundling goods. While most sellers specialize in individual products, customers' preferences vary over sets of products. Value is added as products in each set complement each other. Each customer will prefer a different product bundle, and the perceived value of the same product may vary from one bundle to another.

In the digital economy, negotiated trading mechanisms may allow consumers to bid for bundles according to their preferences; an efficient algorithm can match bundles to facilitate trades that increase the value for both sellers and buyers. In securities markets, for example, the bundle trading mechanism (patent pending) developed by Omega Consulting allows traders to submit a valuation to a complete portfolio of assets, instead of requiring asset-by-asset pricing (Whinston et al., 2000).

However, online business firms need to face the challenge of building emotional, social, and psychological benefits into the customer experience, especially for the elderly and handicapped segment of customers. The low degree of interpersonal interaction in web-based buying experience makes it difficult, if not impossible, to enhance the non-economic aspects of the customer experience (Mohammed et al., 2003).

Offering Tangible vs. Intangible Products

Physical goods represent offerings that cannot be touched, seen, or stored in inventory for later use or traded in for another model. In the CKM context, the challenge is to use ICTs to add value to customers. For example, customers who have ordered their computers, from DELL, for example, can follow their computers along the various stages of the production process in real time on their personalized website. Computers as well as many other appliances can be configured remotely and fixed over the network today. Airlines now communicate special fares to preferred customers through e-mails and special websites. Customers can also be involved in the early stages of product development so that their inputs can shape product features and functionality. For example, pharmaceutical companies are experimenting with the possibility of analyzing patients' genes to determine precisely what drugs should be administered and in what dosages (Venkatraman and Henderson, 2000).

The value-adding transformation in physical goods can be seen in college textbook publishing. This industry-which has seen little innovation since the advent of the printing press-is now in the midst of major changes. Publishers are creating supplementary website links to provide additional aids for students and professors. The publisher's role, which traditionally was selling textbooks at the beginning of term, is becoming that of a value-adding partner throughout the term (Venkatraman and Henderson, 2000).

However, the situation in the service industry is quite different. When purchasing a service, customers usually do not buy physical goods only, rather they buy a service package, or bundle of goods, that are composed of the following (Reid and Sanders, 2007):

- The *physical goods* (tangible aspects such as the food consumed, as well as facilities such as comfortable tables and chairs, table cloths, and fine china).
- The *sensual benefits* (intangible items that we experience through our senses such as taste and smell of the food).

- The *psychological benefits* (intangible items such as the promptness, friendliness, ambiance of the service provider, as well as status, mind comfort, and well-being of the experience).

In designing customer service offerings, focus should not be only on tangible aspects of the service package. Often, the intangible-sensual and psychological-benefits are the deciding factors in the success of the service. Therefore, the service design needs to be designed carefully in a way that defines what the customer is supposed to experience (e.g., relaxation, comfort, efficiency, and speed of service).

Customizing Physical vs. Non-Physical Products

The new business platform recognizes the increased importance of customization of products and services in maximizing value for customers. Performance objectives of customization, e.g. short development and delivery time and low unit cost, can be plotted against the customization value chain. Purely customized items require high delivery time and high unit cost but enjoy higher flexibility and higher customer satisfaction, whereas purely standardized items are associated with lower delivery time and lower unit cost, but lower flexibility and lower customer satisfaction.

Customization refers to the degree to which buyers perceive products from alternative suppliers to be different. The buyers of differentiated products may have to pay a higher price when satisfying their preference for something special, in return for greater added-value. The connection between the producer and buyers may be reinforced, at least to the level of customer loyalty, and perhaps to the point of establishing a partnership between them. Product differentiation also serves as an entry barrier due to the 'switching costs' imposed on the buyer, because internal processes of the buyer-producer relationship become adapted to the special benefits of the particular factor of production, and use of an alternative would force internal changes. Besides, a continuous process of product differentiation may produce an additional cost advantage over competitors and potential entrants, through intellectual property copyright protections, such as patents.

Customization is most powerful when backed up by a sophisticated analysis of customer data. Mass manufacturing experts, such as Nike and Levi Strauss, are experimenting with ways of using digital technology to enable customization. For example, Websites that can display three-dimensional images certainly will boost the attractiveness of custom-tailored offerings. Such experimentation is advisable because the success of MTO models such as Dell's represents a challenge to current MTS business platforms. Dell is not eliminating only the non-value-adding steps in its supply chains but is also leading the way in learning about profiles of customers who visit its website. Such analysis enhances its ability to price and promote different configurations assertively. Another example is Amazon.com that makes recommendations to individual customers on the basis of not only what they have browsed through and bought but by integrated data from customers with similar patterns (Venkatraman and Henderson, 2000).

Bases of customization may be in product (quality, features, options, style, brand name, packaging, sizes, services, warranties, returns), price (list, discounts, allowances, payment period, credit terms), promotion (advertising, personal selling, sales promotion, publicity); and physical channels (channels, coverage, locations, inventory, and transport). More specifically, there are several customization areas, other than customizing physical products, which are as follow (Peppers and Rogers, 1999):

- *Bundling (cross-selling and up-selling)*: Refers to selling two or more products together. Examples are:

  - Bundling related products or accessories (e.g., sweat socks with sneakers, monitors with computers, and insurance with automobiles).
  - Bundling consumable or replenishable supplies with a product (e.g., disks with computers and gas with automobiles).
  - Offering certain high-volume customers a greater quantity than everyone else gets (e.g., a dozen bars of soap, two dozen tennis balls, or a full truckload of products rather than half a truckload).

- *Configuration*: Preconfigure a system according to customer's specifications without changing the physical product itself. Examples are:

  - Computer and office machine makers.
  - Phones are arriving with preset speed dials and preconfigured feature sets.
  - Developing a personalized daily vitamin prescription based on an extensive health questionnaire and an analysis of a single strand of the customer's hair.

- *Packaging:* How many variations of packaging add value to the consumer, *and* are there specific relationships or linkages between consumer types and packaging types? Do seniors want smaller, lighter packages with instructions in larger type? Do professionals seek different product information than other customers? Which customers would prefer multi-packs and which would prefer mini-packs?

- *Delivery and Logistics:* Is the product delivered at the convenience of the customer's schedule or the firm's schedule? Does the product arrive exactly where it is needed or at a general location? Do delivery options vary based on customer value? At what point might a customer qualify for on-site inventory? Even the U.S Post Office has mastered the concept of the on-site service representative, providing postal inspectors at the nation's largest magazine-printing plants to speed catalogues and publications directly to customers' mailboxes and help manage the postal needs of the very largest customers.

- *Ancillary Services:* Does the new car come with bi-weekly wash-and-wax or automatic pickup and delivery when it is time for maintenance? Extended warranties are a great mechanism for enhancing the core product, and a warranty can easily be customized based on intended use, whether measured in copies-per-month, hours-per-day, or miles-per-year. Ancillary services provided by strategic alliance partners are often best sold as part of the business transaction in order to address seamlessly the customers' preferences.

- *Service enhancements:* Time-sensitive businesses and firms that buy mission-critical products or services for their operations appreciate the option of offering special services on a 'one stop' basis. Laptop makers quickly embraced the 'next-day over-haul,' at an additional fee, which promises major or minor laptop repairs in less than twenty-four hours. In most cases, these services are delivered only at premium prices, but the availability and convenience of the service offers tremendous value to some customers.

- *Invoicing:* Are invoices sent at the convenience of the customer or at the firm's own convenience? Are they developed in the optimum, most desirable format for a customer or for ease of issuance by the accounting department? Could the firm provide the invoice digitally or over the Web? Could the firm provide flexible invoice details, set up to help a customer distribute its own costs? Does the business facilitate all types of EDI with your customers? Are cash discounts anticipated? Do bills offer favorable processes and terms of payment to the customer? Is the customer aware of these options and their value, and reminded regularly in case needs change?

- *Payment terms:* Terms can vary widely to increase the flexibility of payment schemes and methods that suit individual needs and preferences, e.g., some buyers prefer smaller payments and longer terms, while others seek to jump in before payment and will gladly pay the price.

- *Preauthorization:* Working with the customer's management team, some markets enforce preset authorizations and limits and customize the corporate approval system to meet the different needs of different customers. Vice presidents are allowed to order leather desk sets and unlimited paper supplies from an executive version of the office supply catalogue, while secretaries perhaps find themselves limited to a certain amount per month.

- *Streamlining services:* Does the new shipment address of a long-time customer really need all that paperwork? Can you your accounting and credit-granting systems be streamlined to make it easier for long-standing customers? Why not use e-commerce systems to empower customers or staff to reduce paperwork and processing time for customer orders meeting a certain set of criteria, pre-approving them wherever possible?

Selecting Product vs. Process Customization Strategies

MC is an alternative strategy to mass manufacturing as a paradigm of management that has dominated the world industrial production since World War II. MC aims at providing goods and services that best meet individual customer's requirements in high volumes and with near mass production efficiency. So, it represents a continuum of production approaches ranging from pure customization of individual units to mass production of standardized products. However, MC is neither a simple marketing strategy to undertake organizationally and operationally, nor a simple concept to comprehend.

Several authors contributed to the definition of MC, e.g. Hart (1995), Browne et al. (1996), and Gilmore and Pine (1997). Hart (1995) defined MC using two distinct definitions:

- The visionary definition: The ability to provide customers with anything they want profitably, any time they want it, anywhere they want it, any way they want it.
- The practical definition: The use of flexible processes and organizational structures to produce varied, and often individually customized, products and services at the low cost of a standardized, mass production system.

According to Hart (1995), the goal in the first definition of MC was considered a transcendent, absolute idea that exists solely as an ideal that rarely will be achieved by an organization. The goal in the second definition is not the 'anything-at-any-time' promised by the visionary definition. It is 'to ascertain, from the customer's perspective, the range within which a given product or service can be customized meaningfully (i.e. differentiated) for that customer, and then to facilitate the customer's choice of options from within that range.' He argued that the concept of producing 'tailor-made' or partially 'tailor-made' goods or services according to customer desire, with very short cycle times and mass production efficiencies, is a more realizable goal than that offered by the visionary definition.

Browne et al. (1996) presented a framework of decoupling points in different levels of MC. Four different designs are represented by varying the position of the decoupling point (Alfnes and Strandhagen, 2000). These designs range from providing unique customized products via two customization levels, viz. MTO and assemble-to-order (ATO), to providing standardized MTS products. Lampel and Mintzberg (1996) defined a continuum of five MC strategies involving different configurations of processes, products, and customer transactions.

Two MC dimensions of change/no change in product and its presentation (process) were identified by Gilmore and Pine (1997). These two dimensions create four generic MC options (Figure 9.3): cosmetic, adaptive, transparent, and collaborative MC (representation service, process, and product). However, these four dimensions are not independent, but rather interwoven. Besides, the qualities and design of production largely define the extent of product's customization alternatives, and vice versa. Also the representation of a product is interwoven with the service dimension (Riihimaa, 2004).

- *Cosmetic MC.* This approach is appropriate when customers use a standardized product the same way and differ only in how they want it presented. It is used when one customer group does not have special needs and only customizing some surface features of the product drives equal value from the customer's perspective (*standardizing core features of products but customizing surface features, e.g., products are packaged differently for different customers*).
- *Adaptive (Modular) MC.* This approach offers one standardized product that is designed so *old* customers can alter it themselves. This approach is appropriate for businesses whose customers want the product to perform in different ways on different occasions, and available technology makes it possible for them to utilize a learning relationship with customers to customize the product easily on their own (*standard products can be altered by customers themselves*).
- *Transparent MC.* This design is appropriate when customers' needs are predictable or can be deduced easily, especially when customers do not want to state repeatedly their needs, and offerings are customized within a standard package for individual customers (*customizing offerings for customers by observing their behavior*).
- *Collaborative MC.* This approach follows three steps: conduct a dialogue with *new* customers to help them articulate their needs; identify the precise offering that fulfills those needs (colors, logos, locations, and so on); and make customized products for them (*designers dialogue with customers to identify their precise needs*).

When designing or redesigning a product/service, or a process, companies should choose one or more of the four approaches to serve their particular customer segments. It is believed that that qualities and design of production largely define

Figure 9.3. Mass customization alternatives

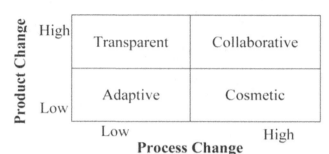

Source: Adapted from Gilmore, J.H. and Pine II, B.J. (1997). Four faces of mass customization. Harvard Business Review, Jan-Feb, 91-101.

the extent of a product's customization alternatives, and vice versa. Also, the representation of product is interwoven with the service dimension. Change in product design may be due to fact that sometimes a company that adopts one generic MC strategy may not be satisfied with it forever. When experiences from one strategy are accumulating, companies may want to develop their strategies and try a more sophisticated approach to customer service.

The four types of MC introduced by Gilmore and Pine (1997) represent 'pure' or generic MC strategies. Different MC approaches are needed in manufacturing and marketing strategic decisions. A company may want to change the emphasis from one 'pure' MC strategy to another. Theoretically there are twelve variations of transitions modified from Gilmore and Pine (1997) MC strategies. These twelve variations are shown in Figures 9.4, Figure 9.5, Figure 9.6, and Figure 9.7 (Riihimaa et al., 2004).

The value of MC strategy, when making a transition from one 'pure' MC strategy to another, depends to a great extent on how much the firm wisely utilizes the available e-business system infrastructural requirements (Lee et al., 2000). Furthermore, the transition among different MC strategies puts extra pressures on technical, organizational, and managerial competencies (Riihimaa et al., 2004).

The different scenarios of transitions among MC designs necessitate changes in ICT infrastructure. Major ICT requirements for transitions among MC are as follow (Riihimaa et al., 2004):

- *Moving to Collaborative MC:* Cooperative customization is implemented jointly with the customer. However, cooperative customization cannot be carried on forever, at least not for the same customers, since product standardization occurs

Figure 9.4. Transition from cosmetic MC

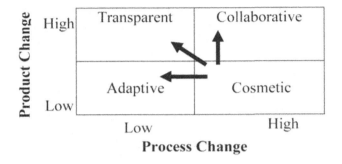

Figure 9.5. Transition from adaptive MC

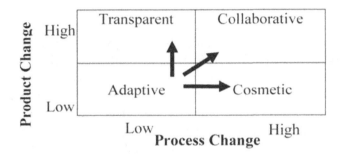

Figure 9.6. Transition from transparent MC

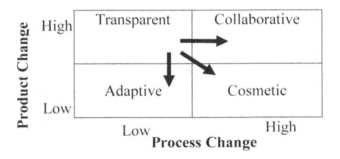

Figure 9.7. Transition from collaborative MC

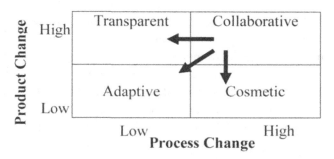

Source (Figures 9.4, 9.5, 9.6, 9.7, and 9.8): Adapted from Riihimaa, J.; Ruohonen, M., & Makipaa, M. (2004). Transitions in mass customization strategies: requirements for information systems, Frontiers of e-Business Research, pp. 373-384.

almost in all industries. When customers are very demanding and require deeper customization of core features (basic structure) collaborative customization can be considered. This requires development of product configuration tools that can be offered directly to customers or to professional salespeople. In this case, the ICT infrastructure in focus is product configuration tool integrated with the PDM system. Moving to collaborative customization can be seen as concentrating on new customer or product segments where enough knowledge has not yet been accumulated. However, collaborative customization is the highest-priced way; hence a company should be able to apply other MC means as well.

- *Moving to Transparent MC:* If a company considers that sufficient CK has been created long enough, it might consider a transparent strategy. Transparent MC requires the use of a large and diversified DW, which contains detailed customers' product and service needs, and a CRM system integrated to the PDM-system to develop advanced knowledge systems.

- After using transparent MC strategy for a while, a company might notice that it is not cost-efficient to serve all customers with the same level of service. Some customer groups might be satisfied with customization of surface features (cosmetic MC), while others could be satisfied with adaptive (modular) customization. There might also be certain customer group needs that require special attention and collaborative work. At this point, it is important to identify customer groups and offer the cost-efficient service required.

- *Moving to Adaptive (Modular) MC:* In adaptive customization, customer needs and preferences are not always known, but the customization level increases by increasing the modularity of products or services. A company can therefore develop customers' needs fulfilling combinations of product qualities with superior PDM in order to develop different kinds of product lines. When moving to adaptive MC, ICT development in focus is mainly PDM. This means that a company has learned enough about customer needs and recognized core features of the product that can satisfy different needs with a customized combination of standard modules. In key focus is learning more from customers and learning to anticipate his or their needs even before they do.

- Moving to an adaptive strategy can be supplementary, seeking cost-efficiency in some old customer segments. It can also be a required transition if customer satisfaction is decreasing and company can no longer anticipate customer needs. Thus learning from customer needs is required and customer satisfaction can be increased with a greater variety of offerings. However, if a company is using adaptive customization, but perceives that it does not fulfill customers' needs or is too complicated (for example, maintaining complicated modular structure enabling over millions of variations), it might also consider other MC alternatives.

- *Moving to Cosmetic MC*: If modular MC is seen as too complex to maintain (i.e., interdependencies of modules, or customers do not get real value from such a variety, cosmetic MC might be considered. Moving to cosmetic MC usually is considered when no real value is offered with expensive collaborative customization and when focus of MC strategy is on cost-efficiency. In this case, core features of the product are standardized, whereas some surface features are customized. Cosmetic product changes usually are done at the end of the manufacturing process, e.g. in the assembly line of the car industry (Riihimaa et al., 2004).

- Cosmetic MC can be seen as a supportive and complementary strategy, for example, used for matured product groups, where product standardization has started to occur. Cosmetic MC can be used first as a tool to collect customer data (Gilmore & Pine, 1997) and later on another strategy may be chosen to learn from customers' preferences by customizing surface features of the product.

All the transitions between MC designs are possible (Figure 9.8). Different MC strategies may suit different products, customers, or times. Some designs (e.g., collaborative MC) may be used first with new customers. After learning about customers, it is possible to move to more profitable, but more sophisticated, designs such as transparent MC (Riihimaa et al., 2004).

Figure 9.8. Dynamic transition in MC strategies

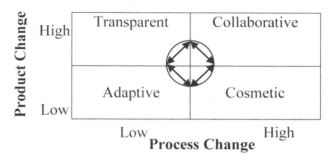

Valuing Benefits vs. Costs of MC

MC provides businesses and customers with various benefits such as the following:

- Enhancing manufacturers' profitability through a synergy of flexibility advantage, increased customer-perceived value, and reduced costs of production and logistics.
- Reducing the reliance of companies on the traditional marketing channels and would gaining more market shares.
- Capitalizing on the key strengths of the modern manufacturing industry well known for its dynamic flexibility and responsiveness.
- Helping to attract and retain individual customers by retailers. Reductions in inventory and working capital allow customized goods to be produced at the same or lower cost than mass-produced products.
- Applicability in a wide variety of industries such as clothing, electronics, watches, machinery, and appliances as well as to service sectors such as software industry, hospitality industry, etc.

However, the MC production strategy usually faces the following pitfalls:

- Unnecessary running costs due to the vast differences in customer preferences, and complexity although it provides several benefits.
- Problems in demand prediction - forecast errors are greater when forecasting individual products versus a group of products.
- Complicated manufacturing operations and decisions - MC complication creates problems in decisions related to the following:

- Inventory level of raw materials, work-in-process, and subassemblies.
- Production volume of made-to-order or made-to-stock items
- Production capacity level.

As for the 1-to-1 strategy, it is especially difficult to justify because its benefits are centered primarily on the revenue side. Investments in such strategies/capabilities (technologies, processes, and people) should be evaluated based on the strategic advantage over competition, evaluating anticipated ROI, and long-term value of the customer base (Peppers and Rogers, 1999). The costs of the 1-to-1 strategy are quantifiable and easy to calculate, but their strategic benefits are intangible and often difficult to measure.

To maintain customer satisfaction and loyalty, companies should serve every customer as an individual offering customized products and services at a reasonable price (Pine, 1993). This contradiction of offering personalized products, and yet keeping reasonable prices, can be solved with an MC strategy (Davis, 1987). However, the decision to adopt MC is not a simple one. It is crucial that managers examine thoroughly what kind or level of customization their customers would value before they adopt a particular customization strategy. Before deciding to pursue MC strategy in particular, four key decision factors need to be considered (Hart, 1995):

- *Customer sensitivity.* The first question companies need to ask themselves is: Do customers care whether a company offers more customization? If the answer is yes, the MC potential is high.
- *Process amenability.* The first question is: Does the existing process technology, allow for customization of products and/or services to individual customer preferences? If it does, the next question is: How extensive an overhaul is required to incorporate this technology into the existing process and how much investment will be required? Another part of process amenability is marketing. Since the goal of MC is products or services tailored to individual customers, an important question for companies to ask is: Does the marketing department have access to the level of detail regarding customer preferences and the capacity to analyze such information? A third consideration is design. Is the company capable of translating customer general preferences into specific technical specifications? The last consideration under this factor is production and distribution. Partly depending on the form and nature of product or service, the flexibility/agility of the production system to handle MC is a critical point to consider here.
- *Competitive environment.* The major question here is: Are there competitive forces that would enhance or hinder the advantage that one company would gain from implementing MC? In other words, would a particular

company lead its market with a mass-customized product? How long would it take for competitors to react? And how will customers of the company's rivals react?

- *Organizational readiness.* The last decision factor requires a transparent and precise assessment of the strengths and weaknesses in the company's resources, capabilities, core capabilities, and DCCs (e.g., in technology, processes, structure, people, culture, etc). Is the company able and ready to capitalize on the opportunity inherent in MC? Organizational change requires enlightened leadership, open-minded management, and financial resources. An MC strategy is unique to the company developing and implementing it. MC strategy that works well for one company may not work well for another. Hence, there is no 'cook-book' approach to creating such a strategy.

Influencing Customer Expectations vs. Customer Experiences

Product or service quality from the customer's point of view relates to the consumer's perceived quality based on judgement about a product's overall excellence or superiority. Service quality is believed to depend on the gap between expected and perceived performance, in order to determine if customers are happy and satisfied with the service; while a comparison is made between the service being given and the level at which the same service is extended toward their customers in other companies (Reid and Sanders, 2007).

The challenge that faces service designers revolves around meeting customers' expectations that vary depending on the types of customers and customers' demographics (age, gender, experience, education, etc.). For services to be successful, the customers' experiences that need to meet or even exceed their expectations (Reid and Sanders, 2007). Offering higher value products and/or services is likely to make customers happier, which in turn leads to greater customer retention and loyalty. Satisfied customers may even turn into endorsements for the product and company, spreading favorable 'word-of-mouth' to colleagues or friends about their experiences.

What aggravates the situation further is in fact related to the presence of the customers while the service is being delivered, such as at a theatre, a restaurant, or a bank. The customer contact with the service provider is often the service itself, such an experience at a doctor's clinic. Unfortunately, since services often have multiple service providers, there can be great variation in the type of service delivered depending on the skills of the service provider, such as hairdressers, food servers, and physicians (Reid and Sanders, 2007).

For a service to be successful, the service experience must be consistent at all times. This requires quality management to ensure high consistency and reliability, standardization and simplification of procedures in services (e.g., fast-food restaurants), training of employees on skills that include courtesy, friendliness, and overall disposition, and monetary incentive systems may be used to motivate employees to excel in the delivery of services (Reid and Sanders, 2007).

Fostering High vs. Low Customer-Centered Culture

The challenge for companies in the Internet-based, customer-company connection is to learn about customers' preferences and to be active in providing offerings that meet or exceed their expectations. However, in the delivery of value-added offerings to customers, corporate culture plays a significant role in facilitating or hindering the delivery process, and ultimately accomplishment of SCA. National and corporate cultures have an influence on people's behavior and many aspects of organizational life, starting from product or service planning, designing, and development, and ending up with marketing, sales, delivery, and customer service.

In some corporate or national cultures, customer-centric, cultural values prevail or fail. In some national as well as corporate cultures, some questions might arise such as: 'Is it ethical to provide preferential treatment for some customers but not for others'? and 'Is providing personalized service considered discriminatory in nature'? Corporate culture's concern with customers varies from one business organization to another. For example, the value-adding, customer-centric service culture emphasizes promptness, quality, responsiveness, integrity, flexibility, and consistency.

In the CKM context, it is extremely essential for businesses to realize the importance of shifting their corporate culture from internally-oriented to customer-oriented in order to be able to create SCA. CKM change requires an analysis of the level of commonality of culture (breadth of widely shared beliefs, values, and norms) and plan for implementation of a cultural transformation program at the individual, team, and organizational levels. However, it should be noted here that cultural change programs that address all three levels of depth of culture may require a two- to five-year implementation program (Davenport, 1993).

Therefore, in order to add value to customer relationships, training should be provided for everyone in the organization who will come in contact with customers. Every employee, regardless of position, can make a contribution to the creation of customer-centric culture through adding excellence to process-based teams in such areas as customer care abilities, problem solving skills, or product and technical knowledge. By adding excellence to their own teams, employees help their companies to stand out competitively and to achieve SCA. For example, customer-service, call centre staff who answer phone calls should be trained on how to reflect customer-centric culture, not only in the content and promptness of the response itself, but also in the way calls are answered and by the tone of the voice used in the response.

RECOMMENDED SOLUTION: A PROPOSED CKM MODEL FOR MASS CUSTOMIZATION

With the advancement of web technologies, businesses can use CKM to meet customer's needs for MC more effectively and efficiently, making interactions faster and easier and, consequently, increasing customer satisfaction and loyalty. CKM process dimensions are proposed for MC according to CK categories (knowledge for, from, and about customers, and knowledge co-creation).

The following CKM dimensions are proposed and described below (Figure 9.9): a) product configuration, customization, and logistics, b) customer demographics, preferences, and experiences c) customer profiling, segmentation, and prediction of behavior, and d) collaborative planning, design, development, and replenishment.

Product Configuration, Customization, and Logistics

Dissemination of information/knowledge for customers about product configuration represents an essential step in MC. For example, textbook publishers provide information/knowledge for students and professors about supplementary websites and additional ancillary aids. Product configuration information is especially needed for new customers in collaborative MC wherein customers are involved in the early stages of product development so that their inputs can shape product features and functionality.

Product development process can be followed by customers in real time on their personalized website (e.g., Dell's modular MC). Airlines industry communicates special fares to preferred customers through e-mails and special websites. Information/knowledge provided for customers may also relate to logistics. Special packaging and/or delivery options comprise important information for customers in cosmetic MC when it is used as a supportive and complementary strategy for product lines that reached maturity and standardization has started to occur.

Customer Demographics, Preferences, and Experiences

Companies can adopt any MC and still learn from demographics, life style, and preferences of their customers who visit their website. Such analysis enhances their ability to price and promote different configurations assertively. For example, customer data can be collected first in cosmetic MC (Gilmore & Pine, 1997) and

Figure 9.9. A proposed CKM model for mass customization

	Categories of CK			
MC Design	Knowledge for Customers	Knowledge from Customers	Knowledge about Customers	Knowledge Co-creation with Customers
CKM Process	Product Configuration, Customization, and Logistics	Customer Demographics, Preferences, and Experiences	Customer Profiling, Segmentation, and Prediction of Behavior	Collaborative Planning, Design, Development, and Replenishment

later on another strategy may be chosen to learn from customers' preferences by customizing surface features of the product.

In addition to their background information and needs/preferences, customers can be a good source to learn about their good and bad experiences with a company. Studies have shown that when companies listen to their customers, and take their complaints and suggestions seriously, customers are impressed and feel more loyal (Gibbert et al., 2002). Feedback from customers helps companies to segment and profile their customers more effectively and continuously improve their products and services (Rowley, 2002).

Customer Profiling, Segmentation, and Prediction of Behavior

Customer profiling and segmentation is helpful in any MC design, but customer needs are predictable or deducible only in transparent MC. For example, pharmaceutical companies are experimenting with the possibility of analyzing patients' genes to determine precisely what drugs should be administered and in what dosages (Venkatraman and Henderson, 2000). Products are customized, but customization is unknown to customers. This may apply to customers that do not want to be interfered or repeat their needs. Recommendations of customized offerings are made to individual customers on the basis of not only what they have browsed through and bought but by profiling and predication of purchasing behavior from customers' data with similar purchasing patterns.

Collaborative Planning, Design, Development, and Replenishment

This dimension of CKM involves collaboration with individual customers as well as business partners. Collaboration with customers is referred to as Collaborative Product Customization, whereas collaboration with suppliers is referred to as Collaborative Planning, Forecasting, and Replenishment. Details of the two dimensions are as follows:

- *Collaborative Design and Customization:* to determine the exact configuration of products that customers want, knowledge co-creation is undertaken in close B2C interactions, especially when their needs are not clear, cannot easily articulate what they want, or require very special product and/or service designs. This approach requires businesses to conduct co-create knowledge along with individual customers to help them articulate their needs. Then, the precise offering that fulfills those needs is to be identified and customized products are made for them.
- *Collaborative Planning, Forecasting, and Replenishment (CPFR):* Knowledge co-creation in CPFR takes place in a B2B practice that combines the intelligence of multiple suppliers in the planning and fulfillment of customer demand. Suppliers can be also empowered to monitor inventory level via the Internet and replenish according to a predetermined Vendor Managed Inventory (VMI) contract. CPFR links sales and marketing best practices to supply chain planning and execution processes. A company can sends forecasts to its suppliers and get responses back about their ability to support those requirements. A company's ability to strengthen the knowledge co-creation with its suppliers is essential for successful inbound and outbound logistics management in its supply chains. The advantages of CPFR knowledge co-creation is to increase availability to the customer while reducing inventory, transportation, and logistics costs

FUTURE TRENDS

The future trends discussed in maximizing value-adding customer products and/or services are: a shift from customer disempowerment to customer empowerment, a shift from 1-to-1 customization to MC, and a shift from generic to intelligent MC strategies.

A Shift from Disempowerment to Empowerment of Customers

Customers in the future will have more opportunities to be connected more closely to the product-delivery chain and will be able to customize offerings and serve themselves. Many organizations opt for empowerment of their customers, not only to secure their satisfaction, but to secure their loyalty by getting them involved directly in value-added processes such as product order, design, and delivery. Organizations that move to self-service provision of products may use technologies such as ATMs, Web sites, IVR, information kiosks, as well as other methods. Self-serve may be also applicable in pure-service areas such as restaurants (e.g., in salad bars, food buffets, and drinks), grocery stores, and hotels (e.g., in-room coffee makers).

Customer empowerment, or governance, improves quality of service, takes a large burden away from the service provider, makes the service delivery time faster, and cost lower due to lowered staffing requirements. Empowering customers provided them with a great deal of convenience and increases their satisfaction. However, as different types of customers have different preferences, many facilities are finding that it is best to offer full-service (labor or machine-based) and self-service (customer-based) options.

Furthermore, automation of business processes provides timesaving in terms of time and number of people needed to complete a particular task. Virtual (click-and-click) business transactions provide faster, self-service twenty-four-hours-a-day and save time of employees, customers, and suppliers. In order to develop useful CK, segmentation of customers (the focus of Chapter Seven) is critical to secure a better understanding of customer needs, deliver the right good or service, and serve them well.

A Shift from 1-to-1 to Mass Customization

Although many customers may still recall earlier days of customer service when sales clerks called customers by their names and customized transactions to them, 1-to-1 model is not very popular model for manufacturers nowadays. The inhibitors to 1-to-1 customization are its high perceived cost and the required big push in the strategic direction of manufacturing organizations.

MC is an emergent concept that is expected to expand in the future to provide customized products or services through flexible processes in high volumes and at reasonably low costs. The advancement of e-commerce capabilities enables companies to create and maintain global reach with customers and suppliers and to gather preferences of customers that support customized preferences. CKM makes MC a viable production model as it seeks to meet changing customer needs and desires.

A Shift from Generic to Intelligent Customization Strategies

Presently, MC seems to be the practice with the strongest likelihood of being a continued trend of the future, but with new enhancements. A DSS or BI could prevail in the future for facilitating design and customer collaboration in the process of selecting product configuration in MC environments. The DSS-based MC integrates object-oriented programming, multi-attribute decision analysis, and integer linear programming to support product/service customization where customer choice is managed by the relative relevance of a set of attributes as well as a set of component combinations offered by the company. However, these programs are restrained by a set of technical, aesthetical, and financial constraints defined interactively by designers and customers (Frutos and Santos, 2004).

A recent framework of GSS for MC may present a significant development in the future. A GSS for MC allows multiple decision makers to cooperate in the MC-related problems. The system provides a set of artificial intelligent approaches, such as CBR for case learning and data mining tools, in addition to the synchronous and asynchronous communication groupware. The model base contains a state-of-the-art set of MC-specific models as well as the generic models for operational management (Huang et al., 2003).

CONCLUSION

Customers of the 21st century face a vast array of products, services, brand choices, prices, and suppliers. In such a business context, the first task of this century's businesses is not to develop products, but to be creative in formulating competitive strategies that deliver the highest value to customers through customized products and/or services. The ultimate aim of business organizations is to create SCA by creating and maintaining value-adding offerings that enable businesses to compete with, and outperform, other rivals. Customer loyalty is the road for achieving SCA. Customer loyalty expresses an intended overall customer behavior related to patronage to a particular business organization and its products and/or services as reflected in future revisit and/or expansion of purchases through up-selling or cross-selling.

The importance of customization of offerings is emphasized by the fact that the buyers of a product or a service are not a homogenous group. Actually, it is difficult to find the 'one size that fits all' as every buyer has individual needs, preferences, resources and behaviors. Since it is impossible to cater for every customer's individual characteristics, companies group customers into segments by variables their customers have in common. These common characteristics allow a standardized marketing mix for all customers in a segment to be developed or to deliver purely personalized offerings for a focused market which allows for development of '1-to-1' customer relationship.

Following the logic of the segmentation theory, organizations use MC as an approach to recognize individual differences among customers and to modify the offerings accordingly.

A customization continuum has two opposite extremes: one extreme point represents mass production of purely standard MTS items while the other extreme point represents manufacturing of purely customized handcrafted items. In between these two extreme come MTO and ATO strategies.

MC can occur at various points along the value chain, ranging from simple 'adaptation' of delivered products by customers themselves, up to the total customization of product sale, design, fabrication, assembly, and delivery. MC can fit well anywhere along the customization value chain, and can provide value-added content without trade-off in performance objectives of customization, e.g. providing companies with advantages of both MTS (lower cost) and MTO (shorter delivery time) at the same time.

Maximizing the experience of customers through introduction of products and/or services that meet their desired needs and preferences would increase operating costs of companies. This is attributed to having to make a unique or distinctive product for each market segment rather than enjoying economies of scale when making one low-priced product for the whole market. Therefore, it seems that the choice here is between 'more-for-less' versus 'less-for-more' resulting from business strategies in their focus on 'cost leadership' versus 'differentiation'.

One of the most crucial problems that face organizations is the degree to which they should customize their offerings. The contradiction of offering individualized products, and yet keeping reasonable prices, can be solved with a MC strategy. The decision on degree of customization must be designed in a way that meets a particular organization's customers, production capabilities, competitive situation, and the new technology available to them. Organizations that are well prepared for customization will be rewarded in customer loyalty, market leadership, productivity, and profitability.

Different product/service customization strategies require quite different ICT requirements; therefore, companies need to be able to manage transitions among different MC approaches. Collaborative MC requires some kind of product configuration tool. Modular (adaptive) MC strategy requires implementation of some sort of PDM-system, which may require massive development efforts from the company. When moving to more sophisticated MC strategies, such as a transparent strategy, new ICT development is needed. In this transition, integration of CRM and PDM is required. Cosmetic customization will also require some developments in a company's ICT infrastructure (Riihimaa et al., 2004).

Two major interdisciplinary infrastructure elements that facilitate MC strategies are e-commerce and KM. The linkages between these two serve to validate the strategic shift toward MC. E-commerce provides capabilities for firms to reach global buyers and suppliers and is recognized increasingly as a way to support the gathering of knowledge, specifically customer preferences. KM provides the framework needed to manage intellectual capital as a valuable organizational resource for supporting customized preferences. CKM makes MC a more viable strategy for manufacturers as they work to meet changing customers' needs and desires.

CKM shows how a business potentially could leverage its DCCs to reach an optimal level of customer satisfaction and loyalty by offering customers more value-added products, services, and processes at less cost. In essence, the approach of minimizing costs and maximizing returns for customers is essential to attract, satisfy, and retain those customers. The use of CKM to provide added value to customers is linked directly to improved profitability and is value-based for the company. This concept will be discussed in Chapter 10.

REFERENCES

Alfnes, E., & Stranhagen, J. O. (2000). Enterprise design for mass customization: The control model methodology. *International Journal of Logistics: Research and Applications*, 3(2), 111-125.

Bourke. (1999). *Mass customization: Survival and growth in the to-order sector:* A QAD white Paper. Bourke Consulting Company www.bourkeconsulting.com/documents/mass_customization.pdf (Retrieved on 10 February, 2008).

Browne, J., Harren, J., & Shivan, J. (1996). *Production management systems. An integrated Perspective*. Harlow: Addison-Wesley.

Davenport, T. H. (1993). *Process innovation*. Boston, MA: Harvard Business School Press.

Davis, S. M. (1987). *Future perfect*. Reading, Massachusetts: Addison-Wesley.

Earl, M. (1994). The new and the old of business process redesign. *Journal of Information Systems*, 3(1), 5-22.

Frutos, J. D., & Santos, E. R. (2004). Decision support system for product configuration in mass customization environments. *Concurrent Engineering*, 12(2), 131-144.

Gibbert, M., Leibold, M., & Probst, G. (2002). Five styles of customer knowledge management and how smart companies use them to create value. *European Management Journal*, 20(5), 459-469.

Gilmore, J. H., & Pine II, B. J. (1997). Four faces of mass customization. *Harvard Business Review*, Jan-Feb, 91-101.

Hart, C. W. L. (1995). Mass Customization: Conceptual underpinnings, opportunities and limits. *International Journal of Service Industry Management*, 6(2), 36-45.

Heizer, J., & Render, B. (2006). *Operations management.* 8th edition, New Jersey: Prentice-Hall.

Hill, C. W., & Jones, G. R. (2007). *Strategic management: An Integrated Approach.* 7th edition, Boston, MA: Houghton Mifflin.

Huang, H., Wang, L., & Gu, Z. (2003). A Web-based GDSS for mass customization: Framework and functionalities. *Systems, Man and Cybernetics*, IEEE International Conference on, *5*(5-8), 4791–4796.

Knox, S., Maklan, S., Payne, A., Peppard, J., & Ryals, L. (2003). *Customer relationship management: Perspectives from the marketplace.* Oxford, UK: Butterworth-Heinemann.

Kotler, P. (2006). *Marketing management*, Upper Saddle River, N.J.: Prentice Hall.

Lampel, J., & Mintzberg, H. (1996). Customizing customization. *Sloan Management Review*, Fall , 21-30.

Lee, C-H.S., Barua, A., & Whinston, A. B. (2000). The complementary of mass customization and electronic commerce. *Economics of Innovation and New Technology*, *9*(2), 81-109.

Mendonca, J. (2003). A model and sample case for teaching the business value of information technology. *Journal of Information Technology Education, 2*, 61-72.

Mohammed, R., Fisher, R., Jaworski, B., & Cahill, A. (2003). *Internet marketing: Building advantage in a networked economy.*2nd edition, Boston, MA: McGraw-Hill.

Mok, C., Alan, S., & Wong, L. (2000). Mass customization in the hospitality industry: Concepts and applications. Fourth International Conference '*Tourism in southeast Asia & Indo-China: Development, marketing and sustainability'*, June 24-26.

Peppard, J., & Ronald, P. (1995). *The essence of business process re-engineering.* Upper Saddle River, NJ: Prentice-Hall.

Peppers, D., Rogers, M., & Dorf, B. (1999). *The one-to-one field book.* New York: Doubleday.

Pine II, B. J. (1993). *Mass Customization: The new frontier in business competition.* Boston, Massachusetts: Harvard Business School Press.

Porter, M. E. (1985). *Competitive advantage: Creating and sustaining superior performance.* New York: The Free Press.

Porter, M. (1998). *Competitive strategy.* New York: The Free Press.

Rainer, K., Turban, E., & Potter, R. (2007). *Introduction to information systems.* Hoboken, NJ: John Wiley.

Reid, R. D., & Sanders, N. R. (2007). *Operations management: An integrated approach.* 3rd edition, New York: John Wiley.

Riihimaa, J.; Ruohonen, M., & Makipaa, M. (2004). Transitions in mass customization strategies: requirements for information systems. *Frontiers of e-Business Research*, 373-384.

Rowley, J. (2002). Eight questions for customer knowledge management in E-Business. *Journal of Knowledge Management, 6*(5), 500-511.

Slack, N., Chambers, S., Johnston, R., & Betts, A. (2006). *Operations and process management: principles and practice for strategic impact. Essex*, England: Pearson Education.

Swift, R. (2001). *Accelerating customer relationships: Using CRM and relationship technologies.* Upper Saddle River, NJ: Prentice-Hall.

Treacy, M., & Wiersema, F. (1995). *The discipline of market leaders: Choose your customers, narrow your focus, and dominate your market.* Boston, MA: Addison-Wesley.

Venkatraman, N., & Henderson, J. C. (2000). Business platforms in the 21st century. In D. Marchand, T. Davenport, & T. Dickson (Eds.). *Mastering information management: Your single source guide to becoming a master of information management* (pp. 283-289). London: U.K: FT-Prentice Hall.

Whinston, A., Paramenswaran, M., & Stallaert, J. (2000). Markets for everything in the networked economy. In D. Marchand, T. Davenport, & T. Dickson, T. (Eds.). *Mastering information management: Your single source guide to becoming a master of information management* (pp. 210-216), London: UK: FT-Prentice Hall.

Chapter X
Measuring Return on Relationships with Customers

INTRODUCTION

Effective development of customer products and/or services requires valid and up-to-date CK in order to target the right customer with the right offering at the right time and through the right channel. Increasing value-adding content of customer offerings is hoped to be reflected on major gains in cost, time, and quality of products and/or services. Doing good things for customers is doing good things good for business. This chapter addresses customer value reciprocity for business represented by durable and profitable customer relationship.

CONCEPTUAL FOUNDATIONS

The buyer-seller relationship has been likened to a marriage since it decreases uncertainty, allows a sharing of tasks, and provides and intimacy. However, like a marriage, it also increases personal responsibilities, requires care and nurturance and can end with a costly dissolution. To a larger (B2B) and smaller (B2C) degree, these same costs and benefits often apply, for example, the revenue-sharing alliance pioneered by Amazon.com where a seller pays a commission to an Internet partner on the basis of click-throughs, sales leads, or actual sales that originate from the partner's site. These alliances require both parties to agree to investments of time and resources, such as technical capabilities, reporting system, and marketing (Mohammed et al., 2003). This section discusses the concept of customer 'relationship' and customer life cycle (CLC).

Customer Relationship

A relationship is a bond or connection between a firm and its customers. It may be strong, weak or nonexistent. It can be intellectual, emotional or both. Relationship can be intellectual, emotional or both. Intellectual: 'I know I cannot get a better deal elsewhere'. Emotional: 'I feel good when I am wearing my Nikes' (Mohammed et al., 2003).

Two categories of relationships are observed: type and involvement. Relationship exists along a continuum of types ranging from communal to exchange based. A purely communal relationship is altruistic in that each person is focused on meeting the needs and wants of the other(s) in the relationship, e.g. parent and child. In contrast, an exchange relationship is based on the giving of one thing in return for another, e.g. buyer-seller relationships (Mills et al., 1994).

Relationship involvement is defined as the degree to which a relationship is relevant to the consumer, viz. the extent to which it relates to consumers' values, interests, or needs. Involvement is a function not only of product characteristics, but also of the purchase situation and the consumer's personal needs.

Customer Life Cycle

CLC is a term used to describe the progression of steps a customer goes through when considering, purchasing, using, and maintaining loyalty to a product or service. Sterne and Cutler (2000) have developed a matrix that breaks the customer life cycle into five distinct steps: reach, acquisition, conversion, retention, and loyalty. This means getting a potential customer's attention, teaching them what you have to offer, turning them into a paying customer, and then keeping them as a loyal customer whose satisfaction with the product or service urges other customers to join the cycle. The customer life cycle is often depicted by an ellipse, representing the fact that customer retention truly is a cycle and the goal of effective CRM is to get the customer to move through the cycle repeatedly (Sterne and Cutler, 2000).

By examining customer relationships via the CLC model, companies can determine when opportunities (or threats) exist for improved or new knowledge-based exchanges that will also affect which specific customer products/services and/or processes should be developed. According to Knox et al., (2003) CLC include suspects, prospects, customers, and advocates. The CLC passes through the following three major stages: acquisition, retention, and expansion/winback (Zikmund et al., 2003).

- *Acquisition:* Customers recognize that the firm is a possible exchange partner, but not initiated any exchange with the firm or purchased any of its products. In this stage, suspects may turn into prospects. However, in many instances, a single exposure creates awareness but will not translate into traffic and ultimately revenue. Customer is motivated to develop ties to the firm only to the extent that the firm is an attractive exchange offer, at a minimum, values that are perceived as superior to competition. Attributes of acquisition are provided in Table 10.1.
- *Retention:* Once exchange is made, the objective is to offer customers a better product and/or service to retain profitable customers and ultimately have customers chose to become loyal advocates or at least intends to repeat another exchange with the same organization. Attributes of retention are provided in Table 10.1.
- *Expansion/Winback:* Expansion in B2B and B2C may take the form of up-selling and cross-selling. Cross-selling focuses on the marketing of complementary products to customers, whereas up-selling emphasizes the marketing of higher-value products and services to new or existing customers. Winback strategies may be used to regain high-value lost customers. To determine whether or not to engage in winback strategies, organization first need to consider the lost customer to be a 'suspect,' ask whether or not the customer should be retained.

Table 10.1. Characteristics of acquisition and retention

Acquisition	Retention
Acquiring potential relationships	Nurturing relationships
External analysis	Internal analysis
Demographic profiles	Demographics and transactional history
Potential needs driven	Actual needs driven
Contacts can be less personal	Contacts must be personal
Inaccuracy tolerated	Accuracy required
Offer driven	Offer relationship-driven
Offers can be events	Offers must be integrated
Relatively low response	Relatively high response
Supports assimilation	Supports reactivating
Synergistic with retention	Synergistic with acquisition

Source: From Swift, R. (2001). Accelerating Customer Relationships: Using CRM and Relationship Technologies. Upper Saddle River, NJ: Prentice-Hall, p.78.

CRITICAL ISSUES

This section discusses the following issues: targeting delighted versus devoted customers, building online versus offline customer relationships, measuring a customer's lifetime value (CLV), increasing value of the CLV, using metric versus non-metric customer valuation measures, using local versus global customer valuation, determining the value of CRM systems, and maximizing return on customer (ROC) versus return on CRM investment.

Targeting Delighted vs. Devoted Customers

It has been argued that what firms should target are not satisfied, not even delighted customers, but devoted customers (Hanselman, 2007). Some customer shave high expectations, some customers have low expectations, all customers either have a 'great' experience, or a 'poor' experience. So companies need to go for 'delighted', aim for 'devoted', spot 'disappointed', and avoid 'disaffected' (Figure 10.1). Delighted customers are positively surprised by the level of service provided, so they represent a good start. But, with time, expectations will rise, and the challenge will be to deliver consistently a 'great' experience. The ultimate aim of businesses is to establish relationships with devoted customers. Devoted customers stick with the business, spend more, and spread the word about the business to others. Therefore, the goal is to be engaged more with customers to determine what should be done to make them 'devoted' or loyal (Hanselman, 2007).

There are some common key terms involved in measuring and building customer loyalty and satisfaction. Businesses can derive information about customer satisfaction and loyalty by measuring their customer churn. The attrition rate, or churn, is defined as the percentage of customers lost in a given period, typically a year (number of customers who discontinue a service in a given period, typically a year, divided by the average total number of customers over that same period). The retention rate is then 1- the attrition rate (Zikmund et al., 2003);

In many industries, customer churn remains a pressing concern, and an expensive one. Global competition has raised the cost of acquiring new customers and made it imperative to determine which customers are likely to churn, and which are likely to be kept. Although they are extremely difficult undertakings, firms need to analyze customer profiles in order to predict churn and design cost-effective strategies to combat it. The challenge is that such projects require organizing and analyzing huge volumes of data that are frequently inaccurate, fragmented, inaccessible, and difficult to consolidate.

Figure 10.1. Creating devoted customers

	A 'Great' Experience	A 'Poor' Experience
High Expectation	Devoted	Disappointed
Low Expectations	Delighted	Disaffected

Source: Adapted from Hanselman, A. (2008). How to create 'devoted' customers: A practical guide. http://www.andyhanselman.com, accessed on 25 July, 2008.

Building Online vs. Offline Customer Relationships

In B2B and B2C transactions, effective integration of the online and offline experience is necessary for effective customer experience and effective CKM. In this regard, customer-facing and back-office transactions need to be integrated. Back-office transactions are concerned with transfer of data between the business and its suppliers and the integration of supplier, distribution systems and other data-centric systems, and with database integration.

The Web is unique in creating customer relationships due to its interactivity and individualization (Mohammed et al., 2003):

- *Interactivity:* It is defined as the extent to which a two-way flow of communication occurs between the firm and the customer. It is not enough that communication flows are frequent; it requires a dialogue between firm and customer in which both parties listen to, respond to and serve the needs of the other. Although not fully developed, mechanisms that facilitate a marriage between the Internet and human involvement include:

  - Retail selling systems in which store personnel are responsible for customer service over the Internet. Video cameras at both ends provide real-time virtual interaction.
  - Coordination between the Internet and retail service personnel.
  - Chat room for various product-related issues of interest to some customers.

- *Individualization:* It refers to the degree to which firm-customer interactions are tailored or customized to the individual user. Low individualization information is distributed to a set of users in much the same way as a newspaper- for example, Dow Jones, NASDAQ, automatic newsletters for seat sales or vacation packages to travelers. High individualization interactions transmit information that is customer-specific, ranging from account information, transaction statements, billing statements to a customized selection of reports from the public domain such as Yahoo! search results.

Measuring a Customer Lifetime Value (CLV)

The quality of customer experience is reflected in CLC. More and better customer experience is likely to be reflected in more profitable and durable relationship with customers. When a company aims to have more customers, it can get them, but they may not be profitable. If company aims at higher sales, it can boost them, but at what cost? What a company usually looks for is profitable and durable customer relationship. The value of a customer relationship takes three forms along the customer profitability cycle composed of the following stages: reach, acquire, expand, retain, decline, and churn (Figures 10.2):

- Increasing ROC investment (*Reach* and *Acquire* phases)
- Optimum ROC (point A)
- Constant ROC (in-between *Expand and Retain* phases)
- Decreasing ROC (*Decline and Churn* phases)

Customer valuation is a scoring process used to help a company determine which customers the company should target in order to maximize profit. Customer valuation requires that the company evaluate past data to learn which customers purchased recently, which customers purchased frequently and which customers

Figure 10.2. Profitability across customer lLfe cycle

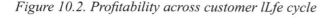

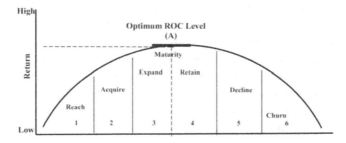

spent the most money, in hopes that the company can forecast future purchase potential and make sure time and resources are spent only on its best customers. Customer valuation is based upon the 80/20 rule in marketing, whereby a company spends the majority of its time working with its best customers.

When measuring a CLV, relationship depth, as reflected by the frequency and magnitude of purchases, is a critical component of customer profitability. Besides, firm must first develop and maintain a well-organized customer recency, frequency, and monetary (RFM) analysis. RFM is a function of three components (Strauss et al., 2006):

- Recency (how long): the average elapsed time between purchasing events.
- Frequency (how often): number of purchasing events.
- Monetary (how much): dollar value spent on customer purchase.

In the calculation of CLV, several issues are likely to emerge (Mohammed et al., 2003):

- Active/Inactive Customers: determining active versus inactive customers is very challenging since each customer's individual purchase activity is difficult to predict and firms cannot directly observe defections, or customers who switch to another firm.
- Customer's Net-Present Value (NPV): calculating a customer's NPV needs to consider the likely cost of keeping the customer and what will the customer purchase pattern will be over its lifetime?
- Critical assumptions: assumptions must be made about the time horizon, marketing and service costs per customer, expected gross contributions and interest rates.

Increasing the CLV

Effective retention tactics for Best Customers include acknowledgement and recognition that they are deserving customers. Of all customers, Best Customers are most worthy of appreciation and special treatment. While such rewards may include preferential discounts, Best Customers are more likely to feel appreciated through higher-quality or more frequent communications, timely information about new products or services, and special events that allow them to relate to the business and other customers who share their interests (Mohammed et al., 2003). For Frequent Customers, who have proven their loyalty via repeat purchases, the best strategy is to increase the average purchase amount via bundling, cross-selling, and up-selling (Figure 10.3).

Using Local vs. Global Customer Valuation

In a world of increasing diversity and intense competition, a marketer, using any segmentation technique with a perspective broader than local, runs the risk of missing opportunities or not identifying potential problem areas. Even the most sophisticated segmentation schemes, if applied on a global or national basis, are not likely to pick up on important local nuances. Customers can differ greatly from one part of the country to another. Even within a major city, there can be significant differences. Such differences are likely to go beyond demographics and may include purchase behavior and product usage. The local competitive environment can also impact local customer differences. In one store's trade area there may be few competitors, while in another, competition may be quite intense. The Customer Value Matrix (CVM) is used to help to differentiate between local and global customer values. The CVM is best applied at a local level, focusing on the customer base for a single store, rather than averaging across multiple stores. In doing so, the local segments derived truly reflect the specifics of the local customer base within the context of the local market environment (Marcus, 1998).

Understanding the consequences of aggregating outlets into a single value (best customer or average customer) is important because corporate marketer's desire for centralized control can impact local performance. When corporate marketers focus on a broad, centralized segmentation, they can end up favoring strong outlets while assisting to perpetuate problem outlets. In addition, due to the scale cost advantage and logistics of implementation, centralized marketing efforts tend to have a bias against very small targeted efforts. Put simply, it is unlikely that centralized efforts would generate local, personalized communications targeting multiple groups of customers who share some relevant characteristics. It is also unlikely that centralized, corporate efforts would be able to take advantage of truly local, event-driven opportunities such as local and national celebrations and festivals (Marcus, 1998).

Figure 10.3. Customer-offerings lifetime matrix

	New Customer	Old Customer
Old Offering	1. Acquisition	2. Retention
New Offering	3. Horizontal Expansion	4. Vertical Expansion

Even in the case of a centrally-driven, multi-outlet franchised business, there is great value to using the CVM to segment and target customers at a local level. Although there are significant challenges to proper implementation, taking advantage of local relationship, customer valuation requires an approach that is easy and affordable enough to be pursued locally. The local personnel, time constraints and marketing skills must also be considered (Marcus, 1998).

Adopting Metric vs. Non-Metric Customer Valuation Measures

The measurement of CKM's profitability poses an immense challenge for CKM initiatives. Most return on investment (ROI)-oriented valuation measures focus too much on the near term, counting only metric 'hard' benefits and ignoring the more important non-metric 'soft' benefits that relate to customer satisfaction, retention, and lifetime value optimization.

Peppers and Rogers (2004) argue that customers are the only reason companies build factories, hire employees, schedule meetings, lay fiber-optic lines, or engage in business activities. Without customers, there is no business. Therefore, customer valuation should be focused much more on the softer benefits, especially maximizing CLV, and the ROC measure is one way to help the team balance the short-term and long-term investments and impacts around this initiative (Peppers and Rogers, 2004).

ROC is calculated as the firm's current-period cash flow from its customers, plus any changes in the underlying customer equity, divided by the total customer equity at the beginning of the period. Customer equity is the net present value of all the cash flows a company expects its customers to generate over their lifetimes. The formula takes into account the short-term sales from customers, as well as factoring in changes to lifetime expectations. Even though sales may be good today, if a customer decides to not purchase in the future because of something that damages the relationship with the customer, whether a market brand issue or a competitive trump, the formula takes this into account by lowering the ROC (Peppers and Rogers, 2004).

The hard part in working with the ROC formula; however, is that the expected lifetime customer value is often hard to estimate, and therefore the equation has risk in its accuracy, and there is a tendency to be uncomfortable with these estimates. This is especially true when the team is asking for large hard-dollar investments to be made today, with a prediction of some future value. With ROC the value of using the equation outweighs these risks. Using ROC as an important element in the CRM decision process can help the team maintain customer focus and better balance investments for long-term value achievement (Peppers and Rogers, 2004).

However, there is an ongoing debate on the metric measurement of KM and CRM initiatives. Today's units of analysis come from the old ICT world and are not appropriate to knowledge. The value of knowledge cannot be fixed; it depends on its context and on the knower (Glazer, 1998). Cohen (1998:33) reports Jan Torsilibri (of Booz Allen & Hamilton) saying that "... the value of knowledge cannot be measured directly, but it is possible to measure outcomes: changes in profitability, efficiency, or rate of innovation that follow from knowledge efforts."

As an alternative to 'hard' approaches to measuring KM and CRM, three general-purpose 'soft' non-metric approaches to measuring the impact of KM initiatives are presented, viz. House of Quality, QFD, BSC, and American Productivity Center (APQC) benchmarking approach (Tiwana, 2000). The House of Quality (Hauser & Clausing, 1988) method involves the development of a metrics matrix (house). The desirable outcomes of KM initiatives are listed on the left wall of the house, the roof consists of the performance metrics, the right wall consists of the weights (relative importance of the outcomes), and the base of the house consists of targets, priorities, and benchmark values. By looking at the correlations within the body of the quality matrix, management can decide to focus on those areas of CKM that are most likely to affect overall firm performance.

Whether it is the more general purpose 'non-metric' or the more CKM specific 'metric' techniques for business performance evaluation, the efficacy of all techniques depends on the competence of management in applying these techniques. Although the metric techniques attempt to provide systematic and comprehensive indicators, there are a number of subjective judgments that need to be made in applying these techniques, e.g. determining which objectives are more important than others and which indicators need to be given greater weight. A lack of standards of terms or measures used leads to proliferation of measures and difficulty in comparison. Therefore, there is a lack of generalizable results on this topic as most of the evidence on KM assessment is on a case-by-case basis (Kankanhalli and Tan, 2005).

Maximizing ROC vs. Return on CRM Investment

There has not been an effective way to evaluate the overall long-term benefits of current and future business programs such as CRM. The idea of ROC has been introduced in the same way that the financial profitability of a company is calculated using ROI technique. The concept of ROC is based on identifying the needs and problems of each individual customer, and treating different customers differently, which is the key concept of 1-to-1 marketing. Peppers and Rogers (2004) define ROC as the sum of a firm's current-period profit from its customers, plus any changes in customer equity (the sum of the lifetime values of all current and future customers served by the firm), divided by the total customer equity at the beginning of the period.

The concept of ROC sounds a lot like the concept of CLV, mostly because CLV is part of the equation. Then, the application of the same financial metrics is used in ROI calculations to determine an ROC. Sounds simple enough, just measure the change in the current and future profit from each customer, and then sum all those profits. But the expected future profit from each customer must be included, which is not yet known. Even though it is difficult to implement, the benefits of adopting the ROC concept can be tremendous. It can help marketers identify how much to invest in each customer, and how much to expect to get back from each customer now and in the future (Peppers and Rogers, 2004).

The ROC concept is built on thinking about customers as economic assets, much the same way that financial managers think about whether to invest in a new warehouse, a new plant, or a new type of manufacturing equipment. In ROC, Peppers and Rogers (2004) encourage marketers to do the same thing for each customer. This means allocating revenue generated by a customer, and the expenses incurred in obtaining and supporting that customer, in order to calculate the net cash flow from each customer, for every activity, response, behavior, and interaction with each customer.

By calculating the sum of all cash flows from all present and future customers, the "customer equity" can be estimated. As more and more historical data is collected on revenue and marketing expenses by customer, it will become possible to develop a ROC model that can help in predicting how proposed marketing programs will affect both short-term and long-term customer equity. In turn, total customer equity, the present value of all future net revenues, is a key component in determining shareholder value. By calculating the long-term future benefits from current marketing programs, it becomes quite easy to justify investing in, say, a brand awareness campaign, adding a new product line, or expanding sales into a new country (Peppers and Rogers, 2004).

Companies frequently focus their investments on quick payback periods implementing projects and initiatives that in the short term may yield a quick ROI by saving the company money or driving short-term sales, but in the long run, yield strategic issues. As for ROC, it requires a strategic decision by top management to apply it across all CRM activities: marketing, sales, and customer service. If a company is to have long-term success, and not be panicked by short-term profitability variations in the market, it's important to take a long-term view toward increasing customer equity, and, therefore, shareholder value.

Justifying CRM Initiatives

After measuring customer value, the next issue to address is to manage customer value, viz. to make money by creating very high ROI customer marketing campaigns. However, many KM and CRM initiatives receive the go-ahead more on gut instinct than hard facts. Capital budgeting techniques such as ROI, payback period, discounted cash flow, and net present value, have been, in many cases, ignored. Knowledge-enabled CRM can deliver the following benefits (Spira, 2004):

- *Expanded Knowledge about Customers:* CRM systems allow users to get to know customers closely. CRM software tracks and analyzes the customers' buying and interaction patterns, from which new opportunities to make more sales, or save money, emerge. It also raises flags at signs of danger and helps the enterprise anticipate customer requirements and preferences. Furthermore, CRM software captures knowledge from the interaction of agents with other agents and customers, adding value to the organization's CK.
- *Increased Customer Satisfaction:* With prompt answers to their questions, customers are more likely to be happy and increased customer satisfaction leads to greater customer retention and loyalty. Satisfied customers may turn ultimately into endorsers for the product and company, speaking favorably to colleagues about their experience. An example of what this means can be found in the typical mail-order company, where the product return rate can may reach as high as 20 percent, due mostly to the customers' questions remaining unasked, unanswered, or answered unsatisfactorily. By providing better answers, the company should be able to cut the rate in half, perhaps to 10 percent. This may translate into the doubling of an organization's annual revenues.
- *Up-selling and Cross-selling Opportunities:* Vendors can up-sell to delighted customers; so increased up-selling and cross-selling opportunities are an additional benefit of CRM software. CRM software also helps uncover customer purchasing patterns, enabling the enterprise to identify up-selling and cross-selling opportunities.
- *Improved Response Time:* The direct, metric benefits of CRM software can be measured in the number of minutes that each representative spends with each customer; the lower the number, the better the CRM software is doing its job. With the adoption of KM search and document management technology, CRM software decreases the response time for each inquiry since better search helps the representative find the needed information more quickly. CRM software also makes it possible to find and contact experts more efficiently,

which also improves response time.

- *Reduced Time to Market*: By staying close to its customers, an organization can collect feedback more quickly and reduce the time it takes to develop and introduce new or revised products. CRM offers ways to maximize customer information through KM applications that enable companies to collect, classify, and distribute customer profiles to research and development teams within the enterprise.

- *Fewer Escalated Enquiries*: CRM software, allows more enquiries to be answered without the need to escalate them by providing more accurate search, document management, and expert interaction and opinion. In the average calling center, approximately 20 percent of the enquiries are escalated to the second level. With a comprehensive CRM implementation, this can be reduced to 5 percent. Since the escalation of an enquiry is the most expensive and time and resource-consuming part of the customer service cycle, this will reduce significantly the customer service cost.

- *Competitive Intelligence*: With CRM, companies can develop customer profiles about themselves, what products they want and what they think of them. CRM systems can also provide valuable intelligence on a company's competitors, through interactions with service representatives or surveys on self-service sites. Once CRM is used smartly, it can become an important component of an organization's competitive intelligence strategy.

- *Improved Supply Chain Integration*: As mentioned earlier, CRM software can generate valuable intelligence on customer desires and purchasing patterns. By integrating this into the supply chain, the organization can better anticipate its needs for new or revised products, services, and/or processes.

RECOMMENDED SOLUTION: A PROPOSED CKM MODEL FOR CUSTOMER LIFE CYCLE

Business organizations use CK to meet customer's needs effectively and efficiently, increase their satisfaction and loyalty, and develop durable and profitable CLC. A model for CKM process dimensions according to CLC stages (customer acquisition, retention, and expansion) and CK categories (knowledge for, from, about, and co-creation with customers) is proposed (Figure 10.4).

There dimensions that emerge from the proposed model are as follows:

- *Customer Acquisition*

Figure 10.4. A proposed CKM model for customer life cycle

		Categories of CK			
	CLC Phase	**Knowledge for Customers**	**Knowledge from Customers**	**Knowledge about Customers**	**Knowledge Co-creation with Customers**
CKM Process	**Acquisition**	Marketing, Sales, and Services	Customer Demographics and Needs	Customer Profiling and Segmentation	Collaborative Planning, Forecasting, and Replenishment
	Retention	Differentiated Product/ Service Offers	Listening to the VOC	Customer Satisfaction and Complaining Behavior	Collaborative Planning, Design, Development, and Replenishment
	Expansion	Cross-Selling and Up-Selling Offers	Customer Demographics, Experiences, and Preferences	Customer Portfolio, Profitability, and Churn Analysis	Collaborative Planning, Design, Development, and Replenishment

- ○ *Marketing, Sales, and Service:* providing information for prospective customers on various dimensions related to products (usually through direct interactive and individualized or segment-specific customer contacts). Such knowledge is usually provided through acquisition campaigns that cover offer price, contract details, distribution and delivery, other logistics, and service activities.

- ○ *Customer Demographics, Needs, and Preferences:* capturing data/information on personal demographics and needs/preferences of customers (e.g., channel preferences) to identify strategically significant prospective customers.

- ○ *Customer Profiling and Segmentation:* developing a 'one-stop-shop' profile of customers (e.g., high/low potentials) through slicing and dicing of customer data that cut across a company's geographic, product, and channel silos. This CK helps companies personalize the relationship with their customers and to improve organizational response to customers' needs and preferences by offering customized products/services with the purpose of retaining customers.

- ○ *Collaborative Planning, Forecasting, and Replenishment* (explained in Chapter IX).

- *Customer Retention*

  ○ *Differentiated Product/Service Offers:* providing existing customers with information on customization options available in product/service features, packaging, delivery, etc.

  ○ *Listening to the VOC:* listening to suggestions, and/or complaints from existing customers with the purpose of retaining them. Companies need to learn not only from transactional data (numerical and content-based) stored in databases or in DWs, but from non-transactional (textual and contact-based) knowledge generated through collaborative CRM system, for instance. Such knowledge is essential to understand emotional and qualitative aspects of customers' experiences (e.g., knowledge acquired through open-ended/essay-style questions) and to develop a holistic view of customers.

  ○ *Customer Satisfaction and Complaining Behavior:* complaints and suggestions received through listening to the VOC are, in turn, used to develop knowledge about customers' satisfaction and complaints.

  ○ *Collaborative Planning, Design, Development, and Replenishment* (as explained in Chapter IX)

- *Customer Expansion:*

  ○ *Cross-Selling and Up-Selling Offerings:* companies may design expansion campaigns. Knowledge on cross-selling and up-selling campaigns is provided for existing customers.

  ○ *Customer Demographics, Experiences, and Preferences:* capturing data/information from customers on their demographics, experiences, preferences, and level of product/service usage.

  ○ *Customer Portfolio, Profitability, and Churn Analysis:* segment customers according to purchasing history and portfolio, profitability analysis (e.g., high/low CLV users), and possible churn decisions (e.g., high/low churn potentials and voluntary/forced churns).

  ○ *Collaborative Planning, Design, Development, and Replenishment* (as explained in Chapter IX)

FUTURE TRENDS

The following future trends in measuring return on CRM are discussed: a shift from customer satisfaction to customer loyalty, a shift from fragmented to integrated CRM, and a shift from Web-based CRM to Mobile-based CRM.

A Shift from Increased Customer Satisfaction to Increased Customer Loyalty

The company-customer relationship is predominantly unidirectional and dynamic in nature, but it is less certain that it will continue to be so in the future in the future. Some customers just want the business transaction the transaction, but others are willing to be engaged in an enduring relationship with which they deal. Customer segments vary in their desire to have relationships with suppliers. In the banking industry, for instance, small private account holders have no need for the additional services that a relationship provides; large corporations have their own treasury departments and often have little value from a bank relationship. At one extreme, small and medium-sized enterprises and high net-worth individuals may have the most to gain from a closer relationship (Buttle, 2004).

Customers, sometimes, feel that they influence organizations when they make them change their business value chain, e.g. order, development, and delivery processes. Growing number of customers are demanding more one-stop-shop business services that integrate ordering, delivery, and post-sale cross-functional processes. A front office may integrate sales, marketing, and service functions across media (call centers, people, stores, Web). Customers lack of control over fragmented cross-functional processes, absence of a single point of contact, longer flow cycle times, as well as many non-value adding steps may add to the dissatisfaction of customers.

Some customers may even feel that the concept of lifetime customer is not be appealing to them, thinking that it represents a sort of control over their 'destiny', threat to their privacy, and contradiction to the spirit of free-market economies when they miss the opportunity to buy from other suppliers. Furthermore, there are those who may question the finite longevity of customer relationships. A lasting relationship usually requires give and take from both parties involved, viz. customers and companies.

On the other hand, successful future organizations usually involve customers more in the planning, design, development, and delivery process of products or services. With this involvement comes customer control of this relationship, and at the same time corporate control through accumulation of information for the personalization of products or services. What is more likely to continue in the future is a bidirectional rather than a unidirectional customer-company's control over each other's 'destiny'. Customers, for instance, may not expect to have un-limited customer care, and companies cannot reasonably expect to have infinite customer commitment.

A Shift from Fragmented to Integrated CRM

The development of CRM as a new business strategy is beginning to drive change in most leading organizations. These companies are tending to use a cross-functional process approach, rather than the traditional approach to managing customers which divides up responsibility for various aspects of the relationship with the customer between different departments.

To manage the whole customer relationship, marketing and ICT departments will have to work together more closely; the key to successful CRM implementation is an integrated approach. Participation is required from people from marketing and sales people, quality management operations, market research and financial accounting, as well as ICTs. Organizations may therefore have to restructure in order to maximize the ROC ratios.

Post-dot.com reality has proven that the Web site cannot be dealt with as an isolated island; rather, it should be considered as one of many channels. Business organizations of the future will have a Web channel responsible for all aspects of the customer life cycle (e.g., engage, transact, fulfill, service). Most Web sites will complement other channels in a hybrid-channel market strategy designed to help customers learn about product and service offerings.

A Shift from Web-Based to Mobile-Based CRM

Developments in ICT systems have made customer contact easier than ever before. Key customer contact systems include the Internet, call centers, and other direct sales/service channels. The Internet is regarded widely as the most significant of these. The use of call centers as a means of customer contact has also increased massively, as has the number of bank cashpoint machines, ATMs.

Customer contact technology applications in the cyberspace began as passive means of making customer contact – they were designed so that customers could visit the website, or call the call centre, or drop by the cash point. Increasingly, however, companies are using their customer contact systems actively to do business. Customers who used to search the Internet for product information increasingly are buying directly over the net. Call centers are switching to out-bound calling and selling. ATMs are being linked to DWs so that messages or product offers can be displayed to customers. Consumers prefer to shop elec-tronically rather than physically visit the retailing shops. Customers like using web sites to buy because they are convenient. Companies win, too, because it is cheaper for them to acquire and service customers via a web site than by traditional means.

However, mobile marketing is expected to be the hype of the new frontier, so is the m-CRM. The ability to communicate and do business directly with customers can be more valuable, cheaper, and more convenient with WAP-enabled mobile CRM systems. The capabilities offered by the DW and by mobile customer contact systems create more value for customers and the company if the management is able to use technology to develop and deliver new marketing strategies through mobile-CRM systems.

CONCLUSION

The migration towards CKM enables organizations to be led by customers, not by their internal processes and requirements. The goal of such a transformation is to provide the best possible experience for customers whenever and wherever they interact with the business (directly, through the contact center, through the Web, or through e-mail). The best experiences result in the most satisfied and loyal customers, and the most satisfied and loyal customers are willing to repeat their purchase and expand it as well, which means ultimately achieving SCA. Therefore, nurturing value-adding customer relationships provides returns for both customers as well as companies.

Strategies for Frequent Customers need to leverage their relative familiarity with and loyalty to the business, with the objective of increasing their average purchase amounts. Typical tactics to accomplish this include the cross-selling and up-selling of products and services. CKM offers the opportunity to develop CK and to understand the impact of marketing on purchase behavior. The CK enables better matching of marketing offers to prospects, as well as tracking the effectiveness of marketing programs as the basis for future planning.

Once CRM is adapted throughout the customer's life, it allows the average customer to acquire a product that has been produced to meet his or her own particular needs and provides exceptional value for money for that customer. Leading customers provide a rich source of new ideas that can also be exploited with other customers or with new prospects. This results in a lower risk of failure and a higher chance of beating the competition.

CRM creates value for the customer. The customer benefits from product and/or service offers which are targeted to meet individual needs and from improvements in customer service. Companies will form close relationships with their suppliers, distributors and customers as they return time and time again for further unique products. Satisfied and loyal customers provide excellent references and referrals.

One of the basic notions of CRM is to attract and keep "Economically Valuable" customers and repelling and eliminating "Economically Invaluable" ones. Customer acquisition incurs cost of convincing a consumer to buy your product or service. This can include research, marketing and advertising costs. As an important business metric, customer acquisition cost should be considered along with other data, especially the value of the customer to the company and the resulting ROI of acquisition. The calculation of customer valuation helps a company decide how much of its resources can be profitably spent on a particular customer.

In the context of CRM, the concept of ROC is introduced to measure to help companies quantify the returns from various CRM activities: marketing, sales, and customer service. The idea of ROC is not new as it resembles financial metrics like net present value, discounted cash flow, and ROI for years. What is new is the idea of applying these financial metrics at the individual customer level. However, ROC is challenging to implement because every company implements customer-centric processes and marketing activities differently.

However, developing performance metrics to assess CRM success poses a challenge to business organizations. Benefits of CRM investment typically are realized immediately after project completion in the short run, or in a mid-range time. Sometimes, intangible benefits of CRM cannot be quantified, or that benefits cannot be proved or achieved at all.

REFERENCES

Cohen, D. (1998). Toward a knowledge context. *California Management Review*, *40*(3), 22-38.

Glazer, R. (1998). Measuring the knower: Towards a theory of knowledge equity. *California Management Review*, *40*(3), 175-194.

Hanselman, A. (2008). *How to create 'devoted' customers: A practical guide.* http://www.andyhanselman.com, retrieved on 25 July, 2008.

Hauser, J., & Clausing, L. (1988). The house of quality. *Harvard Business Review*, May-June, 63-73.

Kankanhalli, A., & Tan, B. C. Y. (2005), Knowledge management metrics: A review and directions for future research. *International Journal of Knowledge Management*, *1*(2), 20-32.

Kaplan, R., & Norton, D. (1996). *Translating strategy into action: The balanced scorecard.* Boston, Harvard Business School Press.

Knox, S., Maklan, S., Payne, A., Peppard, J., & Ryals, L. (2003). *Customer relationship management: Perspectives from the marketplace.* Oxford, UK: Butterworth-Heinemann.

Marcus, C. (1998). A practical yet meaningful approach to customer segmentation. *Journal of Consumer Marketing, 15*(5), 494-504.

Mills, J., & Margaret, S. C. (1994). Communal and exchange relationships: Controversies and research. In R. Eber, & R. Gilmour (Eds.), *Theoretical frameworks for personal relationships* (pp. 29-42). Hillsdale: Lawrence Eribaum Associates.

Mohammed, R., Fisher, R., Jaworski, B., & Cahill, A. (2003). *Internet marketing: Building advantage in a networked economy.*2nd edition, Boston, MA: McGraw-Hill.

Peppers, D., & Rogers, M. (2004). *Managing customer relationships: A strategic framework.* Hoboken, NJ: John Wiley.

Spira, J. (2004). Justifying a knowledge-enabled CRM initiative, *CRM Today*, www.crm2day.com, accessed on 10/25/2004

Sterne, J., & Cutler, M. (2000). *E-metrics: Business metrics for the new economy.* White Paper. Cambridge, MA: NetGenesis Corp.

Strauss, J., El-Ansary, A., & Frost, R. (2006). *E-marketing.* 6th edition, Upper Saddle River, NJ: Pearson.

Swift, R. (2001). *Accelerating customer relationships: using CRM and relationship technologies.* Upper Saddle River, NJ: Prentice-Hall.

Tiwana, A. (2000). *The knowledge management toolkit: Practical techniques for building a Knowledge management system.* Upper Saddle River, N.J.: Prentice Hall.

Zikmund, W., McLeod, R., & Gilbert, F. (2003). *Customer relationship management: Integrating marketing strategy and information technology.* Hoboken, NJ: Wiley.

Chapter XI
Managing Learning throughout CKM Change

INTRODUCTION

The previous chapter focuses on creating value-added products and/or services to customers. As the management of a CKM change is a journey, not a destination, this chapter is concerned with learning and adapting throughout the life of CKM change. It focuses on the accumulated knowledge and experience in implementing CKM, wherein end product learning is back channeled into the early planning stages of CKM. The aim of this CKM value chain phase is to sustain CKM performance.

CONCEPTUAL FOUNDATIONS

This section presents the following conceptual foundations for managing learning throughout the CKM change: CKM implementation, modes of learning, and OL.

CKM Implementation

There have been a lot of misconceptions surrounding the concept of CKM. Many of the early implementations projects were seen as ICT initiatives (Buttle, 2004). Sometimes, business firms have mistakenly dealt with CKM as an ICT project not as a business program. Snyder and Davidson (2003) suggest that up to 80 percent of CRM projects fail, and such failure in implementation may be attributed to several reasons, such as the lack of CRM understanding, the failure to adopt a clear strategy, failure to make appropriate changes to its business processes, and focusing on technology to the exclusion of people, process, and organizational changes required (Bolton, 2004; and Xu and Walton, 2005).

As customer-facing processes depend on structure, structure depends on strategy, and strategy depends on environment, therefore, there is a huge potential for business organizations to have a far more responsive organization through learning from CKM change at an accelerated pace for change. Responsiveness could make every aspect of the good or service configuration unique, and could enable customers to receive customized and individualized treatment. The ability to meet customers' preferences in dynamic and competitive environments is based on the ability of organizations to leverage CK generated through DCCs, e.g. people, technologies, and facilities, which are capable of designing, developing, and delivering adaptable and successful CKM change.

Modes of Learning

The three major approaches to learning to be reviewed are as follows: adaptive learning, generative learning, and U learning.

- Adaptive or 'single-loop' learning: is a mode in which organizations cope with situations within which they find themselves, whereas generative or 'double-loop' learning requires new ways of looking at the world, and challenging assumptions to introduce new innovations, products and/or services, processes, as well as organizational transformations.
- Generative learning: change that results from generative learning is usually conducted best in a team setting in which participants can review collective memories, archival and new data, and by discovery, experimentation, and reflection find solutions to current problems or develop plans to seek newly recognized opportunities. Change that results from generative learning is difficult to master but tends to be profound and long-lasting as it transforms the learner through the learning process (Senge, 1990). Generative learning tends to be continuous, while adaptive learning is more episodic. Pursuing change through generative learning requires companies to look at the world in new ways. This new perspective will change the way the company views and understands its customers, as well as enable better business management (Senge, 1990). Generative learning develops the capability to diagnose future problems and opportunities, plan and implement change, and evaluate outcomes. A company that is pursuing change through generative learning will see things and begin to transform its structures and processes to allow it

to take advantage of previously unforeseen opportunities. When companies observe signals like declining market share, revenue or profits, it is a reasonably safe bet that change utilizing generative learning is in order.

• The U-theory may be viewed as an advanced mode of generative learning that emphasizes learning from future. It consists of three basic aspects which are (Scharmer, 2007):

  • *Sensing* (Observation): the person(s) in this place has a growing awareness that something is not quite right. There is a sense that there is more than what has been currently known or experienced. This is a somewhat de-constructive process – an awakening to the possibility of greater oneness with the world. This is a downward move as it begins to strip away what has been 'known'; the previously unquestionable are beginning to be questioned; the fundamentals are seen with a fresh lens.

  • *Pre-sensing* (Reflection): represents a space of chaos, marked by uncertainty and the choice between running back to what has been known or sitting with the uncertainty, and retreating to reflect on what might be. The bottom of the 'U' is neither to be rushed through nor avoided but fully engaged in contemplating and mediating on thoughts. Instead of analyzing and referring to old patterns of the past, which are often inadequate in addressing the current challenges and which might be even part of the problem itself, the new focus rather is on learning from and bringing into life the best of all future possibilities.

  • *Realizing* (Learning): The upward swing of the 'U' involves bringing something new into reality. This process may be a relatively swift process and stands in direct relation to the sitting with the 'chaos' of the bottom of the 'U'. A painter may be taken as an example: to 'see' an artist sit and stare/study/become one with a mountain for a week and to 'see' the artist swiftly paint. Something new is born and reconstructed, thus the right side of the 'U' cannot be the same as the 'left' side of the 'U'.

  The starting point of the U learning journey is less a question of what we do or how we do something, but much more a question of how to approach or attend to a situation before actually doing something: it is the interior condition, the so-called inner place where any social action is generated and comes into being. It is that perspective which is missing in perception or management of the globalized business world which Scharmer (2007) called the blind spot. However, becoming aware of the blind spot helps organizations to discover their untapped resources and power, develop their absorptive learning capability, and live up to the best future leverage of DCCs in the design and development of innovative customer offerings.

Organizational Learning (OL)

OL has been defined as a quantifiable improvement process in activities, increased available knowledge for decision making, or SCA, and uses OM as its knowledge base (Jennex et al., 2005). Another perspective on OL is that organizations do not learn; rather, only individuals learn. During work, people gain experience, observe, and reflect in making sense of what they are doing. As they analyze these experiences into general abstractions, their perceptions on how work should be done changes. As these individuals influence their co-workers, the "organization" learns, and the process is changed gradually (Jennex et al., 2005). Learning in this perspective also is based on Kolb's (1984) model of experiential learning: 'grasping experience' (doing or watching), and 'transforming experience' (feeling or thinking).

OL takes place in systems of interrelated roles, both formal and informal, and is conducted in the social fabric of the organization involving both cognitive and social communication bases (March, 1991, and Simon, 1991). Individuals are socialized to organizational ideologies and beliefs, values, and norms. Ideologies and beliefs, values, and norms are antecedents, as well as consequences, of lower, higher, and future-oriented levels of OL:

- Lower level or single-loop adaptive (exploitation or behavioral learning) learning: it occurs through repetition, in a well-understood context, focuses on behavioral outcomes, and institutionalizes formal rules. In single-loop learning, organizations cope with situations within which they find themselves. For example, they maintain the organization's ideologies and beliefs, values, and norms (Argyris, 1991; March, 1991; and Klempa, 1995).
- Higher-level or double-loop generative (exploration or cognitive) learning: it requires new ways of looking at the world, and questioning of assumptions, beliefs, values, and norms (Argyris, 1991; and March, 1991). Double-loop learning seeks detection of contradictions, in order to resolve them. The detection of contradictions produces learning, resulting in individual and organizational beliefs, values, and norms. Thus, double-loop learning develops understandings of causation and complex associations involving new actions (Fiol and Lyles, 1985). Higher-level LOs are characterized by their absorptive capacity, diversity of knowledge, creative redundant knowledge (Cohen and Levinthal, 1990), regenerative learning, and creative tension (Senge, 1990b). These five properties facilitate application of new knowledge to innovation, knowledge

transfer, shared understanding, an ability to assess systemic sources of problems, and enable process innovation, and BPR implementation effectiveness (Klempa, 1995).

- Future-centered learning: in highly turbulent and uncertain environmental conditions and emerging complexities and challenges in the age of globalization, organizations find it inevitable to create profound product, process, and/or service innovation and change into technologies, processes, working teams, cultures, and even whole organizations systems. In creating future customer-centric change drawn from insights from the future, a journey to discover and fully use sometimes hidden inner sources of generative DCCs, e.g., power, creativity, and adaptability is required.

KM is highly interwoven with OL. KM may be viewed as a process used to make knowledge actionable to members of the organization; it involves capturing, storing, retrieving, and using knowledge. KM also involves the creation of a KM system and seeks to improve organizational effectiveness as it promotes knowledge reuse to improve decision making. As the KM system includes an environment that promotes OL, KM can be seen as an organizational change or transformation tool that can help management to create an LO culture (Jennex et al., 2005).

Although organizational learning is essentially people-based, it may benefit from the utilization of ICT-enhanced learning (e.g., corporate portals, e-Learning, and CRM). The recent dramatic rise in Internet and Intranet use is one manifestation of the expanding role of electronic technology in communication and knowledge-seeking. Firms are becoming aware both of the potential of this technology to enhance knowledge work and of the fact that the potential can be realized only if they understand more about how KW is actually developed and shared. Although the ICT ingredient is a necessary ingredient for successful KM projects, many authors (e.g., Davenport and Prusak, 2000) caution against a technology-centered KM approach. Technology alone does not make a knowledge-creating business context. Behavioral, cultural, and organizational changes are required.

CRITICAL ISSUES

The issues and challenges addressed in this section are: emphasizing ICT-based versus knowledge-based LO, meeting the challenges of CKM implementation, and identifying CSFs of CKM implementation.

Emphasizing ICT-Based vs. Knowledge-Based LOs

It has been argued by Senge (1990) that organizations seeking to manage knowledge have placed too much emphasis on ICTs and information management. Instead, he advocated learning, which places too little emphasis on structured knowledge and use of technology to capture and leverage it. According to Senge (1999:3), LOs are 'organizations where people continually expand their capacity to create the results they truly desire, where new and expansive patterns of thinking are nurtured, where collective aspiration is set free, and where people are continually learning to see the whole together'. On a personal level, an individual in an LO works on developing 'personal mastery' of his or her capacities, which refers to the spiritual inner drive to learn and to be the best that he or she can be through developing personal vision, abilities, and focus of energy (Senge, 1990).

Siemens, one of the top KM-driven companies worldwide, has also affirmed its stand that the role of people is more important than technology. Siemens KM program focused on a culture of sharing, synergy, and customer focus, especially in markets and fast-moving technology areas where the customer needs are greater for total business solutions and sector intelligence than mere technology (Davenport and Probst, 2002).

An LO is one that works to achieve continuous improvement in quality of goods and services delivered to customers through continuous employee learning and development. Continuous improvement requires constant development and updating of employees' talents, skills, and knowledge, in order to translate the knowledge they gain on a day-to-day basis into new things they learn into new or improved work related practices (Griffin, 2005). The LO is the ultimate form of organization that customer-centric businesses may aspire to in terms of flexibility, adaptability, creativity, responsiveness, efficiency, and competitiveness.

An LO is one that works to facilitate the lifelong learning and personal development of all of its employees while continually transforming its response to changing demands and needs. The main characteristics of LOs according to Peppard and Rowland (1995) are as follow:

- Commitment to collection and dissemination of knowledge.
- A mechanism for renewal (incorporate knowledge into processes).
- Openness/responsiveness to the outside world.
- Many organizations have implemented information systems to improve OL (e.g. Lotus Notes, Intranets).

Senge (1990) saw organizations as products of how people think and how they interact. LOs are organizations in which people continually expand their capacity to create the results they desire, where new and expansive patterns of thinking are nurtured, where collective aspiration is set free, and where people are continually learning to see the whole together. More specifically, Senge (1990) identified five disciplines to be the foundation for LOs:

- Personal mastery: relates to the development of people's capacity to clarify what is important to them in terms of the link to everyone's personal vision and goals. This helps to develop a 'creative tension' between current reality and future vision.
- Team learning: seeks to develop people's capacity to be engaged in conversation and balancing dialogue and discussion, where different views are presented and defended.
- Systems thinking: is the conceptual cornerstone of the fifth discipline as it provides the incentives and means to integrate disciplines and recognize the whole. It is concerned with developing people's capacity for putting pieces together and seeing wholes rather than disparate parts. The lack of systems thinking is seen as the major drawback of traditional management approaches that produce simplistic frameworks to understand complex and dynamic systems and processes (Jashapara, 2004).
- Mental models: is concerned with usage of people's capacity to reflect on internal situations, and involves balancing skills of inquiry and advocacy as well as understanding how mental models influence people's actions. An example of mental models is the development of scenario planning by managers as a precautionary measure to deal with different conditions in the future.
- Shared vision: refers to the building of shared visions and a sense of commitment that are rooted deeply in personal visions of employees.

Traditional organizations cope with major changes by assigning functional units to selected parts of the issue or problem - temporarily removing the burden from view. But for a new form of organization to be a true 'LO,' it must develop an atmosphere that is conducive to long-term rather than short-term benefits (Wysocki and DeMichiell, 1997). In new forms of organizations, the role of people has shifted from doing to improving the work. If 'improving' is becoming an equal to 'doing' for each employee, then 'learning' as well as 'performing' is becoming a key objective for the company as a whole (Peppard and Rowland, 1995).

It is very essential to develop a learning absorptive capacity for anticipating, reacting, and responding to business environment change, complexity, and uncertainty. Such an absorptive capacity can be developed through reorganization of people, knowledge sharing, and building a customer-centric LO. The rate of learning in organizations may become the most critical source of SCA (Awad and Ghaziri, 2004). In recent years, many organizations of different types have implemented this approach. Notable examples are IBM, Microsoft and many large oil companies such as British Petroleum (BP), Shell, and Chevron oil companies.

Meeting Challenges in CKM Implementation

Change occurs frequently in most large and small companies. The problem arises when it is not always well planned or deliberately executed. This is especially true when change is reactive to events rather than proactive in anticipating or even creating them. The situation aggravates when organizations do not invest much in planning, pursue change haphazardly, and adopt ICT-based generic or ready-made change initiatives.

The CKM change arena describes the triggers, targets, and types of change that occur in customer-centric companies. Change is always occurring in companies. Companies usually benefit more from change they are prepared for versus change that is imposed on them. In addition to preparing for change, companies should also learn how to identify the need for change, how to manage it successfully, and how to learn lessons from its successes as well as failures. This learning capability will allow companies to address future problems and take advantage of opportunities more quickly and effectively than their competitors.

The majority of CRM implementations are considered failures (Rowley, 2002, Bose and Sugumaran, 2003). CKM implementation may fail because the failure of organizations to adopt a clear strategy and failure to make appropriate changes. The most common fault was to focus on technology in setting out to implement CRM, to the exclusion of people, process and organizational changes required (Bolton, 2004).

CRM projects fail because they do not serve customers any better and fail to integrate data sources or provide the right kind of information to the right people at the right time (Bose and Sugumaran, 2003). Additionally, one of the major problems with CRM is the large investment to build and maintain a customer database which requires computer hardware, database software, analytical programs, communication links, and skilled personnel. Also, there is the difficulty of getting everyone in the organization to be customer oriented and to get everyone actually to use the customer information that is available. Providing adequate training so that personnel feel comfortable using a new system is critical. As well, not all customers want a relationship with the company, and some may resent the organization collecting information about them and storing it in a database. Another problem is the long-term wait for return on CRM investments.

Building the customer-centric knowledge-intensive enterprise is a process that poses real challenges to organizations. Although CKM change is sound theoreti-cally, its implementation suffers in practice from some pitfalls. Implementing a CKM strategy represents a real challenge as it does not happen over a short period of time like implementation of any ICT-based project. Knowledge-enabled CRM systems frequently have been accused for over-promising but under-delivering. The transformation towards a knowledge-enabled, customer-centric organization may face a number of challenges in such areas as absence of an overall KM strat-egy, knowledge hoarding corporate culture, inaccurate identification of business requirements, stovepipe or functional structure, lack of business process integra-tion, weak customers' expectations and satisfaction, shortage in meeting knowledge needs of power users, poor quality of data, inertia/resistance to change, fear of job loss, excessive vendors' involvement, and ineffective formal organizational roles (Al-Shammari, 2005).

Smith and McKenn, (2005) found out that the most significant challenges in implementing CKM effectively are organizational, not technical. They found that the four major hurdles that must be overcome are as follows:

- *Structural Challenges.* Transforming a product-centric organization into a customer-centric organization is easier said than done as companies may end up becoming customer-focused only by terms that are defined by the companies themselves not by their customers. Some companies may be concerned about the profitability of focusing on customers rather than on selling products, or may have poor alignment of their rewards and goals with a customer perspective.
- *Cultural Challenges.* Some companies may shy away from customer-centric-ity because of corporate narcissism, i.e., a sense that 'we know better than our customers' (Gibbert et al., 2002). Furthermore, not all companies want to hear what their customers really think of their products, services, image, and credibility.
- *Competency Challenges.* Skills and competencies for CKM must be used in the collection, creation, dissemination, and usage of CK. However, companies do not often take full advantage of the knowledge sources they have – com-munities of practice, alumni, retirees, and front line workers.
- *Privacy Concerns.* . Since much of CKM is based on developing a trusting relationship with each customer, organizations should take privacy dimension into consideration. Companies must understand not only the legal guidelines around how customer data is protected but also how customers feel about how

a firm uses their information. For example, too much customization may make some customers feel uncomfortable with what a company knows about them

Paquette (2005) identified several challenges in CKM implementation. He argued that CKM faces cultural challenges of sharing CK at the individual, group, or organizational level. Firms may experience a challenge of perceiving customers as a source of knowledge, not just revenue as reflected in the 'not invented here' concept, which demonstrates an unwillingness to accept externally generated ideas (Paquette, 2005). Other companies fear showing internal processes to customers such as suppliers or alliance partners, so they control what the customer sees to be afraid of giving away strategic secrets to the marketplace (Gibbert et al., 2002).

Besides cultural influences, a firm may face the obstacle of not having the competency required to absorb and utilize the external knowledge. Cohen and Levinthal (1990) argue that a firm's absorptive capacity, or its ability to absorb new knowledge, is a function of the firm's prior knowledge that allows it to recognize and synthesize new knowledge. Also, ICTs may not be able to handle the transfer of knowledge from external sources, as most knowledge sharing support systems are only designed for internal use. Control of content may be lost, as external knowledge transfer can push the locus of control beyond a firm's boundaries (Gibbert et al., 2002). Thus, organizations can be quite reluctant to open up these systems, as technical challenges occur without a universal integration and security mechanism that interfaces with both parties' systems (Paquette, 2005).

A further challenge exists when the customer can solely derive innovations from their knowledge and the need for a partner becomes insignificant. Von Hippel (1988) argues that innovators must have a poor ability to gain from their knowledge regarding innovations in order to share this information with others, or else they would capitalize on their knowledge independently and realize higher revenues. Factors such as manufacturing capability, geography, market knowledge, or supply chain requirements can increase an innovator's ability to bring their development to market, and prevent the opportunity for a formalized knowledge sharing alliance (Paquette, 2005).

Desouza and Awazu (2005) identified four major challenges to CKM: segmentation, integration, distribution, and application. The challenge in information-rich culture is to find the right categories on which to segment data prior to analysis. The attributes used to segment customer data are transient; an attribute that is important today may not be so tomorrow. The problem with dialogue is that customers cannot articulate what they want – they don't realize they need something until the innovative product offers it to them. Novice computer shoppers will need more handholding in terms of knowledge management than the superior ones. So providing the same level of knowledge to both customer groups will lead to frustrated user experiences. In the context of from knowledge, the business firm must be able to segment its users based on how they consume the product and/or service, i.e. into beginners, intermediate, expert and lead users. Segmenting users in this manner allows the business firm to get a better sense of how to manage the incoming knowledge from each group.

The challenge for from knowledge is to integrate the various contact/delivery channels. It is more common to find discrepancies in the information than to find that customer information coming from multiple sources synchronized. The challenge is to integrate the various channels, media, and methods for delivery of CK. With the internet and mobile phones, customers are no longer restricted in the media they can use to find information about products and/or services. To ensure a company can communicate with its customers through disparate mediums and in multiple languages, its CRM systems must be compatible with multiple environments, platforms, and systems.

Distribution calls for movement of CK within and across the organization. The challenge in distribution of about knowledge is to communicate it in usable formats according to different requirements and uses for the knowledge. Not being aware of these different needs risks subjecting staff to information overload, which could lead them to abandon the knowledge channels and try to work without them.

A significant problem with about knowledge is privacy. How does a company ensure it uses the information it gathers in a responsible way? Customers share information willingly when they believe it will be used to provide them with better support, products, and services. They are reluctant to share it when they think it will be used in unauthorized or hidden ways.

Identifying Critical Factors for CKM Success

The implementation of CKM initiatives is often in line with corporate vision and strategy, yet the majority of companies may not be fully prepared to make the necessary changes needed for successful CKM implementation. However, organizations can take several fundamental steps to move closer to a successful CKM change (Smith and McKeen, 2005):

- *Envision what could be done.* To help managers better understand how KM could help organizations meet their goals, develop knowledge about customers, use knowledge to support customers and enhance their experience with the firm, learn from customers, and co-create new knowledge. KM could be brought to customers through developing communities of practice for customers, developing content for customers, and building a platform (website) for customers.

- *Plan for and manage different types of relationships.* Some organizations may wish to use CKM selectively to serve them differently - both because their needs and preferences are different and because their value to the organization is different. Different types of 'customers', i.e. companies, individuals, middlemen, retirees, former employees or communities, require different type of knowledge relationship. Therefore, it may be a practical way to introduce CKM concepts into an organization with customers with whom the firm enjoys a high value relationship.
- *Knowledge development.* Once a customer group is identified and a data collection approach selected, a KM manager must determine how best to obtain and present the knowledge needed. In many cases, this begins with simple data collection and ensuring it is consistent and accurate. The knowledge manager must also work with the business functions involved and meet with customers to learn where and how tacit or 'soft' CK can be developed and used appropriately.
- *Effective Execution.* Poorly conceived and executed CKM initiatives could be problematic for organizations. Any CKM initiative touching end customers is especially sensitive. Therefore, it is essential that time and effort be spent to ensure that a CKM venture is successfully executed both from the customer and the company points of view. Building CKM into normal workflows and processes are usually the most effective ways to do this because it then becomes the way people work.
- *Measure.* Companies use different ways to measure CKM's effectiveness and value to the organization. Many companies use periodic surveys and tracking opinions, satisfaction, and loyalty over time. However, newer techniques include building in feedback loops so that measurement is more dynamic. These approaches are particularly effective when evaluating online tools. Usage, navigation, and satisfaction metrics as well as customer comments can be built into these tools and monitored continually, to enable companies to be responsive to their customers.

Gibbert et al. (2002) argued that although CKM can provide a significant competitive advantage to companies, its possible stumbling blocks have to be appreciated and circumvented. They have identified four major stumbling blocks as follows:

- *Application of CKM with an inappropriate mindset.* CKM need to be used as a long-term customer value-creation mechanism for SCA, rather than as a tool for leveraging knowledge from customers. For CKM to be effective, companies have to value and nurture their customers as knowledge partners, instead of knowledge sources.

- *Underestimating customer diversity.* Customers differ, even in the same industry segments, and this variety among customers requires different CKM approaches.
- *Inappropriate incentives for customers and organizational entities to leverage CMK to its full potential.* Under-estimation of incentives, as well as over-estimating them, can work as disincentives if not properly sensed, devised and implemented.
- *Inadequacies in organizational infrastructure and processes to handle the leveraging of knowledge from customers.* The inadequacy of organizational infrastructure and processes to accommodate diverse CK inputs poses a challenge to CKM implementation. BSCs may be used in organizations to emphasize business processes and enable customer satisfaction. Companies need to avoid falling into the 'trap' of over-reliance on (existing) CK (danger of being excessively 'customer-led' and not broader 'market-led'), without appropriate sensing of wider environmental impacts and influences.
- *Trust and protection issues not adequately emphasized.* CKM creates new knowledge sharing platforms and processes between companies and their customers. Openness in mutual sharing of knowledge and cultural issues of respect, trust, and confidentiality must be consistently implemented.

As for measuring returns on CKM change initiative, it is no different from other business-wide change programs that have preceded it, since returns in the short-run fall below expectations. Many of the benefits of the CKM change take longer to realize than what was initially planned for by organizations. Every CKM change program should be examined in a business case before it is launched, i.e., a recognized and identifiable business problem to solve, and measurable benefits to justify the investment (Gentle, 2002). In order to secure a successful implementation, a business case should be SMART:

- S - specific
- M - measurable
- A – actionable
- R - realistic
- T - timely.

RECOMMENDED SOLUTION: A PROPOSED CKM-BASED LEARNING ORGANIZATION

In order to deal with various issues and challenges associated with CKM implementation, a CKM-based LO model is presented. The model is analogous to a human body as an organizational system can be analyzed using this analogy. De Wit and Meyer (2004) offered a way to divide organizational systems into three parts: anatomy (structure), physiology (processes), and psychology (culture). Salaman and Asch (2003) classified organizations based on three components through which the capability of organizations is produced, i.e. organization structures, systems and processes, and cultures.

Due to today's dynamic business environments and the shift towards knowledge-based, customer-centric organizations, the above classifications may not suffice to analyze organizational dynamics, and thus need to be expanded. The proposed framework presents a seven sub-system classification of organizational systems that is analogous to the human body (Figure 11.1 and Table 11.1).

The components of the framework are as follow:

- Psychological (soul): people, culture, and internal work atmosphere
- Social (social interactions): exchange relationships with the external environment, i.e. customers, suppliers, business partners, and the like.
- Analytical (mind): intelligence, absorptive capacity, knowledge, and continuous learning
- Physical (bones): form (structure), technology, and other tangible resources
- Physiological (flesh): process and content
- Managerial (heart): planning, coordination, command, control, and adjustment
- Informational (blood): data and information

Figure 11.1. Anatomy of a knowledge-based, customer-centric LO

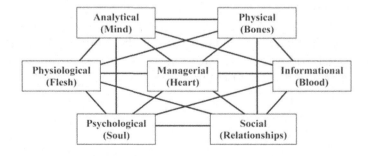

Table 11.1. Components of knowledge-based customer-centric LO

Element	Description
Physical	o Workplace is global, virtual, less hierarchical, and ICT-enabled. o Control is distributed throughout a networked structure made up of self-control units or teams.
Physiological	o Customer-facing processes are knowledge-based, innovative, and value-driven. o Based on continuous learning, processes are reviewed, redesigned, and continuously improved. o Customer-centric, redesigned processes are value-adding, flexible, objective, and timely.
Psychological	o Democratic governance based on distributed locus of control. o Share a common customer-centric vision, values, culture. o Culture fosters communication and collaboration anytime, any place. o Culture stimulates creativity, innovation, continuous learning, and sharing of information and knowledge.
Informational	o Workers are empowered to act using Computer Supported Collaborative Work (CSCW). o Acquiring, developing, and coordinating customer data, information and knowledge from integrated customer touch-points and databases.
Analytical	o ICT networks are used to integrate and manage CK across customer contact and delivery touchpoints. o Learning is continuous, life-long, and integrated into work experiences
Social	o Community is created through alliance with customers and suppliers. o Customer loyalty is assessed and improved.
Managerial	o Managing proactive, customer-based adaptation to changing environment. o Planning is used to create strategic organizational alignment and cohesion, both internally and externally. o Knowledge sharing and teamwork initiatives are valued and rewarded. o Workforce empowerment, satisfaction, and retention are emphasized.

FUTURE TRENDS

The trends thought to be possible to materialize in the future are a shift from contact/content based learning to blended learning, a shift from single-loop to double-loop learning, and a shift from e-Learning to m-Learning.

A Shift from Contact/Content Based Learning to Blended Learning

OL should not be based on the contact/content 'either-or' duality. Blended learning is expected to flourish as a pragmatic option that uses a combination of face-to-face and online methods to facilitate learning.

With the advent of technology, it is logical and convenient to adopt ICT as a learning tool to cater for diversity in preferences of customers for one or more touch-points. Blended learning offers unlimited ways to offer businesses that facilitate creativity and critical thinking and will become one of the most practical learning strategies for years to come.

A Shift from Single-Loop to U-Loop Learning

Future business organizations are expected to adopt generative learning more than adaptive learning as external environments continue to accelerate and complicate at exponential rates. When generative learning is applied to business, it involves examining the company's most basic assumptions about itself and how it does business. For example, who are a company's customers, how do their products and services create value for them, what is the best way to deliver value to customers, and what are a company's beliefs about how to treat customers, suppliers and employees? Re-examination of existing practices is essential to see if their current practices are consistent with their assumptions. Correcting any possible inconsistencies can impact profoundly a company's structure, processes, products, services, and ultimately customer loyalty and business profitability.

Adaptive learning is valuable, too, although it takes for granted assumptions about business environments and focuses instead on how to deliver value more efficiently and effectively to current customers. Many companies are already clear about their assumptions and act consistently on them. They also may be just plain lucky that their unexamined assumptions are not out of synch with their customers' perceptions of value and with their environment.

These companies can focus on making better, and perhaps less expensive, products and services, and delivering them to their customers in a timelier manner. The dilemma is that most companies would be better off examining their assumptions by engaging in generative learning. However, it is a time-consuming process, and many companies are not prepared to act appropriately on what they learn from this process.

However, change via generative learning may be an enormous leap for small- and medium-sized enterprises (SMEs) that face both financial and human capital constraints, or when senior managers are risk averse, that limit how much they can change. Sometimes, mature companies become unwilling to introduce major changes because of preferred life-style and family considerations (Gray, 2002). Another consideration is that generative learning often leads to change that is company-wide. When a department or activity is targeted initially, the consequences of change probably cannot be contained locally, but will reverberate throughout the entire company.

Therefore, adaptive learning and generative learning may be treated as complementary approaches. Generative learning may lead the company to identify new customers and markets to serve and new products and services to offer to them and existing customers. Adaptive learning may lead the company to identify ways to deliver more efficiently and effectively these new products and services to all customers.

Therefore, SMEs are expected to be more engaged in a proactive manner, which means they cause something to happen rather than wait to respond to it after it happens. Owners and managers of SMEs are more likely to engage in generative learning when they are proactive because they have time to explore potential problems and opportunities. SMEs that are reactive do not have adequate time to explore problems and to explore opportunities. Learning under these conditions tends to be adaptive to solve problems, but this may not contribute to long-term survival or prosperity (Gray, 2002).

A Shift from E-Learning to M-Learning

The innovative learning theory and practice is expected to play a significant role in an increasingly customer-centric, mobile and pervasive technological environment. Whilst there have been many successful implementations of mobile learning systems, perhaps the most interesting, challenging and innovative research has been in the area of blended learning, where mobility is but one aspect of a richer and more complex learning environment.

The technological development and dissemination of new approaches to both mobile and blended learning will shift the future of CK generation from e-learning to blended learning. As technology enables a more seamless experience of device-supported learning worlds that may integrate mobile, embedded and immersive technologies, we may expect to see increasing interest and activity in blended approaches to customer-centric, continuous learning.

CONCLUSION

Although the ultimate aim of CKM is to achieve organizational effectiveness and competitiveness, CKM success depends on its ability to target the right customer, with the right product, at the right price, at the right time, and through the right channel to improve organizational profitability. The business reflection of OL is in creating CK and in successfully implementing the CKM strategy. Organizational learning should be involved not only in managing task, structure, and people change, but in supporting customer-centric business processes and creating and maintaining SCA. Due to increasing strategic uncertainties, a continuous learning process needs to be added to CKM change that will be extended dramatically towards customer-centric, lifelong relationship. As superior CKM performance depends on superior learning, effective customer-centric OL requires organizations and their staff members to shift from traditional training on how to do the work to continuous learning and innovative performance.

Continuous learning throughout the CKM development and implementation journey needs revising efforts, building learning into the business processes, and institutionalizing the CK generation, applications, and management processes and the CSFs. Of paramount importance is the ability to monitor business environmental trends, to evolve and adapt quickly as changes to situational context and to make intelligent, customer-centric decisions on strategic uncertainties. Leadership of organizations plays a significant role in gaining employees' buy-in of the CKM change, diffusing customer-centric thinking in organizations, and in removing preconditions that block or hinder learning to reach new understandings of customers. For effective and adaptable transformation to customer-centric organizations, the people, culture, processes, structure, and technology should all be aligned to the requirements of the CKM strategy.

To succeed in CKM implementation, an organization must be ready to learn as well as teach. It is easy to put technology in place but getting the organization to contribute to a successful usage of the technology content, learn from implementation lessons, and accept change implications as a behavioral challenge. So, corporate culture needs to be assessed and revamped before launching a CKM initiative. What makes CK valuable to organizations is its ability to be engaged ultimately in a continuous learning process that helps in making better strategic decisions, conducting successful CKM initiatives, and maximizing experience of customers.

REFERENCES

Alavi, M., & Leidner, D.E. (1999). Knowledge Management Systems: Emerging Views and Practices from the Field. *32nd Hawaii International Conference on System Sciences*, IEEE Computer Society.

Al-Shammari, M. (2005). Implementing a knowledge-enabled CRM strategy in a large company: A Case study from a developing country. In M. E. Jennex (Ed.), *Case studies in knowledge management* (pp. 249-278). Hershey, PA: Idea Group Publishing.

Argyris, C. (1991). Teaching smart people to learn. *Harvard Business Review, 69,* 99-109.

Awad, E., & Ghaziri, H. (2004). *Knowledge management.* Upper Saddle River, NJ: Prentice Hall.

Barna, Z. (2003). *Knowledge management: A critical E-Business strategic factor.* Unpublished Masters Thesis, San Diego State University.

Bolton, M. (2004). Customer centric business processing. *International Journal of Productivity and Performance Management, 53*(1), 44-51.

Bose, R., & Sugumaran, V. (2003). Application of customer knowledge technology in customer relationship management. *Knowledge and Process Management, 10*(1), 3-17.

Buttle, F. (2004). *Customer relationship management: Concepts and Tools.* Oxford, England: Elsevier Publishing.

Davenport, T., & Prusak, L. (2000). *Working knowledge.* 2nd edition, Boston, MA: Harvard Business School Press.

Davenport, T. H. (1993). *Process innovation: Reengineering work through information technology.* Boston, MA: Harvard Business School Press.

Davenport, T. H., & Probst, G. J. B. (2002). *Knowledge management case book.* Weinheim: John Wiley.

Davenport, T. H., DeLong, D. W., & Beers, M. C. (1998). Successful knowledge management projects. *Sloan Management Review, 39*(2), 43-57.

De Wit, B., & Meyer, R. (2004). *Strategy: Process, content and context.* London: Thomson Learning.

Deal, T. E., & Kennedy, A. A. (1982). *Corporate cultures: The rights and rituals of corporate life*. Reading, MA: Addison-Wesley.

Desouza, K. C., & Awazu, Y. (2005). What do they Know? *Business Strategy Review, 16*(1), 41-.45.

Gentle, M. (2002). *The CRM project management handbook: Building realistic expectations and managing risk*. London: Kogan Page.

Gibbert, M., Leibold, M., & Probst, G. (2002). Five styles of customer knowledge management and how smart companies use them to create value. *European Management Journal, 20*(5), 459-469.

Ginsberg, M., & Kambil, A. (1999). Annotate: A Web-based knowledge management support system for document collections. *The 32nd Hawaii International Conference on System Sciences*, IEEE Computer Society Press.

Gray, C. (2002). Entrepreneurship, resistance to change and growth in small firms. *Journal of Small Business and Enterprise Development, 9*(1), 61-72.

Griffin, R. (2005). *Management*. 8th edition, Boston: Houghton Mifflin Company.

Holsapple, C. W., & Joshi, K. D. (2000). An investigation of factors that influence the management of knowledge in organizations. *Journal of Strategic Information Systems, 9*, 235-261.

Hughes, M. (2006). *Change management: A critical perspective*. London: CIPD Publications.

Jashapara, A. (2004). *Knowledge management: An integrated approach*. Harlow, England: Prentice-Hall.

Jennex, M. E., Croasdell, D., Olfman, L., & Morrison, J. (2005). Knowledge management, organizational memory, and organizational learning at the Hawaii International Conference on System Sciences. *International Journal of Knowledge Management, 1*(1), 1-7.

Jennex, M. E., & Olfman, L. (2001). Development recommendations for knowledge management/organizational memory systems. *Contemporary trends in IS development* (pp. 209-222). Norewll, MA: Kluwer Publishing.

Klempa, M. (1995), Understanding business process reengineering: A sociocognitive contingency model. In V. Grover & W. Kettinger (Eds). *Business process change: reengineering concepts, methods and technologies* (pp. 78-122). Pershey, PA: Idea Group Publishing.

Kolb, D. A. (1984) *Experiential learning: experience as the source of learning and development*. New Jersey: Prentice-Hall Inc.

Koskinen, K. U. (2001). Tacit knowledge as a promoter of success in technology firms. *The 34th Hawaii International Conference on System Sciences*, IEEE Computer Society.

Malhotra, Y., & Galletta, D. (2003). Role of commitment and motivation as antecedents of knowledge management systems implementation. *36th Hawaii International Conference on System Sciences*, IEEE Computer Society.

March, J. G. (1991). Exploration and exploitation in organizational learning. *Organization Science*, *2*(1), 71-87.

McAfee, A. (2006). Mastering the three worlds of information technology. *Harvard Business Review*, November, 141-149.

Morgan, G., & Sturdy, A. (2000). *Beyond organizational change: structure, discourse and power in UK financial services*. London: Macmillan.

Ogbonna, E., & Wilkinson, B. (2003). The false promise of organizational culture change: a case study of middle managers in grocery retailing. *Journal of Management Studies*, *40*(5), 1151-78.

Paquette, S. (2005). Customer knowledge management. In D. Schwartz (Ed.), The *Encyclopedia of knowledge management* (pp. 90-96), Hershey, PA: Idea Group.

Peppard, J., & Ronald, P. (1995). *The essence of business process re-engineering*. Upper Saddle River, NJ: Prentice-Hall.

Rowley, J. (2002). Eight questions for customer knowledge management in E-Business. *Journal of Knowledge Management*, *6*(5), 500-511.

Sage, A. P., & Rouse, W. B. (1999). Information systems frontiers in knowledge management. *Information Systems Frontiers*, *1*(3), 205-219.

Salaman, G., & Asch, D. (2003). *Strategy and capability: sustaining organizational change*. Oxford: Blackwell.

Scharmer, C. O. (2007). *Theory U: Leading from the future as it emerges*. Cambridge, MA: SoL, the Society for Organizational Learning.

Senge, P. (1990). *The fifth discipline: The art and practice of the learning organization*. New York: Doubleday Currency.

Simon, H. A. (1991). Bounded rationality and organizational learning. *Organization Science*, *2*(1), 125-134.

Smith, H. A., & McKeen, J. D. (2005). Developments in Practice XVIII - Customer Knowledge Management: Adding Value for Our Customers. *Communications of the Association for Information Systems, 16,* 744-755.

Snyder, M., & Davidson, I. (2003). In trouble? *Conspectus- The IT Report for Directors and Decision Makers,* (pp. 30-32).

Susman, G., Jansen, K., & Michael, J. (2006). Innovation and change management in small and medium-sized manufacturing companies. *Research report published by the college of business.* PA: Pennsylvania State University Publication.

Xu, M., & Walton, J. (2005). Gaining customer knowledge through analytical CRM, *Industrial Management & Data Systems, 105*(7), 955-971.

Wysocki, R. K., & DeMichiell, R. L. (1997). *Managing across the enterprise.* New York: John Wiley.

Yu, S., Kim, Y., & Kim, M., (2004). Linking organizational knowledge management Drivers to knowledge management performance: An exploratory study. *The 37th Hawaii International Conference on System Sciences,* HICSS36, IEEE Computer Society.

About the Author

Dr. **Minwir Al-Shammari** is a professor of operations management & technologies at the University of Bahrain's College of Business Administration. He holds a PhD in industrial management from University of Glasgow, UK (1990) and MS in industrial management from University of Central Missouri, USA (1986). He has been involved for about 20 years in teaching, research, training, and/or consultancy in the areas of operations management, knowledge management, management information systems, business process re-engineering, project management, spreadsheet decision models, management science, and research methodology. Prof. Al-Shammari served as a member of a number of national, regional, and international professional associations. He has received a number of local, regional, and international research awards, grants, and scholarships. He served as a consultant to the UN on a knowledge management project in the ESCWA region. He served on the editorial board of such refereed international publications as *Journal of Systems and Management Sciences*, *International Journal of Applied Decision Science*, *International Journal of Management Innovation Systems*, and *Cross-Cultural Management: An International Journal*. He has authored/co-authored over 30 research papers, and served as a reviewer for several regional and international research journals such as *Logistics Information Management*, *International Journal of Production Economics*, *Journal of Information Systems Education*, and *International Journal of Production & Operations Management*. Al-Shammari's publications have appeared in such refereed international publications as *International Journal of Knowledge Management*, *Logistics Information Management*, *International Journal of Infor-*

mation Management, European Journal of Operational Research, Expert Systems with Applications, Journal of Computer Information Systems, International Journal of Operations and Production Management, Production and Inventory Management Journal, International Journal of Commerce and Management, International Journal of Computer Applications in Technology, Cross-Cultural Management, International Journal of Management, Leadership and Organization Development Journal, and *Creativity and Innovation Management.*

Index